identity

 Other titles in this
series include:

Culture: A Reader for Writers,
John Mauk
(ISBN: 9780199947225)

Language: A Reader for Writers,
Gita DasBender
(ISBN: 9780199947485)

Sustainability: A Reader for Writers,
Carl Herndl
(ISBN: 9780199947508)

Globalization: A Reader for Writers,
Maria Jerskey
(ISBN: 9780199947522)

identity

A READER *for* WRITERS

John Scenters-Zapico

University of Texas at El Paso

New York   Oxford
Oxford University Press

Oxford University Press publishes works that further Oxford University's
objective of excellence in research, scholarship, and education.

Oxford   New York
Auckland   Cape Town   Dar es Salaam   Hong Kong   Karachi
Kuala Lumpur   Madrid   Melbourne   Mexico City   Nairobi
New Delhi   Shanghai   Taipei   Toronto

With offices in

Argentina   Austria   Brazil   Chile   Czech Republic   France   Greece
Guatemala   Hungary   Italy   Japan   Poland   Portugal   Singapore
South Korea   Switzerland   Thailand   Turkey   Ukraine   Vietnam

Published by Oxford University Press.
198 Madison Avenue, New York, New York 10016
http://www.oup.com

Oxford is a registered trademark of Oxford University Press

Library of Congress Cataloging-in-Publication Data
Scenters-Zapico, John.
   Identity : a reader for writers / John Scenters-Zapico, University of Texas at El Paso.
      pages cm
   Includes bibliographical references and index.
   ISBN 978-0-19-994746-1 (pbk.)
   1. College readers. 2. English language--Rhetoric--Handbooks, manuals, etc.
3. English language--Grammar--Handbooks, manuals, etc. 4. Report writing--
Handbooks, manuals, etc. 5. Identity (Philosophical concept) in literature. I. Title.
   PE1417.S357 2014
   808'.0427--dc23
                                                             2013037246

Printing number: 9 8 7

Printed in the United States of America
on acid-free paper

brief table of contents

contents

"For me it's those who name. That's really what we do. And that's what we do as artists, that's what we do in our lives, with metaphor. So, so I think we are the ones who name."

"As Hispanic/Latinos bear a plural identity, ethnic names that are appropriate today may be obsolete or even offensive tomorrow. The mediating factors in self-designation are gaining a voice and power to name one's identity and define one's reality."

"When they were young, one of my children's favorite games was reciting the family lineage. In our culture a person's full name is a combination of his paternal parentage."

"The Kiowas could not remember a time of glory in their racial life; they knew only that they were the 'coming out' people, according to the name which they gave to themselves, *Kwuda*, who in their origin myth had entered the world through a hollow log."

"But why, in 2013, does getting married mean giving up the most basic marker of your identity? And if family unity is so important, why don't men ever change their names?"

"It's my mother tongue. Her language, as I hear it, is vivid, direct, full of observation and imagery. That was the language that helped shape the way I saw things, expressed things, made sense of the world."

"To anglophones, 'Yes we want' may seem funny, and Spanish authorities may even find it embarrassing, but whatever happens to the slogan, its very existence is one more sign that English, now that its global, is no longer the exclusive property of English-speaking nations."

2   Where Are You From? Notions of Identity & Place   41

"And there was a phase in African-American history, especially in the '60s and '70s, where parents were trying to get back to Africa, and if they couldn't physically do it, they did it by naming their child something African. So they were flipping through books looking for a name that had a particular meaning."

"America this is quite serious.
America this is the impression I get from looking in the television set.
America is this correct?"

"Entrance to school brings with it forms and releases and assessments. Mercy relied on a series of tests . . . for placement, and somehow the results of my tests got confused with those of another student named Rose. "

"Most people believe that, for any given student, going to an institution with all (or most) of the conventionally accepted earmarks of 'quality' will lead to greater learning and development. The fact of the matter is that it probably won't."

"We conclude that, in the field of public education, the doctrine of 'separate but equal' has no place. Separate educational facilities are inherently unequal."

"In the street, I had been the most articulate hustler out there—I had commanded attention when I said something. But now, trying to write simple English, I not only wasn't articulate, I wasn't even functional."

"His first school in California is Compton Senior High School. The halls don't look much different from Hamilton. The difference is that Compton seems exclusively African American, none of the poor Irish, the Italians, the Puerto Ricans of Hamilton, not even California's Mexicans. He is alone."

"For although I was a very good student, I was also a very bad student. I was a 'scholarship boy,' a certain kind of scholarship boy. Always successful, I was always unconfident. Exhilarated by my progress. Sad. I became the prized student—anxious and eager to learn. Too eager, too anxious—an imitative and unoriginal pupil."

"What in the world is going on? In the past in America, times of enormous innovation in the rest of society, including in technology and in industry, have also been times of tremendous innovation in education. What has happened to us? Rather than thinking of ways we can be preparing our students for their future, we seem determined to prepare them for our past."

"Watch your back, cover your butt—a very good six word life lesson."

"Now, as this greatest generation grows up, the culture of praise is reaching deeply into the adult world. Bosses, professors and mates are feeling the need to lavish praise on young adults, particularly twenty somethings, or else see them wither under an unfamiliar compliment deficit."

"Now, we have a reversal of the normal situation, where young people migrate into a workplace manned by seasoned natives. Instead, in this digitalized age, this 21-year-old and his peers are showing up in human resources offices as digital natives in a workplace world dominated by digital immigrants—that is, elders who often feel less at ease with new technologies."

"To earn $600, he has to work at least 10 hours a day, six days a week, and that does not happen every week. Sometimes he is paid overtime for the extra hours, sometimes not. And, as he found out in May, he can be fired at any time and bring in nothing, not even unemployment, until he lands another job."

"I went to work for Blue Cross. It's 1969. The Great Society is in full swing. Those who never thought of being minorities before are being turned on. Consciousness raising is going on. Black programs are popping up in universities. Cultural identity and all that. But what about the one issue in this country: economics? There were very few management jobs for minorities, especially blacks."

"In the United States, the emerging aristocracy remains staunchly convinced that it is not an aristocracy, that it's the result of hard work and talent. The permanent working poor refuse to accept that their poverty is permanent. The class system is clandestine."

"You probably don't think of construction managers, sales representatives, or quality assurance engineer as the most cheerful employees. But as it turns out, they are."

"Working Identity is constituted by a range of racially associated ways of being, including how one dresses, speaks, styles one's hair; one's professional and social affiliations; who one marries or dates; one's politics and views about race; where one lives; and so on and so forth."

"When we're with our friends, when we're with people we're just meeting for the first time, even when we're with our spouses and loved ones, the lies are thick and furious."

"Three mouse clicks put me into 'w4m' (women for men). I hadn't thought it through but managed a serviceable ad on my feet. It read: 'Freshly divorced and want my confidence back! I'm 5'10", long sandy blond hair. I'm new at this, a little nervous. I don't know what to put down.'"

"I believe these systematic differences in childhood socialization make talk between women and men like cross-cultural communication, heir to all the attraction and pitfalls of that enticing but difficult enterprise."

"But those who are non-lovers, and whose success in love is the reward of their merit, will not be jealous of the companions of their beloved, and will rather hate those who refuse to be his associates, thinking that their favourite is slighted by the latter and benefited by the former; for more love than hatred may be expected to come to him out of his friendship with others."

"A recent survey of married people in the United States found that when asked the question 'What is very important for a successful marriage?' the quality mentioned most frequently—by 93 percent—was 'faithfulness,' while 'happy sexual relationship' came in with only 70 percent. In other words, to 23 percent of the respondents, it seemed more important that they and their partner should not have sex with others than that they themselves should enjoy sex."

"While our concept of the family has grown and diversified since the days of Mrs. Cleaver, for households striving toward advancement, our labor market and social policy remain stuck in the past."

"Sibling rivalry is a normal aspect of childhood, experts say. Our siblings are our first rivals. They competed with us for the love and attention of the people we needed most, our parents, and it is understandable that we occasionally felt threatened. Much of what is written about sibling rivalry focuses on its effects during childhood."

"Love begins in a country
Where organs weep sweetness
And men piss in the street"

". . . Twitter and social media in general is kind of blurring the boundary between like this private intimate space and public space, right?"

"The tools we use to think change the ways in which we think. The invention of written language brought about a radical shift in how we process, organize, store, and transmit representations of the world. Although writing remains our primary information technology, today when we think about the impact of technology on our habits of mind, we think primarily of the computer."

"How much, I began to wonder, was I shaping my Twitter feed, and how much was Twitter shaping me?"

"Weibo can be used for frivolous socializing and celebrity watching, but what has caught the world's attention is the site's powerful twin forces of subversion and surveillance."

"The Electronic Communications Privacy Act (ECPA) is a 1986 law that Congress enacted to protect your privacy in electronic communications, like email and instant messages. ECPA provides scant protection for your identifying information, such as the IP address used to access an account. While

Paula Broadwell reportedly created a new, pseudonymous account for the allegedly harassing emails to Jill Kelley, she apparently did not take steps to disguise the IP number her messages were coming from. The FBI could have obtained this information with just a subpoena to the service provider. But obtaining the account's IP address alone does not establish the identity of the emails' sender."

Dan Fletcher, **"How Facebook Is Redefining Privacy"** *Time*   362

"Facebook has changed our social DNA, making us more accustomed to openness. But the site is premised on a contradiction: Facebook is rich in intimate opportunities—you can celebrate your niece's first steps there and mourn the death of a close friend—but the company is making money because you are, on some level, broadcasting those moments online."

Alan Norton, **"10 Reasons Why I Avoid Social Networking Services"** *TechRepublic*   372

"Our image is, in part, defined by our words. Each of us should ask how much of ourselves we want to give to people we don't even know. Once gone, that private piece of our lives can never be retrieved."

rhetorical contents

interview

academic research

definition

classification and division

narration

argument and persuasion

example and illustration

comparison and contrast

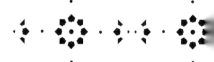

preface

In the United States, we are constantly defining and redefining who we are to each other. As quick as we are to pull ourselves together as "Americans" in times of war or natural disaster, we also incessantly define the other, at times favorably, at other times not so much. We band together as "us" to defend our freedoms and safety from outside threats, yet we also move away from each other and maintain our differences, our uniqueness, our independence. We are a nation of commonalities, differences, natives, immigrants, and visitors.

We recognize that our strength is our ability to intelligently negotiate our independence and dependence, and similarities and differences with each other. The negotiation process takes place because we are a nation of readers and writers. We inform ourselves to understand issues important to us, and we then share our thoughts with others, trying to inform or persuade them of what we believe is the correct way to understand or act in a situation. To understand our ever-changing society, the issues important to it, and take stands on issues, we by necessity must read. To get our views out there, we write. In order to read and write well, we must understand rhetorical principles, our roles and identities, and the writing processes that are the foundations of literacy and writing practices.

Why learn to read and write, or become more sophisticated readers and writers? Take a moment to think about what we could not do if we could not read or write. Could we shop online? Could we read the text that helps as we play a video game? Could we read or send an e-mail, a text or tweet, or post to our Facebook or Skype accounts? The answer to all of these is, No. Nothing in these environments would make any sense.

Imagine trying to make a résumé or write a research paper or lab report. Our world and work possibilities would diminish substantially from how we experience them now. The more schooling we have the better and more varied are our reading and writing skills, and from these refined skills more opportunities exist for us. The processes that we go through to become highly literate are many and complex.

Traditional literacies, the abilities to read and write, and digital or electronic literacies, the abilities to communicate and understand using multimodal means, are a vast network of possibilities and challenges that we must learn at increasing levels of sophistication and complexity. Throughout our years in school we will need to advance our critical reading and writing skills through study and practice. Each chapter's title in *Identity: A Reader for Writers* is a question about our identity, from "What's in a Name? The Role of Language and Identity" to "Where Do You Draw the Line? Privacy, Socializing, and Life without Boundaries." The variety of readings explore each chapter's question through a diversity of texts, essays, court decisions, visuals, and poetry, imparting knowledge about the changing literacies we practice while fostering skills to make us aware of how to negotiate our views and identity in order to succeed and excel in an increasingly demanding world.

Identity: A Reader for Writers is part of a series of brief single-topic readers from Oxford University Press designed for today's college writing courses. Each reader in this series approaches a topic of contemporary conversation from multiple perspectives:

- **Timely** Most selections were originally published in 2010 or later.
- **Global** Sources and voices from around the world are included.
- **Diverse** Selections come from a range of nontraditional and alternate print and online media, as well as representative mainstream sources.

In addition to the rich array of perspectives on topical (even urgent) issues addressed in each reader, each volume features an abundance of different genres and styles—from the academic research paper to the pithy Twitter argument. Useful but nonintrusive pedagogy includes:

- **Chapter introductions** that provide a brief overview of the chapter's theme and a sense of how the chapter's selections relate both to the overarching theme and to each other.

- **Headnotes** introduce each reading by providing concise information about its original publication, and pose an open-ended question that encourages students to explore their prior knowledge of (or opinions about) some aspect of the selection's content.
- **"Analyze" and "Explore" questions** after each reading scaffold and support student reading for comprehension as well as rhetorical considerations, providing prompts for reflection, classroom discussion, and brief writing assignments.
- **"Forging Connections" and "Looking Further" prompts** after each chapter encourage critical thinking by asking students to compare perspectives and strategies among readings both within the chapter and with readings in other chapters, suggesting writing assignments (many of which are multimodal) that engage students with larger conversations in the academy, the community, and the media.
- **An appendix on "Researching and Writing about Identity"** guides student inquiry and research in a digital environments. Coauthored by a research librarian and a writing program director, this appendix provides real-world, transferable strategies for locating, assessing, synthesizing, and citing sources in support of an argument.

about the author

John Scenters-Zapico (PhD Arizona 1994) is a professor of rhetoric and writing studies (RWS) at the University of Texas at El Paso, where he teaches in the PhD and MA Programs in RWS, and is the director of the University Writing Center. He has published widely, from *American Indian Quarterly* and *Rhetoric Society Quarterly* to *Computers and Composition*.

acknowledgments

I dedicate *Identity: A Reader for Writers* to my vibrant mother, Betty Joe Scenters, and to the memory of my father, John Wallace Scenters. They helped shape who I am today by always pushing education, personal

betterment, and reasoned decisionmaking. Finally, the generous and in-depth feedback, suggestions, and critique from a group of outstanding reviewers helped me make significant improvements to *Identity: A Reader for Writers*. I thank Guy Shebat, Youngstown State University; Cindy King, University of North Texas-Dallas; Yavanna Brownlee, University of Alaska-Fairbanks; Krista Callahan-Caudill, University of Kentucky; Carl Ostrowski, Middle Tennessee State University; Sally Palmer, South Dakota School of Mines and Technology; Kara Poe Alexander, Baylor University; Jessica Fordham Kidd, University of Alabama; Amber Buck, College of Staten Island; Laurah Norton, Georgia State University; Erin Dietel-McLauglin, University of Notre Dame; Aaron Matthew Percich, West Virginia University; Amy Patrick Mossman, Western Illinois University; Erin Griesser, and Patricia Houston, University of Cincinnati.

What's in a Name? The Role of Language & Identity

Names serve as labels for things in our lives, and even for us. Think of all the names we experience, process, and make choices on every day, such as our own name, the name of the city where we live, the type of car we drive, the brand of clothes we wear, or even our tattoos. Every named person, place, and thing has a story to tell, and that story creates an identity full of meanings.

When we are able to call something or someone by a name, to describe them, we have an empowering ability. This power helps us shape our lives, and it even helps us to understand and control them better. The way in which we use words to identify people, places, and things brings with it great responsibilities, and we need to study these responsibilities in order to use them effectively.

Names serve a useful purpose, on the one hand, in creating common characteristics and themes. They can unite us and make us feel good about our nation, its peoples, and ourselves. Think of when a country wins a gold medal at the Olympics. The citizens of that country do not care about the winners' ethnic or cultural backgrounds. The winners simply become the uniforms and flag of that country. On the other hand, when something bad happens, such as 9/11, we suddenly begin to focus negatively on race and ethnicity. Despite diverse multigenerational histories, families, and contributions, we label and identify all members of particular groups with negative traits. After 9/11, names that identified people with the Middle East, and who were darkskinned, became part of a news story that made them seem like a threat.

In the readings and exercises that follow, we discover the power and complexities of names, naming, identity, and how language works in shaping these. Names, and the ways we are identified because of them, are the focus of this chapter. We will see how they can empower and how they can hurt. The writers in this chapter discuss several of the implications that names and naming have had on their own identities. Because these writers target different audiences, the forms of their writing, the words they use, and the appeals they evoke are all different, yet effective. Pay attention to how some authors define their subjects, some with documentation to support what they say while others employ emotional appeals and personal stories to help us understand the suffering or growth they have experienced.

In the first reading, "Getting Called Fag," Dorwick reflects on the power of words both to hurt and also to self-educate. In her academic article, "Hispanics, Latinos, or Americanos: The Evolution of Identity," Comas-Díaz creates a robust taxonomy of the many titles and types that exist for the various Latinos in the United States. The importance of names is continued in Kuttab's "We Are Palestinians," which looks at the wealth of knowledge we can gain by exploring the history of our last names, as well as the complications associated with place. In an excerpt from Momaday's *Names*, the author takes great pride in sharing his family's last name creation tale and the unique stories that accompany the members of his family.

Arguing last names are important to our identity, "Why Should Married Women Change Their Names? Let Men Change Theirs," Filipovic explores why women who marry should not have to shed a part of who they are. In a story of growth, Tan realizes in "Mother Tongue" that our names

and accents can cause people to interpret us in negative ways and this also can damage our self-esteem and respect for our culture. Rounding off the readings is Baron's blog post, "Who Owns Global English?" In it he explores how nonnative English-speaking countries are creatively using and evolving English. In the way some native English speakers critically respond to Global English, we see how language and identity are closely intertwined.

Keith Dorwick
"Getting Called Fag"

The author of this literacy narrative shares a story about getting called "fag" in the 1970s when he was around fifteen years old. Despite the hurt the event caused him, he maturely contemplates the process of naming things and of others naming us as an act of rhetoric. This story comes from the Digital Archives of Literacy Narratives (DALN) and is available for open-access download in video, audio, text, or all three at the Digital Archive of Literacy Narratives at Ohio State University (http://daln.osu.edu/). If you read the text below first and then listen to the audio of it, you will find that you pick up on different points.

While this narrative has the potential to appear negative or even sad, how does Dorwick make it into a story of growth and strength?

Ok, so I'm maybe 15, maybe 16 at the time of the story and I'm living out in Glendale Heights, Illinois, and Crane's Chicago Business once described it as a hardscrabble factory town, but it wasn't. It was a bedroom community, kinda working class I guess, yeah. Certainly my parents were, certainly I am, I consider myself that way anyway. And I'm walking down the street, all of a sudden this car goes screeching past me. And then as in lots of small towns I guess, you kind of drive

> "I didn't know anybody who was gay and I was worried that I was the only one."

around. You drive around a lot, go back and forth here and there. Anyway, there were maybe 8, 9, maybe 10 kids, crammed, all guys, into this car. It made me kind of think of one of those cars in the circus with all the clowns. Well I laughed, and when I laughed, they got kind of upset on one of their passes. And so they zoomed around again just so they could yell: "Faggot! Fag!" "Queer!" Now, at the time I hadn't really dealt with the fact that I was gay, I kinda sorta was wondering it, and I knew I was kinda intrigued, and interested in men. But I didn't really know what to do about it, or even if I wanted to do anything about it. So, so I was kind of appalled, like, "How did they know?" "How do they know? I haven't said anything about this to anybody? How do they know?" But then the other thing is that I kinda was feeling pretty liberated. Because I had been worried, this is 1975, there wasn't any Will and Grace, you know. There weren't a whole lot of media role models for young gay guys, and I didn't know anybody who was gay, and I was worried that I was the only one. And the minute that they called me those names, I started to think "Oh my God, I'm not the only one." "There are people out here, there are people like me." And that was totally cool, that was in fact liberating. And so I kinda started trying to figure out where I could run into guys, and I kinda figured out where I could run into guys. And one thing led to another and it was all pretty fun. Well years later, years and years later. I think it was maybe even in one of my courses, at the University of North Chicago, where I did my MA and my PHD. So maybe it was Bill Cavino, or maybe it was David (. . .). And anyway we got onto the subject of naming and what people are called and the implications for naming, as an act of rhetoric. And I thought back to that story, at that moment, and I connected to that story right then. And I realized that that was the first act that I consider myself as a Rhetorician, because it's the first time that I thought of that language in that way. Not as something solid, where this word means that word, but I had actually thought about what the language means and how it operates. And what it's implications were. And if there were names for these things, then there must be things connected to these things, to these concepts. And so that's it, the more I . . . The older I get, you know, the more I think that it's naming, and language that makes us who we are. I mean, you know, there's an old Biblical story, that one of Adam's gifts and tasks and duties, was to name everything that hadn't yet had a name. It came straight out of God's mind into being, and now it needed to be called something, and

that was Adam's job. So you know, we've been called The Human, one of the definitions is the Man who Laughs, another is the Man who Plays, another is Homosapiens, The Wise Ones, all those names. Some sexist, some not. For me it's those who name. That's really what we do. And that's what we do as artists, that's what we do in our lives, with metaphor. So, so I think we are the ones who name. Thanks.

Analyze

1. What lesson does Dorwick draw from his encounter with the young men in the car?

2. The young men in the car use the derogatory word *fag* to label the author. At the time, he was trying to figure out his sexuality, so how did being named this actually help him?

3. The writer uses the rhetorical mode description to share how he saw the carload of young men. How does he use this mode to show where the event took place as well as to criticize the young men?

Explore

1. By using compare and contrast, make a list of the ways that Dorwick presents the positive and negative of his experience as a young man. Share these in class.

2. The author takes a highly insensitive comment about his sexuality and seems to make us forget about the negative connotations of the experience. He turns the occurrence around and shows us the power of words and language to lead us to new understandings of the dimensions of language. Using the power of language, he took something that was intended to be destructive and turned it into something constructive in his life. Have you ever been called something negative that you turned into a positive? Or have you ever read, heard, or watched an event from a book, short story, newspaper, blog, Facebook, or movie that was intended to cause one reaction—positive or negative—and ended up causing the opposite?

3. Using Dorwick's talk as an example, and keeping in mind the fact that names have the power to bring up many emotions, argue why it is so important to be aware of the multiple ways in which words can have power.

Lillian Comas-Díaz
"Hispanics, Latinos, or Americanos: The Evolution of Identity"

Comas-Díaz, originally from Puerto Rico, lives in the United States. From her own work, and from her involvement with the American Psychological Association (APA) and the Committee on Women in Psychology (CWP), she began seeing how psychology, politics, and social organizations are intimately intertwined. In this essay, Comas-Díaz creates a taxonomy that names and defines a robust array of labels given to Latinos and Hispanics. It is important, Comas-Díaz argues, for any population to self-designate (name) itself in order to gain a voice and describe its experiences.

How do you think members of Latino and Hispanic communities accept or reject Comas-Díaz's taxonomy?

Identity is the number-one national problem here.

(Hoffman, 1989, p. 262)

One of the fastest growing ethnic minority groups in the United States is in search of a name. Or so it appears, given the multiple terms used for its designation. Historically, such an amalgamation of people was referred to as Spanish speaking, a current misnomer, given that a significant segment of this population is English dominant. Hispanics, Latinos, Hispanos, Latins, Central Americans, or South Americans—to name a few—are some of the general terms used to designate this diverse ethnic collage. Many individuals prefer to politically affirm their ethnic identity by using terms such as Chicanos, Xicanos, Ricans, or Boricuas, whereas others affirm their national origins by using terms such as Mexicans or Mexican Americans, Cubans or Cuban Americans, Colombians, Dominicans, Peruvians, Salvadorans, or Venezuelans, among many others.

Encased within historical eras, ethnic self-designation reflects the dialectics between dominance and self-determination. Because the systematic negation and oppression of people of color result in pervasive identity conflicts (Fanon, 1967), Latinos' power to name themselves advances liberation by rejecting colonization (Castillo, 1994). Searching for a name to designate

this heterogeneous group can be a challenging and confusing ordeal. Because self- and other identification is a developmental process, naming evolves in response to psychosocial and geopolitical factors.

In this essay I present a brief taxonomy of terms in an attempt to clarify the complexity of ethnic identification. Such presentation is situated within the current historical and political context. As Hispanic/Latinos bear a plural identity, ethnic names that are appropriate today may be obsolete or even offensive tomorrow. The mediating factors in self-designation are gaining a voice and power to name one's identity and define one's reality. I conclude with a discussion of the evolution of the Latino identity.

A Taxonomic Panorama

I offer a taxonomy of ethnic terms used to designate the generic Hispanic/Latino population in addition to specific names used to designate distinct groups. Besides the references cited, the interested reader can consult Internet resources, such as the Chicano-Latino Network (CLNET), accessible through the University of California, Los Angeles gopher server (gopher.ucla.edu 70), the Encyclopedia.com, and The Hispano Crypto-Jewish Resource Center (located at the Ira M. Beck Memorial Archives, University of Denver Main Campus, Penrose Library Special Collections, Denver, Colorado), and other related links.

Generic Terms

Hispanic

The generic term *Hispanic* was officially created by the United States Bureau of the Census to designate people of Spanish origin who identified themselves as such in the 1970 census (COSSMHO, 1986). Often used to refer collectively to all Spanish speakers, it connotes a lineage or cultural heritage related to Spain. Indeed, the term Hispanic can be related to internalized colonization because it is strongly supported by politically conservative groups who regard their European ancestry as superior to the conquered indigenous peoples of the Americas (Falicov, 1998). An example of identity imperialism, the term Hispanic is inaccurate, incorrect, and often offensive as a collective name for all Spanish speakers or Latinos.

Many millions of Spanish-speaking people—such as Native Americans—are not of true Spanish descent, and millions of Latin Americans do not speak Spanish or claim Spanish heritage (e.g., Brazilians); therefore, they are not Hispanics.

Latino(a)

Recognizing the diversity of this ethnic minority group, Latino (male) or Latina (female) is used to refer to people originating from or having a heritage related to Latin America. Acting as a superset of many nationalities, Latino is preferred by many over the term Hispanic because it excludes Europeans such as Spaniards from being identified as ethnic minorities in the United States while it includes Brazilians, who do not qualify as Hispanics because their mother tongue is Portuguese. Many politically correct people prefer Latino because it reaffirms their native pre-Hispanic identity (Falicov, 1998). The term Latin comes into use as the least common denominator for all peoples of Latin America in recognition of the fact that some Romance language (Spanish, Portuguese, French) is the native tongue of the majority of Latin Americans.

Shorris (1992) argued that the term Latino is linguistically correct in Spanish because it has gender, contrary to the term Hispanic that follows the English usage of nongendered grammar. However, as the current term used to designate the vast majority of this ethnic group, Latino(a) is not appropriate for the millions of Native Americans who inhabit the Americas.

La Raza

La Raza (literally meaning "the race") is a widespread term in use among Spanish-speaking and Spanish-surnamed people in the United States. La Raza emerges as a designation acceptable to many Latino, Caribbean, Chicano, and Mexican Americans born in the United States or Latin America.

The term La Raza has been intricately involved in political activism. In the 1960s and 1970s, The Brown Power grew politically active, demanding equal opportunities and rights. Cesar Chavez organized the United Farm Workers in 1962, obtaining victories against large California growers. Although La Raza Unida, a party formed in 1970, has won local elections, greater political success has come to Mexican Americans in mainstream U.S. political parties.

Hispano(a)

The term *Hispano* or *Hispana* comprises those individuals who trace their 10
history to the Spanish conquistadores and settlers who arrived in 1494
and occupied and dominated what is known today as Mexico, California,
Texas, Florida, New Mexico, and Arizona in the 1600s to the 1800s
(SOSSMHO 1986). Comprising the Creole Spanish-Native American
race, Hispanos tend to identify with their Spanish heritage as opposed to
the Mexican settlers. A traditionally closed and conservative group,
evidence suggests that many Hispanos may be descendants of persecuted
Jews who fled Spain during the 16th and 17th centuries seeking refuge
in what were then the farthest reaches of the known world. They survived
by minimizing their contact with outsiders and by hiding or disguising
their religious and cultural identities as much as possible. They are what
historical researchers call "cryptic or crypto Jews," meaning hidden Jews
(Bloom & Bloom, 1993).

"Spanish People"

This term is frequently used in the United States to refer indiscriminately
to any person who speaks Spanish. As an ethnic term, "Spanish People" is
imprecise and often inappropriate in that it includes people from the
Americas continent, the Caribbean, and Spain. The term, however, is a
proper designation for the people of Spain, as some Spaniards or native
people of Spain do reside in the United States. Nonetheless, some of
the "Spaniards" living in the United States, such as Basques, Catalonians,
and Spanish gypsies, do not consider themselves Spaniards. As an illustration, Basques and Catalonians each have a different culture and language
from Spain, in addition to separatist political movements to become independent republics. The originators of flamenco, *gitanos* or Spanish gypsies,
do not consider themselves Spaniards, and many call themselves the
Roma people.

Americano(a)

This term is traditionally used to designate Americans who are not of
Hispanic/Latino extraction. However, it has been used recently to designate Latinos living in the United States. The term Americano embraces and
celebrates the diversity and energy of the contemporary Latin American
community wedded through a wealth of nationalities (Olmos, Ybarra, &

Monterey, 1999). Moreover, Americano describes a group people bound together by their languages and traditions, as varied as America itself.

Specific or National Terms

Mexican

The nationality of the inhabitants of Mexico, *Mexicans* is the term used appropriately for Mexican citizens who visit or work in the United States. However, it is an ineffective name to designate those people who are citizens of the United States—either born in the United States or naturalized citizens of the United States who are of Mexican ancestry. Some Mexicans maintain strong family ties in Mexico (by visiting periodically and by investing economically and emotionally in Mexico), and they usually intend to return to Mexico provided they can become economically secure. Therefore, these people maintain and nurture their offspring in their language, religion, and culture.

Mexican American

Following the pattern sometimes used to identify the extraction of other ethnic Americans (African American, Italian American, etc.), Mexican American refers to those individuals of Mexican descent who are U.S. citizens. This term is acceptable to many Mexican descendants, with the exception of those who do not identify with a Mexican heritage but rather with a Spanish heritage (such as Hispanos). Also, for those who do not view themselves as "Americans" by choice, this designation is problematic, and still others reject a hyphenated identity.

Chicano(a)

15   Used to describe Mexican Americans, Chicano (male) and Chicana (female) were originally pejorative. Brown Power movement activists of the 1960s and 1970s in the United States adopted this designation with a sense of pride. One theory of its etymology traces its origin to the 1930s and 1940s period when poor, rural, indigenous Mexicans came to the United States as seasonal migrant workers. The term seems to have come into first use in the fields of California in derision of the inability of native Nahuatl speakers to refer to themselves as "Mexicanos" and instead spoke of themselves as "Mesheecanos," in accordance with the pronunciation rules of

their language. Another theory of the etymology of Chicano is that in vulgar Spanish it is common for Mexicans to use the "ch" conjunction in place of certain consonants to create a term of endearment. Among some Mexican Americans, the term still retains an offensive connotation, particularly because it is used by activists and by those who seek to create a new identity for their culture rather than to subsume it under the mainstream culture.

Xicano(a)

Like Chicano(a), the word *Xicano* derives from the Nahautl pronunciation of Mexica or Mexicanos, the group of indigenous people commonly referred to as the Aztecs. In using Xicano, which replaces the "ch" in Chicano with the "x," the person affirms his or her indigenous heritage (Castillo, 1994).

Boricua

This Taino name refers to the inhabitants of Borinquen, the island that became Puerto Rico, a colony of Spain, in 1493. Neither a state nor a republic, Puerto Rico is a free associated state, an American commonwealth, whereby political power remains with the United States government (Comas-Díaz, Lykes, & Alarcon, 1998). The island has limited political self-determination because of its colonial status. The terms used by Puerto Ricans for self-designation tend to reflect an identity crisis borne by their country's uncertain political status. Boricua emphasizes a political identification with a Spanish-speaking Latin American identity, as opposed to an English-speaking United States one. During the late 1960s and 1970s, the phrase "Boricua, defiende lo tuyo" (Boricua, defend what is yours) was used as a revolutionary cry. Boricua is also an endearing expression used by Puerto Ricans to designate each other.

Nuyorican

This term refers to Puerto Ricans born in the continental United States, particularly in New York City. A separate ethnic identity from island Puerto Ricans who are members of a majority group, many Nuyoricans' identity is colored by being an ethnic minority population (Algarin & Pinero, 1975). Indeed, some Nuyoricans are politically radicalized within their experiences as people of color in the United States society. Continental

Puerto Ricans are also born outside of New York; therefore, the collective term used to designate them is Ricans. As an illustration, whereas a Nuyorican is a Rican born and raised in New York, a Chicagorican is a Rican born and raised in Chicago.

Rican

Rican refers to the second-and third-generation Puerto Ricans on the U.S. mainland. Like Nuyoricans, many Ricans maintain close contact with island Puerto Rican communities through migration and reverse migration. Regardless of their birthplace, Puerto Ricans are United States citizens since 1917. Ricans embrace a cultural identity different from Puerto Ricans. Like Spanglish, Rican culture synthesizes Puerto Rican and United States cultures into a brand new one. For instance, contrary to the dominant ideology on Puerto Rico, which has deemphasized the role of slavery in Puerto Rican history and the presence of African traits and cultural elements, many Ricans tend to underline their debt to Africa, affirming their Black heritage (Klor de Alva, 1997).

LatiNegro(a)

20   This term was coined to designate the African Latino (a) who is perceived beyond any doubt as Black by both the North American and the Latino communities (Comas-Díaz, 1994). This term avoids the partial or total negation of the Latinness in African Latinos by the Latino community. The offspring of African American (Caribbean or North, Central, and South American) and Latino parents, some LatiNegros are immersed in the African American community. Also known as Afro Latinos, this segment of the Latino population bears a racial identification based on the combined and class discrimination they experience from the mainstream society as well as from the Hispanic/Latino community.

Caribeño(a)

This term refers to the Latinos from the Caribbean. Acknowledging that the Caribbean region provides a specific worldview, many Spanish-speaking Caribbean groups, such as Cubans, Dominicans, and Puerto Ricans, are additionally using this self-designation, recognizing their emotional-geographic locale. The term Caribeño(a) also embraces the psychology of being an islander.

"Epilogue or Prelude: La Raza Cosmica/The Cosmic Race"

The Latino mosaic reflects a plural, dynamic, and evolving transformation. An apt metaphor for the development of the United States, Latino identity evolution offers a parallel to the collective identity redefinition. Historically, some Latinos were indigenous to this land, whereas others arrived searching for the immigrant golden dream of opportunities, and still others continue to be washed up on American shores searching for freedom and political asylum.

The high rates of Latin American immigration, Latino birth, and growing numbers of mixed marriages accentuate the emerging Latino preponderance in the United States. No longer "strangers among us," Latinos transform the North American ethnic makeup and economy (Suro, 1999). As both outsiders and insiders, many Latinos live in the hyphen (Stavans, 1996), creating a space whereby transculturation changes both the Latino and mainstream cultures. The concept of transculturation involves an adaptive, dynamic, evolutionary, and dialectical process (Comas-Díaz, 1987). It differs from acculturation in that it gives birth to a distinct culture emerging from conflicting cultural values (De Granda, 1968).

Likewise, Latino identity evolution underscores mestizaje, or the mixing of races to produce a new one. As early as 1925, Jose Vasconcelos (1997), a Mexican philosopher, presented his racial theory of the cosmic race—the future of humankind—as emanating out of the synthesis of Indian, White, "Mongol," and African races. Arguing that mestizaje promoted civilization, Vasconcelos believed that the Spanish Empire in Europe, connected, for the first time, all of the major racial groups. Contrary to other Christian religions, he asserted the Spanish Catholic Church enhanced racial unification by including the Indians through religious conversion and education.

Regardless of calling themselves Hispanics, Latinos, Americanos, or la Raza Cosmica, this ethnic group continues searching for the evolution of 25 identity. As people of all colors, they transform every inch of the Americas' spiritual, physical, and emotional geography.

Analyze

1. Why do you think it is important for Hispanics, Latinos, or Americanos to have a name to label themselves?
2. What other ethnic groups are engaged in a similar search? Can you create a taxonomy for another group?

3. The author uses definition to tease out all of the terms she uses. What effect does this have on you as a reader? Does she seem thorough or superficial? How is the effect different from a dictionary definition?

Explore

1. Comas-Díaz states, "As Hispanic/Latinos bear a plural identity, ethnic names that are appropriate today may be obsolete or even offensive tomorrow. The mediating factors in self-designation are gaining a voice and power to name one's identity and define one's reality." Imagine you are Dorwick today. Write an essay using a taxonomy like Comas-Díaz's describing how you would self-identify in as many ways as you can think of. One way to start this essay is to write, "I am . . ." and then begin listing all the things you are and by doing this you would show someone a robust image of who you are.
2. What is *mestizaje*? Discuss what it means and argue whether you are or are not *mestizaje*.
3. Write an essay that details the various historical admixtures of the race or races with which you identify. Make sure to create a taxonomy for your major categories, and support each one.

Daoud Kuttab
"We Are Palestinians"

Kuttab was born in Jerusalem and is a Palestinian journalist. He has worked on and been involved in many projects across the Arab world, including Jordan and Palestine, and he has published widely. This article comes from *The International Herald Tribune*. Like Comas-Díaz in the previous reading, Kuttab speaks about the cultural significance of surnames and how they create an identity for Palestinians. He argues that their identity must be derived from within the Palestinian community, not from outside communities such as the Israelis.

Do you think many Americans would go to the extent the author did in order to find out the meanings of their last names?

JERUSALEM—When they were young, one of my children's favorite games was reciting the family lineage. In our culture a person's full name is a combination of his paternal parentage. My son, born in Jerusalem in 1988, would say his name is Bishara Daoud George Musa Qustandi Musa Kuttab.

Our family name came from the profession two brothers had a long time ago. The first Kuttabs were scribes who sat outside the court and wrote up petitions for people who had a claim with the authorities. Kuttab is Arabic for writers or scribes.

Upon graduating from North Park University in Chicago and returning to Palestine, Bishara visited the St. James Orthodox Church in the Old City of Jerusalem. He met with the head of the local Palestinian Christian parish. Using extensive baptismal records, they were able to patch together the history of Kuttabs in Jerusalem for hundreds of years. This turned into a family tree that has been circulated on Facebook to all Kuttabs.

My son's visit had another reason: He wanted to collect rent on our family's property. On the eve of World War I, many Palestinian families turned their properties over to local churches or the Islamic Waqf (trust) for safekeeping. The properties were controlled by the churches but the owners were able to collect a meager rent. Our history is typical of many Palestinians.

When my father was born in 1922, the world was abuzz with the self-determination doctrine advanced by President Woodrow Wilson. Palestinian Arabs attempted to become independent after the British mandate ended, but the British pledged Palestine simultaneously to Jews and Arabs. 5

In addition to owning property, my father had a passport issued by the government of Palestine and he often showed us Palestinian coins that he had used before the 1948 Arab-Israeli war. Dad, his brother Qustandi, and their mother escaped the violence to Zarqa in Jordan. Their sister, Hoda, decided to stay on with her family and lost her husband, Elias Awad, in the fighting that broke out in the Musrara district just outside Jerusalem's Damascus Gate.

My grandmother's family, the Fatallehs, left their home in the Katamon neighborhood of Jerusalem and, as Palestinian refugee, have been barred by Israel from returning. Their house still stands, not far from the King David Hotel.

With the unification of the Palestinians under the Palestine Liberation Organization, and with the Arab and international recognition the P.L.O. acquired, questions began to arise over Palestinian identity and nationhood. In 1969, for example, the Prime Minister Golda Meir of Israel declared, "There were no such thing as Palestinians."

Nearly 25 years later, in 1993, Meir's successor, Yitzhak Rabin, shook hands with Yasir Arafat after the P.L.O. and Israel exchanged letters of recognition. The handshake on the South Lawn of the White House was witnessed by President Bill Clinton and leading Jewish and non-Jewish American leaders and members of Congress.

10   Newt Gingrich attended that ceremony, and reportedly shook hands with Arafat. Now, as a Republican candidate for president, he is claiming that the Palestinian people were "invented" because there was never a Palestinian state. The 107 states that recognized Palestine as a full member of Unesco would seriously disagree with this logic.

Gingrich never does say what should happen to this "invented" people if he is elected president.

The people themselves are the best authority on what a people is. If the learned Republican nominee really wants to know who Palestinians are, I would suggest he listen to what they say about themselves.

The historian Rashid Khalidi, in his book "Palestinian Identity: The Construction of Modern National Consciousness," argues that the fierce conflict between Palestinians and Israelis is one reason why the Palestinian identity is so poorly understood. He traces the development of the Palestinians' identity to the late Ottoman area, "when they had multiple loyalties to their religion, the Ottoman state, the Arabic language, and the emerging identity of Arabism, as well as their country and local and familial foci."

In the end, however, Gingrich's attempt to deny Palestinians their identity has nothing to do with history. It is simply political pandering.

15   The majority of Israelis and Palestinians understand that they must share the land between the Mediterranean and the River Jordan. The last thing we need is for American politicians to use our lives and future as a political football.

Analyze

1. In the opening of this essay, Kuttab writes, "My son, born in Jerusalem in 1988, would say his name is Bishara Daoud George Musa Qustandi Musa Kuttab." Many of us have several last names, in the way the author says or with hyphens. What effect and what are the reasons why people have multiple last names, especially with hyphens? Does this practice say anything about family history and identity?

2. What effect does Kuttab's use of chronological narrative have on the way you read his story?

3. The author looks up his last name and finds that the word *Kuttab* is Arabic for "writers or scribes," ones "who sat outside the court and wrote up petitions for people who had a claim with the authorities." How does Kuttab create a sense of dignity and respect because his family has a lineage of literate members? Do you think Kuttab would feel the same if the family name had other roots?

Explore

1. Write an essay about your last name's historical meaning using Kuttab's essay as an example. Has your family had any political experiences because of its last names?

2. The author says, "The people themselves are the best authority on what a people is. If the learned Republican nominee really wants to know who Palestinians are, I would suggest he listen to what they say about themselves." Taking into account the roles of names and naming in this chapter, what are some of the differences that occur when we define ourselves as opposed to when others define us? Use readings from the chapter or others you are familiar with to support your argument.

3. How does the author make a last name into several political issues? What are they and what does it say about the relationship of names to places?

N. Scott Momaday
Excerpts from *The Names: A Memoir*

Momaday, a Native American of Kiowa descent, received the Pulitzer Prize for Fiction for his novel *House Made of Dawn* and a National Medal of Arts. He is Professor Emeritus of English from the University of Arizona. In the excerpt that follows, Momaday tells the tale of his ancestry through the stories and tales that accompany his family's names and history.

How does the form and style of writing affect you compared to the other essays in the chapter?

In devotion to those whose names I bear and to those who bear my names.

My name is Tsoai-talee. I am, therefore, Tsoai-talee; therefore I am.

The storyteller Pohd-lohk gave me the name Tsoai-talee. He believed that a man's life proceeds from his name, in the way that a river proceeds from its source.

In general my narrative is an autobiographical account. Specifically it is an act of the imagination. When I turn my mind to my early life, it is the imaginative part of it that comes first and irresistibly into reach, and of that part I take hold. This is one way to tell a story. In this instance it is my way, and it is the way of my people. When Pohd-lohk told a story he began by being quiet. Then he said Ah-keah-de, "They were camping," and he said it every time. I have tried to write in the same way, in the same spirit. Imagine: They were camping.

Prologue

*You know, everything had to begin, and this is how it was: the Kiowas came one by one into the world through a hollow log. They were many more than now, but not all of them got out. There was a woman whose body was swollen up with child, and she got stuck in the log. After that, no one could get through, and that is why the Kiowas are a small tribe in number. They looked all around and saw the world. It made them glad to see so many things. They called themselves **Kwuda**, "coming out."*

—Kiowa folk tale

About the year 1850 in Kentucky a daughter was born to I. J. Galyen and his Cherokee wife, Natachee, newcomers to the knobs from the foothill of the Great Smoky Mountains. Very little is known of I. J. Galyen, and even less is known of his bride. Perhaps there was Indian blood in his veins, too; family tradition has it that he was predominantly French (Gallien?). He settled in the countryside known as "the knobs," for its numerous abrupt hills, in southwestern Kentucky. Natachee bore him four children, one of whom was Nancy Elizabeth, my great-grandmother. Nancy was frail, sallow-skinned, altogether quiet. She married George Scott of Woodbury and bore him five children. Her first son was Theodore, my grandfather.

My mother tells me that the ancestral house at Scott's Landing was built in 1784. Charles Scott was a general in the Revolutionary War and the fourth governor of Kentucky (1808–1812); he commanded Kentucky troops in the War of 1812.

> *There is a roiling rain, so fine that it remains in the air like a scent. There are barns in the trees, smoking. Smoke, a little darker, denser than the sky, rises from the cracks in the walls and hangs above the woods. The broad sidings are gray and black slats, rough-surfaced, frosted with age like old men. In the dark doors the big brown and yellow sheaves hang heavy and still, shriveled, yet swollen with smoke and damp.*

I have been to the graves of the two of my great-great-grandparents, one on each side of my family. I. J. Galyen and his daughter Nancy are buried close together on the edge of a thick, tangled woods. There are trees in Smith Cemetery, but they are apart from the woods, which are wild. Trees that stand among tombstones are singular and discrete in their definition; their roots extend into the strict society of the dead.

My mother and I once stood at the foot of Nancy Scott's grave. A man approached through the fields, a long way, and greeted us. He was large, rude in appearance; a shotgun lay in the crook of his neck. He was dressed in a plaid shirt and overalls, high, heavy shoes, and a rumpled brown felt hat. His face was almost perfectly round, and his teeth were remarkably small and brown-stained. He did not smile, but he was amiable. I thought: This man must know odd and interesting things and he must know them well.

Reckon it's son' rine. M'nime's Belcher. Y'all got folk hyere? They's wald   5
chickens in them woods.
Y'all listen; you c'n hyear them wald chickens by.
It's gon' rine.

Theodore Scott was born in 1875. He was a third child and first son. Before him were born Olivia and Myrtle; after him Granville and Elizabeth. When the children were very young their father worked on the railroad, and the family lived at Henderson, on the Ohio River. There George Scott died about 1885 of tuberculosis. Nancy returned with her children to her father's house (I. J. Galyen died in 1878) at Costellow, above Chandler's Chapel.

Tuberculosis ravaged Nancy's family. Her mother the old Cherokee woman is thought to have died of it (but when? and where is she buried?); it is likely that her father was infected; her husband and all three of her daughters were destroyed by it. Only her sons, Theodore and Granville, were spared. They lived to be old men.

Mammedaty was my grandfather, whom I never knew. Yet he came to be imagined posthumously in the going on of the blood, having invested the shadow of his presence in an object or a word, in his name above all. He enters into my dreams; he persists in his name.

Mammedaty was the son of Guipagho the Younger and of Keahkinekeah, one of the wives of Poh-lohk. His grandfather Guipagho the Elder was a famous chief, for whom the town of Lone Wolf, Oklahoma, is named, and like his father, Mammedaty lived in the reflected glory of a large reputation. All in all, he bore up under that burden, they say, with courage and good will. His mother, Keahdinekeah, was the daughter of Kau-au-ointy, a woman of strong, foreign character. There was a considerable vitality in him, therefore, and a self-respect that verged upon arrogance. He was born in 1880.

10   Just before Mamaedaty's time the Kiowas had been brought to their knees in the infamous winter campaigns of the Seventh Cavalry, and their Plains culture, which was relatively new to them, virtually destroyed. Nomads, they had come upon the Southern Plains at about the time of the Revolutionary War, having migrated from the area of the headwaters of the Yellowstone River, in what is now western Montana, by way of the Black Hills and the High Plains. Along the way they had become a people of the deep interior, the midcontinent-hunters, warriors, keepers of the sacred earth. When at long last they drew within sight of the Wichita Mountains, they had conceived a new notion of themselves and of their destiny.

> *There are many levels to the land, and many colors. You are drawn into it, down and away. You see the skyline, and you are there at once in your mind, and you have never been there before. There is no confinement, only wonder and beauty.*

The Kiowas could not remember a time of glory in their racial life; they knew only that they were the "coming out" people, according to the name which they gave to themselves, *Kwuda*, who in their origin myth had entered the world through a hollow log. Now it must have seemed to them that in the Southern Plains of 1800, they had reached the time and place of their fulfillment; and so it was indeed. In the course of their long journey they had acquired horses, the sun dance religion, and a certain love and possession of the prairies. They had become centaurs in their spirit. For a hundred years, more or less, they ruled an area that extended from the Arkansas River to the Staked Plains, from the rain shadow of the Rocky Mountains to the Gulf of Mexico, and in them was realized the culmination of a culture that was peculiarly vital, native, and distinct, however vulnerable and ill-fated. But by the time Mammedaty was born the Kiowas had been routed in the Indian wars, the great herds of buffalo had been destroyed, and the sun dance prohibited by law.

Nonetheless Mammedaty had his own life to live, and he thought of   15
being a farmer. The thought must have galled him at first, for the Kiowas were hunters and had never had an agrarian tradition, and indeed they were at best disdainful of their neighbors the Wichitas, Creeks, and Osages, who were planters. And yet he had to contend with the matter of his own survival—a practical matter first, then a spiritual one—and with the example of his closer forebears as well. His grandmother Kau-au-ointy was headstrong and indomitable still, in her sixties, careless of all custom and tradition, and his mother, Keahdinekeah, before she was married, had run her own herd of cattle, riding harder and better than the men who watched her, with grudging admiration, out of the corners of their eyes. And on the other side, too, there was likewise precedent, enough to bridle a young man. Guipagho the Elder was known to make the best of a bad situation, having counseled his people in defeat, urging them simply to hold together when dissolution and degeneration threatened to destroy them. If it came to that, Mammedaty could swallow his pride and be proud of it. Moreover, he had very little choice in the matter. Under the allotment system he had too little land to raise cattle as a business, and the whites had long since begun to close in on all sides, building roads and fences, churches and towns. While many of his kinsmen gave themselves up to self-pity and despair, Mammedaty sowed cotton and wheat, melons and beans.

Shortly after the turn of the century Mammedaty married Aho, the daughter of Gaa-kodalte. She had been a schoolgirl at Rainy Mountain, and somewhere there was in her breeding—as there was in his own—a sheer and separate vitality. It was said that one of her grandfathers was a French Canadian who had come to trade for horses on the Brazos in the 1830s. But for all that she was a Kiowa, sure enough, and a black-eyed beauty besides. And for Mammedaty that was that. In the space of twenty years she bore him six children, two daughters and four sons. Her spirit was whole and hard to bend, and she should certainly have dominated a weaker character—she found in her eldest son a temperament that she could own and manage precisely—but Mammedaty was his own man. He knew of the gentleness in her and brought it out, as he brought a harvest from the seed. Perhaps he saw at once that beneath the hard surface of her will there was a reserve and thoughtfulness that should—and did in fact—succeed and commemorate him, that she should keep possession of his name in all her ways.

> *The dark came first into the house. It was so gradual, then there was nothing to see except the windows, the dusk on the grass, the arbor like a great skeleton. Someone touched a match to the wick and fitted the globe down and yellow light grew up in the room. The shadows were thrown up high on the walls; the oilcloth on the oval table gleamed; the flame was like a great yellow tooth.*

Mammedaty was shrewd in matters of the world; he spent little and traded well, and so he prospered. There were times when he was out of sorts, and his temper got the better of him on occasion, but in the main he was stead enough. He worked hard and believed in his work, and yet there were more important things in his life. It was in his nature to be religious, and he looked deeply into the spiritual part of things. For a time he wore a medicine bundle around his neck, and he prayed to the sun. At odd moments he beheld strange things, visions to which he attached great, supernatural significance. He was a peyote priest in his prime and a Christian in his last years. His character was such that it could not have been easy for him to give up the one way for the other; he must have been for a long time on the edge of eternity.

20   How was it then?

We used to go to Cache, to Quanah Parker's house. There were peyote meetings there. Quanah Parker had a beautiful house; there was a big white star on the roof.

Mammedaty built a house for his mother on the north side of Rainy Mountain Creek, and when he died Keahdinekeah buried him in a bronze casket and covered it with her favorite shawl, and then she lived out her life there in a room of that house, a room that was at last like the shadow in her sightless eyes. And there she dreamed of him, of winter mornings and autumn afternoons in which he was a child, and of the child's delights: new moons and rainbows and wheeling birds.

On a high knoll across the creek Mammedaty built a house for himself and his wife and children. This was 1913, the year in which my father, while the house was under construction, was born in a tipi on the north side of the site, where later the arbor was to be. The youngest of Mammedaty's children, Ralph, was born in the house in 1920, and all but one, a daughter who died in infancy, grew up in it.

Mammedaty went on with his farming as long as he lived, and one by one he put his sons to work in the fields, but it came to nothing in the end. When he died the fields were left fallow, or else they were given under lease to the white farmer of the neighborhood, and so it was from then on.

John, how much do you want for that hog?   25
Twenty-five dollars.
It ain't worth that, John. It ain't worth more than seventeen, eighteen
dollars; I'll give you twenty.
It is worth twenty-five dollars.
How much for that hog, your bottom price?
Twenty-five dollars.   30
Like hell.

Mammedaty died of Bright's disease in 1932.

Well, have you thought it over, John? _Now_ how much do you want for that
there hog?
I have thought it over.
Yes?   35
I want what I wanted yesterday, twenty-five dollars.
All right. All right.
All right.

Analyze

1. The way Momaday presents his story about names to us is different from the essays we have read so far. How is it different from those that discuss family history? Do you find it more or less effective?

2. Momaday starts his *Names* by invoking others who have named him. What effect does this have on his name? Compare his approach to how other essays in this chapter have viewed it as negative when others name them.
3. What makes this essay a narrative form?

Explore

1. Momaday uses a Kiowa folk tale as one of the reasons for the existence of his race. Find or invent a folk tale about your heritage and use it to create a narrative of your family history. Use family pictures to compliment your story, or create a comic book that tells your family identity story. For help with creating a comic book, see *How to Create a Comic Book* (http://www.wikihow.com/Make-a-Comic-Book).
2. At one point the author says, after Mammedaty married Aho, that "Perhaps he saw at once that beneath the hard surface of her will there was a reserve and thoughtfulness that should—and did in fact—succeed and commemorate him, that she should keep possession of his name in all her ways." In this statement there is pride in adopting the man's name yet a hint also that she would adapt them. How does this view stand in contrast with some of the other essays in the chapter or with today's society? Write a Cause/Effect essay pointing out the results of the ways we keep, adapt, or discard last names.
3. This essay goes through the author's real and imagined history. A critical part of it is the intermixing of races to make family. Like the earlier essay's use of *Raza Cosmica*, discuss how such intermixing of names makes up our American cultures. Bring in your own family names if you can.

Jill Filipovic
"Why Should Married Women Change Their Names? Let Men Change Theirs"

Filipovic writes for her political blog, *Feministe*, and is a freelance writer. As a law student focusing on international human rights, her goal is to help with women's issues. In her essay below she questions why, even in the twenty-first century, women are so willing to give up their names, asking, "does getting married mean giving up the most basic marker of your identity?" The logic she uncovers is a wish for family unity, but with the same logic she asks, are men averse to changing their names?

When you marry, will you change your name, and why or why not?

Excuse me while I play the cranky feminist for a minute, but I'm disheartened every time I sign into Facebook and see a list of female names I don't recognize. You got married, congratulations! But why, in 2013, does getting married mean giving up the most basic marker of your identity? And if family unity is so important, why don't men ever change their names?

On one level, I get it: people are really hard on married women who don't change their names. Ten percent of the American public still thinks that keeping your name means you aren't dedicated to your *marriage*. And a full 50% of Americans think you should be legally required to take your husband's name. Somewhere upwards of 90% of women do change their names when they get married. I understand, given the social judgment of a sexist culture, why some women would decide that a name change is the path of least resistance.

But that's not what you usually hear. Instead, the defense of the name change is something like, "We want our family to share a name" or "His last name was better" or "My last name was just my dad's anyway"—all reasons that make no sense. If your last name is really your dad's, then no one, including your dad, has a last name that's actually theirs.

It may be the case that in your marriage, he did have a better last name. But if that's really a *gender*-neutral reason for a name change, you'd think that men with unfortunate last names would change theirs as often as women do. Given that men almost never change their names upon marriage, either there's something weird going on where it just so happens that women got all of the bad last names, or "I changed my name because his is better" is just a convenient and ultimately unconvincing excuse.

Not that I'm unsympathetic to the women out there who have difficult 5 or unfortunate last names. My last name is "Filipovic." People can't spell it or pronounce it, which is a liability when your job includes writing articles under your difficult-to-spell last name, and occasionally doing television or radio hits where the host cannot figure out what to call you. It's weird, and it's "ethnic," and it makes me way too easily Google-able. But Jill Filipovic is my name and my identity. Jill Smith is a different person.

That is fundamentally why I oppose changing your name (and why I look forward to the wider legalization of same-sex marriage, which in addition to just being good and right, will challenge the idea that there are naturally different roles for men and women within the marital unit). Identities matter, and the words we put on things are part of how we make them real. There's a power in naming that *feminists* and social justice activists have long highlighted. Putting a word to the most obvious social dynamics is the first step toward ending inequality. Words like "sexism" and "racism" make clear that different treatment based on sex or race is something other than the natural state of things; the invention of the term "Ms" shed light on the fact that men simply existed in the world while women were identified based on their marital status.

Your name is your identity. The term for you is what situates you in the world. The cultural assumption that women will change their names upon marriage—the assumption that we'll even think about it, and be in a position where we make a "choice" of whether to keep our names or take our husbands'—cannot be without consequence. Part of how our brains function and make sense of a vast and confusing universe is by naming and categorizing. When women see our names as temporary or not really ours, and when we understand that part of being a woman is subsuming your own identity into our husband's, that impacts our perception of ourselves and our role in the world. It lessens the belief that our existence is valuable unto itself, and that as individuals we are already whole. It disassociates us from ourselves, and feeds into a female understanding of self as relational— we are not simply who we are, we are defined by our role as someone's wife or mother or daughter or sister.

Men rarely define themselves relationally. And men don't tend to change their names, or even let the thought cross their mind. Men, too, seem to realize that changing one's name has personal and professional consequences. In the internet age, all the work you did under your previous name isn't going to show up in a Google search. A name change means a new driver's license, passport, professional documentation, the works. It means someone trying to track you down—a former client, an old classmate, a co-worker from a few years back with an opportunity you may be interested in—is going to have a tough time finding you. It means lost opportunities personally and professionally.

Of course, there's also power in a name change. Changing your name if, for example, you change your gender presentation makes sense—a new, more authentic name to match the new, more authentic you. But outside of the gender transition context, marriage has long meant a woman giving up her identity, and along with it, her basic rights. Under coverture laws, a woman's legal existence was merged with her husband's: "husband and wife are one," and the one was the husband. Married women had no right to own property or enter into legal contracts. It's only very recently that married women could get their own credit cards. Marital rape remained legal in many states through the 1980s. The idea that a woman retains her own separate identity from her husband, and that a husband doesn't have virtually unlimited power over a woman he marries, is a very new one.

Fortunately, feminists succeeded in shifting the law and the culture of   10 marriage. Today marriages are typically based on love instead of economics. Even conservative couples who still believe a husband should be the head of the household have more egalitarian marriages than previous generations, and are less likely than their parents or grandparents to see things like domestic violence as a private matter or a normal part of family life.

Unfortunately, despite all of these gains, the marital name change remains. Even the small number of women who do keep their names after marriage tend to give their children the husband's name. At best there's hyphenation. That's a fair solution, but after many centuries of servitude and inequality, allow me to suggest some gender push-back: Give the kids the woman's last name.

Allow me to suggest an even stronger push: If it's important to you that your family all share a last name, make it the wife's. Yes, men, that means taking your wife's name. Or do what this guy did and invent a new name with your wife. And women, if the man you're set to marry extols the virtues of sharing a family name but won't consider taking yours? Perhaps ask yourself if you should be marrying someone who thinks your identity is fundamentally inferior to his own.

The suggestion that men change their names may sound unfair given everything I just wrote about the value of your name and identity, and the psychological impact of growing up in a world where your own name for yourself is impermanent. But men don't grow up with that sense of psychological impermanence. They don't grow up under the shadow of several thousand years of gender-based discrimination. So if you'd rather your family all shared a name, it actually makes much more sense to make it the woman's. Or we can embrace a modern vision of family where individuals form social and legal bonds out of love and loyalty, instead of defining family as a group coalesced under one male figurehead and a singular name.

At the very least, everyone keeping their own name will make Facebook less confusing.

Analyze

1. What percent of women in America change their name when they get married?
2. How did the invention of the term "Ms" help the equality cause?
3. What is gender push-back? Can you think of any other examples of push-back?

Explore

1. Filipovic argues that when women change their name, they are subsuming their own identity into their husband's, and this impacts their self-perception, what she calls being "defined by our role as someone's wife or mother or daughter or sister." Individually or in small groups, interview married women to see if they agree with Filipovic. Present the reasons you discover in a PowerPoint to the class.
2. When women marry (or divorce), they often have to change many legal documents to their new/old name. Filipovic believes the change in names could inhibit professional opportunities. Do you agree with her and why? Make sure to include examples that support your view. Do you know of any other cultures that change names differently at marriage?
3. Filipovic states at one point, "everyone keeping their own name will make Facebook less confusing." The implication is that everyone uses his/her real name on Facebook, married or not. Explore your Facebook site(s) and take a tally of how many of your friends use their real names. Share the results with the class, and why you feel people do or do not create pseudonyms on Facebook.

Amy Tan
"Mother Tongue"

Tan was born in California and is the daughter of Chinese immigrants who had fled China's Cultural Revolution in the 1940s. While at one point in her life she worked to separate herself from her ethnicity, she came to realize that a combination of experiences and things make us who we are. In her case, she came to accept her Chinese side. This is embraced in her well-known novel, *The Joy Luck Club.* Below, Tan shares her language experiences growing up in an immigrant household. Through the differences of language in her home, she becomes sensitive to language manifested in different ways.

From the ways that language was used around her, how does Tan come to understand that identity and language interconnect and make us who we are?

I am not a scholar of English or literature. I cannot give you much more than personal opinions on the English language and its variations in this country or others.

I am a writer. And by that definition, I am someone who has always loved language. I am fascinated by language in daily life. I spend a great deal of my time thinking about the power of language—the way it can evoke an emotion, a visual image, a complex idea, or a simple truth. Language is the tool of my trade. And I use them all—all the Englishes I grew up with.

Recently, I was made keenly aware of the different Englishes I do use. I was giving a talk to a large group of people, the same talk I had already given to half a dozen other groups. The nature of the talk was about my writing, my life, and my book *The Joy Luck Club.* The talk was going along well enough, until I remembered one major difference that made the whole talk sound wrong. My mother was in the room. And it was perhaps the first time she had heard me give a lengthy speech, using the kind of English I have never used with her. I was saying things like "The intersection of memory upon imagination" and "There is an aspect of my fiction that relates to thus-and-thus"—speech filled with carefully wrought grammatical phrases, burdened, it suddenly seemed to me, with nominalized forms, past perfect tenses, conditional phrases, all the forms of standard English that

I had learned in school and through books, the forms of English I did not use at home with my mother.

Just last week, I was walking down the street with my mother, and I again found myself conscious of the English I was using, the English I do use with her. We were talking about the price of new and used furniture and I heard myself saying this: "Not waste money that way." My husband was with us as well, and he didn't notice any switch in my English. And then I realized why. It's because over the twenty years we've been together, I've often used that same kind of English with him, and sometimes he even uses it with me. It has become our language of intimacy, a different sort of English that relates to family talk, the language I grew up with.

5   So you'll have some idea of what this family talk I heard sounds like, I'll quote what my mother said during a recent conversation which I videotaped and then transcribed. During this conversation, my mother was talking about a political gangster in Shanghai who had the same last name as her family's, Du, and how the gangster in his early years wanted to be adopted by her family, which was rich by comparison. Later, the gangster became more powerful, far richer than my mother's family, and one day showed up at my mother's wedding to pay his respects. Here's what she said in part:

"Du Yusong having business like fruit stand. Like off the street kind. He is Du like Du Zong—but not Tsung-ming Island people. The local people call putong, the river east side, he belong to that side local people. That man want to ask Du Zong father take him in like become own family. Du Zong father wasn't look down on him, but didn't take seriously, until that man big like become a mafia. Now important person, very hard to inviting him. Chinese way, came only to show respect, don't stay for dinner. Respect for making big celebration, he shows up. Mean gives lots of respect. Chinese custom. Chinese social life that way. If too important won't have to stay too long. He come to my weddings. I didn't see, I heard it. I gone to boy's side, they have YMCA dinner. Chinese age I was nineteen."

You should know that my mother's expressive command of English belies how much she actually understands. She reads the *Forbes* report, listens to *Wall Street Week,* converses daily with her stockbroker, reads all of Shirley McLain's books with ease—all kinds of things I can't begin to understand. Yet some of my friends tell me they understand 50 percent of what my mother says. Some say they understand 80 to 90 percent. Some say they understand none of it, as if she were speaking pure Chinese. But to me, my mother's English is perfectly clear, perfectly natural. It's my mother tongue. Her language, as I hear it, is vivid, direct, full of observation and imagery. That was the language that helped shape the way I saw things, expressed things, made sense of the world.

Lately, I've been giving more thought to the kind of English my mother speaks. Like others, I have described it to people as "broken" or "fractured" English. But I wince when I say that. It has always bothered me that I can think of no way to describe it other than "broken," as if it were damaged and needed to be fixed, as if it lacked a certain wholeness and soundness. I've heard other terms used, "limited English," for example. But they seem just as bad, as if everything is limited, including people's perceptions of the limited English speaker.

I know this for a fact, because when I was growing up, my mother's "limited" English limited my perception of her. I was ashamed of her English. I believed that her English reflected the quality of what she had to say. That is, because she expressed them imperfectly her thoughts were imperfect. And I had plenty of empirical evidence to support me: the fact that people in department stores, at banks, and at restaurants did not take her seriously, did not give her good service, pretended not to understand her, or even acted as if they did not hear her.

My mother has long realized the limitations of her English as well.   10 When I was fifteen, she used to have me call people on the phone to pretend I was she. In this guise, I was forced to ask for information or even complain and yell at people who had been rude to her. One time it was a call to her stockbroker in New York. She had cashed out her small portfolio and it just so happened we were going to New York the next week, our very first trip outside California. I had to get on the phone and say in an adolescent voice that was not very convincing, "This is Mrs. Tan."

And my mother was standing in the back whispering loudly, "Why he don't send me check, already two weeks late. So mad he lie to me, losing me money."

And then I said in perfect English, "Yes, I'm getting rather concerned. You had agreed to send the check two weeks ago, but it hasn't arrived."

Then she began to talk more loudly. "What he want, I come to New York tell him front of his boss, you cheating me?" And I was trying to calm her down, make her be quiet, while telling the stockbroker, "I can't tolerate any more excuses. If I don't receive the check immediately, I am going to have to speak to your manager when I'm in New York next week." And sure enough, the following week there we were in front of this astonished stockbroker, and I was sitting there red-faced and quiet, and my mother, the real Mrs. Tan, was shouting at his boss in her impeccable broken English.

We used a similar routine just five days ago, for a situation that was far less humorous. My mother had gone to the hospital for an appointment, to find out about a benign brain tumor a CAT scan had revealed a month ago. She said she had spoken very good English, her best English, no mistakes. Still, she said, the hospital did not apologize when they said they had lost the CAT scan and she had come for nothing. She said they did not seem to have any sympathy when she told them she was anxious to know the exact diagnosis, since her husband and son had both died of brain tumors. She said they would not give her any more information until the next time and she would have to make another appointment for that. So she said she would not leave until the doctor called her daughter. She wouldn't budge. And when the doctor finally called her daughter, me, who spoke in perfect English—lo and behold—we had assurances the CAT scan would be found, promises that a conference call on Monday would be held, and apologies for any suffering my mother had gone through for a most regrettable mistake.

15   I think my mother's English almost had an effect on limiting my possibilities in life as well. Sociologists and linguists probably will tell you that a person's developing language skills are more influenced by peers. But I do think that the language spoken in the family, especially in immigrant families which are more insular, plays a large role in shaping the language of the child. And I believe that it affected my results on achievement tests, IQ tests, and the SAT. While my English skills were never judged as poor, compared to math, English could not be considered my strong suit. In grade school I did moderately well, getting perhaps B's, sometimes B-pluses, in English and scoring perhaps in the sixtieth or seventieth percentile on achievement tests. But those scores were not good enough to override the opinion that my true abilities lay in math and science, because in those areas I achieved A's and scored in the ninetieth percentile or higher.

This was understandable. Math is precise; there is only one correct answer. Whereas, for me at least, the answers on English tests were always a judgment call, a matter of opinion and personal experience. Those tests were constructed around items like fill-in-the-blank sentence completion, such as "Even though Tom was ---, Mary thought he was ---." And the correct answer always seemed to be the most bland combinations of thoughts, for example, "Even though Tom was shy, Mary thought he was charming," with the grammatical structure "even though" limiting the correct answer to some sort of semantic opposites, so you wouldn't get answers like "Even though Tom was foolish, Mary thought he was ridiculous." Well, according to my mother, there were very few limitations as to what Tom could have been and what Mary might have thought of him. So, I never did well on tests like that.

The same was true with word analogies, pairs of words in which you were supposed to find some sort of logical, semantic relationship—for example, "*Sunset* is to *nightfall* as --- is to ---." And here you would be presented with a list of four possible pairs, one of which showed the same kind of relationship: *red* is to *stoplight, bus* is to *arrival, chills* is to *fever, yawn* is to *boring.* Well, I could never think that way. I knew what the tests were asking, but I could not block out of my mind the images already created by the first pair, "*sunset* is to *nightfall*"—and I would see a burst of colors against a darkening sky, the moon rising, the lowering of a curtain of stars. And all the other pairs of words—*red, bus, stoplight, boring*—just threw up a mass of confusing images, making it impossible for me to sort out something as logical as saying: "A sunset precedes nightfall" is the same as "a chill precedes a fever." The only way I would have gotten that answer right would have been to imagine an associative situation, for example, my being disobedient and staying out past sunset, catching a chill at night, which turns into feverish pneumonia as punishment, which indeed did happen to me.

I have been thinking about all this lately, about my mother's English, about achievement tests. Because lately I've been asked, as a writer, why there are not more Asian Americans represented in American literature? Why are there few Asian Americans enrolled in creative writing programs? Why do so many Chinese students go into engineering? Well, these are broad sociological questions I can't begin to answer. But I have noticed in surveys—in fact, just last week—that Asian students, as a whole, always do significantly better on math achievement tests than in English. And this makes me think that there are other Asian American students whose English spoken in the home might also be described as "broken" or "limited." And perhaps they also have teachers who are steering them away from writing and into math and science, which is what happened to me.

Fortunately, I happen to be rebellious in nature and enjoy the challenge of disproving assumptions made about me. I became an English major my first year in college, after being enrolled as pre-med. I started writing non-fiction as a freelancer the week after I was told by my former boss that writing was my worst skill and I should hone my talents towards account management.

20   But it wasn't until 1985 that I finally began to write fiction. And at first I wrote using what I thought to be wittily crafted sentences, sentences that would finally prove I had mastery over the English language. Here's an example from the first draft of a story that later made its way into *The Joy Luck Club,* but without this line: "That was my mental quandary in its nascent state." A terrible line, which I can barely pronounce.

Fortunately, for reasons I won't get into today, I later decided I should envision a reader for the stories I would write. And the reader I decided upon was my mother, because these were stories about mothers. So with this reader in mind—and in fact she did read my early drafts—I began to write stories using all the Englishes I grew up with: the English I spoke to my mother, which for lack of a better term might be described as "simple"; the English she used with me, which for lack of a better term might be described as "broken"; my translation of her Chinese, which could certainly be described as "watered down"; and what I imagined to be her translation of her Chinese if she could speak in perfect English, her internal language, and for that I sought to preserve the essence, but neither an English nor a Chinese structure. I wanted to capture what language ability tests can never reveal: her intent, her passion, her imagery, the rhythms of her speech and the nature of her thoughts.

Apart from what any critic had to say about my writing, I knew I had succeeded where it counted when my mother finished reading my book and gave me her verdict: "So easy to read."

Analyze

1. What are the Englishes Tan speaks of?
2. What made Tan realize that her Englishes make her who she is and make her a better writer? How does she compare/contrast the Englishes in her life?
3. How did imagining an audience change Tan's approach to writing? Who was her audience?

Explore

1. What Englishes do you speak? Share some examples in the form of a story.
2. Have you ever felt uncomfortable because of the way you talk, or someone in your family? Describe the experience to your classmates and why you felt this way.

3. While growing up, Tan felt embarrassed by her mother's English, what she called broken and fractured. She also includes other labels that make her sound limited. Write about an experience you have had where you felt limited because of your way of talking, or share an experience where you made someone else feel like this, or of an example of this from something you have read or seen such as a novel, short story, or movie.

Dennis Baron
"Who Owns Global English?"

Dennis Baron is a professor of English and Linguistics at the University of Illinois at Urbana-Champaign. In his recent book, *A Better Pencil: Readers, Writers, and the Digital Revolution* (OUP 2009), he points out that pencils and computers were not created for what we associate them with: writing. In much of his work he explores how computers are used as writing tools. This piece is originally from his blog, "The Web of Language," and here he explores how English, now a global language, is taking on a life of its own and causing quite a stir among language purists.

Why do you think English, or any language for that matter, could be considered pure?

A 1.8 million Euro advertising campaign for Madrid's new Spanish-English public schools is being ridiculed for its slogan "Yes, we want," which critics are calling bad English.

English is what the chanters of "Yes, we want," want to learn, because English is the new global language. The ads, which evoke Barack Obama's "Yes, we can," have appeared on Spanish television, radio, billboards, and buses, prompting complaints that the Education Ministry should be promoting its bilingual public elementary and high schools in correct English if it wants pupils to pick them.

After all, one professional translator sniffed, "any of the students in these schools would be suspended if they repeated this slogan on a test." But a representative of the Ministry of Education insisted that "Yes, we want," is not a test item, it's a "creative publicity slogan, one of the best in recent years."

Is the slogan really bad English, or is it simply new English? Now that English is a global language, it's taking on a life of its own in non-English-speaking countries, and the question of correctness is taking on a new spin. There are plenty of websites chronicling the depredations of "Engrish," Asian signs and product labels translated into inadvertently funny English.

5   The proliferation of non-idiomatic English in international settings is hardly new, and it's not confined to East Asia or to former British colonies. Thirty years ago, in a small French city, my daughter's sixth-grade English teacher marked *phone number* wrong on a test. The correct idiom, Mme la prof told me when I complained, was "number phone," a translation of the French idiom *numéro de téléphone. Phone number* might be "O.K." in American English, she conceded, but only British English was acceptable in her class. She had been to England, and she had it on good authority that the Queen said "number phone." She didn't change the grade.

While much of the world has joined Spain in chanting, "What do we want? English! When do we want it? Now!" or words to that effect, some governments are trying to stop global English before it undermines their own national language.

Recently a Slovak television station came under fire for three untranslated English sentences uttered on a talk show. A guest, British musician Andy Hillard, a Bratislava resident fairly fluent in Slovak, had trouble understanding a question in Slovak, so the host translated it into English. Hillard automatically answered in English, violating the new official language law requiring that only Slovak be used in public. Someone complained, and the government quickly launched an investigation which could result in a $7,300 fine for "misusing the language." While English is taught in almost every Slovak school, the government doesn't want English on the air.

In another move to combat the spread of English, the Chinese government has ordered its television stations to stop using English abbreviations, including GDP (gross domestic product), CPI (consumer price index), and NBA (National Basketball Association). Supporters of the English ban see it protecting the purity of Chinese, while opponents of the restriction point out that Chinese was never a pure language: up to 30,000 ancient

Chinese words, like *shijie*, 'world,' and *zhendi*, 'truth,' come from Sanskrit and Pali, while more recent borrowings include *gongchandang*, 'communist,' which comes from Japanese. Not to mention that, as in Spain, Slovakia, and France, English is the most widely studied foreign language in China.

What's also curious, considering the global status of English, is that some English speakers actually fear that their language is threatened by other languages. Just as Slovakia and France declared their languages official in order to protect them from English, and from the languages of indigenous minorities and immigrants, anglophones think that making English official will protect it, though it's not clear what protection the global language needs.

In some cases the protectionists go even further, campaigning to get   10 rid of borrowed words in English. So Oliver Kamm complained when the London *Times* TV critic, reviewing the new actor playing Dr. Who, wrote, "Plus ça change, plus c'est la même Doctor Who." Kamm, a *Times* leader writer, believes that to be correct, the reviewer should have written "le même Dr. Who," since Dr. Who is a male character. But Kamm would prefer no French at all, or any other foreign language, for that matter, since in his view, readers of the *Times,* who don't attend bilingual schools and aren't very good at languages, won't understand foreignisms unless they're translated (*The Times,* Mar. 27, 2010, p. 107; *leader writer* is British for op-ed columnist).

No matter how much we object to "mistakes" in other people's language, there doesn't seem to be much we can do about it. Plus English speakers, who can't effectively control the English of fellow anglophones, are actually in a much weaker position when trying to control the English of foreigners. And objecting to the English of advertising seems hopeless. To anglophones, "Yes, we want" may seem funny, and Spanish authorities may even find it embarrassing, but whatever happens to the slogan, its very existence is one more sign that English, now that it's global, is no longer the exclusive property of English-speaking nations.

The ancient Romans may have felt a similar loss of linguistic control as their empire slipped away and Latin started its long segue into Italian, Spanish, French, Portuguese, Romanian, Catalan, and the other Romance tongues. For now it doesn't look like English is breaking up the way Latin did. But it could. As the Queen might put it, it's early days yet. And that's British for "it's too soon to tell."

Analyze

1. What happened on Slovak television?
2. What other civilization does Baron say might have felt other civilizations were ruining its language?
3. What is the Spanish campaign slogan, and what is the missing piece Baron points out?

Explore

1. Imagine you are Amy Tan and you just read Baron's essay. What would you argue? Would you agree or disagree with the flow of the language or with those trying to maintain it?
2. While Baron talks about English usage in foreign countries, the United States is a country of immigrants and the language is bound to mix with other languages. Write an essay to your teacher arguing why you feel writing teachers should or should not allow more flexibility in the Englishes of this country.
3. Go to a local market where they sell foreign goods and write or take pictures of products that have English translations, or find some instructions (e.g., how to assemble) for products from a foreign country, or something that has been translated and falls into what might be a controversial use of English. Write an essay or produce a PowerPoint pointing out why the language is acceptable or why it is not, especially with dangerous situations.

Forging Connections

1. Drawing from two to three of the essays from this chapter as models, write about an experience with names and identity you had in a city where you have lived or presently live. For example, you might discuss the various ways a community within your city (e.g., Little Italy) is talked about from the outside, and then how the members of Little Italy name those who are not from it. How do the different perspectives of insiders and outsiders compliment and criticize each other? Include images to show what the place, the people, foods, and so on, are like as part of the storyline you create.
2. Create a comic book based on the topic in Prompt One above.

3. Communicate the same message as on previous page, but in four different formats for four different readers or audiences. (1) Write a formal three- to five-page letter to one of the essayists in this chapter telling him/her what you know about the power of naming and being named; make sure you draw from several of the essays in the chapter. (2) Write a tweet expressing the same point (140 characters). (3) Compose a text addressed to your classmates on the same point, and then (4) Create a mostly visual message using Tumblr to express the same point. When you complete these tasks, write down the strengths and weaknesses of each form (letter, tweet, text, and Tumblr) for communicating your views. What were the adjustments you made for each and why? Time allowing, discuss the four adapted messages in class.

Looking Further

1. How do the writers in this chapter agree with each other in terms of the power of names and naming, and of those who have the power over language? Create a list of the ways they agree, and another where they do not (Classification/Division). Make sure to draw conclusions from your findings. Depending on your instructor's wishes, this can be done as either an essay or as a PowerPoint.

2. How has society shaped who you are, either in a way that you like or a way that you dislike? Write or record with audio or video a specific positive or negative experience you have had with names (if you use audio or video to record, keep the completed, final time under two minutes). Compare and contrast the effects that naming has had on you. For example, in this chapter, most of the writers extol the power of what names can do for us. In contrast, in Chapter 4, in Zaslow's "The Most Praised Generation Goes to Work," the author criticizes a generation that needs constant praise, even when unwarranted.

Where Are You From? Notions of Identity & Place

2

While Chapter 1 explored the role and power of names, Chapter 2 asks us to consider where we are from, including our ancestry, and the ways that our past shapes notions of our identity, through our own eyes and from others' viewpoints. The readings in this chapter share a multitude of approaches that writers and speakers use to make sense of their relationship to the United States, as natives, citizens, and immigrants. These readings run the spectrum from joyful and heartwarming to painful and saddening.

As our essays reveal, names can quickly be associated with a place and, consequently, a certain unique cultural identity. In the first reading, Thurston uses humor to draw our attention to how blacks are stereotyped as all being the same and, because they are black, all from Africa. We also introduce a poem in this chapter, "America." In it Ginsberg brings social issues to light by looking at New York America—not *Real Housewives of New York*, but a gritty working and artistic class. We will hear how, as a poet, his use of language to establish his identity and connection to place establishes his use of language as well.

On a different note, this chapter contains two essays that explore what the United States means from several ideological, political, and personal angles. In "Deconstructing America," Buchannan argues that America is deconstructing itself. He bases this on the increasing diversity making up the population of the United States, having changed from its majority European descent. Meyer explores what he sees as a new type of immigrant to the United States, the Mexican who only wants to work here, not stay, in "Why Americans Hate This 'Immigration' Debate."

The final three readings explore how identity becomes shaped in new, real worlds from immigration, or in digital ones. In Mengestu's "Home at Last" we discover how he finally feels grounded to place by identifying with the experiences of other people who are also immigrants. In "Unravelling the Social Network: Theory and Research," Merchant explores how social networking sites (SNSs) have many of the same characteristics that reinforce our identity(ies) as do real-life ones. Unlike Meyer's findings, our last essay, "Rhode Island," by Lahari explores her life as a one-time foreigner growing up in Rhode Island, and how her family became an integral part of America's diversity.

Baratunde Thurston
"How to Be Black"

Baratunde Thurston is a stand-up comic and directs *The Onion*, a satirical newspaper. We have included here "How to Be Black," a performance mixing satire with memoir. For more on this story, go to National Public Radio at http://www.npr.org. In the style of memoir, he reflects on the cultures he has experienced, and using satire, he gives his take on being black today. At one point in his interview, Thurston talks about how he adapts his messages among different groups of people. For more on this interview in audio and text from National Public Radio, visit http://www.npr.org.

How do you adjust who you are among the different groups of people you are around?

GROSS: Baratunde Thurston, welcome to FRESH AIR.

BARATUNDE THURSTON: It is great to be here. Thanks, Terry.

GROSS: So I'd like you to do a reading from your new book, *How to Be Black*, and it's a very autobiographical part of the book.

THURSTON: Yes, it is.

GROSS: Would you read it for us?

THURSTON: Absolutely. My name is Baratunde Thurston, and I've been black for over 30 years. I was born in 1977 in Washington, D.C., in the wake of civil rights, black power and "Sanford and Son." My mother was a pro-black, pan-African, tofu-eating hippy who had me memorizing the countries of Africa and reading about Apartheid before my 10th birthday. My Nigerian name was not handed down to me from any known lineage but rather claimed and bestowed upon me by parents who demanded a connection, any connection at all, to mother Africa.

> "I was born in 1977 in D.C., in the wake of civil rights, black power and 'Sanford and Son.'"

Yes, I grew up in the inner city at 1522 Newton Street, and I survived D.C.'s drug wars. Yes, my father was absent. He was shot to death in those same drug wars. But it's also true that I graduated from Sidwell Friends School, the educational home of Chelsea Clinton and the Obama girls, and Harvard University. I love classical music, computers and camping.

I've gone clubbing with the president of Georgia, the country, twice. My version of being black adheres as much to the stereotypes as it dramatically breaks from them, and that's probably true for most of you reading this, if not about blackness itself than about something else related to your identity. Through my stories, I hope to expose you to another side of the black experience while offering practical comedic advice based on my own painful lessons learned.

GROSS: Great, thanks for reading that. And that's from Baratunde's— Baratunde Thurston's new book, *How to be Black*.

So let's start with your name, which you say some really interesting things about in the book, the name being Baratunde Thurston, very African first name, very . . .

THURSTON: Not African last name.

(SOUNDBITE OF LAUGHTER)

GROSS: Not African second name, yes. And you say my name has served as a perfect window through which to examine my experience of blackness.

10   **THURSTON:** Yes.

GROSS: So how were you named Baratunde?

THURSTON: So I was named, as most children, by my parents, and for them it wasn't simply a name, and it wasn't grabbing an ancestral name or a grandfather or grandmother. They were—it was a political act on their part. My mother was very much this pan-African hippy type of woman, and she marched in the streets, and I have photos of her taking over radio stations.

And there was a phase in African-American history, especially in the '60s and '70s, where parents were trying to get back to Africa, and if they couldn't physically do it, they did it by naming their child something African. So they were flipping through books looking for a name that had a particular meaning.

And in my case, my mother had had a series of miscarriages before I was born, and so they were looking for something extra-deep, and they found this name, Babatunde. Babatunde is a very common Nigerian name. It means the spirit of my mother's grandfather returns in me.

In the same book, they also saw Baratunde, a slight derivation, a little tweak with an R instead of the B. And the book also explained that Baratunde means one who was chosen, which I have to clarify with people. It doesn't mean the chosen one. That's a lot of pressure. It's one who was chosen. There could be like 50 chosen people, 1,000. The chosen one, usually life ends poorly for that person.

(SOUNDBITE OF LAUGHTER)

THURSTON: So I'm happy to be one who was chosen. And my middle name is actually Arabic, it's Rafik(ph), and Rafik means friend or companion. So the combination of Baratunde Rafik is to mean kingly companion, and that's the total history of how I got that name.

GROSS: So what reaction did you get to your name typically from white people, from African-Americans and from Africans?

15   **THURSTON:** So very early on, teachers started shortening my name. They didn't want to deal with Baratunde. It was a little strange even for them. So they called me Barry. Actually, Barrington was the first name a teacher . . .

GROSS: That's the same with Barack Obama, right? He was Barry.

THURSTON: Yeah, yeah, so I'm just like the president. I control the nuclear arsenal, I occasionally disappoint my progressive base, but I'm generally a good guy.

(SOUNDBITE OF LAUGHTER)

THURSTON: So yeah, I was Barrington, and then I was Barry, and half-way through my middle school time at Sidwell Friends, it was seventh grade, and it just clicked in me, my name's Baratunde. That's a great name. People should call me that. And I had to actually convert the school to call me not Barry but Baratunde, because once people know what they call you, even if you don't approve of it, you know, nicknames, Chester is Chest Hair, right, just stuff like that, it takes a long time to kind of undo that.

So it took a couple of years to retrain people, but I finally fully asserted Baratunde as the name I should have. So people, usually they assume there's a nickname, and they'll just jump to it, or they say: What do people call you for short? And I say Baratunde, just say it faster. You can save time and be a little bit more efficient if you're really worried about the time it takes to say the name.

GROSS: So what assumptions were made about you because of your name?

THURSTON: Well, so it's really, I have different audiences that take it [20] differently. First of all, I meet Nigerians, and many of them are initially really excited because they're like, oh, one of our brothers. But then they're like, wait, Baratunde, you mean Babatunde. I'm like, no, I mean Baratunde. Well, where'd you get the name, and who did this?

And so they have excitement, then frustration, then judgment often from the Nigerian community.

GROSS: And the judgment is, like, you're not really Nigerian.

THURSTON: Exactly, and I'm not authentically Nigerian. I'm not really African, which is just fun given the idea of why I was given the name, because I'm not really fully American either because of the history—this was my mother's attempt, and I didn't have any say in it, but I like the sound, and I like the meaning.

So I have that community. Then you have kind of the more American-born black people who really generally don't have that much of a reaction because I think American blacks are used to very interesting names in our community, whether they're derived from Africa or just made up from cars plus like a candy bar and the name of the street you grew up on. Like that's a pretty unique tradition.

And then, you know, from white Americans it's often the assumption of, well, you've got to have a nickname, or what does it mean. It's got to have some super-deep meaning. And in my case it actually does.

GROSS: Because it was an African name, meant to connect you to Africa, because your parents, or at least your mother, was interested in that connection, did you feel that connection when you were growing up?

THURSTON: I did, and my mother wouldn't let me not feel that connection either. It was a part of my programming as a kid growing up. So I grew up in D.C. in the Columbia Heights neighborhood, before it became as shiny as it is today, and my mother after sixth grade enrolled me in Sidwell Friends School, which is a great private school.

The Obama girls go there now. But she also at the same time enrolled me in what's known as a Rights of Passage program. And in the '60s, you know, along with black power, there was even a subset of pan-Africanism, where people were really trying to reclaim this connection and borrowing and learning from traditions.

So you could think of it sort of as Hebrew school or a bar mitzvah for blackness.

(SOUNDBITE OF LAUGHTER)

25   **THURSTON:** And every, you know, weekday I'd be at Sidwell learning Sidwell-type things, and it's field hockey and lacrosse and the sons of presidents and daughters of World Health Organization people. And then every Saturday morning, from maybe 7 a.m. to 1 p.m., we'd have physical training, we'd read books like *The Isis Papers*, we'd read Toussaint Louverture, and we would dance and do all sorts of cultural and intellectual activities to try to ground us in what they thought was a more appropriate Africanness in that era.

It was also a time when crack was ravaging communities, and there was a special focus on how do we preserve young black boys and prevent them from ending up in the criminal justice system. So that was also an angle.

So I had this balanced experience of Sidwell. By weekday (unintelligible), which is the name of the program, on the weekends, and that was kind of my strongest grounding. But then even at home, it didn't stop. My mom had this big map of Africa on her bedroom wall, and it had all the nations carved out. She would actually quiz me.

GROSS: And you keep describing your mother as like a hippy and, you know, tofu and carob and all that. How was she accepted in your neighborhood? Was she considered like the hippy of the neighborhood, and was that a bad thing?

THURSTON: She was not in any way ostracized. I mean, my mom also had this sort of hybrid personality. When she grew up, I think it was Fourth Street Northwest, I'd have to double-check, I didn't get that deep into her bio, but she had—you know, she ran the streets. She was in gangs. She was also super-political, and she was a crunchy hippy lady.

She went through her own evolution, grew up in a Baptist church, kind of rejected that because of the images of whiteness all around. She's like, what, they can't all be white. You know, if civilization began in Africa, the logical conclusion is—so she was kind of ahead of her time on that.

Then she became vegetarian and started hanging out with the hippy-type people, but that wasn't the full extent of her personality, and she was still kind of a bad-ass as well. So I think she had, from my young eyes and recollection, a lot of respect in the neighborhood.

GROSS: If you're just joining us, my guest is Baratunde Thurston. His new book is called *How to Be Black*. He's the director of digital for the satirical newspaper *The Onion*, co-founder of the blog Jack and Jill Politics. Let's take a short break here. Then we'll talk some more.

THURSTON: All right.

GROSS: OK. This is FRESH AIR.   30

(SOUNDBITE OF MUSIC)

GROSS: My guest is Baratunde Thurston. He's the author of the new book *How to Be Black*. It's a memoir, it's satirical also. He's the director of digital for the satirical newspaper *The Onion*, co-founder of the blog Jack and Jill Politics. He also does stand-up comedy.

So in the reading that you did at the beginning of the show, you kind of like drop in that your father was killed during the crack epidemic, and he was murdered during a drug deal that went bad, and he was the person buying, not selling.

THURSTON: Right.

GROSS: And you say in your book the only thing that could have been more cliched at the time—and you say this with great sorrow—but that the only thing that could be more cliched at the time was that the deal had gone down at a KFC.

THURSTON: Yes, I did write that.

GROSS: How old were you when that happened, six?   35

THURSTON: I was five or six years old, yeah.

GROSS: How did your mother tell you what happened?

THURSTON: So there was a—there was a phone call that she had received, and you have to understand, my father did not live with us at the time. So I had very few memories and interactions with him. But I knew I had a father, and I'm pretty sure he loved me a lot, and I probably loved him in any way a four- or five-year-old kid can actually know what love means for a father.

But she got a call, and she said Arnold Robinson is dead. And I started crying, and I still—you know, it's such a strange thing to think about because I know what those words mean now, I've experienced death as an adult, of my own mother, of really close friends, and hearing those words and having those feelings at five or six years old, they're a little different. So I know I had an immediate physical, emotional reaction, but it wasn't until years later that I fully understood what that meant.

This to me at the time just meant, oh, my daddy's not around anymore, that's bad.

GROSS: Did she explain that he was shot?

40   **THURSTON:** I found—I don't remember in the moment, and a young child's memory is a little fudgy. What I do remember is actually not knowing how he died when she told me, but coming across—we had a big file cabinet in our house, a big black file cabinet, I think five drawers—very, very deep; smooth rolling wheels with these chrome label-holders you could slide an index card into.

And we had a file subsection within it called vital statistics, and I remember it so specifically because statistics was spelled with an X at the end because my mom thought that was fun. And I used to think it was vittle(ph) statistics.

And so I was going through the vittle(ph) statistics file one afternoon, as a kid does, rifling through papers, and I found my father's death certificate. And I had never known in that detail what had happened.

And death certificates are just—it's the first time I'd ever seen one. I haven't seen very many in my life, but the death certificate from a gunshot wound is a horrible, horrible representation of mortality, and it's cold, and it's clinical, and you basically watch the body shutting down in text.

GROSS: You quote it in the book. You want to read it?

THURSTON: Yeah. Here's what the death certificate said: Bullet wound of chest, lungs, spine and spinal cord followed by paraplegia and bronchial pneumonia.

GROSS: Right.

THURSTON: That's—I don't know, it's just, it's a strange medical dark poetry, and what I'd understood is he was shot, which translated into something much more troubling yet also richer and just strange. So I don't remember knowing in the very moment that he was shot. I know I found out in the intervening years, and then coming across this document was sort of another shock to my system of just what that actually meant.

45   **GROSS:** So what did it do to your sense of, like, violence in the neighborhood, how drugs can actually lead to death? You know, it's the kind of like potentially "Scared Straight" type of thing that, you know, a lot of parents and law officers and stuff try to like instill in young people. This is the consequence.

THURSTON: Right.

GROSS: So like at age six, your father's shot to death in a drug deal. What impact did that have in terms of how one goes about living in the world?

THURSTON: So I don't think it was an explicit, like, red flag in my head. I was a nerdy kid. I was a studious kid. I did have friends as well, I wasn't totally isolated and alone, but I was in the gifted and talented program in the public school system and did extracurricular activities, paying bass in the D.C. Youth Orchestra program, Boy Scouts.

And again, this was in part my mother just throwing activities at me to keep me drowning in busy-ness.

GROSS: Keep you off the streets.

THURSTON: Exactly, so I wouldn't have time, literally didn't have time   50
to do any crime because I had assignments backed up from all these different activities. You know, and it wasn't just a matter of not having time, it was being engaged in things that actually stimulated the mind. And I think that probably lifted any burden off of me where it might have been so easy to kind of fall into the statistical future that lay before me of hold this bag, deliver this thing and then look out for that and then collect this.

It just didn't interest me as much, and it was never this loud voice of my dead father saying don't do this, but that probably had a subconscious effect, at least.

GROSS: In your book, in talking about growing up during the crack epidemic and that epidemic affecting your neighborhood, you write—you compare it to the HBO series "The Wire."

(SOUNDBITE OF LAUGHTER)

GROSS: And you write: When the HBO series "The Wire" came out, I recognized so much of what was on my TV screen from my memories of my own neighborhood. We had everything "The Wire" had except for universal critical acclaim and the undying love of white people who saw it.

(SOUNDBITE OF LAUGHTER)

GROSS: I love that.

THURSTON: That's true, we did not have the ratings or the Netflix popularity that "The Wire" did.

GROSS: So how did the crack epidemic affect your neighborhood?   55

THURSTON: It was—I think the first thing I remember was not being . . .

GROSS: And do you know one of the reasons why I'm so interested? I remember like during the height of the crack epidemic, like always thinking what's it like for the kids who are growing up in this, you know, and like now we can talk to the kids because they're adults and find out, you know?

THURSTON: Exactly. Let me—I remember not being able to go outside. I remember specifically not being allowed to sit on our front stoop. And on the weekends I used to sometimes sit on the stoop and eat breakfast outside, especially in the summertime. We didn't have air conditioning, it's hot, it's a nice day.

And there was a period of time when that was no longer allowed. I remember not playing outside as much and being told go to so-and-so's house but stay inside, there's a sort of captivity. And I also have a very particular memory of watching some of my friends walk down that road that I didn't walk down.

And there was a family of brothers who lived across the street from us, and there may—there were at least three of them, I'm pretty sure there were four, and you could just watch them almost like that image of evolution, which shows kind of a hunched-over ape evolving into man.

You could watch the older brother get into the drug business, and then the next one and the next one and then the youngest one, and it was just—that was the pattern established.

And I remember when those guys used to deliver pizza for Domino's, and that was their way of making money, and that was their job, and they had rigged up a lawnmower engine to their 10-speed bikes to turn them into motorcycles and would zip down 16th Street—I lived at 16th and Newton—and I thought that was so cool.

And then I remember when those same kids set up a lemonade stand. And then I remember when their jackets got nicer, their boots got nicer, and they were selling drugs. And that was a—I don't know, such a strong memory in my head of, well, they used to that, and now they do this. And I used to be able to do this, and now I can't do that. Those are some of the effects I remember kind of growing up in a neighborhood that was being corrupted and poisoned by crack cocaine.

GROSS: In seventh grade, you moved to a different neighborhood.

60   **THURSTON:** Yeah, the end of seventh grade, we moved out of northwest Washington, D.C., to Tacoma Park, Maryland. And essentially it had become too much for my mother, and I think it was very stressful for her raising me. She was raising me alone. So she was working a lot of hours to pay for all these things, including private school at the time.

And I was pretty cool with it because, again, as a kid, whatever you grow up in feels normal. So this is where my friends are, this is the neighborhood I know. I'm not feeling so dramatic about the situation. But as a parent, you're probably just seeing risk, risk, risk, risk, risk—everywhere.

So we moved out to a more suburban area, still a black neighborhood, actually, but we had a little plot of land, free-standing house and . . .

GROSS: Did you like it?

THURSTON: I did like it. I didn't spend much time there. And it was quiet. It was quieter than I was used to, especially growing up at a major intersection in a city. You have cops and ambulances and people yelling, and that's a sign of life. So we moved out to—near a park, and there's deer that run across the street.

(SOUNDBITE OF LAUGHTER)

THURSTON: That's actually a little alarming, you know, even for a kid who was a Boy Scout and went camping. I wasn't used to sleeping in silence. So the first while was a bit different. And then I did so many school activities that home really was where I slept and not much more. But it was nice.

GROSS: What kind of work was your mother doing to support you?

THURSTON: So she evolved a lot throughout her life. I think she started doing domestic work, and then she was a secretary, and then she was a paralegal. And she—she never got a full college degree, but she took a lot of classes at the University of District of Columbia and at Montgomery Community College and ended up essentially learning computer programming and taking—you know, sliding from the paralegal department within the federal government to the programming department.

And I don't remember what level grade she made in the government, but it was a pretty good one. So she worked for something called the Office of the Comptroller of the Currency; it's a division of the Treasury Department, and they were charged with overseeing the national banks.

So she programmed in a language called COBOL, this mainstream computer language, and wrote software and inspected software that in turn inspected national banks. She was a big geeky nerd.

GROSS: And you got deep into computers too.

THURSTON: Yeah, because of her. I mean, she—that was so fortunate for her to have discovered that. It really magnified her earning power, but it also positioned both of her kids—I have an older sister who lives in Michigan—and both of us, because of our mother, got early access to computers. She knew it was important. So we were one of the first households in our neighborhood to have a computer, to get online.

I was doing bulletin boards and early Internet before it became anywhere near front-page news.

GROSS: Baratunde Thurston will be back in the second half of the show. His new book is called *How to Be Black*. I'm Terry Gross and this is FRESH AIR.

(SOUNDBITE OF MUSIC)

GROSS: This is FRESH AIR. I'm Terry Gross, back with Baratunde Thurston, author of the new book *How to Be Black*. It's part memoir, part satirical guidebook. Stand-up comic, the director of digital for the satirical newspaper *The Onion*, and co-founder of the blog Jack and Jill Politics. When we left off, we were talking about the different cultures he grew up in.

So you were describing, earlier, how your mother really wanted to give you a very complete education and some like historical rooting . . .

70   **THURSTON:** Yeah.

GROSS: . . . and what it means to be African-American. So she sent you to Sidwell Friends School, a fine school that the Obama children go to . . .

THURSTON: Yeah.

GROSS: Chelsea Clinton went there. But on weekends you'd go to this, like, Afrocentric school and learn all about like African history and . . .

THURSTON: Yeah. Yeah.

75   **GROSS:** . . . and so on. Were you able to be the same person in both those settings? Or did you have to like adjust who you were? I mean because a lot of us are, that's how we are.

THURSTON: Yeah.

GROSS: You know, you have different friends and you're slightly different with different friends, you're slightly different in different contexts.

THURSTON: Yeah, no, the code switching is a real thing and I think there was a Baratunde from Newton Street who learned to walk those streets and navigate that world and be very comfortable with all the stuff that's happening in the street. And then there was the academic library, studious, you know, high school newspaper Baratunde; and then there was the, like, black power Tunde.

(SOUNDBITE OF LAUGHTER)

THURSTON: That was also going down. And those worlds often collided. I remember I wrote a paper once for an English class, that was extremely radical. It was the type of paper that I won't be president because I wrote this thing.

(SOUNDBITE OF LAUGHTER)

80   **THURSTON:** It was one of those things that they dig up, like Rush Limbaugh would have a field day.

GROSS: No, you should read—you have to—you reprint some of it in the book. You have to read some of it.

THURSTON: Yeah. Yeah. I'm be happy to. I'd be happy to . . .

GROSS: You have to read some of it from the book. It's very conspiracy.

(SOUNDBITE OF LAUGHTER)

THURSTON: So the title of this piece is "The U.S. Propaganda Machine," and that's what I submitted to my English teacher.

85   **GROSS:** Find a really good excerpt in there.

THURSTON: Yeah. Let me jump to a hyper-inflammatory section, which . . .
(SOUNDBITE OF LAUGHTER)
THURSTON: All right. This is fun. (Reading) Now, my brothers and sisters, I will tell you—and what you also have to understand I wrote this as if it were a major speech . . .
(SOUNDBITE OF LAUGHTER)
THURSTON: . . . that I was delivering to all black people. I imagined kind of a State of the Black Union with everybody around the world, and especially the U.S., tuned into my words.

(Reading) Now, my brothers and sisters, I will tell you ways that the white man has led our people into this epidemic—this epidemic of violence. If you want to go way back: It all started when the Europeans invaded our rich, prosperous motherland and robbed her of her people. At the time of the slave trade, there were Africans who sold their own people for beads and jewelry. This was the beginning of our self-destruction.

(Reading) Another possibility is found by looking at the brutal times of slavery. During slavery, some of the brutalities were earthshaking and unfathomable.

And I remember being so proud of using the word *unfathomable*. And so I go on and I blame the white man. I basically call for a reverse revolution against white people. And I turned in this paper, very proudly, not at all conscious that this wasn't a normal thing to submit to a middle school English class at a place like Sidwell Friends. That was the black power Tunde speaking. And my English teacher came to be the next day, asked me to stay after class, and said hey, some pretty radical stuff you put in that paper. Would you have written that if I weren't black? And I was like absolutely not. And I expect you to keep our secret. But that was the moment—a flashpoint for me, of conflict, of kind of, using the ability to manipulate words that I was picking up at Sidwell, but with the ideas that I was sucking up Saturdays at this Ankobea Society and it turned out into this, kind of, militant speech that I hypothetically delivered.
GROSS: Were you taught that all of black people's problems were really a conspiracy by white people?
THURSTON: Well, so here was the beauty. And this is why the mix is so 90 important—and even I talk about my mother's evolution in her life. I talk about my mix in these neighborhoods. I was taught extremes, and able to balance them because I was taught multiple extremes. So at a place like Sidwell, and Sidwell's a great school. It really is. But it was also a tough place to be one of the few minority kids, one of the few poorer kids, and there's a big social adjustment. And one of the arguments there was we

need more black faculty, we need more black subjects in the curriculum. That always happens at any sort of school, especially kind of elite secondary and then colleges. Meanwhile and the Ankobea environment, it was Africa did this, Africa invented that, Imhotep this, blah, blah, blah and the white men cause these problems. Those either cancel each other out or they drive the bearer of both ideas insane.

GROSS: Right.

THURSTON: I didn't go insane.

(SOUNDBITE OF LAUGHTER)

THURSTON: And fortunately. And I think most people in that situation probably wouldn't, so a sort of encouraged to me both see the good in old sides, and also challenge both perspectives.

GROSS: OK. So we've established that you were exposed to really different ways of seeing history?

95 **THURSTON:** Mm-hmm.

GROSS: Of seeing being black in America.

THURSTON: Yeah.

GROSS: And that that was a really good thing for you.

THURSTON: Yeah. Absolutely. Absolutely.

100 **GROSS:** And then you went to Harvard.

THURSTON: I did.

GROSS: And you say at Harvard is where you learned that some people could see your black skin is just a cover for the whiteness underneath. Not necessarily you, but ones like skin. So was that like your introduction to the whole, you know, quote, "Oreo" concept?

THURSTON: Well, the Oreo concept was, I was introduced to that at Sidwell.

GROSS: Oh, OK.

105 **THURSTON:** Sidwell was boot camp for me.

GROSS: Right.

THURSTON: It was, OK, you're going to go train here so that you can enter the world, you know, the mainstream world of America. And it was actually my first, possibly my second day, but I'm pretty sure it was my first day at Sidwell, that a black student who had been at the school for a really long time was assigned to be my buddy and adjust me to the environment. And he asked if I knew what an Oreo was. I actually—it's such a strong memory. We were in the first floor stairwell of the upper-school building, southwest corner, I remember all this—southeast corner. I really thought he was talking about cookies. I said, yeah, it's the cream-filled cookie from Nabisco. And he's like, no, no man. Oreo's somebody's who is black on the outside and white on the inside. And then he made an example. And he's like you see that kid across the way. And he pointed across the dining hall a little later, he said, that kid's an Oreo. And I didn't even know the kid's name at the time—I saw this nerdy black kid with glasses hanging out with white friends and I was like he could be president someday. It's a good way to fundraise, you know, make white friends early. And that was the first introduction of this concept of, sort of, inauthentic blackness because you're comfortable around whiteness.

GROSS: And if you were either introverted or, like, intellectual bookish, would that add to an Oreo image?

THURSTON: It, I mean I think and again, I wish I almost have in my head an image of the layers of expectations around your identity. So at a school like Sidwell, first let's just take the fun fact of a black kid who's been at Sidwell his entire life judging another black kid at Sidwell's blackness. It's like you've both been steeped in this environment so are you picking on that kid. But then you have the, you know, take someone like me who would go to Sidwell by day and then go back to my neighborhood and the black kids there, and their judgment of someone like me who goes off to the fancy white private school . . .

GROSS: Right. Yeah. What was that judgment?   110

THURSTON: Well, so and I never got hit with a heavy like you think your white, in part because I think I, these kids just knew me—at least from the kids that actually knew me. But you will get it from kids who don't know you. I mean we're—as people who are really good at judging people we don't know, that's part of how we move through the world and were programmed to do it. So you see some black kid in this environment like, sellout, Oreo. It's just an instant, mild envy, misunderstanding and judgment about someone who you don't really get. And when you start equating success and literacy and achievement and hard academic work with white, and more importantly, with not black, then it becomes a little troubling, or actually, I'd say, very troubling. So I experienced a little dose of that but mostly because I was interacting with kids who knew me and I had made that transition, they saw me make it, they were less harsh.

GROSS: And I'm also wondering if the African name Baratunde . . .

(SOUNDBITE OF LAUGHTER)

THURSTON: My black pass. Yes.

GROSS: Seriously. And also everything that you knew about like African history, because of your Afrocentric schooling on the weekends . . .

THURSTON: Yeah.   115

GROSS: I mean, you know, I mean come on.

(SOUNDBITE OF LAUGHTER)

GROSS: You know what I mean? Like you . . .

THURSTON: Actual knowledge never prevents people from judging you.

(SOUNDBITE OF LAUGHTER)

GROSS: That's true, isn't it?

120　**THURSTON:** There was a great moment in the book—I interviewed people and this book, as well—and one of them was a friend Derrick Ashong, who was born in Ghana. And he described an experience of being judged by black Americans, saying he wasn't black enough because he wasn't radical enough, because he hadn't written some middle school paper calling for the death of all white people.

(SOUNDBITE OF LAUGHTER)

THURSTON: And he's like slow down. I was born in Africa. Like, I can trace my family back generations. You can't out black me. It's impossible. I am definitely, definitely black.

GROSS: If you're just joining us, my guest is Baratunde Thurston, and he's the author of the new book *How to Be Black*, which is part memoir, part satire, part satirical self-help book. He's also the director of digital for the satirical newspaper *The Onion*, and the co-founder of the blog Jack And Jill Politics. Let's take a short break here and we'll talk some more.

THURSTON: All right.

GROSS: This is FRESH AIR.

(SOUNDBITE OF MUSIC)

125　**GROSS:** If you're just joining us, my guest is Baratunde Thurston. He's the author of the new book *How to Be Black*. He's also director of digital for the satirical newspaper *The Onion*, and the co-founder of the blog Jack And Jill Politics.

At Harvard you say you learned how important and powerful the role of black friend to white people could be. Explain that.

THURSTON: A lot of white people like black people, right? They buy hip-hop, they watching black athletic and sports figures, and this black culture it's super popular—from jazz through hip-hop and everything else that's come in between and beyond. And so having a black friend, which I think is actually in the book *Stuff That White People Like* that Christian Lander wrote, is a mark of progressive success as a white person. And the black friend that they have is usually seen as their asset. It's like oh, I'm cooler by proxy, I can get my questions answered, I'm hip.

What I try to describe in the book a little more is like what black people get out of having emissaries in the white community as the black friend.

GROSS: What do they get?

THURSTON: Well, you have a covert operative behind enemy lines. You've got a trusted source who can shuttle information back and forth.

It's like the Cold War. It's basically a back channel that prevents race wars from blowing up. So if your white friend has a question about something, they can ask you, their trusted black friend, and you can feed them real or false information, depending on your purposes, but they don't necessarily have to just make an assumption or a leap that ends up in some even more awkward, more public moment. So it's actually very important to have this cross-cultural exchange of actual friendship going on and the black friend is a really, really big part of preventing that conflagration.

GROSS: I want to quote something else from the book. You write about, I write that upon graduation from Harvard, you say I was conscious of the fact that I could be me and thus be black, but not have to be black in order to be me.

THURSTON: Yeah.   130

GROSS: Talk about that.

THURSTON: Harvard was a liberating experience, which I don't know many black people who would say that. But it was because of Sidwell. I spent six years at Sidwell Friends going through—there is a typical lifecycle kind of minority in private schools. You know, first they challenge your right to be there and say it's all affirmative action, you feel awkward, your friends back home judge you as selling out, you have the black student union, you probably protest something, someone writes the N-word on the wall or in the bathroom, or in your locker, like these things are going to happen. And by the time I got to Harvard, I had been through all of that. And then I could just—Harvard's a great place. It can be a really great place if you can enjoy it and take advantage of it and I was able to do that there. So I was involved in the Black Student's Associations at Harvard but at Sidwell I felt this like absolute obligation to like fight and lead and protest and write reports.

And at Harvard I still was actively involved in that black community, but it wasn't the core source for, like, my full identity and I felt as comfortable hanging out with the kids at the newspaper, hanging out with the kids with the computer society, and the theater kids. And black became more of a part of my identity and less of kind of an ongoing protest movement, which it can often be because you often can feel besieged. And I was able to let go of that feeling of being besieged and just sort of be instead. And so there were protests and there were controversies but I think I was able to not let them define me or limit my definition of myself, certainly not affect my feeling of a right to be there.

And so many folks that's a harsher transition when they haven't had the boot camp of some kind of private school to prepare them.

GROSS: We were talking earlier a bit about your, the Afrocentric part of your education.

THURSTON: Yeah.

135   **GROSS:** Jack & Jill politics is not in Afrocentric title by any means.

(SOUNDBITE OF LAUGHTER)

THURSTON: No it's not.

GROSS: What does Jack . . .

. . . the Afrocentric part of your education.

THURSTON: Yeah.

GROSS: "Jack and Jill Politics" is not an Afrocentric title.

(SOUNDBITE OF LAUGHTER)

140   **THURSTON:** No, it's not.

GROSS: By any means. What does "Jack and Jill Politics" supposed to mean as a title?

THURSTON: Sure. It is, first of all, a political blog that I helped found with Cheryl Contee who's my co-founder and also featured significantly in the book. We started it in the summer of 2006 as a platform for black— we were called the black bourgey(ph), black middle class people to talk politics. The blogging was really taking off and had taken off by that point, but among black people in the world of politics, there wasn't a big home.

There were a few places and where black people did blog at the time, there was a lot of entertainment and hip hop and there was a lot about being gay and black. Actually, I think you find in blogging, people are able to build communities virtually that they may not have in their physical home. It made a lot of sense for homosexual/lesbian black people to find that common ground.

So we started this in '06 as a way to just throw down and talk about what's going on, politically, in the country. What are these policies doing? What's the state of black leadership and the congressional black caucus and the name was a subtle nob—nod to and mild jab at an organization that exists within upper middle class black America called Jack and Jill.

And this has existed for a couple of generations and the idea was for pretty well-to-do black people—you're often alone. You're one of the few black families in this neighborhood. You have a few black kids in this type of school. And so for the parents who want their kids to still experience a black community, but at a certain class level, they kind of create this forum and this organization.

I was never a member of Jack and Jill. My co-founder was not a member of Jack and Jill, but it's a mild signal to those who know about it that, OK, we're kind of coming from this perspective while also messing with the idea of a class-based race organization. We have a gigantic watermelon as our logo, which is to signify intelligence, people who are really smart love watermelon.

And that's the only possible thing that could mean; anyone who thinks otherwise is a racist. So I think we're sending a bunch of different signals. For people who have no idea, she's a woman, I'm a man. Jill and Jack. And it doesn't go any farther than that. But for certain types of black people it's like, oh, so are you in Jack and Jill? You're kind of making fun of Jack and Jill? You're representing that? And it's yes to all of the above.

GROSS: So between "Jack and Jill Politics" . . .

THURSTON: Yeah.

GROSS: . . . and you work at *The Onion* as director of digital, you must   145
have to follow politics pretty closely.

THURSTON: I try not to lately because it's just so much. But, yeah, absolutely. I mean, I've been political my whole life. I grew up in D.C. with a mother that we're all getting to know a little bit through this conversation, so it's hard to put that down.

GROSS: And your favorite headlines, recently, from *The Onion*?

(SOUNDBITE OF LAUGHTER)

THURSTON: Oh, man. Let me think. I mean, I'll go back to two old ones and they're so different. One was—it kind of relates well to this book—I will mash up—I will mess up the headline, but it was essentially the idea of Obama as an elite is a great boon for African-Americans. And it was an Onion News Network satirical video news report where they had this panel discussion.

And they're saying: for years, black people were seen as not good enough for white folks and now they're saying this guy is too smart? Too educated? Eats arugula, too elite?

(SOUNDBITE OF LAUGHTER)

THURSTON: That is an amazing step forward for black people to be seen as too good for white people. And I love that that . . .

GROSS: Yeah.   150

THURSTON: . . . kind of satire came out of *The Onion*. Obviously our election headline of Black Guy Given Nation's Worst Job . . .

(SOUNDBITE OF LAUGHTER)

THURSTON: . . . is probably the most accurate news headline real or satirical ever printed, I'd say humbly. And this is actually pretty non-sequitur, but we have a magazine cover which is my own personal favorite and it's in the style of like a Sunday magazine, *New York Times* and it says Enough—in large font and then smaller beneath that: Is it Enough?

(SOUNDBITE OF LAUGHTER)

GROSS: My guess is Baratunde Thurston, author of the new book *How to Be Black*. We'll talk more after a break. This is FRESH AIR.

(SOUNDBITE OF MUSIC)

GROSS: If you're just joining us, my guest is Baratunde Thurston, author of the new book *How to Be Black*. He's also director of digital for the satirical newspaper, *The Onion*, and cofounder of the blog, Jack and Jill Politics. Your book *How to Be Black* is part-satirical self-help book.

155   **THURSTON:** Yeah.

GROSS: And one of the chapters is about how to take advantage of the booming black spokesperson market.

THURSTON: Yes.

GROSS: And provide a valuable service to the nation's clueless media outlets. What's the kind of spokespersons you're thinking of there?

THURSTON: So I'm thinking of, first of all, of a spokesperson who fills a void. And I think, actually, the world is getting better at this, but for most of media history there would be a pile of things happening called black things. And they would be associated with, OK, there's this drug problem, there's a crime thing, there's some sports thing, there's some R&B soul/hip hop thing. We've got to get—there's a riot somewhere.

Quick, grab a black guy, throw him on air. And that was often some reverend type figure: Al Sharpton, Jesse Jackson. And they would be looked to, to kind of fill that void and speak for all black people. And ever since King and X, people have—in the mainstream, have been like well, who speaks for black people now? Farrakhan maybe had the last go-around with the Million Man March.

And people still try to ascribe all black thought, occasionally, to him. So this black spokesperson idea in the book is to kind of mock that desperation, that, OK, we've got to get somebody to explain all of blackness. I don't care who it is. I don't care what the qualifications are. Is it a dude in a suit who ran some kind of organization with the words national and organization in it?

(SOUNDBITE OF LAUGHTER)

160   **THURSTON:** Put them on, mic them up, get some foundation makeup on them, and let's just have him talk. And it's almost always a him.

GROSS: My impression, now, is that in part, ever since Obama was elected...

THURSTON: Yeah.

GROSS: ... that there's a much, like, wider—like on the news channels, for instance...

THURSTON: Yeah.

165   **GROSS:** ... a much wider representation of African-American, like, pundits and experts.

THURSTON: Yeah.

GROSS: And think tank people and bloggers and so on.

THURSTON: I actually agree with you, and I think that's part of the transition we're in, because we're entering a world where we need less to ask permission from, sort of, centralized authority. Whether it's media authorities to get a certain image out, whether it's political authorities to promote a certain policy, whether it's religious authorities to express a certain type of spirituality, the range of black thought—and Jack and Jill Politics is a part of this booming tradition—of black people just representing themselves.

And when that happens and when we're all given, not just the right to demand change or the right to work from the inside to adjust the system or protest, but to actually build native systems, to build your own perspective and voice using these tools—a lot of them technologically based—you can't help but diversify the range of that conversation.

I've been—you know, this chapter also kind of mocks myself a bit, because I've been that black pundit. And they go, oh, now we have Baratunde Thurston from Jack and Jill Politics to talk about something related to blackness. And Rod Blagojevich, former governor of Illinois, said something dumb which should not be news-making at a certain point, because that's what he does. And he said: I'm blacker than Obama.

And some cable news outlet, they said we'd love you to come on and talk about Rod Blagojevich's comment that he's blacker than Obama. I said what? There's nothing to say. Just let the dumbness stand on its own sometimes, and just sit out there—

GROSS: So you declined?

THURSTON: I declined because the idea of Rod Blagojevich, who was   170
an attention-seeking dude saying absurd, and a white guy saying he's blacker than a black guy, which has been done before—it's kind of hacked, too—just wasn't that interesting.

GROSS: So it strikes me that as an African-American memoirist, and—

THURSTON: Ooh, I'm a memoirist. Nice.

(SOUNDBITE OF LAUGHTER)

GROSS: Yes. And blogger and, you know, pundit . . .

THURSTON: Yeah.

GROSS: . . . that you're in a kind of interesting spot, in the sense on the   175
one hand, you're satirizing the whole idea of, like, spokespeople speaking about the black community . . .

THURSTON: Yeah.

GROSS: . . . and, you know, spokespeople being, in a way, confined to talking about the African-American issues of the day. But at the same time, you know, you start Jack and Jill Politics to specifically address what a certain socioeconomics bracket of African-Americans are thinking.

THURSTON: Yeah.

GROSS: And your book is called *How to Be Black* and it's all about your experiences as a black boy, as a black man.

180　**THURSTON:** Yeah.

GROSS: And it's satirical, but there's a lot of real genuine emotion in it, too.

THURSTON: Yeah.

GROSS: I'm not sure exactly what the question is, but I think it has to do with being at that point in time where you can kind of stand back and satirize the whole idea of, like, the black spokespeople, but at the same time feel like—but that's still needed.

THURSTON: Yeah.

185　**GROSS:** Do you know what I mean? That you still have to be there representing African-American points of view in what is still a kind of white dominant culture, politically.

THURSTON: Yeah.

GROSS: And socially.

THURSTON: Part of the mission of this book, besides being uproariously funny and occasionally tear-jerkingly emotional, is as I said in the intro, to re-complicate blackness and to just put out some other examples. Because we're at a time where the gap between who we really are and who the world expects us to be can be closed, because we can articulate who we are much more loudly than any of our ancestors.

We can paint ourselves better. And so this book, what I hope—it's definitely steeped in blackness because a part of me has been. But there's also so many quote/unquote "non-black things." All the gardening stuff, and the computer science-y stuff. You don't see those held up as shining examples of blackness. But I'm black and I do those things. And Elon James White, who I interviewed, he had a great line to, kind of, sum this up.

He said, you know, you don't have to do any particular thing to be black. Right? You do what you do and you open up the doors to blackness. And that's kind of a fun way to think, not just about blackness, about the self, and about identity in general. And so this book could be "How to Be Jewish." It could be "How to Be a Woman." It could be "How to Be Gay."

And I probably should buy all those domain names right now.
(SOUNDBITE OF LAUGHTER)
THURSTON: So I can cash in—cha-ching—and make money off my tweets. But I think that everyone has had some kind of experience like, well, I'm not who people think I am or think I should be because their information about me is so off. We can kind of change that information.
GROSS: Baratunde Thurston, thank you so much. It's really been a pleasure to talk with you. Thank you.
THURSTON: Thank you. This has been a life goal. I'm checking this off the bucket list.
(SOUNDBITE OF LAUGHTER)
THURSTON: Thank you so very much, Terry.
GROSS: Thank you. Baratunde Thurston is the author of the new book *How to Be Black*. You can read an excerpt on our website freshair.npr .org where you can also download Podcasts of our show.

190

Analyze

1. What are some of the places Thurston has lived and why did he move?
2. What type of role does Thurston's mother play in his life?
3. How does Thurston describe his schooling experiences? In Chapter 3 we look at the role that schooling plays in creating who we become. One example is with the Supreme Court's decision, *Brown v. Board of Education*, which explores the types of hardships Thurston would have encountered if this decision had not happened. What would Thurston's schooling experiences have been like if *Brown v. Board of Education* had not been decided as it was?

Explore

1. Thurston talks about the ways he adapts in a variety of settings and with different people. Compare and contrast the ways that you adapt when in different settings and with different people.
2. Thurston begins his talk by telling us about his name, its meaning, and how it needed to be identified by place, Africa. In a group, explore your names to see if anyone has a name that their parents selected because of a place. If you are not sure about a name and have access to the Internet, look up the meaning and etymology of the name.

3. In a group, discuss what Thurston means when he says, "Because we're at a time where the gap between who we really are and who the world expects us to be can be closed, because we can articulate who we are much more loudly than any of our ancestors." Then, based on the makeup of your class group, pick an agreed-upon identity to write about in a humorous fashion. Thurtson mentions "How to Be Jewish," "How to Be a Woman," and "How to Be Gay," but you can decide on one everyone agrees upon. Additionally, if you listen to Thurston's interview, another way to approach the assignment is to prepare an interview script and produce your own NPR interview based on your "How to Be" assignment.

Allen Ginsberg
"America"

Allen Ginsberg was born in Newark, New Jersey, and attended Columbia University. He was a member of the well-known "Beat Generation," a term coined by his friend and fellow writer Jack Kerouac (*On the Road*) to capture the spiritual tiredness they felt and their rebellion against the general conformity they saw around them. *America*, written while he lived in San Francisco, is a challenge to broken dreams and personal freedom.

Thinking about the types of questions Ginsberg asks in his poem, what are some questions you would ask of America?

America I've given you all and now I'm nothing.
America two dollars and twenty-seven cents January 17, 1956.
I can't stand my own mind.
America when will we end the human war?
Go fuck yourself with your atom bomb
I don't feel good don't bother me.
I won't write my poem till I'm in my right mind.
America when will you be angelic?
When will you take off your clothes?

5

When will you look at yourself through the grave?   10
When will you be worthy of your million Trotskyites?
America why are your libraries full of tears?
America when will you send your eggs to India?
I'm sick of your insane demands.
When can I go into the supermarket and buy what I need with my   15
    good looks?
America after all it is you and I who are perfect not the next world.
Your machinery is too much for me.
You made me want to be a saint.
There must be some other way to settle this argument.
Burroughs is in Tangiers I don't think he'll come back it's sinister.   20
Are you being sinister or is this some form of practical joke?
I'm trying to come to the point.
I refuse to give up my obsession.
America stop pushing I know what I'm doing.
America the plum blossoms are falling.   25
I haven't read the newspapers for months, everyday somebody goes
    on trial for murder.
America I feel sentimental about the Wobblies.
America I used to be a communist when I was a kid and I'm not
    sorry.
I smoke marijuana every chance I get.
I sit in my house for days on end and stare at the roses in the closet.   30
When I go to Chinatown I get drunk and never get laid.
My mind is made up there's going to be trouble.
You should have seen me reading Marx.
My psychoanalyst thinks I'm perfectly right.
I won't say the Lord's Prayer.   35
I have mystical visions and cosmic vibrations.
America I still haven't told you what you did to Uncle Max after he
    came over from Russia.

I'm addressing you.
Are you going to let our emotional life be run by Time Magazine?
I'm obsessed by Time Magazine.   40
I read it every week.
Its cover stares at me every time I slink past the corner candystore.

I read it in the basement of the Berkeley Public Library.
It's always telling me about responsibility. Businessmen are serious.
    Movie producers are serious. Everybody's serious but me.
45   It occurs to me that I am America.
I am talking to myself again.

Asia is rising against me.
I haven't got a chinaman's chance.
I'd better consider my national resources.
50   My national resources consist of two joints of marijuana millions
    of genitals an unpublishable private literature that goes 1400
    miles and hour and twentyfivethousand mental institutions.
I say nothing about my prisons nor the millions of underprivileged
    who live in my flowerpots under the light of five hundred suns.
I have abolished the whorehouses of France, Tangiers is the next
    to go.
My ambition is to be President despite the fact that I'm a Catholic.

America how can I write a holy litany in your silly mood?
55   I will continue like Henry Ford my strophes are as individual as
    his automobiles more so they're all different sexes
America I will sell you strophes $2500 apiece $500 down on your
    old strophe
America free Tom Mooney
America save the Spanish Loyalists
America Sacco & Vanzetti must not die
60   America I am the Scottsboro boys.
America when I was seven momma took me to Communist Cell
    meetings they sold us garbanzos a handful per ticket a ticket
    costs a nickel and the speeches were free everybody was angelic
    and sentimental about the workers it was all so sincere you have
    no idea what a good thing the party was in 1835 Scott Nearing
    was a grand old man a real mensch Mother
Bloor made me cry I once saw Israel Amter plain. Everybody must
    have been a spy.
America you don're really want to go to war.
America it's them bad Russians.
65   Them Russians them Russians and them Chinamen. And them
    Russians.

The Russia wants to eat us alive. The Russia's power mad. She
    wants to take our cars from out our garages.
Her wants to grab Chicago. Her needs a Red Reader's Digest. her
    wants our auto plants in Siberia. Him big bureaucracy running
    our fillingstations.
That no good. Ugh. Him makes Indians learn read. Him need big
    black niggers.
Hah. Her make us all work sixteen hours a day. Help.
America this is quite serious.   70
America this is the impression I get from looking in the television set.
America is this correct?
I'd better get right down to the job.
It's true I don't want to join the Army or turn lathes in precision
    parts factories, I'm nearsighted and psychopathic anyway.
America I'm putting my queer shoulder to the wheel.   75

Analyze

1. Do you think Ginsberg cares for America? Discuss why or why not.
2. Who does Ginsberg see as his enemies?
3. Why does Ginsberg seem angry at America?

Explore

1. Write an essay comparing and contrasting Ginsberg's experience
   with America with another story you have read about someone's
   experience.
2. Write a poem in Ginsberg's style sharing your experiences with
   America.
3. A big part of the story for newcomers to the United States is the trip
   here, why they came, and how they came. Argue why you agree or disagree with this statement: Any newcomers who come to the United
   States should be allowed to stay if they work and pay their bills and
   taxes. Discuss why, during the mass migrations after WWII, we were
   seemingly more receptive to immigrants (even though many came illegally as the essays suggest) as opposed to current immigrants from
   Mexico and Central and South America.

Pat Buchanan
"Deconstructing America"

Writer and politician Pat Buchanan is a nationally syndicated columnist and television political commentator. He was twice a candidate for the Republican presidential nomination and he was the Reform Party's candidate once as well. While serving as President Nixon's speechwriter and President Reagan's White House Communications Director, he coined the term "silent majority," which served to attract many Democrats to Nixon and the Republican party. In this essay he makes the argument that soon America will have nothing to hold it together.

Is the type of unity Buchanan describes still possible in the United States? How so?

I t was in their unity, not their diversity, that the strength of the colonies resided. So Patrick Henry believed, as he declared, "The distinctions between Virginians, Pennsylvanians, New Yorkers and New Englanders are no more. I am not a Virginian, but an American."

National identity must supersede state identity for America to survive.

Yet it has lately become fashionable to say that America is great not because she is united, but because she is diverse. It is because America is a multicultural, multiracial, multiethnic, multilingual nation that she is a great nation. A corollary is that the more diverse America becomes, the better and greater she becomes.

After the Los Angeles riot of 1992, Vice President Dan Quayle was asked by his Japanese hosts if perhaps America did not suffer from too much diversity. "I begged to differ with my hosts," Quayle retorted. "I explained that our diversity is our strength."

5   That America is gone forever.

Last week, we learned that in the last seven years 10.3 million people, almost all from the Third World, entered the United States, more than half illegally. The nation that was one-tenth minority in 1960 is now one-third minority. European-Americans will soon be a minority in the nation, as they are today in California, Texas and most large American cities.

And when that day comes, what then will unite us as a people?

And how can we say diversity is a strength, when the most diverse nations of Europe, Yugoslavia and the Soviet Union, shattered into 22 nations as soon as they became free, and Slovaks and Czechs divorced? Ethnic and linguistic diversity is now pulling Belgium apart, as they tore Cyprus in two.

When Islam arose in the 7th century, our world became more diverse. Fourteen centuries of war followed. When Catholic Europe became more diverse with the Protestant Reformation, a century of war followed, ending in a Thirty Years War that carried away a third of all the German people.

There came a new diversity when the English came to the Red Man's continent in 1607 and Africans were brought as slaves in 1619. From that diversity came the near annihilation of American Indians and a racial divide that led to the American Civil War, bloodiest in the West in the 19th century. 10

Britain is more diverse than in the time of Victoria and Churchill. Is Britain a better, stronger nation now that London is Londonistan, madrassas defend the London bombers and race riots are common in the industrial north? If diversity is a strength, why do Scots wish to follow the Irish and secede?

Has Germany been strengthened by the diversity the Turks brought? Is France a stronger nation for the 5 million to 8 million Muslims concentrated in the banlieus? How have the Japanese suffered from their lack of diversity?

This generation is witnessing the Deconstruction of America. Out of one, many.

Analyze

1. Early on, Buchanan declares, "National identity must supersede state identity for America to survive." What does this mean and is this possible in today's America?
2. According to Buchanan, what happens, historically, to diverse nations? Do you agree with him? Why or why not?
3. Does America fit the model Buchanan argues for, or are we different?

Explore

1. Buchanan argues that diversity in a nation is not a good attribute. What are some of the strengths of our diversity that make us stronger, better? Write a letter to Buchanan arguing against his theory.

2. Write an essay, based on your experiences, describing why diversity has been good or bad for the United States. Use the essays from this chapter to support your points.
3. Write an essay, a tweet, a text, and a Facebook post stating why diversity has been good or bad for the United States. What are some of the choices you make in the different formats you use to express your view?

Herbert E. Meyer
"Why Americans Hate This 'Immigration' Debate"

Meyer served during the Reagan Administration as Special Assistant to the Director of Central Intelligence and Vice Chairman of the CIA's National Intelligence Council. From 1971 to 1981 he was an associate editor for *Fortune* as an international specialist. He has published numerous articles and books on American politics. In this essay, Meyer states that, as in the past, immigrants come to live and be Americans, but, contrary to popular belief, a significant portion of Mexican immigrants do not want to stay here.

Do you agree with Meyer that most immigrants "come here with absolutely nothing except a burning desire to be an American," except a large segment of the Mexican immigrant population?

One of the most striking features of the immigration debate now raging in Washington is that none of the Democratic or Republican proposals seem to hold any appeal for ordinary Americans—which is why this debate is generating so much frustration among voters that no matter which proposal Congress adopts, the issue itself threatens to shatter both parties' bases and dominate the November elections.

Simply put, the debate in Washington isn't about "immigration" at all—and that's the problem.

To ordinary Americans, the definition of "immigration" is very specific: You come here with absolutely nothing except a burning desire to be an

American. You start off at some miserable, low-paying job that at least puts a roof over your family's head and food on the table. You put your kids in school, tell them how lucky they are to be here—and make darn sure they do well even if that means hiring a tutor and taking a second, or third, job to pay for it. You learn English, even if you've got to take classes at night when you're dead tired. You play by the rules—which means you pay your taxes, get a driver's license and insure your car so that if yours hits mine, I can recover the cost of the damages. And you file for citizenship the first day you're eligible.

Do all this and you become an American like all the rest of us. Your kids will lose their accents, move into the mainstream, and retain little of their heritage except a few words of your language and—if you're lucky—an irresistible urge to visit you now and then for some of mom's old-country cooking.

This is how the Italians made it, the Germans made it, the Dutch made   5
it, the Poles made it, the Jews made it, and more recently how the Cubans and the Vietnamese made it. The process isn't easy—but it works and that's the way ordinary Americans want to keep it.

The Two Hispanic Groups

But the millions of Hispanics who have come to our country in the last several decades—and it's the Hispanics we're talking about in this debate, not those from other cultures—are, in fact, two distinct groups. The first group is comprised of "immigrants" just like all the others, who have put the old country behind them and want only to be Americans. They aren't the problem. Indeed, most Americans welcome them among us, as we have welcomed so many other cultures.

The problem is the second group of Hispanics. *They aren't immigrants*—which is what neither the Democratic or Republican leadership seems to understand, or wants to acknowledge. They have come here solely for jobs, which isn't the same thing at all. (And many of them have come here illegally.) Whether they remain in the U.S. for one year, or ten years—or for the rest of their lives—they don't conduct themselves like immigrants. Yes, they work hard to put roofs above their heads and food on their tables—and for this we respect them. But they have little interest in learning English themselves, and instead demand that we make it possible for them to function here in Spanish. They put their children in our schools, but don't always demand as much from them as previous groups demanded of their kids. They don't always pay their taxes—or insure their cars.

In short, they aren't playing by the rules that our families played by when they immigrated to this country. And to ordinary Americans this behavior is deeply—very deeply—offensive. We see it unfolding every day in our communities, and we don't like it. This is what none of our politicians either understands, or dares to say aloud. Instead, they blather on—and on—about "amnesty" and "border security" without ever coming to grips with what is so visible, and so offensive, to so many of us—namely, all these foreigners among us who aren't behaving like immigrants.

The phrase we use to describe foreigners who come here not as "immigrants" but merely for jobs is "guest workers." And we are told—incessantly—that we need these "guest workers" because they take jobs that Americans don't want and won't take themselves. This is true, but it's also disingenuous. Throughout our country's history, immigrants have always taken jobs that Americans don't want and won't take themselves. For crying out loud, no foreigner has ever come to our country out of a blazing ambition to dig ditches, mow lawns, bag groceries, sew clothing or clean other people's houses. If we hadn't always had a huge number of these miserable jobs available that none of "us" would do—there wouldn't have been a way for immigrants throughout the nineteenth and twentieth centuries to step off the boat and find work.

10   A willingness by "immigrants" to start at the bottom—so they can move up the economic ladder or at least give their kids a shot at the higher rungs—is precisely how the system is supposed to work. And it always has. (My own family is one of the tens of millions that did precisely this. My grandfather came from Poland and found work as a pocket-maker in New York's garment district. The pay was low, the hours were long, and when the old man finally retired he could hardly move his fingers or see without thick glasses. Yet one of his sons, my uncle, became a lawyer with a fancy practice on Manhattan's Upper East Side. His kids did even better; his son wound up chairman of Stanford University's history department, and his daughter became a famous art critic, moved to London, and married an Englishman who became a member of the House of Lords. What is astonishing about this story is that—it isn't astonishing. It's the sort of thing that happens all the time, and it's why ordinary Americans don't want to change the system that made it possible.)

Blame the Birth Rate

One fact that hasn't been part of the immigration debate is this: During the past two decades our national birth rate has dropped to just below the 2.1 births-per-woman replacement rate. So we really do need to "import" people because—to put it bluntly—we haven't bred enough of them ourselves to do all the work that needs to be done in an affluent, ageing society like ours. But then, we've always needed "more" people to do the work we want done. And we've always brought them in from elsewhere—as immigrants.

Yet today we have millions of foreigners among us who have come here to work, but not to immigrate. Our politicians tell us that we must accept this because—for the first time in our history—we've reached that point when we need "guest workers" who aren't immigrants to keep our economy growing. If this is true—and isn't it odd that no one has troubled to explain why it's true—then we must find some way to distinguish between "immigrants" and "guest workers" so that they aren't treated the same just because they both are here. And if it isn't true that our continued economic growth requires "guest workers" that lies at the core of virtually every proposal now before Congress, including amnesty for those who are here illegally, must be abandoned in favor of something that makes sense.

Until our elected officials come to grips with the real issue that's troubling ordinary Americans—not a growing population of foreigners among us, but rather a growing population of foreigners among us who aren't behaving like immigrants—public frustration will grow no matter what bill Congress passes in the coming weeks. It could lead to the kind of political explosion that none of us really wants.

Analyze

1. What are the traditional and historical types of immigrants that come to this country, according to Meyer? Do you agree with him?
2. What two types of Mexican immigrants come to the United States, and what are the differences between them?
3. Why, according to Meyer, aren't these new immigrants behaving in the old model?

Explore

1. Meyer quickly focuses on a split in the norm of Mexicans who illegally immigrate here. In groups, discuss whether you feel as though this is the norm and whether any other groups fit this "norm" as well. Are there any other patterns you see happening that Meyer hasn't brought up?

2. Does the high unemployment rate in Mexico and other parts of the world have something to do with immigration here? Does the high unemployment rate in the United States have something to do with the way we view those who are here "only to work"? Write an essay taking a stand on why anyone who immigrates here should or should not be required to stay here permanently.

3. Based on the argument that Meyer makes, write an essay suggesting ways to solve the two types of immigration he seems to have difficulty with.

Dinaw Mengestu
"Home at Last"

Mengestu is both a journalist and fiction writer. As a journalist, he visited war-torn areas such sub-Saharan Africa, and his publications have appeared in *The New Yorker, Harper's, Rolling Stone, The Wall Street Journal,* and *Granta.* He is the author of *The Beautiful Things That Heaven Bears* and *How to Read the Air.* Mengestu came to the United States from Ethiopia when he was two years old. Coming at such a young age, he experiences a feeling common among immigrants, that they are neither from here (the United States) nor from there (native country). In "Home at Last," he shares how, when living in Kensington, that he finds community, even if those who make up the community are from different countries and speak languages we do not understand.

Despite the fact that Mengestu did not speak the languages of those he would make it a point to be around, do you think, though he was always on the outside, they accepted him?

At twenty-one I moved to Brooklyn hoping that it would be the last move I would ever make—that it would, with the gradual accumulation of time, memory, and possessions, become that place I instinctively reverted back to when asked, "So, where are you from?" I was born in Ethiopia like my parents and their parents before them, but it would be a lie to say I was *from* Ethiopia, having left the country when I was only two years old following a military coup and civil war, losing in the process the language and any direct memory of the family and culture I had been born into. I simply am Ethiopian, without the necessary "from" that serves as the final assurance of our identity and origin.

Since leaving Addis Ababa in 1980, I've lived in Peoria, Illinois; in a suburb of Chicago; and then finally, before moving to Brooklyn, in Washington, D.C., the de facto capital of the Ethiopian immigrant. Others, I know, have moved much more often and across much greater distances. I've only known a few people, however, that have grown up with the oddly permanent feeling of having lost and abandoned a home that you never in fact, really knew, a feeling that has nothing to do with apartments, houses, or miles, but rather the sense that no matter how far you travel, or how long you stay still, there is no place that you can always return to, no place where you fully belong. My parents, for all that they had given up by leaving Ethiopia, at least had the certainty that they had come from some place. They knew the country's language and culture, had met outside of coffee shops along Addis's main boulevard in the early days of their relationship, and as a result, regardless of how mangled by violence Ethiopia later became, it was irrevocably and ultimately theirs. Growing up, one of my father's favorite saying was, "Remember, you are Ethiopian," even though, of course, there was nothing for me to remember apart from the bits of nostalgia and culture my parents had imparted. What remained had less to do with the idea that I was from Ethiopia and more to do with the fact that I was not from America.

I can't say when exactly I first became aware of that feeling—that I was always going to and never from—but surely I must have felt it during those first years in Peoria, with my parents, sister, and me always sitting on the edge of whatever context we were now supposed to be a part of, whether it was the all-white Southern Baptist Church we went to every weekend, or the nearly all-white Catholic schools my sister and I attended first in Peoria and then again in Chicago at my parents' insistence. By that point my father, haunted by the death of his brother during the revolution and the ensuing loss of the country he had always assumed he would live and die in, had taken to long evening walks that he eventually let me accompany him on. Back then he had a habit of sometimes whispering his brother's name as he walked ("Shibrew," he would mutter), or whistling the tunes of Amharic songs that I had never known. He always walked with both hands firmly clasped behind his back, as if his grief, transformed into something real and physical, could be grasped and secured in the palms of his hands. That was where I first learned what it meant to lose and be alone. The lesson would be reinforced over the years whenever I caught sight of my mother sitting by herself on a Sunday afternoon, staring silently out of our living room's picture window, recalling, perhaps, her father who had died after she left, or her mother, four sisters and one brother in Ethiopia—or else recalling nothing at all because there was no one to visit her, no one to call or see. We had been stripped bare here in America, our lives confined to small towns and urban suburbs. We had sacrificed precisely those things that can never be compensated for or repaid—parents, siblings, culture, a memory to a place that dates back more than half a generation. It's easy to see now how even as a family we were isolated from one another—my parents tied and lost to their past; my sister and I irrevocably assimilated. For years we were strangers even among ourselves.

By the time I arrived in Brooklyn I had little interest in where I actually landed. I had just graduated college and had had enough of the fights and arguments about not being "black" enough, as well as the earlier fights in high school hallways and street corners that were fought for simply being black. Now it was enough, I wanted to believe, to simply be, to say I was in Brooklyn and Brooklyn was home. It wasn't until after I had signed the lease on my apartment that I even learned the name of the neighborhood I had moved into: Kensington, a distinctly regal name at a price that I could afford; it was perfect, in other words, for an eager and poor writer with inflated ambitions and no sense of where he belonged.

5   After less than a month of living in Kensington I had covered almost all of the neighborhood's streets, deliberately committing their layouts and routines to memory in a first attempt at assimilation. There was an obvious and deliberate echo to my walks, a self-conscious reenactment of my father's routine that I adopted to stave off some of my own emptiness. It wasn't just that I didn't have any deep personal relationships here, it was that I had chosen this city as the place to redefine, to ground, to secure my place in the world. If I could bind myself to Kensington physically, if I could memorize and mentally reproduce in accurate detail the various

shades of the houses on a particular block, then I could stake my own claim to it, and in doing so, no one could tell me who I was or that I didn't belong.

On my early-morning walks to the F train I passed in succession a Latin American restaurant and grocery store, a Chinese fish market, a Halal butcher shop, followed by a series of Pakistani and Bangladeshi takeout restaurants. This cluster of restaurants on the corner of Church and McDonald, I later learned, sold five-dollar plates of lamb and chicken biryani in portions large enough to hold me over for a day, and in more financially desperate times, two days. Similarly, I learned that the butcher and fish shop delivery trucks arrived on most days just as I was making my way to the train. If I had time, I found it hard not to stand and stare at the refrigerated trucks with their calf and sheep carcasses dangling from hooks, or at the tanks of newly arrived bass and catfish flapping around in a shallow pool of water just deep enough to keep them alive.

It didn't take long for me to develop a fierce loyalty to Kensington, to think of the neighborhood and my place in it as emblematic of a grander immigrant narrative. In response to that loyalty I promised to host a "Kensington night" for the handful of new friends that I eventually made in the city, an evening that would have been comprised of five-dollar lamb biryani followed by two-dollar Budweisers at Denny's, the neighborhood's only full-fledged bar—a defunct Irish pub complete with terribly dim lighting and wooden booths. I never hosted a Kensington night, however, no doubt in part because I had established my own private relationship to the neighborhood, one that could never be shared with others in a single evening of cheap South Asian food and beer. I knew the hours of the call of the muezzin that rang from the mosque a block away from my apartment. I heard it in my bedroom every morning, afternoon, and evening, and if I was writing when it called out, I learned that it was better to simply stop and admire it. My landlord's father, an old gray-haired Chinese immigrant who spoke no English, gradually smiled at me as I came and went, just as I learned to say hello, as politely as possible, in Mandarin every time I saw him. The men behind the counters of the Bangladeshi takeout places now knew me by sight. A few, on occasion, slipped an extra dollop of vegetables or rice into my to-go container, perhaps because they worried that I wasn't eating enough. One in particular, who was roughly my age, spoke little English, and smiled wholeheartedly whenever I came in, gave me presweetened tea and free bread, a gesture that I took to be an acknowledgment that, at least for him, I had earned my own, albeit marginal, place here.

And so instead of sitting with friends in a brightly lit fluorescent restaurant with cafeteria-style service, I found myself night after night quietly walking around the neighborhood in between sporadic fits of writing. Kensington was no more beautiful by night than by day, and perhaps this very absence of grandeur allowed me to feel more at ease wandering its streets at night. The haphazard gathering of immigrants in Kensington had turned it into a place that even someone like me, haunted and conscious of race and identity at every turn, could slip and blend into.

Inevitably on my way home I returned to the corner of Church and McDonald with its glut of identical restaurants. On warm nights, I had found it was the perfect spot to stand and admire not only what Kensington had become with the most recent wave of migration, but what any close-knit community—whether its people came here one hundred years ago from Europe or a decade ago from Africa, Asia, or the Caribbean—has provided throughout Brooklyn's history: a second home. There, on that corner, made up of five competing South Asian restaurants of roughly equal quality, dozens of Pakistani and Bangladeshi men gathered one night after another to drink chai out of paper cups. The men stood there talking for hours, huddled in factions built in part, I imagine, around restaurant loyalties. Some nights I sat in one of the restaurants and watched from a corner table with a book in hand as an artificial prop. A few of the men always stared, curious no doubt as to what I was doing there. Even though I lived in Kensington, when it came to evening gatherings like this, I was the foreigner and tourist. On other nights I ordered my own cup of tea and stood a few feet away on the edge of the sidewalk, near the subway entrance or at the bus stop, and silently stared. I had seen communal scenes like this before, especially while living in Washington, D.C., where there always seemed to be a cluster of Ethiopians, my age or older, gathered together outside coffee shops and bars all over the city, talking in Amharic with an ease and fluency that I admired and envied. They told jokes that didn't require explanation and debated arguments that were decades in the making. All of this was coupled with the familiarity and comfort of speaking in our native tongue. At any given moment, they could have told you without hesitancy where they were from. And so I had watched, hardly understanding a word, hoping somehow that the simple act of association and observation was enough to draw me into the fold.

10   Here, then, was a similar scene, this one played out on a Brooklyn corner with a culture and history different from the one I had been born into, but familiar to me nonetheless. The men on that corner in Kensington, just like

the people I had known throughout my life, were immigrants in the most complete sense of the word—their loyalties still firmly attached to the countries they had left one, five, or twenty years earlier. If there was one thing I admired most about them, it was that they had succeeded, at least partly, in re-creating in Brooklyn some of what they had lost when they left their countries of origin. Unlike the solitary and private walks my father and I took, each of us buried deep in thoughts that had nowhere to go, this nightly gathering of Pakistani and Bangladeshi men was a makeshift reenactment of home. Farther down the road from where they stood were the few remaining remnants of the neighborhood's older Jewish community— one synagogue, a kosher deli—proof, if one was ever needed, that Brooklyn is always reinventing itself, that there is room here for us all.

While the men stood outside on the corner, their numbers gradually increasing until they spilled out into the street as they talked loudly among themselves, I once again played my own familiar role of quiet, jealous observer and secret admirer. I have no idea what those men talked about, if they discussed politics, sex, or petty complaints about work. It never mattered anyway. The substance of the conversations belonged to them, and I couldn't have cared less. What I had wanted and found in them, what I admired and adored about Kensington, was the assertion that we can rebuild and remake ourselves and our communities over and over again, in no small part because there have always been corners in Brooklyn to do so on. I stood on that corner night after night for the most obvious of reasons—to be reminded of a way of life that persists regardless of context; to feel, however foolishly, that I too was attached to something.

Analyze

1. Why did Mengestu's family leave Ethiopia?
2. What were the two places he lived before Brooklyn?
3. What was the train he would take in the morning?

Explore

1. Mengestu says that his parents were "tied and lost to their past; my sister and I irrevocably assimilated." Since he moved to America when he was two, he does not remember where he was born and he never learned the language. When he says, "irrevocably assimilated" do you

think he means this in a good way or, to borrow from Star Trek's Borg, something he could not resist?

2. Kensington, Mengestu tells us, because of the admixture of immigrants there, "had turned it into a place that even someone like me, haunted and conscious of race and identity at every turn, could slip and blend into." When we speak of identity, a significant part of it is how we feel we blend or fit in particular settings, be it a neighborhood, a school, or within a social network site. Write about an experience you have had in which you feel you blended (or not) and why this happened.

3. Mengestu comes to an awareness that, despite where we are from or our pasts, we can "rebuild and remake ourselves and our communities over and over again." In other words, who we are, our sense of self, can evolve. Write about an experience or move that caused you to remake yourself in your new community.

Guy Merchant
"Unraveling the Social Network: Theory and Research"

Guy Merchant, professor of literacy in education at Sheffield Hallam University (UK), researches digital literacy practices in formal and informal educational settings. He coauthored with Julia Davies *Web 2.0 for Schools: Learning and Social Participation*, is coeditor of *Virtual Literacies*, and is a founding editor of the *Journal of Early Childhood Literacy*. In "Unraveling the Social Network" he explores how our online social networks as much create and maintain a sense of belonging as sustain many of our social divisions.

From your experiences, do you agree with Merchant that digital social networks have many of the same qualities as traditional networks?

Despite the widespread popularity of social networking sites (SNSs) amongst children and young people in compulsory education, relatively little scholarly work has explored the fundamental issues at stake. This paper makes an original contribution to the field by locating the study of this online activity within the broader terrain of social network theory in order to inform future educational debate and further research. The first section offers a way of classifying different kinds of online social networking and then places this within the context of the study of social networks. It is argued that relational networks create a sense of belonging and that online networks just as easily trace the contours of existing social divisions as they transcend or transform them. This analysis informs the second section which specifically addresses educational issues, including both the attractions and the limitations of such work. The paper concludes with an exploration of three possible approaches to using SNSs in educational contexts.

Introduction

Those with an interest in how popular engagement with digital technologies generates new socio-cultural practices cannot fail to ignore the rapid absorption of online social networking into the daily lives of friends, families and fellow professionals. Despite the presence of significant numbers who do not engage with *Facebook* and the like, even the 'refuseniks' (Willet 2009) are aware, at least in general terms, of what they are opting out of and why. In the affluent West, social networking sites (SNSs) are the source of media debate, moral panic and day-to-day conversation. Furthermore, they are attracting the attention of educators who are beginning to ask about their relevance to different kinds of learning (Davies and Merchant 2009a; Greenhow and Robelia 2009). It is perhaps surprising then that such a widespread phenomenon has received relatively little theoretical and empirical attention from social scientists and that quite basic definitional frameworks are under-developed in the literature on new technologies (Boyd and Ellison 2008 notwithstanding). In this paper, I explore some fundamental conceptual issues that relate to online social networking and its relationship to wider social networks in an attempt to lay the foundations for future empirical work and to outline some key areas of concern for educators.

What follows falls into two sections: in the first, and longer section, I interrogate the social network concept in order to expose some of its complexities and to caution against some naive assumptions about the power of online social networking and youth engagement with it. On the basis of this critical re-appraisal, the second section addresses key issues for educators, suggesting how they might respond to the widespread adoption of online social networking. This second section concludes by identifying a number of areas in which further empirical research is needed. I begin though by providing an examination of online social networking by focusing attention on the definitional challenges that are raised in current work on the topic. This is developed by suggesting that it may now be helpful to make a distinction between SNSs as online spaces explicitly designed for interpersonal exchange, and the more general ways in which social networks may transfer to, develop or be complemented by online activity. I then address the more fundamental question of what we mean by a social network, how social networks have become a focus of study in recent years and to what extent the various online activities described fit with these conceptions. This leads into a discussion of the idea of 'belonging' and how it comes to be realised through our networks of connection. The first section concludes with a critique of the popular notion of the 'social graph'.

The Social Network

The social network is a way of conceptualising social groupings and interaction; give it capital letters—'The Social Network' and it refers to David Fincher's film biopic of Mark Zuckerberg and the rise of *Facebook*. In an era of technologised sociability, this conflation of everyday human experience with mediated communication is significant in itself as social interaction becomes almost synonymous with, and in some cases indistinguishable from, the technology that enables it. What was said on *Facebook*, who texted who, and the latest celebrity tweets are seamlessly interwoven in face-to-face conversation—yet at the heart of this sort of conversation we see the intersection of two distinct notions of social networking, and it is worthwhile to tease them apart, at least for the purposes of the current analytical work, in the acknowledgement that in everyday life they may blend together in the same sort of way that the fortunes of X Factor contestants, and who has 'added' who to their *Facebook* page, are incorporated into our social world.

Online Social Networking or Social Networks Online?
Social networking could, in general terms, be seen as a way of describing the patterning of everyday practices of social interaction, including those

that take place within family structures, between friends, and in neighbourhoods and communities. In this way, we could talk about the social networks of former school friends, co-workers or those that form within the social institutions of a whole variety of groups, organisations and clubs that serve our varied needs, interests and affiliations. Indeed, social institutions and the informal or casual encounters that occur in and between people provide important contexts for the maintenance and development of relationships including both friendship and casual acquaintance. Wellman (2002) suggests that social networks in traditional societies are characterised by a predominance of face-to-face encounters contained within relatively small geographical areas—and certainly for most of the twentieth century this was true for the majority of the population. The extent to which this is changed by increases in population mobility and developing communications technology is a fertile area for investigation not least because of the likely variation between communities and social groups.

If Wellman's description captures the essence of what we might call 'traditional' face-to-face social networks, then it seems that advances in the   5
technologies of communication have tended to act as accompaniments and sometimes supplements to these patterns of interaction. So, for example, postal systems and telephone networks have, for most of their history, allowed us to sustain and thicken existing social network ties. Literacy scholars will quickly point out the long history of writing in *maintaining* social ties in dispersed networks (Vincent 2000; Gillen and Hall 2010); however, it may be worth noting that although accounts of the use of these communication technologies in *initiating* social relationships do exist, they are by comparison quite rare. Technology may make new connections possible, but there is little evidence that it actually determines them. From this point of view, online social networking could be seen as a newer way of enhancing or modifying pre-existing relations—with the term probably best used as a way of capturing, in a rather general way, the use of web-based communication to build or maintain such things as friendship or interest groups, extended family ties, and professional, political or religious affiliations.

Since its inception, the internet has worked as a channel for communication in connected social networks. In countering some of the more extravagant claims of *Web 2.0* enthusiasts who have written about a paradigm shift that has resulted in the 'social web', Tim Berners-Lee is frequently quoted as saying that 'the internet was always social' (Davies and Merchant 2009a, 3). Yet, it is also argued that the most noteworthy development of recent years is the scale of adoption of technologies and the popular spread of the read/write web. Whichever viewpoint is the more appealing is perhaps less relevant than the general observation that the online textual universe is now extremely large and varied, and encompasses well-established practices such as email groups, listservs and bulletin boards, as well as more recent developments such as music- and photo-sharing sites, massively multiplayer online games (MMOGs) and 3D virtual worlds. These and related practices could be seen as the basis of online social networking as a popular and broad-based activity.

An important subset of online social networking is constituted by those environments that are specifically designed to support and develop friendship and whose overt purpose is to provide a context and appropriate tools for doing so. The term SNSs is used to describe these environments and to distinguish them from other forms of techno-sociability—*Facebook, Bebo, MySpace* and *Twitter* being the most popular examples at this moment in time (see Figure 1 for more). In their intelligent commentary on SNSs, Boyd and Ellison (2008, 211) make a distinction between 'networking', which they argue implies active relationship *initiation*, and 'network', which for them suggests relationship *maintenance*. The distinction is helpful as a way of categorising different kinds of online social activity but glosses over the fact that relationship maintenance and development can be

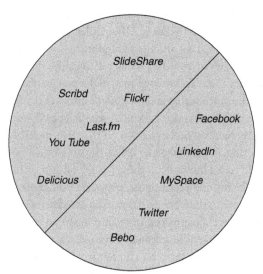

Figure 1 A map of social software showing some popular sites that promote online social networking and on the right some specific SNSs.

just as active and arguably equally as significant as relationship initiation. Boyd and Ellison (2008) tie their definition of SNSs to three core characteristics. These are that:

- Individual users or members construct a public or semi-public profile on the site
- Users/members create and list connections with others (friends, followers or buddies)
- Users/members traverse the site through their own and others' friendlists

Although it could be argued that these characteristics are shared with other environments that may not focus explicitly on friendship (*Blogger, YouTube* and similar applications come to mind), the emphasis on presence, connection and community are certainly germane to understanding of social media. There is clearly a fuzzy boundary between the characteristics of wider online social networking and the smaller area of specific SNSs as defined above. This is most evident in web-based services that have supported the growth of a community, or communities of interest—or what Gee (2004) refers to as an affinity space. Examples of these are the *Flickr* photo-sharing community, music recommending sites like Blip.fm and those other online spaces that benefit substantially from having their own 'in house' communication tools.

It has been argued that it is useful to distinguish between those environments specifically designed to promote social interaction and friendship and those that support social networking around a specific activity, usefully described by Engestrom (2007) as a 'social object' (Ito et al. 2008; Merchant 2010a). In Figure 1, this distinction is represented by the diagonal division of the social software set—this distinction needs, of course, to be conceived of as a weak boundary but helps in characterising the patterning of online interaction.

One of the unifying features of SNSs is the way that they support public displays of friendship and connection. In blogs, this is often shown as a blogroll, in other sites it is a friendlist, whereas in the micro-blogging site *Twitter* this function is fulfilled by the lists of who 'follows' you as well as who you 'follow'. In this way, according to Greenhow and Robelia (2009), users 'make visible their social networks' or, to be more precise, they give an online performance of those connections that they *think are significant* to their imagined audience. The concepts of performance and audience (which have their origins in the work of Goffman 1959) suggest that where individuals use multiple SNSs we might expect to see differences in their friendlists—differences that would reflect their engagement in different communities and different activities. I am not aware of any research that has looked at patterns of affiliation across SNSs, but such work would be very useful if only to begin to explore the real complexity of social networks.

In order to complete this developing picture of SNSs, they must now be placed in what I referred to above as the 'wider textual universe' of online communication in which all the email exchanges, i-m chats, bulletin boards and so on feature. This is important, first in order to be more specific about the difference between SNS activity and social networking online, and secondly to open to a more expansive view of social networks in which activity and interaction across a range of platforms can be conceptualised. This then begs the broader question of how, and in what ways, the social networks enacted online fit into the bigger picture of social networking. In order to approach this topic, we now need a more refined understanding of what it means to talk about a network, and what the strengths and limitations of this perspective might be.

What Is a Social Network?

As a way of describing social interaction, the metaphor of a network is appealing in a number of ways—after all, it suggests connection between points, as well as a sense of fluidity; but it also invites a certain kind of abstraction of the social which is perhaps best captured in the diagrams that are a common characteristic of network analysis (see http://www .neuroproductions.be/twitter_friends_network_browser/). It is also a peculiarly twentieth-century metaphor—one that readily associates with *the network*, itself synonymous with the online world of digital connection. The concept of a social network reduces the human social actor to a point—not even a point of view—but a point that connects in various ways to other points. In essence, it speaks to the patterning and flow of communication and interaction by drawing attention to relationships, social groupings, friendship, intra- and inter-group behaviours as they are enacted in and across different geographical locations and over time.

The work of Wellman and his associates, based on their in-depth studies of a community in metropolitan Toronto, has made a major contribution to our current understanding of social networks—and particularly to the way these may be changing in a time of rapid global communication and increased population mobility. In their body of work, computer-supported networks sometimes receive a lot of attention, even to the extent of generating what seems like quite a narrow definition. Here is one example:

> When a computer network connects people or organisations, it is a social network. (Garton, Haythornthwaite, and Wellman 1997, 1)

In a similar vein, Wellman's theory of how the patterning of relationships may evolve from 'close-knit' groups, to 'glocalised communities' and on to 'networked individualism' (Wellman 2002) has received a lot of attention from those interested in new technology not only because of the way it fits with the rise of mobile computing but also because of the way in which it suggests high levels of agency. So, for example, Benkler argues that networked individuals are able to 'reorganise their social relations in ways that fit them better' and 'loosen bonds that are too hierarchical and stifling' or fill in the gaps where 'their real-world relations seem lacking' (Benkler 2006, 367). Whilst the networked individual *may* be able to do all these things, this idealistic vision tends to over-simplify the complexities of social relations and the ways in which they play out in everyday contexts.

Elsewhere, Wellman's work documents how social networks support the routine life of households, their capacity to cope with adversity, with emotional upheaval, economic hardship, and the everyday challenges of life including everything from child care to house maintenance (e.g., Wellman and Wortley 1990). The theoretical strength of the network metaphor has enabled these researchers to map the extent of social ties, to examine both individual and collective dimensions and to begin to re-theorise the concept of community. In these accounts, communication is fore-grounded as attention is placed on the 'flow of information (and other resources)' within and between groups (Garton, Haythornthwaite, and Wellman 1997, 1). In other words, how social beings are linked and how they participate by creating allegiances and friendships in both formal and informal contexts become important considerations in this tradition. Social network analysis helps us to map the relationship between the individual and the larger social systems in which he or she participates. As a result, the relationships themselves have become the unit of analysis.

As Emirbayer and Goodwin (1994) point out, the concept of the social network emerges at various points in the history of the social sciences but its distinctiveness in terms of theory and analysis first becomes apparent in the sociological literature of the mid-twentieth century (see also Schuller, Baron, and Field 2000). Enthusiastic commentaries have suggested that by emphasising the interdependence of individuals, social network analysis has the potential to bridge micro- and macro-sociological concerns by illustrating how the 'flow of material and non-material resources' is patterned (Schuller, Baron, and Field 2000, 19). As we can see, this is a wider ambition than any number of studies of online behaviour could hope to reveal.

This short overview of theory and research in the substantive field of social network studies highlights a number of important issues that can be brought to bear on the topic of online social networking. The first of these has to be an acknowledgement that there is much more depth and density of activity in social networks than is represented or enacted in SNSs. Social networks may depend on a variety of modes of communication, but they are also necessary to the flow of material resources, activity and action in the physical environment. They are, for example, key to a range of activity from the day-to-day maintenance of household life, to achieving a sense of community cohesion and civic participation (see Putnam 2000). SNSs may have an increasingly significant role to play in this range of activity, but there is insufficient evidence to suggest that they are about to transform existing structures.

The second issue is not entirely unrelated to this, and that is the clear possibility that SNSs *can* provide an arena in which some aspects of wider social networking can be achieved and in which some of the kinds of activity and action referred to above can be negotiated, arranged and co-ordinated. But current research simply does not tell us enough about how social networks are enacted across material and virtual spaces. This interplay between online and offline interaction offers a rich vein for future research along the lines suggested by Leander and McKim (2003). Finally, since social identity shapes and is shaped by the structures and networks in which we are located, these can be seen as conferring a 'sense of place' either in a spatial or a metaphorical sense. It is this sense of place (and lack of it) that I now address.

A New Sense of Place

It has become popular to argue that our identities develop and emerge through interaction and, following the theories of Goffman (1959) and others, that the social self is performed in front of an audience of others.

This point of view is particularly persuasive when applied to online environments in which the individual self-consciously chooses to display biographic data (with varying degrees of accuracy and disclosure), selects an avatar to represent herself on screen (like or unlike the 'real' self), and even a name (real or fictive). Of course, in some online settings, the invitation to play a role is overtly constructed by the design of the environment—this is the case in Second Life and most MMOGs in which an avatar has a fictional identity whose relationship to a real-life person is more complex. Admittedly, there is nothing to prevent one from disclosing personal details in these contexts, an act often achieved through sharing profile data, but there is an important difference between this sort of identity play and what normally occurs on SNSs. The difference can be accounted for in terms of the nature of the relationship between the virtual and material worlds. The highly connected relationships promoted by SNSs allow, and even encourage, users to anchor their relationships and social activities to the real world and this raises new and complex issues concerning privacy and self-expression (Livingstone 2008). In short, the identity work done online has an iterative relationship with offline identity (see Dowdall 2009b for an illustration of this).

This notion of identity anchorage inevitably raises issues of place and belonging. Spencer-Oatey argues:

> Identity helps people 'locate' themselves in social worlds. By helping to define where they belong and where they do not belong in relation to others, it helps to anchor them in their social worlds, giving them a sense of place. (Spencer-Oatey 2007, 642)

As the boundary between online and offline social networking becomes increasingly porous, we might well ask *where* our friends are: in our friendlist or in the 'real' world? The question may well prompt us to investigate how the two arenas of social life may be interwoven or re-integrated (as suggested in the introduction to this paper).

In a careful exploration of the role of the mobile phone in contemporary life, Gergen (2003) uses the metaphor of the 'floating world'. Historically speaking, the floating world refers to the urban lifestyle associated with the Japanese Edo period—an unregulated social world devoted to everyday pleasures and pastimes. The similarities between this informal social world and the floating world of mobile phone users is carefully sketched out by Gergen; yet, the contrast lies in the different conceptions of space and place that are involved. Geography is clearly less significant for networked communities and, as Gergen poetically suggests, these communities are 'elevated from the physical terrain'.

> We may imagine here that dwelling about us at all times are small communities that are unseen and unidentifiable. However, as we stroll the thoroughfare or sip coffee in a café their presence is made constantly known to us. Each mobile phone [. . .] is a sign of a significant nucleus, stretching in all directions, amorphous and protean. (Gergen 2003)

As an increasing number of SNSs are available on 3G mobiles, the idea of a phone as the hub of the individual's portable and dispersed connections, and Gergen's idea of the invisible web (of networks) in the floating world are enduringly powerful images—particularly when the everyday reports of what has taken place 'on Facebook' or 'on Twitter' appear to invest those environments with something rather like a sense of place. At the same time, it is clearly not the case that places in the real world have emptied out, or become bare stages on which absent presence is enacted. It is perhaps more helpful to see how social networks have become more densely layered with the advance of new communicative tools.

But having a sense of place in a social world is at the same time more complex and more varied than the above account might suggest. For the purpose of the current argument I suggest two reasons for this, one general and one more specific to the world of SNSs. Firstly, social networks at large are not entirely neutral. In other words, they constitute or reflect the divisions, diversity and inequities of the social fabric. One has only to read MacDonald's study of networks in the North East of England to understand how a particular social network can simultaneously limit opportunity and re-inforce social exclusion (MacDonald et al. 2005). If networks describe a relational context, then that description must apply equally to criminal activity and legitimate professional interchange, to affluent urban youth as well as those growing up in poor neighbourhoods. Here, Putnam's notion of 'bonding capital' is relevant: networks which connect the like-minded are simply likely to perpetuate or increase social divisions (Putnam 2000). Secondly, it is often assumed that online social networking is in some way a unitary phenomenon, whereas in actual fact SNSs themselves are silos, traversed in particular ways by particular users who are locked into particular sites (Lanier 2010). Even within a single SNS, it is simply not the case that individuals are part of a big happy family. Division continues to perpetuate, interest groups form and dissolve, and levels of use vary widely.

The Problem of the Social Graph

When Facebook founder Mark Zuckerberg was named Time Magazine's   25 person of the year (Time Magazine 2010), he was lauded for 'connecting the world'. He was praised for the way in which *Facebook* had 'wired together a twelfth of humanity into a single network, thereby creating a social entity almost twice as large as the US'. Whilst *Facebook's* success should not be under-played, the claim that it has created a 'single network' or, for that matter, 'a social entity' is a misreading of online social networking for reasons that by now should be quite clear. Nonetheless, the mythology of the single network is pervasive in some quarters in which it is imagined that we might soon inhabit a world in which one's position on the 'social graph' (Fitzpatrick 2007)—the global mapping of everybody and how they're related—seems to count for a lot. The concept of the social graph easily plays into the sort of naive 'cyber-libertarianism' lampooned by Buckingham (2010); but I suspect that for most of those interacting through SNSs, and particularly young people in the education system, more parochial concerns predominate.

However, the concept of the social graph also evokes the idea that who you know matters, and with this the more unsettling idea that making this visible is important. Rather than the globalised egalitarian world suggested by SNS enthusiasts, this could turn out to be how social capital is rendered in the digital age. Take Bourdieu's definition that social capital is:

> the aggregate of the actual or potential resources which are linked to possession of a durable network of more or less institutionalised relationships of mutual aquaintance and recognition [. . .] which provides each of its members with the backing of collectively owned capital. (Bourdieu 1997, 51)

It is not difficult to see from this that social capital can be conceived in terms of the resources that reside in individuals' social networks, and that these resources might be mobilised by them for their own ends. As a result, the totality of our interconnections, both online and offline—our *Facebook* friends as well as our work colleagues—contribute to this capital, and so too do the social institutions and organisations that we participate in. But given the sorts of social divisions and inequities that I referred to in the previous section, it seems unlikely that increased engagement in online social networking will serve to transform or 'bridge' social capital; perhaps at best it will augment it.

Online Social Networking and Education

In a social context of rapid technological innovation and dissemination strongly shaped by consumerism, corporate interest and techno-utopian imaginings, it is vital that we are critically aware of the role that technology plays in all our lives, and particularly in the lives of those we are responsible for, including the children and young people in our education systems. So far, this paper has focused on a single manifestation of new technology, namely the rapidly growing engagement with SNSs. I have argued against simplistic views that tend to exoticise online social networking, to exaggerate its popular appeal, or to ignore its position in wider social networks. Whilst acknowledging the widespread use of SNSs, I have also drawn attention to the realities of occasional, persistent or even reluctant engagement, as well as the existence of those who refuse to participate. In this section, I draw on earlier themes to identify ways in which educators might respond to the phenomenon of online social networking, and the related research questions that need to be asked.

To begin with, it is worth underlining the fact that we simply do not know enough about children and young people's experience of online social networking and how this is interwoven with life offline. Despite the succession of Pew internet reports from the US (e.g., Lenhart et al. 2007), the work of Livingstone and colleagues in the UK (Livingstone, Bober, and Helsper 2005), OfCom studies (OfCom 2008) and the like, we only gain a limited impression of the spread of SNSs. Few studies point to demographic variation—Hargittai (2007) is a notable exception—and even fewer explore the experiences of online social networking and the role it plays in the everyday lives of young people. In this respect, Greenhow, Robelia, and Hughes' argument is supported. We need:

> a stronger focus on students' everyday use and learning with *Web 2.0* technologies in and outside of classrooms. (Greenhow, Robelia, and Hughes 2010, 255)

We also need to know about the part these activities play in their wider 30 social lives and to place this alongside a sensitive exploration of what has been referred to as the 'participation gap' (Jenkins et al. 2006). Some key themes emerging from the earlier overview of social networks in 'The social network' section are applicable here. For example it has been argued that we would profit from a better understanding of: patterns of use *across* SNSs and the ways in which these are located in the wider textual universe of online practices; the nature of the relationships that are formed and maintained and how these relate to activity and action in other contexts; and how online social networks constitute or reflect broader divisions, diversity and inequities in society.

But also, given the growing significance of SNSs in students' lives, it is important to look at the influences that already frame educational responses to digital literacies (see Dowdall 2009b). Some of the difficulties that educators face in tapping into their students' experiences in the context of formal education may be beyond their control, constrained by curriculum and assessment regimes as well as institutional policies—but there are also some other areas of difficulty. First, there is the perceived danger of unfiltered and open access to online interaction, fuelled as it is by moral panic over internet safety. Secondly, there is the suspicion, still felt in some quarters, of anything that smacks of popular culture in which young people are often more expert than teachers. Thirdly, there is a lack of knowledge or familiarity—because, to some extent, online social networking is still seen as the province of the young—a foreign country to some teachers. Fourthly and finally, there are relatively few models of good practice to draw upon.

Yet, when we think that the popularity of SNSs stems from the way they provide a context for friendship, interaction and affinity around shared interest, and see how they become spaces in which self-directed learning *can* take place, they begin to seem more attractive. SNSs clearly do provide opportunities for geographically and temporally dispersed groups and individuals to communicate, exchange information and develop ideas, and from this perspective, we may be able to glimpse some new ways of structuring learning communities (Davies and Merchant 2009b). The innovative work of Hull and Stornaiuolo (2010), discussed below, provides an example of this as they follow the dictum that:

> the rewards could not be greater, or the risk of failure more grave for
> educating a citizenry able and willing to communicate with digital

tools across differences in a radically interconnected yet divided world. (Hull and Stornaiuolo 2010, 85)

Despite the strength and validity of this statement, there is still important work to do in conceptualising the learning that can occur through these sorts of connections. So, although there may be broad agreement that learning is dependent on interaction, we need to be wary of the assumption that all interaction results in learning. Claims that the digital age is characterised by new kinds of learning, although seductive in their appeal, still require empirical support. Here, the work of Ravenscroft, Wegerif, and Hartley (2007) on learning dialogues and Pachler and Daly's (2009) study of narrative as a tool for knowledge construction offer possible ways forward.

Three Approaches to the Use of SNSs in Educational Settings

An initial exploration of how young people and their teachers currently use SNSs (Merchant 2010a) identified a number of areas of interest for educators, and these are broadly suggestive of three different kinds of activity that are relevant to educational settings. These are characterised as *learning about SNSs, learning from SNSs* and *learning with SNSs*. Each is explored, in turn, below.

35   The first of these is to *learn about* SNSs and their role in learners' lives— doing this is crucial in understanding the worlds that our students inhabit as well as in identifying the knowledge, skills and dispositions involved as social and cultural capital. This underlines the imperative to recognise and validate the learning that takes place in SNSs (Owen et al. 2006) and to begin to explore the relationship between casual sociality, informal learning and the endeavours of institutionalised education. Such an approach can involve a benign form of media literacy in which the over-riding purpose is not to evaluate or denigrate the enjoyment of online social networking but merely to exchange experiences and to discuss general issues such as privacy, safety and responsibility (Livingstone 2008) as well as the role of commercial and corporate interest. This kind of activity leads into potentially fruitful explorations, investigating what sort of practices might constitute 'advantageous' online activity (Greenhow and Robelia 2009) and the nature of the influences that shape the presentation of self in SNSs.

The second approach is to *learn from* social networking in order to appreciate the kinds of social interaction and informal learning SNSs can support, and as a result to reflect upon and refresh our own pedagogies and designs for learning. Here, the work of Hull and Stornaiuolo (2010), which chronicles the development of an international SNS to promote 'cosmo-politan' educational practice, is of significance. Although the presentation of self is still important in this work, this takes its place in the context of fostering mutual understanding between students in a variety of dispersed geographical and socio-cultural environments.

The third and final approach is to *learn with* SNSs, and involves making use of learners' existing online social networks to support and extend curriculum-based work. This is an approach perhaps best-suited to older learners who may be encouraged to choose among freely available SNSs to support collaborative learning, but also can include younger children as my own case study work has shown (Merchant 2010b). In a similar vein work by Waller (2010) on the use of *Twitter* with his class of 6 year olds shows the value of online social networking in evaluating and reflecting on learning.

Conclusion

Conceptions of social media that fail to acknowledge the rich body of literature on social networking are likely to provide an impoverished view of the challenges and opportunities that are presented by new tech-nologies of communication. In this paper I have distinguished between dif-ferent kinds of social networking and, in summarising some influential themes in theory and research, I have presented an overview of the key con-cerns for educators. By emphasising the ways in which SNSs may simply re-flect the divisions, diversity and inequities of the social fabric, the paper has explored the notions of 'social capital' and 'belonging', and provided a cri-tique of the popular notion of 'the social graph'. This offers a context for more principled educational approaches to SNSs and one that is cognisant of its relationship to more established networks. The concluding section out-lined three separate approaches to the use of SNSs in educational settings.

Despite claims that the social web is a rich space for informal learning, to date there has been little serious attention paid to the form or nature of that learning. Researchers such as Boyd (2007), Carrington (2008), Davies (2006) and Dowdall (2009a) have all *described* the learning that takes place, but no model has been developed yet to theorise this learning. At the same time, there is growing evidence of innovative educators using *Web 2.0* and social networking in the classroom (Lankshear and Knobel 2006), and a growing body of work that documents the ways in which young people learn informally in online contexts (Ito et al. 2008)—but it must be said that these are small gains in a political and educational environment that often sees new technology as a solution to all its problems—from providing for employment and skills shortages, to 'curing' pupil disaffection and under-achievement.

References

Benkler, Y. 2006. *The wealth of networks: How social production transforms markets and freedom*. London: Yale University Press.

Bourdieu, P. 1997. The forms of capital. In *Education: Culture, economy and society*, ed. A. Halsey, H. Lauder, P. Brown, and A. Stuart Wells. Oxford: Oxford University Press.

Boyd, d. 2007. Why youth (heart) social network sites: The role of networked publics in teenage social life. In *Youth, Identity, and Digital Media*, ed. D. Buckingham, 119–42. Cambridge, MA: MIT Press.

Boyd, D.M., and N.B. Ellison. 2008. Social network sites: Definition, history and scholarship. *Journal of Computer-Mediated Communication* 13: 210–320.

Buckingham, D. 2010. Do we really need media education 2.0? Teaching in the age of participatory media. In *Digital content creation: Perceptions, practices and perspectives*, ed. K. Drotner and K. Schroder. New York: Peter Lang.

Carrington, V. 2008. 'I'm Dylan and I'm not going to say my last name': Some thoughts on childhood, text and new technologies. *British Educational Research Journal* 34, no. 2: 151–66.

Davies, J. 2006. Escaping to the borderlands: An exploration of the internet as a cultural space for teenaged Wiccan girls. In *Travel notes from the new literacy studies: Instances of practice*, ed. K. Pahl and J. Rowsell, 57–71. Clevedon: Multilingual Matters.

Davies, J., and G. Merchant. 2009a. *Web 2.0 for schools: Learning and social participation*. New York: Peter Lang.

Davies, J., and G. Merchant. 2009b. Negotiating the blogosphere: Educational possibilities. In *Digital literacies: Social learning and classroom practice*, ed. V. Carrington and M. Robinson, 81–95. London: Sage.

Dowdall, C. 2009a. Impressions, improvisations and compositions: Reframing children's text production in social networking sites. *Literacy* 43, no. 2: 91–9.

Dowdall, C. 2009b. Masters and critics: Children as producers of online digital texts. In *Digital literacies: Social learning and classroom practice*, ed. V. Carrington and M. Robinson, 43–61. London: Sage.

Emirbayer, M., and J. Goodwin. 1994. Network analysis, culture, and the problem of agency. *American Journal of Sociology* 99, no. 6: 1411–54.

Engestrom, J. 2007. Microblogging: Tiny social objects. On the future of participatory media. http://www.slideshare .net/jyri/microblogging-tiny-social-objects-on-the-future-of-participatory-media (accessed December 30, 2010).

Fitzpatrick, B. 2007. Thoughts on the social graph. http://bradfitz .com/social-graphproblem (accessed December 19, 2010).

Garton, L., C. Haythornthwaite, and B. Wellman. 1997. Studying online social networks. *Journal of Computer Mediated Communication* 3, no. 1. DOI: 10.1111/j.1083-6101.1997 .tb00062.x.

Gee, J.P. 2004. *Situated language and learning: A critique of traditional schooling*. Abingdon: Routledge.

Gergen, K. 2003. Self and community in the new floating worlds. In *Mobile democracy, essays on society, self and politics*, ed. K. Nyiri, 103–14. Vienna: Passagen.

Gillen, J., and N. Hall. 2010. Edwardian postcards: Illuminating ordinary writing. In *The Anthropology of Writing*, ed. D. Barton and U. Papen, 169–89. London: Continuum.

Goffman, E. 1959. *The presentation of self in everyday life*. London: Penguin.

Greenhow, C., and B. Robelia. 2009. Informal learning and identity formation in online social networks. *Learning, Media and Technology* 34, no. 2: 119–40.

Greenhow, C., B. Robelia, and J.E. Hughes. 2010. Learning, teaching and scholarship in a digital age: Web 2.0 and classroom research: What path should we take now?. *Educational Researcher* 38, no. 4: 246–59.

Hargittai, E. 2007. Whose space? Differences among users and nonusers of social network sites. *Journal of Computer-Mediated Communication* 13: article 14.

Hull, G.A., and A. Stornaiuolo. 2010. Literate arts in a global world: Reframing social networking as a cosmopolitan practice. *Journal of Adolescent & Adult Literacy* 54, no. 2: 85–97.

Ito, M., H. Horst, M. Bittanti, D. Boyd, B. Herr-Stephenson, P. Lange, C. Pascoe, et al. 2008. *Living and learning with new media: Summary of findings from the digital youth project.* Chicago: MacArthur Foundation. http://digitalyouth.ischool .berkeley.edu/report (accessed February 26, 2011).

Jenkins, H., R. Purushota, K. Clinton, M. Weigel, and A. Robinson. 2006. *Confronting the challenges of participatory culture: Media education for the 21st century.* Chicago: MacArthur Foundation. http://digitallearning.macfound.org/site/c.enJLKQNlFiG/ b.2108773/apps/nl/content2.asp?content_id=%7BCD911571- 0240-4714 (accessed December 30, 2010).

Lanier, J. 2010. *You are not a gadget: A manifesto.* New York: Alfred Knopf.

Lankshear, C., and M. Knobel. 2006. *New literacies: Everyday practices and classroom learning.* 2nd ed. Maidenhead: Open University Press.

Leander, K., and K. McKim. 2003. Tracing the everyday 'Sitings' of adolescents on the internet: A strategic adaptation of ethnography across online and offline spaces. *Education, Communication and Information* 3, no. 2: 211–40.

Lenhart, A., M. Madden, A. Macgill, and A. Smith. 2007. *Teens and social media.* Washington, DC: Pew Internet and American Life Project.

Livingstone, S. 2008. Taking risky opportunities in youthful content creation: Teenagers' use of social networking sites for intimacy, privacy and self-expression. *New Media & Society* 10, no. 3: 393–411.

Livingstone, S., M. Bober, and E. Helsper. 2005. *Internet literacy among children and young people: Findings from the UK children go online project.* London: London School of Economics.

MacDonald, R., T. Shildrik, C. Webster, and D. Simpson. 2005. Growing up in poor neighbourhoods: The significance of class and place in the extended transitions of "socially excluded" young adults. *Sociology* 39, no. 5: 873–91.

Merchant, G. 2010a. View my profile(s). In *Adolescents' online litera-cies*, ed. D. Alvermann. New York: Peter Lang.

Merchant, G. 2010b. Social media and primary school children. In *Teaching media in primary schools*. ed. C. Bazalgette. London: Sage.

OfCom. 2008. Social networking: A quantitative and qualitative re-search report into attitudes, behaviour and use. http://stakeholders .ofcom.org.uk/market-data-research/media-literacy/medlitpub/ medlitpubrss/socialnetworking (accessed December 20, 2010).

Owen, M., L. Grant, S. Sayers, and K. Facer. 2006. *Social software and learning*. Bristol: Futurelab. http://archive.futurelab.org.uk/ resources/publications-reports-articles/opening-education-reports/ Opening-Education-Report199 (accessed December 20, 2010).

Pachler, N., and C. Daly. 2009. Narrative and learning with Web 2.0 technologies: Towards a research agenda. *Journal of Com-puter Assisted Learning* 25: 6–18.

Putnam, R.D. 2000. *Bowling alone: The collapse and revival of American community*. New York: Simon & Schuster.

Ravenscroft, A., R. Wegerif, and R. Hartley. 2007. Reclaiming thinking: Dialectic, dialogic and learning in the digital age. *British Journal of Educational Psychology Monograph Series: Learning through Digital Technologies* 2, no. 5: 39–57.

Schuller, T., S. Baron, and J. Field. 2000. Social capital: A review and critic. *In Social capital*, ed. S. Baron, J. Field, and T. Schuller. Oxford: Oxford University Press.

Spencer-Oatey, H. 2007. Theories of identity and the analysis of face. *Journal of Pragmatics* 39, no. 4: 639–56.

Time Magazine. 2010. *Person of the Year 2010*. http://www.time .com/time/specials/packages/article/0,28804,2036683_203718 3_2037185,00.html (last accessed June 7, 2011).

Vincent, D. 2000. *The rise of mass literacy: Reading and writing in modern Europe*. Cambridge: Polity.

Waller, M. 2010. "It's very very fun and ecsiting"—using Twitter in the primary classroom. *English* 4–11, no. 39: 14–6.

Wellman, B. 2002. Little boxes, glocalization, and networked indi-vidualism. In Digital cities II: *Computational and sociological approaches*, ed. M. Tanabe, P. Besselaar, and T. Ishida, 1025. Berlin: Springer.

Wellman, B., and S. Wortley. 1990. Different strokes from different folks: Community ties and social support. *American Journal of Sociology* 96, no. 3: 558–88.

Willet, R. 2009. "It feels like you've grown up a bit": Bebo and teenage identity. Paper presented at the ESRC Seminar Series: The educational and social impact of new technologies on young people in Britain. http://www.education.ox.ac.uk/wordpress/wp-content/uploads/2010/07/Seminar-4-Report.pdf (accessed December 20, 2010).

Analyze

1. According to Merchant, what is a "refusenik"?
2. What is a social graph?
3. What does Merchant list as the most popular SNSs at the moment? Would you add any to this list?

Explore

1. Merchant found that what we say on sites like Facebook or as tweets become part of our face-to-face conversations, seamlessly transcending both social realms. Create a comic showing how this intertwining process takes place in your use and experience in digital and face-to-face social interactions.
2. Merchant asks, What is a social network? And then discusses the meaning from scholars' definitions. Use the meanings Merchant uses and expand on them if you think they need expanding. Then, create a visual showing how networks work in your life.
3. Merchant points out that the "highly connected relationships promoted by SNSs allow, and even encourage, users to anchor their relationships and social activities to the real world and this raises new and complex issues concerning privacy and self-expression (Livingstone 2008). In short, the identity work done online has an iterative relationship with offline identity (see Dowdall 2009b for an illustration of this)." In other words the worlds intertwine. Based on your experiences in SNSs, write an essay agreeing or disagreeing with this view.

Jhumpa Lahiri
"Rhode Island"

Jhumpa Lahiri was born in London to Bengali Indian immigrants and raised in Rhode Island. She received a Guggenheim Fellowship and in 1999 published her first short story collection, *Interpreter of Maladies*, which received several prestigious awards, among them the Pulitzer Prize, the PEN/ Hemingway Award, and The New Yorker Debut of the Year. Similar to Mengestu's story of displacement, immigration, and struggle to fit in the United States, Lahiri's short story, "Rhode Island," also explores in first-person narration the social and geographical impact Rhode Island had in shaping her sense of identity.

How does Lahiri show us that, despite being a nonnative, she became a Rhode Islander?

Rhode Island is not an island. Most of it is attached to the continental United States, tucked into a perfect-looking corner formed by the boundaries of Connecticut to the west and Massachusetts above. The rest is a jagged confusion of shoreline: delicate slivers of barrier beach, numerous inlets and peninsulas, and a cluster of stray puzzle pieces, created by the movement of glaciers, nestled in the Narragansett Bay. The tip of Watch Hill, in the extreme southwest, extends like a curving rib bone into the Atlantic Ocean. The salt ponds lining the edge of South Kingstown, where I grew up, resemble the stealthy work of insects who have come into contact with nutritious, antiquated paper.

In 1524, Giovanni Verrazzano thought that the pear-shaped contours of Block Island, nine miles off the southern coast, resembled the Greek island of Rhodes. In 1644, subsequent explorers, mistaking one of Rhode Island's many attendant islands—there are over thirty of them—for another, gave the same name to Aquidneck Island, famous for Newport, and it has now come to represent the state as a whole. Though the name is misleading it is also apt, for despite Rhode Island's physical connection to the mainland, a sense of insularity prevails. Typical to many island communities, there is a combination of those who come only in the warm months, for the swimming and the clam cakes, and those full-time residents who seem never to go anywhere else. Jacqueline Kennedy Onassis and Cornelius Vanderbilt were among Rhode Island's summer people. Given its diminutive proportions there is a third category: those who pass through without stopping. Forty-eight miles long and thirty-seven wide, it is a brief, unavoidable part of the journey by train between Boston and New York and also, if one chooses to take I-95, by car.

Historically it has harbored the radical and the seditious, misfits and minorities. Roger Williams, the liberal theologian who is credited with founding Rhode Island in 1636, was banished from the Massachusetts Bay Colony by, among others, Nathaniel Hawthorne's great grandfather. Williams's unorthodox views on matters religious and otherwise made him an enemy of the Puritans. He eventually became and remained until his death a Seeker, rejecting any single body of doctrine and respecting the good in all branches of faith. Rhode Island, the thirteenth of the original thirteen colonies, had the greatest degree of self-rule, and was the first to renounce allegiance to King George in 1776. The Rhode Island Charter of 1663 guaranteed "full liberty in religious concernments," and, to its credit, the state accommodated the nation's first Baptists, its first Quakers, and is the site of its oldest synagogue, dedicated in 1763, A different attitude greeted the indigenous population, effectively decimated by 1676 in the course of King Philip's War. Rhode Island is the only state that continues to celebrate, the second Monday of every August, VJ Day, which commemorates the surrender of Japan after the bombings of Hiroshima and Nagasaki. On a lesser but also disturbing note, it has not managed to pass the bottle bill, which means that all those plastic containers of Autocrat Coffee Syrup, used to make coffee milk (Rhode Island's official beverage), are destined for the purgatory of landfills.

Though I was born in London and have Indian parents, Rhode Island is the reply I give when people ask me where I am from. My family came in the summer of 1970, from Cambridge, Massachusetts, so that my father could begin work as a librarian at the University of Rhode Island. I had just turned three years old. URI is located in the village of Kingston, a place originally called Little Rest. The name possibly stems from accounts of Colonial troops pausing on their way to fight the Narragansett tribe on the western banks of Worden Pond, an event known as the Great Swamp Massacre. We lived on Kingston's main historic tree-lined drag, in a white house with a portico and black shutters. It had been built in 1829 (a fact stated by a plaque next to the door) to contain the law office of Asa Potter, who was at one point Rhode Island's secretary of state, and whose main residence was the larger, more spectacular house next door. After Asa Potter left Rhode Island to work in a bank in New York, the house became the site of a general store, with a tailor's shop at the front. By 1970 it was an apartment house owned by a fellow Indian, a professor of mathematics named Dr. Suryanarayan.

My family was a hybrid; year-rounders who, like the summer people,   5 didn't fundamentally belong. We rented the first floor of the house; an elderly American woman named Miss Tay lived above us, alone, and her vulnerable, solitary presence was a constant reminder, to my parents, of America's harsh ways. A thick iron chain threaded through wooden posts separated us from our neighbors, the Fishers. A narrow path at the back led to a brown shingled shed I never entered. Hanging from one of the out buildings on the Fisher's property was an oxen yoke, an icon of old New England agriculture, at once elegant and menacing, that both intrigued and seared me as a child. Its bowed shape caused me to think it was a weapon, not merely a restraint. Until I was an adult, I never knew exactly what it was for.

Kingston in those days was a mixture of hippies and Yankees and professors and students. The students arrived every autumn, taking up all the parking spaces, crowding the tables in the Memorial Union with their trays of Cokes and French fries, one year famously streaking on the lawn outside a fraternity building. After commencement in May, things were quiet again, to the point of feeling deserted. I imagine this perpetual ebb and flow, segments of the population ritually coming and going, made it easier for my foreign-born parents to feel that they, too, were rooted to the community in some way. Apart from the Suryanarayans, there were a few other Indian families, women other than my mother in saris walking now and then across the quad. My parents sought them out, invited them over for Bengali dinners, and consider a few of these people among their closest friends today.

The gravitational center of Kingston was, and remains, the Kingston Congregational Church ("King Kong" to locals), where my family did not worship but where I went for Girl Scout meetings once a week, and where my younger sister eventually had her high-school graduation party. Across the street from the church, just six houses down from ours, was the Kingston

Free Library. It was constructed as a courthouse, and also served as the state house between 1776 and 1791. The building's staid Colonial bones later incorporated Victorian flourishes, including a belfry and a mansard roof. If you stand outside and look up at a window to the right on the third floor, three stern while life-sized busts will stare down at you through the glass. They are thought to be likenesses of Abraham Lincoln, Oliver Wendell Holmes, and John Greenleaf Whittier. For many years now, the bust of Lincoln has worn a long red-and-white striped hat, *Cat in the Hat*—style, on its head.

From my earliest memories I was obsessed with the library, with its creaky, cramped atmosphere and all the things it contained. The books used to live on varnished wooden shelves, the modest card catalog contained in two bureau-sized units, sometimes arranged back to back. Phyllis Goodwin, then and for decades afterward the children's librarian, conducted the story hours I faithfully attended when I was little, held upstairs in at vaulted space called Potter Hall. Light poured in through enormous windows on three sides, and Asa Potter's portrait, predominantly black apart from the pale shade of his face, presided over the fireplace. Along with Phyllis there were two other women in charge of the library—Charlotte Schoonover, the director, and Pam Stoddard. Charlotte and Pam, roughly my mother's generation, were friends, and they both had sons about my age. For many years, Charlotte, Pam, and Phyllis represented the three graces to me, guardians of a sacred place that seemed both to represent the heart of Kingston and also the means of escaping it. They liked to play Corelli or Chopin on the little tape recorder behind the desk, but ordered Patti Smith's *Horses* for the circulating album collection.

When I was sixteen I was hired to work as a page at the library, which meant shelving books, working at the circulation desk, and putting plastic wrappers on the jackets of new arrivals. A lot of older people visited daily, to sit at a table with an arrangement of forsythia or cattails at the center, and read the newspaper. I remember a tall, slightly harried mother with wire-rimmed glasses who would come every two weeks with many children behind her and a large canvas tote bag over her shoulder, which she would dump out and then fill up again with more volumes of *The Borrowers* and Laura Ingalls Wilder for the next round of collective reading. Jane Austen was popular with the patrons, enough for me to remember that the books had red cloth covers. I was an unhappy adolescent, lacking confidence, boyfriends, a proper sense of myself. When I was in the library it didn't matter. I took my cue from the readers who came and went and understood that books were what mattered, that they were above high school, above an adolescent's petty trials, above life itself.

By this time we no longer lived in Kingston. We had moved, when I was 10 eight and my sister was one, to a house of our own. I would have preferred to stay in Kingston and live in an enclave called Biscuit City, not only because of the name but because it was full of professors and their families and had a laid-back, intellectual feel. Instead we moved to a town called Peace Dale, exactly one mile away. Peace Dale was a former mill town, an area where the university didn't hold away. Our housing development, called Rolling Acres, was a leafy loop of roads without sidewalks. The turn into the neighborhood, off the main road, is between a John Deere showroom and a bingo hall. Our house, a style called Colonial Garrison according to the developer's brochure, was historical in name only. In 1975 it was built before our eyes—the foundation dug, concrete poured, pale yellow vinyl siding stapled to the exterior,

After we moved into that house, something changed; whether it was my growing older or the place itself, I was aware that the world immediately outside our door, with its red-flagged mailboxes and children's bicycles left overnight on well-seeded grass, was alien to my parents. Some of our neighbors were friendly. Others pretended we were not there. I remember hot days when the mothers of my American friends in the neighborhood would lie in their bikinis on reclining chairs, chatting over wine coolers as my friends and I ran through a sprinkler, while my fully dressed mother was alone in our house, deep-frying a carp or listening to Bengali folk songs. In Rolling Acres we became car-bound. We couldn't walk, as we had been able to do in Kingston, to see a movie on campus, or buy milk and bread at Even's Market, or get stamps at the post office. While one could walk (or run or bike) endlessly around the looping roads of Rolling Acres, without a car we were cut off from the rest of the world. When my parents first moved to Rhode Island, I think they both assumed that it was an experiment, just another port of call on their unfolding immigrant journey. The fact that they now owned a house, along with my father getting tenure, brought the journey to a halt. Thirty-seven years later, my parents still live there. The Little Rest they took in 1970 has effectively become the rest of their lives.

The sense of the environment radically shifting from mile to mile holds true throughout Rhode Island, almost the way life can vary block by block in certain cities. In South Kingstown alone there is a startling mixture of the lovely and the ugly—of resort, rural, and run-of-the-mill. There are strip malls, most of them radiating from a frenetic intersection called Dale Carlia corner, and no one who lives in my town can avoid negotiating its many traffic lights and lanes on a regular basis. There are countless housing developments, filled with energy-efficient spilt-levels when I was growing up, these days with McMansions. There are several Dunkin' Donut shops (Rhode Island has more per capita than any other state). There are also quiet farms where horses graze, and remote, winding roads through woods, flanked by low stone walls. There are places to buy antiques and handmade pottery. Along South Road is a sloping, empty field that resembles the one where Wyeth painted *Christina's World*. There is a house on Route 108, just after the traffic light on 138, with the most extraordinary show of azaleas I have ever seen. And then, of course, there are the beaches. We did not live on the ocean proper, but it was close enough, about five miles away. The ocean was where we took all our visitors from Massachusetts (which was where the majority of my parents' Bengali friends lived), either to Scarborough, which is the state beach, or to Point Judith Light. They used to sit on the grassy hill speaking a foreign tongue, sometimes bringing a picnic of packaged white bread and a pot of *aloo dum*. On the way back they liked to stop in the fishing village of Galilee, where the parking lots of the shops and restaurants were covered with broken seashells. They did not go to eat stuffies, a local delicacy made from quahogs and bread crumbs, but to see if the daily catch included any butterfish or mackerel, to turn into a mustard curry at home. Occasionally my mother's best friend from Massachusetts, Koely Das, wanted to get lobsters or crabs, but these, too, received the curry treatment, a far, fiery cry from a side of melted butter.

The Atlantic I grew up with lacks the color and warmth of the Caribbean, the grandeur of the Pacific, the romance of the Mediterranean. It is generally cold, and full of rust-colored seaweed. Still, I prefer it. The waters of Rhode Island, as much a part of the state's character, if not more, as the land never asked us questions, never raised a brow. Thanks to its very lack of welcome, its unwavering indifference, the ocean always made me feel accepted, and to my dying day, the seaside is the only place where I can feel truly and recklessly happy.

My father, a global traveler, considers Rhode Island paradise. For nearly   15
four decades he has dedicated himself there to a job he loves, rising through
the ranks in the library's cataloging department to become its head. But in
addition to the job, he loves the place. He loves that it is quiet, and moder-
ate, and is, in the great scheme of things, uneventful. He loves that he lives
close to his work, and that he does not have to speed a significant portion of
his life sitting in a car on the highway, or on a crowded subway, commuting.
(Lately, because my parents have downsized to one car, he has begun to take
a bus, on which he is frequently the sole passenger.) Though Rhode Island
is a place of four proper seasons, he loves that both winters and summers,
tempered by the ocean breezes, are relatively mild. He loved working in his
small garden, and going once a week to buy groceries, coupons in hand, at
Super Stop&Shop. In many ways he is a spiritual descendant of America's
earliest Puritan settlers: thrifty, hard-working, plain in his habits. Like
Roger Williams, he is something of a Seeker, aloof from organized religions
but appreciating their philosophical worth. He also embodies the values of
two of New England's greatest thinkers, demonstrating a profound lack of
materialism and self-reliance that would have made Thoreau and Emerson
proud. "The great man is he who in the midst of the crowd keeps with
perfect sweetness the independence of solitude," Emerson wrote. This is
the man who raised me.

My mother, a gregarious and hard-wired urbanite, has struggled; to hear
her recall the first time she was driven down from Massachusetts, along
I–95 and then a remote, lightless stretch of Route 138, is to understand
that Rhode Island was and in many ways remains the heart of darkness for
her. She stayed at home to raise me and my sister, frequently taking in other
children as well, but apart from a stint as an Avon Lady she had no job. In
1987, when my sister was a teenager, my mother finally ventured out, directing a day care and also working as a classroom assistant at South Road
Elementary School, which both my sister and I had attended. One day, after
she'd been working at the school for a decade, she started to receive anonymous hate mail. It came in the form of notes placed in her mailbox at
school, and eventually in her coat pocket. There were nine notes in total.
The handwriting was meant to look like a child's awkward scrawl. The content was humiliating, painful to recount. "Go back to India," one of them
said. "Many people here do not like to see your face," read another. By then
my mother had been a resident of Rhode Island for twenty-seven years. In

Rhode Island she had raised two daughters, given birth to one. She had set up a home and potted geraniums year after year and thrown hundreds of dinner parties for her ever-expanding circle of Bengali friends. In Rhode Island she had renounced her Indian passport for an American one, pledged allegiance to the flag. My mother was ashamed of the notes, and for a while, hoping they would stop, she kept them to herself.

The incident might make a good start to a mystery novel, the type that always flew out of the Kingston Free Library: poison-pen letters appearing in a quaint, sleepy town. But there was nothing cozily intriguing about the cold-blooded correspondence my mother received. After finding the note in her coat pocket (it was February, recess time, and she had been expecting to pull out a glove), she told the school principal, and she also told my family what was going on. In the wake of this incident, many kind people reached out to my mother to express their outrage on her behalf, and for each of those nine notes, she received many sympathetic ones, including words of support from the former president of the university, Francis Horn. The majority of these people were Americans; one of the things that continues to upset my mother was that very few members of Rhode Island's Indian community, not insignificant by then, were willing to stand by her side. Some resented my mother for creating controversy, for drawing attention to their being foreign, a fact they worked to neutralize. Others told her that she might not have been targeted if she had worn skirts and trousers instead of saris and bindis. Meetings were held at the elementary school, calling for increased tolerance and sensitivity. The story was covered by the *Providence Journal-Bulletin* and the local television news. Montel Williams called our house, wanting my mother to appear on his show (she declined). A detective was put on the case, but the writer of the notes never came forward, was never found. Over ten years have passed. South Road School has shut down, for reasons having nothing to do with what happened to my mother. She worked for another school, part of the same system, in West Kingston, and has recently retired.

I left Rhode Island at eighteen to attend college in New York City, which is where, following a detour up to Boston, I continue to live. Because my parents still live in Rhode Island I still visit, though the logistics of having two small children mean they come to me these days more often than I go to them. I was there in August 2007. My parents, children, sister, and I had just been to Vermont, renting a cabin on a lake. There was a screened-in porch, a Modern Library first edition of *To the Lighthouse* in the bookcase, and a severe mouse problem in the kitchen. In the end the mice drove us away, and during the long drive back to my parents' house, I was aware how little Vermont and Rhode Island, both New England states, have in common. Vermont is dramatically northern, rural, mountainous, landlocked. Rhode Island is flat, briny, more densely populated. Vermont is liberal enough to sanction gay marriage but feels homogenous, lacking Rhode Island's deep pockets of immigration from Ireland, Portugal, and Italy. Rhode Island's capital, Providence, was run for years by a Republican Italian, Buddy Cianci. In 1984 he was convicted of kidnapping his then-estranged wife's boyfriend, beating him with a fire log, and burning him with a lighted cigarette. In 1991 he ran again for mayor, and the citizens of Rhode Island handed him 97 percent of the vote.

It was hotter in Rhode Island than it had been in Vermont. The Ghiorse Beach Factor, courtesy of John Ghiorse, the meteorologist on Channel 10, was a perfect 10 for the weekend we were there. On my way to buy sunscreen at the CVS pharmacy in Kingston, I stopped by the library, excited to see the sign outside indicating that the summer book sale was still going on. The library has been expanded and renovated since I worked there, the circulation desk much larger now and facing the entering visitor, with a computer system instead of the clunky machine that stamped due date cards. The only familiar thing, apart from the books, was Pam. "Just the dregs," she warned me about the book sale.

As we were catching up, an elderly couple with British accents approached, "Excuse me," the woman interrupted. "Can you recommend something decent? I'm tired of murder mysteries and people being killed. I just want to hear a decent family story." Pam led her away to the books on tape section, and I went upstairs to Potter Hall to look at the sale. It was just the dregs, as Pam had said, but I managed to find a few things I'd always meant to read—a paperback copy of Donna Tartt's *The Secret History*, and *Monkeys* by Susan Minot. The curtained stage that used to be at one end of the room, on which I had performed, among other things, the role of the Queen of Hearts in *Alice in Wonderland*, was gone, so that the space seemed even bigger. The grand piano was still there, but Asa Potter's portrait was at the Museum of Fine Arts in Boston, Pam later explained, for repairs. She told me she was thinking of retiring soon, and that Phyllis, who had retired long before, had discovered a late-blooming talent for portrait painting.

"It's a quirky place," Pam reflected when I asked her about Rhode Island, complaining, "There's no zoning. No united front." And practically in the same breath, proudly: "Kingston is the melting pot of the state."

20   In the afternoon I took my children, along with my mother and sister, to Scarborough. The beach was packed, the tide high and rough. As soon as we set down our things, a wave hit us, forcing us to pick up a drenched blanket and move. Scarborough is a large beach with a paved parking lot that feels even larger. The parking lot itself is also useful in the off-season, for learning how to drive. Scarborough lacks the steep, dramatic dunes and isolated aura of lower Cape Cod, a stretch of New England coastline I have come, in my adult life, to love more than the beach of my childhood. The sand at Scarborough is extremely fine and gray and, when moist, resembles wet ash. A large tide pool had formed that day, and it was thick with young muddied children lying on their bellies, pretending to swim. My son darted off to chase seagulls. The breeze blew impressively in spite of the sultry weather, justifying Ghiorse's ten out of ten. In the distance I could see Point Judith Light. The giant billboard for Coppertone, the Dr. T.J. Eckleburg of my youth, has vanished, but I imagined it was still there—the model's toasted bikini-clad seventies body sprawled regally, indifferently, above the masses.

An announcement on the loudspeaker informed us that a little girl was lost, asking her to meet her mother under the flag on the boardwalk. Another announcement followed: The men's hot water showers were temporarily out of service. The population was democratic, unpretentious, inclusive: ordinary bodies of various sizes and shades, the shades both genetic and cultivated, reading paperback bestsellers and reaching into big bags of chips. I saw no *New Yorker* magazines being read, no heirloom tomato sandwiches or organic peaches being consumed. A trio of deeply tanned adolescent boys tripped past, collectively courting, one could imagine, the same elusive girl. The sun began to set, and within an hour the crowd had thinned to the point where a man started to drag his metal detector through the sand, and the only kids in the tide pool were my own. As we were getting up to go, our bodies sticky with salt, it occurred to me that Scarborough Beach on a summer day is one of the few places that is not a city but still manages, reassuringly, to feel like one. Two days later, I headed home with my sister and my children to Brooklyn. On our way through West

Kingston to catch the highways, a lone green truck selling Dell's, Rhode Island's beloved frozen lemonade, beckoned at an otherwise desolate intersection, but my sister and I drove on, accepting the fact that we would not taste Dell's for another year.

As long as my mother and father live, I will continue to visit Rhode Island. They are, respectively, in their late sixties and seventies now, and each time I drive by the local funeral home in Wakefield, I try to prepare myself. Just after I'd finished a draft of this essay, early one November morning, my mother had a heart attack at home. An Indian doctor at Rhode Island Hospital, Arun Singh, performed the bypass operation that has saved her life. When I was a child, I remember my mother often wondering who, in the event of an emergency or other crisis, would come running to help us. During the weeks when I feared she might slip away, everyone did. Our mailbox was stuffed with get-well cards from my mother's students, the refrigerator stuffed with food from her friends. My father's colleagues at the library took up a collection to buy my family Thanksgiving dinner. Our next door neighbor, Mrs. Hyde, who had seen the ambulance pulling up to our house, crossed over to our yard as I was heading to the hospital one day, and told me she'd said a special prayer for my mother at her church.

Due to my parents' beliefs, whenever and whenever they do die, they will not be buried in Rhode Island soil. The house in Rolling Acres will belong to other people; there will be no place there to pay my respects. At the risk of predicting the future, I can see myself, many years from now, driving up I–95, on my way to another vacation on the Cape. We will cross the border after Connecticut, turn off at exit 3A for Kingston, and then continue along an alternative, prettier route that will take us across Jamestown and over the Newport Bridge, where the sapphire bay spreads out on either side, a breathtaking sight that will never grow old. There will no longer be a reason to break the journey in Little Rest. Like many others, we will pass through without stopping.

Analyze

1. Who were some of the famous people who called Rhode Island home in the summer?
2. Who is credited with founding Rhode Island and what is his story?
3. How does Lahiri describe the Atlantic Ocean off of Rhode Island?

Explore

1. In her writing Lahiri describes and narrates Rhode Island as a part of her identity. What are some of the things she describes that make us feel like we are being led into her own private Rhode Island?

2. Write an essay of a place that you feel is a part of you. Show how this place has shaped you through some of your experiences and why some of the places are special.

3. Create a collage of images of your special place, making sure it reveals something about you.

Forging Connections

1. The essays in this chapter explore a variety of ways to think about how and why we are here in the United States, as well as the types of experiences we have. Write an essay that uses the writings from this chapter to stress the importance that these writers give to place, that is, that place is not just geographical, but that it is also the types of experiences—good and bad—that we have once we are here. Be sure to answer the question: how does where we are from, how we get here, and what we experience here shape who we become?

2. A few of the essays in this chapter argue that "our" forefathers came here knowing they would be the lowest part of society, but they worked hard, and succeeding generations climbed the ladder of success. Other writers suggest that such sugarcoated views do not account for the hardship and discrimination that immigrants have experienced. Using the readings to inform your view, write an essay in which you discuss how immigrants might be integrated (or not) into U.S. society.

3. This chapter asks the question: Where are you from? It then showcases a variety of ways in which writers establish this. Write a poem about where you are from and use many of the techniques you studied and learned from the readings. Alternatively, create a comic book to develop this.

Looking Further

1. Interview a senior member from your family or someone from a senior assisted living center. Before you do the interview, create a list of ten questions. Focus on asking half of the questions that tie into the person's name and the issues we covered in Chapter 1, and the other half on ideas about place and identity that we discussed in this chapter. Also, ask the person whether he or she is willing to share any pictures with you. Put together a story about this person based on the information he or she shares with you and offer to give a copy to your interviewee.

2. Create a collage that shows where you are from, drawing from the points we learned about our identity in Chapters 1 and 2. This can be created with cutouts from newspapers, magazines, and your own pictures placed on poster board, or it can be a digital collage in PowerPoint, Prezi, or Keynote.

3. Create a three-minute movie telling a story of the positive and negative power of names and place in your or someone else's life. Draw from the readings and ideas you learned from discussion and class exercises from Chapters 1 and 2.

3

Where Did You Go to School? Education in America

If you are reading this book, you most likely are taking a class, so this chapter will have some important insights for you. Our overarching question for this chapter is one we have all asked others at some point, and, in turn, they have asked us: Where did you go to school? In the context of a conversation, our responses could include our elementary school, middle school, high school, or college experiences. In many cases, depending on where we went to school, we make judgments about where we or others went to school, based on criteria such as which side of town the school is on, whether it is a smart or athletic school, whether it is a band or engineering school, and so forth. So even though the question seems straightforward, the responses and the meanings behind them reveal a lot about us. The factor that unites all these types of questions is that they all characterize us in some way: we make judgments about those we ask, and those who ask us do the same.

These readings reveal experiences and attitudes that the writers have had while in or out of school, studies gauging perceptions of school experiences, and critiques of the way we are standardized in our schools. In the first reading, "Could Have Done Better," an interview, the speaker indicates that he could have done better in school (an experience many of us share). However, his interviewer encourages him; when he says that he did not care for reading and writing but liked math, she pushes him to think how accurate it is to believe there is no writing or reading in math, as students oftentimes mistakenly believe.

In "I Just Want to Be Average," Rose shares his high school experience of being mistakenly placed in the wrong classes. The mistake was discovered and he was moved into the correct classes, but getting caught up in more advanced classes later posed new issues. He shows us how the system allows us to underachieve once we are labeled. The next essay is a scholarly article, "Living with Myths," and it debunks through research the myths about where we can attain a quality education. Many families believe that the more prestigious sounding schools offer a better education because of their elevated tuitions. As we discover, this might not be the case. Introducing a visual for our reading, we include a chart showing the range of salaries that come with more advanced education in "Education Pays: Education Pays in Higher Earnings and Lower Unemployment." How do we read visuals? When are visuals more powerful than words? How do words and visuals work together?

This chapter introduces a new type of reading: a Supreme Court ruling. *Brown v. Board of Education* is an important decision that ended segregation in schools based on race. This decision has changed education for many students. "Learning to Read," by Malcolm X, is another example of how, when desire to learn is present, we can turn even a bad situation into a good one. In this case, Malcolm X learns to read while in prison. Villanueva's "Spic in English!" explores the process of assimilating into America while maintaining his sense of his Puerto Rican identity. We see some of the results of this journey in the ways that his school peers treat him and by the way the school system labels him, like Rose, as noncollege material. In contrast to Villanueva, in "Achievement of Desire" we follow Rodriguez in his process of assimilating into American culture and education by rejecting his Mexican identity, family, and roots. Our last essay, Davidson's "Project Classroom Makeover," argues against the way we are taught in our schools, with a focus on standardization that circumvents the creative inquiry-based problem solving needed in our twenty-first-century classroom and workforce.

These essays encourage us to think about our schooling experiences from several perspectives. We are asked to think about issues of equality and race, the economic impact of schooling on our salaries, of the effects of placement in schools, of perceptions of what is a good school and the education such schools provide, and how, perhaps, our schooling system has failed to adapt to the needs of the twenty-first century.

As we dive into these readings, we are asked to think about our past, current, and future educational experiences in order to understand what we have and what we can change. We also think about our educational experiences in order to be informed about the changes we would like to make on personal and societal levels. Although not all of the readings will reflect all of our experiences, as individual readings and as a collection, they do reveal something about us, about our classmates, and about why we are sitting in the classrooms in which we are currently reading these essays.

Taylor Garcia
"Could Have Done Better"

Cindy Selfe video interviewed Taylor Garcia for the Digital Archive of Literacy Narratives project, which is an online research site dedicated to collecting all sorts of literacy narratives, ranging from views about the impact of reading and writing, like this one, to music and digital literacy learning experiences. In this interview at Garcia's graduation he admits he never liked reading or writing and, in hindsight, he could have put more effort into his studies. For more on this story, go to http://daln.osu.edu/. In our selection, Taylor Garcia describes his narrative as "a story about growing up fast."

What do you think are the most important skills to have for college and your intended career?

INTERVIEWER: Can you tell me your name?

TAYLOR: Taylor Garcia.

INTERVIEWER: Talk to me about what's happening to you today and how you, you know, feel on this day.

TAYLOR: I am going through my graduating ceremony for getting my GED. And, it's exciting.

5   **INTERVIEWER:** How old are you?

TAYLOR: Seventeen

INTERVIEWER: Ok, tell me what role reading and writing has played in your life. Do you read a lot? Are you a reader or a writer?

TAYLOR: No, I actually don't like reading or writing.

INTERVIEWER: Tell me about why.

10   **TAYLOR:** I don't know. I'm good at reading and writing both, real good. I just don't like those. I'm more of a math and science guy.

INTERVIEWER: How did you come to be a math and science guy and not a reading and writing guy?

TAYLOR: I don't know. I just, ever since I started school in kindergarten, I liked math and science a lot more than reading and writing.

INTERVIEWER: Can you tell us a story about that? Like, something that happened in school or something that made you like that?

TAYLOR: I guess, I just, I like, I like excel really, really, well, really fast in math and science and I was interested in, you know, doing different things in numbers and money and just stuff like that.

15   **INTERVIEWER:** Can you tell us a story about something that you did that made you interested in math and science?

TAYLOR: No, there's not really a story.

INTERVIEWER: Ok. Can you talk to us about maybe a story about how you grew up and something that you did at home?

TAYLOR: I grew up, I like, used to play outside a lot and I never really liked school all that much. I did good but I didn't like going there, except for friends and stuff.

INTERVIEWER: Why didn't you like school?

20   **TAYLOR:** It was boring. 'Cause none of my classes were high enough for me to where, like I was always more advanced than the classes I was in. So, I got bored and I acted up and that's what led to me having to get my GED in the end.

INTERVIEWER: Did, um, so when you were bored in class, it was just too slow for you?

TAYLOR: Yeah.

INTERVIEWER: Can you remember any particular teacher or class that made you make up your mind to drop out or not to go?

TAYLOR: Uh, well no, I got in trouble in the ninth grade, well trouble started in the eighth grade. I had a drug and alcohol problem and that carried on for a while. Then I went to the ninth grade and ended up leaving that school and I had to go, I went to an in-patient treatment, and then I came out of that and went to a different school, and I ended up getting in trouble there and had to leave there too and went to a computer school, and it just wasn't cutting it for me, so I decided to leave.

INTERVIEWER: Why? How come? What was the computer school? Was that not what you wanted to do?   25

TAYLOR: It was just, I was not very good at, like, working on computer just sitting there and then doing something like that. It was just boring and there was no push forward or anything like that. And I had to catch the bus an hour and a half to get there. And then to work on a computer which is something that I could have done at home if I wanted to. So, I quit that and decided to get my GED.

> "So, I quit that and decided to get my GED."

INTERVIEWER: And now what do you want to do with your life after graduation?

TAYLOR: Uh, I plan on going to college in the fall and getting a business degree. Or a degree in political science.

INTERVIEWER: Where do you want to go to college?

TAYLOR: Uh, I'm going to start out at Columbus State and hopefully transfer to OSU.   30

INTERVIEWER: And what is it that you want to study? Talk to me about why you want to study business or political science.

TAYLOR: Well I've always loved politics and what's going on in the world. I have very strong views and opinions about that. And business, like I said in the beginning, I love math and I like money and different stuff like that. I've always thought about doing realty or owning my own business or just something like that since I was a little kid.

INTERVIEWER: And can you tell me what you think of the current political state of the world?

TAYLOR: It's not good, I don't, uh, agree with the war, I don't agree with where our soldiers are and how they're being used, and how everything is going on in this world. All our money problems are all wrong.

INTERVIEWER: Do you read a lot of newspapers or listen to the news?   35

TAYLOR: Yeah. I listen to the news just about every day.

INTERVIEWER: And if you were president what would you do?

TAYLOR: Uh, if I were president there would be tons of different things. Um, I don't know, I can't really say. But, I would do whatever I can do to fix the economy and put our troops in the right places, help our own country more than, I mean we've got people here starving in our own country that don't have clothes on their backs and I don't see why we send money to other countries when we have all those problems right here; diseased kids with no homes or families.

INTERVIEWER: How about funding for education?

40   **TAYLOR:** Education is important, I feel, I feel bad that I didn't go through with whole, my whole high school career because, you know, there's a lot of things you learn, not just book wise, but social wise and other things just from being in high school and what-not and, you know, going to school, it's a good thing. We need funding for school 'cause there's so many classes getting cut like art classes and music classes and those are essential, you know, growing up and getting smarter too.

INTERVIEWER: What kinds of classes do you look forward to taking in college?

TAYLOR: Um, I don't know, I don't really know. College has so many different classes to offer, I don't, I don't know; a lot of 'em.

INTERVIEWER: What kinds of things do you look forward to in college just generally?

TAYLOR: Just, college life, I am glad that I am going to be out on my own soon and trying something different. I've always heard college is so much more different than grade school. It's a lot funner. The work's harder, but it's also more interesting and all that. And that's what I've heard and that's what I look forward to.

45   **INTERVIEWER:** Tell me about, do you have any stories about your GED program and how you did in the GED program? What's that been like for you?

TAYLOR: I did real well in the GED program, and, like I said, I've been real smart really my whole life. I was the class clown, and I got in trouble and stuff, so. But the GED, I went and took the pre-test and I passed that, so I came back and took the actual GED test and I passed that in, like, half the time they gave me to do so. I don't know, I just, I actually, I didn't find the GED test hard at all.

INTERVIEWER: Do you think that the GED program is one that should be continued and supported?

TAYLOR: Oh, of course. I mean, because everybody has their own troubles, you know, inside the home, outside the home at school or somewhere else and people make mistakes and they mess up and, you know, without the GED program there's a lot of people who wouldn't be able to move on to college, you know, or have their high school diploma.

INTERVIEWER: So, you think it's pretty worthwhile?

TAYLOR: Yeah, it's worthwhile. It's a good thing that should be funded   50
by the state.

INTERVIEWER: Thank you very much! That's excellent!

TAYLOR: Thank you!

Analyze

1. Why is Taylor averse to reading or writing, preferring math and science?
2. What was Taylor's view about school when he was growing up?
3. How does Taylor see the current state of the political world?

Explore

1. Interview two of your classmates about a literacy experience they have had. Some areas you can ask them about include the following: Who taught them to read or write, and where? How did they achieve this? Who taught them to use their first computer and software? Report your findings to the class. You might also think about recording your interviews and sharing them on the Digital Archives site.
2. The GED seems to have served as a pressure valve for Taylor; that is, he realizes he was not focused or ready in high school. In groups, discuss the pros and cons of the GED. Do you think it is a fair exam, considering the fact that most students attend four years of high school in order to earn their degree? Look into the requirements for a GED in your area so you can compare a traditional high school degree with it.
3. Taylor seems to shift focus in the interview about what his strengths and interests are and what he eventually wants to earn a degree in. Is the shifting focus of interests common among your peers in class? Based on the responses you come up with, create a Classification and Division chart of what your peers' strengths and interests are and what they eventually want to earn a degree in.

Mike Rose
"I Just Want to Be Average"

Rose, a professor in the School of Education at UCLA, is a prolific writer and has won numerous awards for his work. In his essay below, we find that his start in high school was anything but successful. From his own experience, he shows us what happens to students who are placed in classes with low expectations. "I Just Want to Be Average" comes from his book *Lives on the Boundary* (1989), a book examining the educationally underprivileged.

How do your educational experiences contrast with Rose's?

I t took two buses to get to Our Lady of Mercy. The first started deep in South Los Angeles and caught me at midpoint. The second drifted through neighborhoods with trees, parks, big lawns, and lot of flowers. The rides were long but were livened up by a group of South L.A. veterans whose parents also thought that Hope had set up shop in the west end of the country. There was Christy Biggars, who, at sixteen, was dealing and was, according to rumor, a pimp as well. There were Bill Cobb and Johnny Gonzales, grease-pencil artists extraordinaire, who left Nembutal-enhanced swirls of "Cobb" and "Johnny" on the corrugated walls of the bus. And then there was Tyrrell Wilson. Tyrrell was the coolest kid I knew. He ran the dozens like a metric halfback, laid down a rap that outrhymed and outpointed Cobb, whose rap was good but not great—the curse of a moderately soulful kid trapped in white skin. But it was Cobb who would sneak a radio onto the bus, and thus underwrote his patter with Little Richard, Fats Domino, Chuck Berry, the Coasters, and Ernie K. Doe's mother-in-law, an awful woman who was "sent from down below." And so it was that Christy and Cobb and Johnny G. and Tyrrell and I and assorted others picked up along the way passed our days in the back of the bus, a funny mix brought together by geography and parental desire.

Entrance to school brings with it forms and releases and assessments. Mercy relied on a series of tests . . . for placement, and somehow the results of my tests got confused with those of another student named

Rose. The other Rose apparently didn't do very well, for I was placed in the vocational track, a euphemism for the bottom level. Neither I nor my parents realized what this meant. We had no sense that Business Math, Typing, and English-Level D were dead ends. The current spate of reports on the schools criticizes parents for not involving themselves in the education of their children. But how would someone like Tommy Rose, with his two years of Italian schooling, know what to ask? And what sort of pressure could an exhausted waitress apply? The error went undetected, and I remained in the vocational track for two years. What a place.

My homeroom was supervised by Brother Dill, a troubled and unstable man who also taught freshman English. When his class drifted away from him, which was often, his voice would rise in paranoid accusations, and occasionally he would lose control and shake or smack us. I hadn't been there two months when one of his brisk, face-turning slaps had my glasses sliding down the aisle. Physical education was also pretty harsh. Our teacher was a stubby ex-lineman who had played old-time pro ball in the Midwest. He routinely had us grabbing our ankles to receive his stinging paddle across our butts. He did that, he said, to make men of us. "Rose," he bellowed on our first encounter; me standing geeky in line in my baggy shorts. "'Rose'? What the hell kind of name is that?"

"Italian, sir," I squeaked.

"Italian! Ho. Rose, do you know the sound a bag of shit makes when it   5 hits the wall?"

"No, sir."

"*Wop*!"

Sophomore English was taught by Mr. Mitropetros. He was a large, bejeweled man who managed the parking lot at the Shrine Auditorium. He would crow and preen and list for us the stars he'd brushed against. We'd ask questions and glance knowingly and snicker, and all that fueled the poor guy to brag some more. Parking cars was his night job. He had little training in English, so his lesson plan for his day work had us reading the district's required text, *Julius Caesar,* aloud for the semester. We'd finished the play way before the twenty weeks was up, so he'd have us switch parts again and again and start again: Dave Snyder, the fastest guy at Mercy, mus-cling through Caesar to the breathless squeals of Calpurnia, as interpreted by Steve Fusco, a surfer who owned the school's most envied paneled wagon. Week ten and Dave and Steve would take on new roles, as would we all, and render a water-logged Cassius and a Brutus that are beyond my powers of description.

Spanish I—taken in the second year—fell into the hands of a new recruit. Mr. Montez was a tiny man, slight, five foot six at the most, soft-spoken and delicate. Spanish was a particularly rowdy class, and Mr. Montez was as prepared for it as a doily maker at a hammer throw. He would tap his pencil to a room in which Steve Fusco was propelling spitballs from his heavy lips, in which Mike Dweetz was taunting Billy Hawk, a half-Indian, half-Spanish, reed-thin, quietly explosive boy. The vocational track at Our Lady of Mercy mixed kids traveling in from South L.A. with South Bay surfers and a few Slavs and Chicanos from the harbors of San Pedro. This was a dangerous miscellany: surfers and hodads and South-Central blacks all ablaze to the metronomic tapping of Hector Montez's pencil.

10   One day Billy lost it. Out of the corner of my eye I saw him strike out with his right arm and catch Dweetz across the neck. Quick as a spasm, Dweetz was out of his seat, scattering desks, cracking Billy on the side of the head, right behind the eye. Snyder and Fusco and others broke it up, but the room felt hot and close and naked. Mr. Montez's tenuous authority was finally ripped to shreds, and I think everyone felt a little strange about that. The charade was over, and when it came down to it, I don't think any of the kids really wanted it to end this way. They had pushed and pushed and bullied their way into a freedom that both scared and embarrassed them.

Students will float to the mark you set. I and the others in the vocational classes were bobbing in pretty shallow water. Vocational education has aimed at increasing the economic opportunities of students who do not do well in our schools. Some serious programs succeed in doing that, and through exceptional teachers ... students learn to develop hypotheses and troubleshoot, reason through a problem, and communicate effectively—the true job skills. The vocational track, however, is most often a place for those who are just not making it, a dumping ground for the disaffected. There were a few teachers who worked hard at education; young Brother Slattery, for example, combined a stern voice with weekly quizzes to try to pass along to us a skeletal outline of world history. But mostly the teachers had no idea of how to engage the imaginations of us kids who were scuttling along at the bottom of the pond.

And the teachers would have needed some inventiveness, for none of us was groomed for the classroom. It wasn't just that I didn't know things—didn't know how to simplify algebraic fractions, couldn't identify different kinds of clauses, bungled Spanish translations—but that I had developed various faulty and inadequate ways of doing algebra and making sense of Spanish. Worse yet, the years of defensive tuning out in elementary school had given me a way to escape quickly while seeming at least half alert. During my time in Voc. Ed., I developed further into a mediocre student and a somnambulant problem solver, and that affected the subjects I did have the wherewithal to handle: I detested Shakespeare; I got bored with history. My attention flitted here and there. I fooled around in class and read my books indifferently—the intellectual equivalent of playing with your food. I did what I had to do to get by, and I did it with half a mind.

But I did learn things about people and eventually came into my own socially. I liked the guys in Voc. Ed. Growing up where I did, I understood and admired physical prowess, and there was an abundance of muscle here. There was Dave Snyder, a sprinter and halfback of true quality. Dave's ability and his quick wit gave him a natural appeal, and he was welcome in any clique, though he always kept a little independent. He enjoyed acting the fool and could care less about studies, but he possessed a certain maturity and never caused the faculty much trouble. It was a testament to his independence that he included me among his friends—I eventually went out for track, but I was no jock. Owing to the Latin alphabet and a dearth of Rs and Ss, Snyder sat behind Rose, and we started exchanging one-liners and became friends.

There was Ted Richard, a much-touted Little League pitcher. He was chunky and had a baby face and came to Our Lady of Mercy as a seasoned street fighter. Ted was quick to laugh and he had a loud, jolly laugh, but when he got angry he'd smile a little smile, the kind that simply raises the corner of the mouth a quarter of an inch. For those who knew, it was an eerie signal. Those who didn't found themselves in big trouble, for Ted was very quick. He loved to carry on what we would come to call philosophical discussions: What is courage? Does God exist? He also loved words, enjoyed picking up big ones like *salubrious* and *equivocal* and using them in our conversations—laughing at himself as the word hit a chuckhole rolling off his tongue. Ted didn't do all that well in school—baseball and parties and testing the courage he'd speculated about took up his time. His textbooks were *Argosy* and *Field and Stream,* whatever newspapers he'd find on the bus stop—from the *Daily Worker* to pornography—conversations with uncles or hobos or businessmen he'd meet in a coffee shop, *The Old Man and the Sea.*

With hindsight, I can see that Ted was developing into one of those rough-hewn intellectuals whose sources are a mix of the learned and the apocryphal, whose discussions are both assured and sad.

15   And then there was Ken Harvey. Ken was good-looking in a puffy way and had a full and oily ducktail and was a car enthusiast . . . a hodad. One day in religion class, he said the sentence that turned out to be one of the most memorable of the hundreds of thousands I heard in those Voc. Ed. years. We were talking about the parable of the talents, about achievement, working hard, doing the best you can do, blah-blah-blah, when the teacher called on the restive Ken Harvey for an opinion. Ken thought about it, but just for a second, and said (with studied, minimal affect), "I just wanna be average."

That woke me up. Average? Who wants to be average? Then the athletes chimed in with the clichés that make you want to laryngectomize them, and the exchange became a platitudinous melee. At the time, I thought Ken's assertion was stupid, and I wrote him off. But his sentence has stayed with me all these years, and I think I am finally coming to understand it.

Ken Harvey was gasping for air. School can be a tremendously disorienting place. No matter how bad the school, you're going to encounter notions that don't fit with the assumptions and beliefs that you grew up with maybe you'll hear these dissonant notions from teachers, maybe from the other students, and maybe you'll read them. You'll also be thrown in with all kinds of kids from all kinds of backgrounds, and that can be unsettling—this is especially true in places of rich ethnic and linguistic mix, like the L.A. basin. You'll see a handful of students far excel you in courses that sound exotic and that are only in the curriculum of the elite: French, physics, trigonometry. And all this is happening while you're trying to shape an identity, your body is changing, and your emotions are running wild. If you're a working-class kid in the vocational track, the options you'll have to deal with this will be constrained in certain ways: you're defined by your school as "slow"; you're placed in a curriculum that isn't designed to liberate you but to occupy you, or, if you're lucky, train you, though the training is for work the society does not esteem; other students are picking up the cues from your school and your curriculum and interacting with you in particular ways. If you're a kid like Ted Richard, you turn your back on all this and let your mind roam where it may. But youngsters like Ted are rare. What Ken and so many others do is protect themselves from such suffocating madness by taking on with a vengeance the identity implied in the vocational track. Reject the confusion and frustration by openly defining yourself as the Common Joe. Champion the average. Rely on your own good sense. Fuck this bullshit. Bullshit, of course, is everything you—and the others—fear is beyond you: books, essays, tests, academic scrambling, complexity, scientific reasoning, philosophical inquiry.

The tragedy is that you have to twist the knife in your own gray matter to make this defense work. You'll have to shut down, have to reject intellectual stimuli or diffuse them with sarcasm, have to cultivate stupidity, have to convert boredom from a malady into a way of confronting the world. Keep your vocabulary simple, act stoned when you're not or act more stoned than you are, flaunt ignorance, materialize your dreams. It is a powerful and effective defense—it neutralizes the insult and the frustration of being a vocational kid and, when perfected, it drives teachers up the wall, a delightful secondary effect. But like all strong magic, it exacts a price.

My own deliverance from the Voc. Ed. world began with sophomore biology. Every student, college prep to vocational, had to take biology, and unlike the other courses, the same person taught all sections. When teaching the vocational group, Brother Clint probably slowed down a bit or omitted a little of the fundamental biochemistry, but he used the same book and more or less the same syllabus across the board. If one class got tough, he could get tougher. He was young and powerful and very handsome, and looks and physical strength were high currency. No one gave him any trouble.

I was pretty bad at the dissecting table, but the lectures and the textbook 20 were interesting: plastic overlays that, with each turned page, peeled away skin, then veins and muscle, then organs, down to the very bones that Brother Clint, pointer in hand, would tap out on our hanging skeleton. Dave Snyder was in big trouble, for the study of life—versus the living of it—was sticking in his craw. We worked out a code for our multiple-choice exams. He'd poke me in the back: once for the answer under *A,* twice for *B,* and so on; and when he'd hit the right one, I'd look up to the ceiling as though I were lost in thought. Poke: cytoplasm. Poke, poke: methane. Poke, poke, poke: William Harvey. Poke, poke, poke, poke: islets of Langerhans. This didn't work out perfectly, but Dave passed the course, and I mastered the dreamy look of a guy on a record jacket. And something else happened. Brother Clint puzzled over this Voc. Ed. kid who was racking up 98s and 99s on his tests. He checked the school's records and discovered the error. He recommended that I begin my junior year in the College Prep program.

According to all I've read since, such a shift, as one report put it, is virtually impossible. Kids at that level rarely cross tracks. The telling thing is how chancy both my placement into and exit from Voc. Ed. was; neither I nor my parents had anything to do with it. I lived in one world during spring semester, and when I came back to school in the fall, I was living in another.

Switching to College Prep was a mixed blessing. I was an erratic student. I was undisciplined. And I hadn't caught onto the rules of the game: why work hard in a class that didn't grab my fancy? I was also hopelessly behind in math. Chemistry was hard; toying with my chemistry set years before hadn't prepared me for the chemist's equations. Fortunately, the priest who taught both chemistry and second-year algebra was also the school's athletic director. Membership on the track team covered me; I knew I wouldn't get lower than a C. U.S. history was taught pretty well, and I did okay. But civics was taken over by a football coach who had trouble reading the textbook aloud—and reading aloud was the centerpiece of his pedagogy. College Prep at Mercy was certainly an improvement over the vocational program—at least it carried some status—but the social science curriculum was weak, and the mathematics and physical sciences were simply beyond me. I had a miserable quantitative background and ended up copying some assignments and finessing the rest as best I could. Let me try to explain how it feels to see again and again material you should once have learned but didn't.

You are given a problem. It requires you to simplify algebraic fractions or to multiply expressions containing square roots. You know this is pretty basic material because you've seen it for years. Once a teacher took some time with you, and you learned how to carry out these operations. Simple versions, anyway. But that was a year or two or more in the past, and these are more complex versions, and now you're not sure. And this, you keep telling yourself, is ninth- or even eighth-grade stuff.

Next it's a word problem. This is also old hat. The basic elements are as familiar as story characters: trains speeding so many miles per hour or shadows of buildings angling so many degrees. Maybe you know enough, have sat through enough explanations, to be able to begin setting up the problem: "If one train is going this fast . . ." or "This shadow is really one line of a triangle . . ." Then: "Let's see . . ." "How did Jones do this?" "Hmmmm." "No." "No, that won't work." Your attention wavers. You wonder about other things: a football game, a dance, that cute new checker at the market. You try to focus on the problem again. You scribble on paper for a while, but the tension wins out and your attention flits elsewhere. You crumple the paper and begin daydreaming to ease the frustration.

The particulars will vary, but in essence this is what a number of students go through, especially those in so-called remedial classes. They open their textbooks and see once again the familiar and impenetrable formulas and diagrams and terms that have stumped them for years. There is no excitement here. *No* excitement. Regardless of what the teacher says, this is not a new challenge. There is, rather, embarrassment and frustration and, not surprisingly, some anger in being reminded once again of long-standing inadequacies. No wonder so many students finally attribute their difficulties to something inborn, organic: "That part of my brain just doesn't work." Given the troubling histories many of these students have, it's miraculous that any of them can lift the shroud of hopelessness sufficiently to make deliverance from these classes possible.

Through this entire period, my father's health was deteriorating with 25 cruel momentum. His arteriosclerosis progressed to the point where a simple nick on his shin wouldn't heal. Eventually it ulcerated and widened. Lou Minton would come by daily to change the dressing. We tried renting an oscillating bed—which we placed in the front room—to force blood through the constricted arteries in my father's legs. The bed hummed through the night, moving in place to ward off the inevitable. The ulcer continued to spread, and the doctors finally had to amputate. My grandfather had lost his leg in a stockyard accident. Now my father too was crippled. His convalescence was slow but steady, and the doctors placed him in the Santa Monica Rehabilitation Center, a sun-bleached building that opened out onto the warm spray of the Pacific. The place gave him some strength and some color and some training in walking with an artificial leg. He did pretty well for a year or so until he slipped and broke his hip. He was confined to a wheelchair after that, and the confinement contributed to the diminishing of his body and spirit.

I am holding a picture of him. He is sitting in his wheelchair and smiling at the camera. The smile appears forced, unsteady, seems to quaver, though it is frozen in silver nitrate. He is in his mid-sixties and looks eighty. Late in my junior year, he had a stroke and never came out of the resulting coma. After that, I would see him only in dreams, and to this day that is how I join him. Sometimes the dreams are sad and grisly and primal: my father lying in a bed soaked with his suppuration, holding me, rocking me. But sometimes the dreams bring him back to me healthy: him talking to me on an empty street, or buying some pictures to decorate our old house, or transformed somehow into someone strong and adept with tools and the physical.

Jack MacFarland couldn't have come into my life at a better time. My father was dead, and I had logged up too many years of scholastic indifference. Mr. MacFarland had a master's degree from Columbia and decided, at twenty-six, to find a little school and teach his heart out. He never took any credentialing courses, couldn't bear to, he said, so he had to find employment in a private system. He ended up at Our Lady of Mercy teaching five sections of senior English. He was a beatnik who was born too late. His teeth were stained, he tucked his sorry tie in between the third and fourth buttons of his shirt, and his pants were chronically wrinkled. At first, we couldn't believe this guy, thought he slept in his car. But within no time, he had us so startled with work that we didn't much worry about where he slept or if he slept at all. We wrote three or four essays a month. We read a book every two to three weeks, starting with the *Iliad* and ending up with Hemingway. He gave us a quiz on the reading every other day. He brought a prep school curriculum to Mercy High.

MacFarland's lectures were crafted, and as he delivered them he would pace the room jiggling a piece of chalk in his cupped hand, using it to scribble on the board the names of all the writers and philosophers and plays and novels he was weaving into his discussion. He asked questions often, raised everything from Zeno's paradox to the repeated last line of Frost's "Stopping by Woods on a Snowy Evening." He slowly and carefully built up our knowledge of Western intellectual history—with facts, with connections, with speculations. We learned about Greek philosophy, about Dante, the Elizabethan world view, the Age of Reason, existentialism. He analyzed poems with us, had us reading sections from John Ciardi's *How Does a Poem Mean?,* making a potentially difficult book accessible with his own explanations. We gave oral reports on poems Ciardi didn't cover. We imitated the styles of Conrad, Hemingway, and *Time* magazine. We wrote and talked, wrote and talked. The man immersed us in language.

Even MacFarland's barbs were literary. If Jim Fitzsimmons, hung over and irritable, tried to smartass him, he'd rejoin with a flourish that would spark the indomitable Skip Madison—who'd lost his front teeth in a hapless tackle—to flick his tongue through the gap and opine, "good chop," drawing out the single "0" in stinging indictment. Jack MacFarland, this tobacco-stained intellectual, brandished linguistic weapons of a kind I hadn't encountered before. Here was this *egghead,* for God's sake, keeping some pretty difficult people in line. And from what I heard, Mike Dweetz and Steve Fusco and all the notorious Voc. Ed. crowd settled down as well when MacFarland took the podium. Though a lot of guys groused in the schoolyard, it just seemed that giving trouble to this particular teacher was a silly thing to do. Tomfoolery, not to mention assault, had no place in the world he was trying to create for us, and instinctively everyone knew that. If nothing else, we all recognized MacFarland's considerable intelligence and respected the hours he put into his work. It came to this: the trouble-maker would look foolish rather than daring. Even Jim Fitzsimmons was reading *On the Road* and turning his incipient alcoholism to literary ends.

There were some lives that were already beyond Jack MacFarland's min- 30 istrations, but mine was not. I started reading again as I hadn't since elementary school. I would go into our gloomy little bedroom or sit at the dinner table while, on the television, Danny McShane was paralyzing Mr. Mota with the atomic drop, and work slowly back through *Heart of Darkness,* trying to catch the words in Conrad's sentences. I certainly was not MacFarland's best student; most of the other guys in College Prep, even my fellow slackers, had better backgrounds than I did. But I worked very hard, for MacFarland had hooked me. He tapped my old interest in reading and creating stories. He gave me a way to feel special by using my mind. And he provided a role model that wasn't shaped on physical prowess alone, and something inside me that I wasn't quite aware of responded to that. Jack MacFarland established a literacy club, to borrow a phrase of Frank Smith's, and invited—invited all of us—to join.

There's been a good deal of research and speculation suggesting that the acknowledgment of school performance with extrinsic rewards—smiling faces, stars, numbers, grades—diminishes the intrinsic satisfaction children experience by engaging in reading or writing or problem solving. While it's certainly true that we've created an educational system that encourages our best and brightest to become cynical grade collectors and, in general, have developed an obsession with evaluation and assessment, I must tell you that venal though it may have been, I loved getting good grades from MacFarland. I now know how subjective grades can be, but then they came tucked in the back of essays like bits of scientific data, some sort of spectroscopic readout that said, objectively and publicly, that I had made something of value. I suppose I'd been mediocre for too long and enjoyed a public redefinition. And I suppose the workings of my mind, such as they were, had been private for too long. My linguistic play moved into the world; . . . these papers with their circled, red B-pluses and A-minuses linked my mind to something outside it. I carried them around like a club emblem.

One day in the December of my senior year, Mr. MacFarland asked me where I was going to go to college. I hadn't thought much about it. Many of the students I teach today spent their last year in high school with a physics text in one hand and the Stanford catalog in the other, but I wasn't even aware of what "entrance requirements" were. My folks would say that they wanted me to go to college and be a doctor, but I don't know how seriously I ever took that; it seemed a sweet thing to say, a bit of supportive family chatter, like telling a gangly daughter she's graceful. The reality of higher education wasn't in my scheme of things: no one in the family had gone to college; only two of my uncles had completed high school. I figured I'd get a night job and go to the local junior college because I knew that Snyder and Company were going there to play ball. But I hadn't even prepared for that. When I finally said, "I don't know," MacFarland looked down at me—I was seated in his office—and said, "Listen, you can write."

My grades stank. I had A's in biology and a handful of B's in a few English and social science classes. All the rest were C's—or worse. MacFarland said I would do well in his class and laid down the law about doing well in the others. Still, the record for my first three years wouldn't have been acceptable to any four-year school. To nobody's surprise, I was turned down flat by USC and UCLA. But Jack MacFarland was on the case. He had received his bachelor's degree from Loyola University, so he made calls to old professors and talked to somebody in admissions and wrote me a strong letter. Loyola finally accepted me as a probationary student. I would be on trial for the first year, and if I did okay, I would be granted regular status. MacFarland also intervened to get me a loan, for I could never have afforded a private college without it. Four more years of religion classes and four more years of boys at one school, girls at another. But at least I was going to college. Amazing.

In my last semester of high school, I elected a special English course fashioned by Mr. MacFarland, and it was through this elective that there arose at Mercy a fledgling literati. Art Mitz, the editor of the school newspaper and a very smart guy, was the kingpin. He was joined by me and by Mark Dever, a quiet boy who wrote beautifully and who would die before he was forty. MacFarland occasionally invited us to his apartment, and those visits became the high point of our apprenticeship: we'd clamp on our training wheels and drive to his salon.

He lived in a cramped and cluttered place near the airport, tucked away   35
in the kind of building that architectural critic Reyner Banham calls a
dingbat. Books were all over: stacked, piled, tossed, and crated, underlined
and dog eared, well worn and new. Cigarette ashes crusted with coffee in
saucers or spilling over the sides of motel ashtrays. The little bedroom had,
along two of its walls, bricks and boards loaded with notes, magazines, and
oversized books. The kitchen joined the living room, and there was a stack
of German newspapers under the sink. I had never seen anything like it: a
great flophouse of language furnished by City Lights and Cafe Ie Metro.
I read every title. I flipped through paperbacks and scanned jackets and
memorized names: Gogol, *Finnegans Wake,* Djuna Barnes, Jackson
Pollock, *A Coney Island of the Mind,* F. O. Matthiessen's *American Renaissance,* all sorts of Freud, *Troubled Sleep,* Man Ray, *The Education of Henry
Adams,* Richard Wright, *Film as Art,* William Butler Yeats, Marguerite
Duras, *Red-burn, A Season in Hell, Kapital.* On the cover of Alain-
Fournier's *The Wanderer* was an Edward Gorey drawing of a young man on
a road winding into dark trees. By the hotplate sat a strange Kafka novel
called *Amerika,* in which an adolescent hero crosses the Atlantic to find the
Nature Theater of Oklahoma. Art and Mark would be talking about a
movie or the school newspaper, and I would be consuming my English
teacher's library. It was heady stuff. I felt like a Pop Warner athlete on
steroids.

Art, Mark, and I would buy stogies and triangulate from MacFarland's
apartment to the Cinema, which now shows X-rated films but was then
L.A.'s premier art theater, and then to the musty Cherokee Bookstore in
Hollywood to hobnob with beatnik homosexuals—smoking, drinking
bourbon and coffee, and trying out awkward phrases we'd gleaned from
our mentor's bookshelves. I was happy and precocious and a little scared as
well, for Hollywood Boulevard was thick with a kind of decadence that was
foreign to the South Side. After the Cherokee, we would head back to the
security of MacFarland's apartment, slaphappy with hipness.

Let me be the first to admit that there was a good deal of adolescent passion in this embrace of the avant-garde: self-absorption, sexually charged
pedantry, an elevation of the odd and abandoned. Still it was a time during
which I absorbed an awful lot of information: long lists of titles, images
from expressionist paintings, new wave shibboleths, snippets of philosophy,
and names that read like Steve Fusco's misspellings—Goethe, Nietzsche,
Kierkegaard. Now this is hardly the stuff of deep understanding. But it was

an introduction, a phrase book, a [travel guide] to a vocabulary of ideas, and it *felt* good at the time to know all these words. With hindsight I realize how layered and important that knowledge was.

It enabled me to do things in the world. I could browse bohemian bookstores in far-off, mysterious Hollywood; I could go to the Cinema and see events through the lenses of European directors; and, most of all, I could share an evening, talk that talk, with Jack MacFarland, the man I most admired at the time.

Knowledge was becoming a bonding agent. Within a year or two, the persona of the disaffected hipster would prove too cynical, too alienated to last. But *for* a time it was new and exciting: it provided a critical perspective on society, and it allowed me to act as though I were living beyond the limiting boundaries of South Vermont.

Analyze

1. What was Rose's bus ride like on the way to Our Lady of Mercy Catholic School?
2. What type of jobs does he mention as dead ends and why was he targeted for them?
3. What high school class caused a turning point in Rose's life and why?

Explore

1. Rose makes the comment that "Students will float to the mark you set." What does he mean by this? Apply the idea in a positive and negative way to someone you know, a character on a TV show, or to your own life.
2. Have you or someone you know ever seemed to, as Rose says, "Reject the confusion and frustration by openly defining yourself as the Common Joe"? What does this mean in terms of how we see ourselves and how others see us? Start with a list of definitions for Common Joe and how the term has been used. From the definitions and examples, create a PowerPoint (or something similar) showing the examples. Be sure to make a main point about how a label like Common Joe can serve to limit what we think we are capable of doing and being (or how we think of others).

3. Have you ever had a Mr. McFarland, someone who went that extra yard with you, who saw something in you that others did not? Or, to the contrary, have you ever had a teacher or authority figure who insisted on bringing down your sense of your abilities and your drive? Write an essay like Rose's that shows your experiences, positive or negative, while also making a point about the educational system.

Patrick T. Terenzini and Ernest T. Pascarella
"Living with Myths:
Undergraduate Education in America"

Terenzini is associate director of the National Center on Postsecondary Teaching, Learning, and Assessment at the Pennsylvania State University. Pascarella is the University of Illinois Foundation James T. Towey Scholar and professor of policy studies at the College of Education at the University of Illinois-Chicago. In their essay they deconstruct many of the common myths about what distinguishes a good school education from a bad one.

Why do you think the authors call their subject myths and societal brainwashing?

In early civilizations, myths played important roles in people's lives, bringing order to what would otherwise have been a chaotic and uninterpretable world. The Greeks had to have some plausible explanation for the passage of the sun across the heavens. But when myths continue to guide thought and action, despite evidence that they are without empirical foundation, they become dysfunctional and counterproductive. Persistence in the belief that the sun is actually Apollo's chariot passing across the heavens forecloses geocentric and heliocentric explanations of the movements of the sun and other heavenly bodies.

Does higher education have its own dysfunctional myths? From 1985 to 1990, we reviewed some 2,600 books, book chapters, monographs, journal articles, technical reports, conference papers, and research reports produced over the past two decades describing the effects of college on students (Pascarella and Terenzini, 1991). Based on that literature, we can identify at least five myths about undergraduate education in America. Faculty members and administrators alike embrace these myths, which structure how we think about and design undergraduate educational programs. The evidence also suggests these myths may impede the improvement of teaching and learning in our colleges and universities.

Myth Number 1: Institutional prestige and reputation reflect educational quality.

Most people believe that, for any given student, going to an institution with all (or most) of the conventionally accepted earmarks of "quality" will lead to greater learning and development. The fact of the matter is that it probably won't.

5   The evidence on this point is strikingly clear and cuts across a wide array of educational outcomes, including gains in verbal, quantitative, and subject-matter competence; growth in cognitive complexity and the development of intellectual skills; educationally desirable changes in a wide range of psychosocial traits, attitudes, and values; and the emergence of principled moral reasoning. Across all these outcomes, the net impact of attending (versus not attending) college tends to be substantially more pronounced than the impact attributable to attending one kind of institution rather than another.

After taking into account the characteristics, abilities, and backgrounds students bring with them to college, we found that how much students grow or change has only inconsistent and, perhaps in a practical sense, trivial relationships with such traditional measures of institutional "quality" as educational expenditures per student, student/faculty ratios, faculty salaries, percentage of faculty with the highest degree in their field, faculty research productivity, size of the library, admissions selectivity, or prestige rankings. Even when taking into account several methodological considerations that might partially explain this finding, the evidence is still persuasive: similarities across kinds of colleges substantially outnumber and outweigh their differences in terms of their effects on student learning and other educational outcomes.

It is important to be clear about two things we are not saying. First, we are not suggesting that graduates of all colleges have reached the same level of academic achievement or psychosocial development. The evidence suggests nothing of the kind. Indeed, after four years, the graduates of some colleges reach a level of achievement or development approximately equal to that of freshmen entering some other institutions. The point to remember is that differences across institutions in levels of student performance on outcomes measures (e.g., Graduate Record Examination scores) are attributable not so much to the institutions attended as to the kinds of students who enroll at those institutions in the first place. Most schools that graduate high-performing students also admit high-performing students.

Second, we are not saying that any given institution has no greater educational impact that any other. Indeed, certain individual institutions probably combine many or most of the things that are related to student learning and development (see below) into particularly potent educational programs and environments. Our point is that it is hardly possible to identify the most educationally effective institutions by relying simply on the resource dimensions traditionally used to judge or rank institutions for "educational quality." These widely used indicators of college quality are, more appropriately, measures of institutional advantage. They may look good and have intuitive appeal, but they reveal little of substance in terms of educational impact.

The evidence we reviewed strongly suggests that real quality in undergraduate education resides more in an institution's educational climate and in what it does programmatically than in its stock of human, financial, and educational resources. That is not to say that resources are irrelevant, but that to understand educational quality one must look beyond the obvious and easy measures of institutional wealth, resource availability, and advantage. One must look at factors such as

1. the nature and cohesiveness of students' curricular experiences;   10
2. their course-taking patterns;
3. the quality of teaching they receive and the extent to which faculty members involve students actively in the teaching-learning process;
4. the frequency, purpose, and quality of students' non-classroom interactions with faculty members;
5. the nature of their peer group interactions and extracurricular activities; and
6. the extent to which institutional structures promote cohesive environments that value the life of the mind and high degrees of student academic and social involvement.

What happens to a student after arrival on campus makes a markedly greater difference in what and how much students learn than the prestige, reputations, or resources of the institution. The questionable relevance of the characteristics we conventionally use to differentiate among institutions leads us to ask more about what our colleges do that does make a difference. That brings us to a second myth.

Myth Number 2: Traditional methods of instruction provide proven, effective ways of teaching undergraduate students.

Lecturing is the overwhelming method of choice for teaching undergraduates in most institutions. One study (Pollio, 1984), for example, found that teachers in the typical classroom spent about 80 percent of their time lecturing to students who were attentive to what was being said about 50 percent of the time. The evidence we reviewed is clear that the lecture/discussion mode of instruction is not effective (indeed, we estimate average freshman-senior gains of 20–35 percentile points across a range of content and academic/cognitive skill areas). But the evidence is equally clear that these conventional methods are not as effective as some other, far less frequently used methods.

Long trails of research suggest that certain individualized instructional approaches are consistently more effective in enhancing subject-matter learning than are the more traditional approaches. These more effective approaches emphasize small, modularized units of content, student mastery of one unit before moving to the next, immediate and frequent feedback to students on their progress, and active student involvement in the learning process.

15   Of the five individualized instructional approaches we reviewed, four of them (audio-tutorial, computer-based, programmed, and visual-based instruction) showed statistically significant learning advantages of 6–10 percentile points over traditional approaches. The fifth method, the Personalized System of Instruction (PSI, or "Keller Plan") approach, produced an average learning advantage of 19 percentile points, approximately twice as large as any of the other forms of individualized instruction. (PSI involves small, modularized units of instruction, study guides, mastery orientation and immediate feedback on unit tests, self-pacing through the material, student proctors to help with individual problems, and occasional lectures for motivation.)

The differences in effectiveness between individualized and conventional methods of instruction probably have multiple sources, but two are prominent. First, the lecture/discussion format rests on several assumptions:

1. that all students are equally prepared for the course;
2. that all students learn at the same rate;
3. that all students learn in the same way and through the same set of activities; and
4. that differences in performance are more likely due to differences in student effort or ability than to the faultiness of any of the foregoing assumptions.

If these assumptions are valid, why not deliver course material at the same pace and in the same fashion to all students?

Despite the fact that the research evidence, personal experience, and common sense all suggest these assumptions are untenable, most faculty members persist in teaching (and academic administrators encourage it) as if they were true. Individualized and collaborative approaches to instruction are more effective because they respond better to differences in students' levels of preparation, learning styles, and rates.

Second, in contrast to the passive roles students are encouraged to play 20 in most lecture/discussion classes, individualized and collaborative teaching approaches require active student involvement and participation in the teaching-learning process. Such methods encourage students to take greater responsibility for their own learning; they learn from one another, as well as from the instructor. The research literature indicates active learning produces greater gains in academic content and skills; it clearly supports efforts to employ various forms of "collaborative learning."

Myth Number 3: The good teachers are good researchers.

One of the most frequent criticisms of undergraduate education today is that faculty members spend too much time on research at the expense of their teaching. The typical defense against this charge is that faculty members must do research in order to be good teachers. Faculty members who are researchers, so the argument goes, are more likely to be "on the cutting edge" in their disciplines; they pass their enthusiasm for learning on to their students. This faith in the instructional benefits of research is, of course, reflected in our faculty reward structures.

Proponents of the good-researchers-make-good-teachers point of view usually argue by anecdote; they cite faculty members who are noted scholars and who bring their research to the classroom, there (presumably) intellectually energizing their students. We do not doubt the existence of such faculty members. Indeed, most of us can think of individuals who are both outstanding scholars and extraordinary teachers. But such people are probably outstanding in most every academic thing they do, and the reason they come to mind is precisely because they are extraordinary. And one wonders: is exposure to these exceptional individuals a part of the experience of most undergraduates in today's universities?

The available empirical evidence calls the 'good-researcher = good-teacher' argument sharply into question. Our review indicates that, at best, the association between ratings of undergraduate instruction and scholarly productivity is a small, positive one, with correlations in the .10 to .16 range.

25   In the most comprehensive literature review on this issue, Feldman (1987) reviewed more than 40 studies of the relation between faculty productivity or scholarly accomplishment and instructional effectiveness (as perceived by students). He found the average correlation between scholarly productivity or accomplishment and instructional effectiveness to be +.12. Put another way, scholarly productivity and instructional effectiveness have less than 2 percent of their variance in common. That means that about 98 percent of the variability in measures of instructional effectiveness is due to something other than research productivity or accomplishment. Feldman concluded that "in general, the likelihood that research productivity actually benefits teaching is extremely small or [alternatively] that the two, for all practical purposes, are essentially unrelated." It is worth noting, however, as Feldman points out, that if the evidence does not support the good-researcher = good-teacher argument, neither does it support claims that doing research detracts from being an effective teacher.

So long as the myth that research and teaching are closely and positively related persists, promotion and tenure decisions will continue to be made on the presumption that an institution can have the best of both worlds by allowing research productivity to dominate the faculty reward structure. Why bother to scrutinize both the teaching and research abilities of candidates for appointment, promotion, and tenure if looking mostly at the one will do? Find and reward good researchers, the logic goes, and chances are high you'll find and reward a good teacher.

Where the belief persists that research and teaching effectiveness are opposed to one another, proposed "reforms" of teaching will focus on quantitative solutions, on how much faculty members are required to teach rather than on how well they do it. Many statehouses and coordinating agencies are busy passing faculty workload policies that will require all full-time faculty members to teach a minimum number of credit hours. Such policies are likely to be counterproductive. There's no reason to believe that teaching more courses will result in better instruction. Moreover, since time is a finite commodity, such policies are likely to reduce the amount of research being done, in many cases by the country's best researchers.

In neither case is the teaching of undergraduates likely to improve. Teaching and research appear to be more or less independent activities. Each is essential to the mission of most of our colleges and universities, and each deserves recognition and reward. Until the good-researcher = good-teacher myth is put to rest, however, the research on effective teaching methods will continue to be ignored, reward structures will continue to go unexamined, good researchers will be excused for marginally competent teaching, and good teachers who do not publish will continue to be denied tenure. As for undergraduate instruction, it will be business as usual.

Somehow, as college and university faculty and academic administrators, we must get beyond the smoke of this long-standing myth and turn our energies to what really makes a difference in helping students learn. That leads to a fourth myth.

Myth Number 4: Faculty members influence student learning only in   30 the classroom.

Many faculty members and more than a few administrators appear to believe that faculty obligations to contribute to the education of undergraduate students begin and end at the classroom or laboratory door. If these obligations extend beyond the classroom at all, it is only to the faculty member's office, to class-related questions or academic advising. Faculty workload policies and reward systems implicitly support this narrow conception of the faculty member's sphere of influence. The research literature does not.

What a host of studies demonstrate is that faculty exert much influence in their out-of-class (as well as in-class) contacts with students. "Instruction," therefore, must be understood more broadly to include the important teaching that faculty members do both inside and outside their classrooms.

As a backdrop, remember that as much as 85 percent of a student's waking hours are spent outside a classroom. Common sense should tell us that educational programs and activities that address only 15 percent of students' time are needlessly myopic. What the research tells us is that a large part of the impact of college is determined by the extent and content of students' interactions with the major agents of socialization on campus: faculty members and student peers. Further, faculty members' educational influence appears to be significantly enhanced when their contacts with students extend beyond the formal classroom to informal non-classroom settings.

More particularly, controlling for student background characteristics, the extent of students' informal contact with faculty is positively linked with a wide array of outcomes. These include perceptions of intellectual growth during college, increases in intellectual orientation and curiosity, liberalization of social and political values, growth in autonomy and independence, increases in interpersonal skills, gains in general maturity and personal development, orientation toward a scholarly career, educational aspirations, persistence, educational attainment, and women's interest in, and choice of, a sex-atypical (male-dominated) career field. It also appears that the impact of student-faculty informal contact is determined by its content as well as by its frequency; the most influential forms of interaction appear to be those that focus on ideas or intellectual matters, thereby extending and reinforcing academic goals.

35   Some faculty members consider informal, out-of-class contact with students to be "coddling" or (worse) irrelevant or inappropriate to the role of a faculty member. Such views reflect, at best, little knowledge of effective educational practices and of how students learn, and, at worst, a callous disregard. "Talk with students as persons outside of class? That's the dean of students' job": behind this attitude lies still another myth.

Myth Number 5: Students' academic and non-academic experiences are separate and unrelated areas of influence on learning.

Most theoretical models of student learning and development in no way suggest, much less guarantee, that any single experience—or class of experiences—will be a crucial determinant of change for students. Our review of the evidence indicates that the impact of particular within-college experiences (e.g., academic major, interactions with faculty, living on- or off-campus, interactions with peers) tends to be smaller than the overall net effect of attending (versus not attending) college. That same evidence suggests that a majority of the important changes that occur during college are probably the cumulative result of a set of interrelated and mutually supporting experiences, in class and out, sustained over an extended period of time.

To break this out further, the evidence shows that, compared to freshmen, seniors have a greater capacity for abstract or symbolic reasoning, solving puzzles within a scientific paradigm, intellectual flexibility, organizing and manipulating cognitive complexity, and using reason and evidence to address issues for which there are no verifiably correct answers (e.g., dealing with toxic waste, capital punishment, abortion, or even buying a used car). Students, however, not only become more cognitively advanced (i.e., become better learners), they also demonstrate concurrent changes in values, attitudes, and psychosocial development that are consistent with and probably reciprocally related to cognitive change. While there is insufficient evidence to conclude that changes in some areas actually cause changes in other areas, it is nonetheless abundantly clear that documented change in nearly every outcome area appears to be embedded within an interconnected and perhaps mutually reinforcing network of cognitive, value, attitudinal, and psychosocial changes—all of which develop during the student's college experience. In short, the student changes as a whole, integrated person during college. (All these changes may be independent of one another, but we doubt it.)

Moreover, while intellectual growth may be primarily a function of the student's academic involvement and effort, the content and focus of that same student's interpersonal and extracurricular involvements can have a mediating influence on that growth, either promoting or inhibiting it. In some areas of intellectual development (such as critical thinking), for example, the evidence suggests it is the breadth of student involvement in the intellectual and social experiences of college, and not any particular type of involvement, that counts most. Thus, although the weight of evidence indicates that the links between involvement and change tend to be specific, the greatest impact may stem from the student's total level of campus engagement, particularly when academic, interpersonal, and extracurricular involvements are mutually supporting and relevant to a particular educational outcome.

The Campus's Role

What we've just said stresses the importance of individual student 40 effort and involvement as a determinant of college impact, but it in no way means that particular campus policies or programs are unimportant. Quite the contrary. If individual effort or involvement is the linchpin for college impact, then a key matter becomes how a campus can shape its intellectual and interpersonal environments in ways that do indeed encourage student involvement.

The research on within-college effects suggests programmatic and policy levers. For example, we have long known that students living on-campus enjoy larger and more varied benefits of college attendance than do commuting students. A college might usefully ask, how can the most educationally potent characteristics of the residential experience (e.g., frequent academic and social interaction among students, contact with faculty members, more opportunities for academic and social involvement with the institution) be made more readily available to students who commute?

Research on the impacts of student residence offers more clues. Considerable evidence suggests discernible differences in the social and intellectual climates of different residence halls on the same campus; halls with the strongest impacts on cognitive development and persistence are typically the result of purposeful, programmatic efforts to integrate students' intellectual and social lives during college—living-learning centers are not only a neat idea, they actually work! On relatively few campuses, however, are such programs available to students today.

Plenty of other ways exist for integrating students' classroom and nonclassroom experiences in ways that reasonably reflect how students learn. While a discussion of those ways is beyond the scope of this article, it is useful here to return to our first finding, that the impact of college is more general than specific, more cumulative than catalytic. Real college impact is likely to come not from pulling any grand, specific (and probably expensive) policy or programmatic lever, but rather from pulling a number of smaller, interrelated academic and social levers more often. If a college's effects are varied and cumulative, then its approaches to enhancing those effects must be varied and cumulative, too, and coordinated.

Academic Affairs/Student Affairs

There is an organizational analog to Myth Number 5, that students' academic and non-academic experiences are separate and independent sources of influence on student learning. Since 1870, when Harvard's Charles William Eliot appointed Ephraim Gurney "to take the burden of discipline off President Eliot's shoulders" (Brubacher and Rudy, 1968), the academic affairs and student affairs functions of most institutions have been running essentially on parallel but separate tracks: academic affairs tends to students' cognitive development while student affairs ministers to their affective growth.

This bureaucratization of collegiate structures is a creature of adminis-   45
trative convenience and budgetary expedience. It surely has not evolved
from any conception of how students learn, nor is it supported by research
evidence. Organizationally and operationally, we've lost sight of the forest.
If undergraduate education is to be enhanced, faculty members, joined by
academic and student affairs administrators, must devise ways to deliver
undergraduate education that are as comprehensive and integrated as the
ways students actually learn. A whole new mindset is needed to capitalize
on the interrelatedness of the in- and out-of-class influences on student
learning and the functional interconnectedness of academic and student
affairs divisions.

In describing her efforts to bring together the activities of inner-city
schools, social agencies, and neighborhoods to meet the basic physical, developmental, and educational needs of inner-city children, Cicely Tyson
cites a suggestive African proverb: "It takes a whole village to raise a child."

John F. Kennedy stated that "the great enemy of truth is very often not the
lie—deliberate, contrived and dishonest—but the myth, persistent, persuasive
and unrealistic" (Schlesinger, 1965). It is time we put to use what we know
with some confidence about what constitutes effective teaching and learning
and put to rest educational myths that have outlined their usefulness.

Analyze

1. What role do myths play in the way we determine the quality of
   schools?
2. Discuss each of the five myths and what they are based on.
3. Which of the myths apply to your school?

Explore

1. In small groups, brainstorm the results these myths have had on your
   education. Write a collaborative essay discussing some small changes,
   as the essay suggests, that your school can enhance to better the educational experience for students.
2. In teams, create a visual of the five myths. This can be done either
   digitally in the form of a visual display, or with hard copy images to
   make a collage.
3. Pick one of the myths and argue against it, showing how the myth has
   positive effects on your campus and on your experience as a student.

Bureau of Labor Statistics, Current Population Survey (Chart)

"Education Pays: Education Pays in Higher Earnings and Lower Unemployment"

This chart from the Bureau of Labor Statistics graphically argues our earned income rises with the amount of education and number of degrees we receive.

If you printed out this chart and posted it in different places, where are some locations that it would be most effective? Least effective? Why?

Education pays in higher earnings and lower unemployment rates.

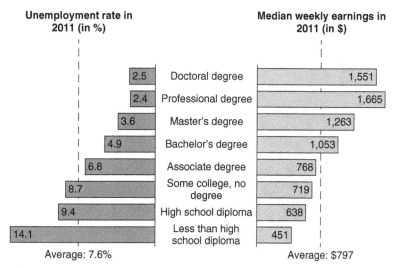

Education Pays

Unemployment rate in 2011 (in %)		Median weekly earnings in 2011 (in $)
2.5	Doctoral degree	1,551
2.4	Professional degree	1,665
3.6	Master's degree	1,263
4.9	Bachelor's degree	1,053
6.8	Associate degree	768
8.7	Some college, no degree	719
9.4	High school diploma	638
14.1	Less than high school diploma	451
Average: 7.6%		Average: $797

Figure 3.1 Note: Data are for persons age 25 and over. Earnings are for full-time wage and salary workers.

Source: Bureau of Labor Statistics, Current Population Survey.

Analyze

1. If you wanted to make the least amount of money you could, what degree would you strive for? How about the most money possible?
2. How effective would this chart be on the students in Rose's Vocational Education Class? How about his College Preparatory classes?
3. Run an informal survey in class to see what level of degree students in your class would like to earn. Discuss whether you want to earn a particular degree for the money or for personal interests.

Explore

1. This chart encourages earning college degrees. How do you think the salaries for technical workers, such as electricians and plumbers, and professional careers, such as firemen and policemen, fit in this chart? Research their salaries and place their earnings in a new chart that combines the Bureau of Labor Statistics findings with yours. Make sure you document your sources.
2. In addition to education, what do you think are factors that determine the income we make?
3. Using the Education Pays chart, create a poster or PowerPoint with images of people who you think fit each educational category. Also include images of their homes, cars, and lifestyles. Make sure to explain your reasons for placing the images in the categories.

Supreme Court of the United States "Brown v. Board of Education"

Brown v. Board of Education, 347 U.S. 483 (1954) (USSC+)
347 U.S. 483
Argued December 9, 1952
Reargued December 8, 1953
Decided May 17, 1954
APPEAL FROM THE UNITED STATES DISTRICT COURT FOR THE DISTRICT OF KANSAS

Brown v. Board of Education (1952) reflects five separate cases (Brown v. Board of Education of Topeka, Briggs v. Elliot, Davis v. Board of Education of Prince Edward County (VA), Boiling v. Sharpe, and Gebhart v. Ethel) on segregation in public schools that were heard by the U.S. Supreme Court. While the cases were different, the root issue under consideration was whether state-sponsored segregation in public schools was constitutional. When the cases came before the Supreme Court, they consolidated them as one case with the Brown v. Board of Education heading. After much debate, all of the Justices unanimously supported a decision declaring segregation unconstitutional in public schools.

Why is it important for our schools to be unsegregated?

S egregation of white and Negro children in the public schools of a State solely on the basis of race, pursuant to state laws permitting or requiring such segregation, denies to Negro children the equal protection of the laws guaranteed by the Fourteenth Amendment—even though the physical facilities and other "tangible" factors of white and Negro schools may be equal.

a. The history of the Fourteenth Amendment is inconclusive as to its intended effect on public education.

b. The question presented in these cases must be determined not on the basis of conditions existing when the Fourteenth Amendment was adopted, but in the light of the full development of public education and its present place in American life throughout the Nation.

c. Where a State has undertaken to provide an opportunity for an education in its public schools, such an opportunity is a right which must be made available to all on equal terms.

5   d. Segregation of children in public schools solely on the basis of race deprives children of the minority group of equal educational opportunities, even though the physical facilities and other "tangible" factors may be equal.

e. The "separate but equal" doctrine adopted in Plessy v. Ferguson, 163 U.S. 537, has no place in the field of public education.

f. The cases are restored to the docket for further argument on specified questions relating to the forms of the decrees.

Opinion
WARREN

M r. Chief Justice Warren delivered the opinion of the Court.

These cases come to us from the States of Kansas, South Carolina, Virginia, and Delaware. They are premised on different facts and different local conditions, but a common legal question justifies their consideration together in this consolidated opinion.

In each of the cases, minors of the Negro race, through their legal representatives, seek the aid of the courts in obtaining admission to the public schools of their community on a nonsegregated basis. In each instance, they had been denied admission to schools attended by white children under laws requiring or permitting segregation according to race. This segregation was alleged to deprive the plaintiffs of the equal protection of the laws under the Fourteenth Amendment. In each of the cases other than the Delaware case, a three-judge federal district court denied relief to the plaintiffs on the so-called "separate but equal" doctrine announced by this Court in Plessy v. Ferguson, 163 U.S. 537. Under that doctrine, equality of treatment is accorded when the races are provided substantially equal facilities, even though these facilities be separate. In the Delaware case, the Supreme Court of Delaware adhered to that doctrine, but ordered that the plaintiffs be admitted to the white schools because of their superiority to the Negro schools.

The plaintiffs contend that segregated public schools are not "equal" and 10 cannot be made "equal," and that hence they are deprived of the equal protection of the laws. Because of the obvious importance of the question presented, the Court took jurisdiction. Argument was heard in the 1952 Term, and reargument was heard this Term on certain questions propounded by the Court.

Reargument was largely devoted to the circumstances surrounding the adoption of the Fourteenth Amendment in 1868. It covered exhaustively consideration of the Amendment in Congress, ratification by the states, then-existing practices in racial segregation, and the views of proponents and opponents of the Amendment. This discussion and our own investigation convince us that, although these sources cast some light, it is not enough to resolve the problem with which we are faced. At best, they are inconclusive. The most avid proponents of the post-War Amendments undoubtedly intended them to remove all legal distinctions among "all persons born or naturalized in the United States." Their opponents, just as certainly, were antagonistic to both the letter and the spirit of the Amendments and wished them to have the most limited effect. What others in Congress and the state legislatures had in mind cannot be determined with any degree of certainty.

An additional reason for the inconclusive nature of the Amendment's history with respect to segregated schools is the status of public education at that time. In the South, the movement toward free common schools, supported by general taxation, had not yet taken hold. Education of white children was largely in the hands of private groups. Education of Negroes was almost nonexistent, and practically all of the race were illiterate. In fact, any education of Negroes was forbidden by law in some states. Today, in contrast, many Negroes have achieved outstanding success in the arts and sciences, as well as in the business and professional world. It is true that public school education at the time of the Amendment had advanced further in the North, but the effect of the Amendment on Northern States was generally ignored in the congressional debates. Even in the North, the conditions of public education did not approximate those existing today. The curriculum was usually rudimentary; ungraded schools were common in rural areas; the school term was but three months a year in many states, and compulsory school attendance was virtually unknown. As a consequence, it is not surprising that there should be so little in the history of the Fourteenth Amendment relating to its intended effect on public education.

In the first cases in this Court construing the Fourteenth Amendment, decided shortly after its adoption, the Court interpreted it as proscribing all state-imposed discriminations against the Negro race. The doctrine of "separate but equal" did not make its appearance in this Court until 1896 in the case of Plessy v. Ferguson, supra, involving not education but transportation. American courts have since labored with the doctrine for over half a century. In this Court, there have been six cases involving the "separate but equal" doctrine in the field of public education. In Cumming v. County Board of Education, 175 U.S. 528, and Gong Lum v. Rice, 275 U.S. 78, the validity of the doctrine itself was not challenged. In more recent cases, all on the graduate school level, inequality was found in that specific benefits enjoyed by white students were denied to Negro students of the same educational qualifications. Missouri ex rel. Gaines v. Canada, 305 U.S. 337; Sipuel v. Oklahoma, 332 U.S. 631; Sweatt v. Painter, 339 U.S. 629; McLaurin v. Oklahoma State Regents, 339 U.S. 637. In none of these cases was it necessary to reexamine the doctrine to grant relief to the Negro plaintiff. And in Sweatt v. Painter, supra, the Court expressly reserved decision on the question whether Plessy v. Ferguson should be held inapplicable to public education.

In the instant cases, that question is directly presented. Here, unlike Sweatt v. Painter, there are findings below that the Negro and white schools involved have been equalized, or are being equalized, with respect to buildings, curricula, qualifications and salaries of teachers, and other "tangible" factors. Our decision, therefore, cannot turn on merely a comparison of these tangible factors in the Negro and white schools involved in each of the cases. We must look instead to the effect of segregation itself on public education.

In approaching this problem, we cannot turn the clock back to 1868, 15 when the Amendment was adopted, or even to 1896, when Plessy v. Ferguson was written. We must consider public education in the light of its full development and its present place in American life throughout the Nation. Only in this way can it be determined if segregation in public schools deprives these plaintiffs of the equal protection of the laws.

Today, education is perhaps the most important function of state and local governments. Compulsory school attendance laws and the great expenditures for education both demonstrate our recognition of the importance of education to our democratic society. It is required in the performance of our most basic public responsibilities, even service in the armed forces. It is the very foundation of good citizenship. Today it is a principal instrument in awakening the child to cultural values, in preparing him for later professional training, and in helping him to adjust normally to his environment. In these days, it is doubtful that any child may reasonably be expected to succeed in life if he is denied the opportunity of an education. Such an opportunity, where the state has undertaken to provide it, is a right which must be made available to all on equal terms.

We come then to the question presented: Does segregation of children in public schools solely on the basis of race, even though the physical facilities and other "tangible" factors may be equal, deprive the children of the minority group of equal educational opportunities? We believe that it does.

In Sweatt v. Painter, supra, in finding that a segregated law school for Negroes could not provide them equal educational opportunities, this Court relied in large part on "those qualities which are incapable of objective measurement but which make for greatness in a law school." In McLaurin v. Oklahoma State Regents, supra, the Court, in requiring that a Negro admitted to a white graduate school be treated like all other students, again resorted to intangible considerations: ". . . his ability to study, to engage in discussions and exchange views with other students, and, in general, to learn his profession." Such considerations apply with added force to children in grade and high schools. To separate them from others of similar age and qualifications solely because of their race generates a feeling of inferiority as to their status in the community that may affect their hearts and minds in a way unlikely ever to be undone. The effect of this separation on their educational opportunities was well stated by a finding in the Kansas case by a court which nevertheless felt compelled to rule against the Negro plaintiffs:

Segregation of white and colored children in public schools has a detrimental effect upon the colored children. The impact is greater when it has the sanction of the law, for the policy of separating the races is usually interpreted as denoting the inferiority of the negro group. A sense of inferiority affects the motivation of a child to learn. Segregation with the sanction of law, therefore, has a tendency to [retard] the educational and mental development of negro children and to deprive them of some of the benefits they would receive in a racial[ly] integrated school system.

20   Whatever may have been the extent of psychological knowledge at the time of Plessy v. Ferguson, this finding is amply supported by modern authority. Any language in Plessy v. Ferguson contrary to this finding is rejected.

We conclude that, in the field of public education, the doctrine of "separate but equal" has no place. Separate educational facilities are inherently unequal. Therefore, we hold that the plaintiffs and others similarly situated for whom the actions have been brought are, by reason of the segregation complained of, deprived of the equal protection of the laws guaranteed by the Fourteenth Amendment. This disposition makes unnecessary any discussion whether such segregation also violates the Due Process Clause of the Fourteenth Amendment.

Because these are class actions, because of the wide applicability of this decision, and because of the great variety of local conditions, the formulation of decrees in these cases presents problems of considerable complexity. On reargument, the consideration of appropriate relief was necessarily subordinated to the primary question—the constitutionality of segregation in public education. We have now announced that such segregation is a denial of the equal protection of the laws. In order that we may have the full assistance of the parties in formulating decrees, the cases will be restored to the docket, and the parties are requested to present further argument on Questions 4 and 5 previously propounded by the Court for the reargument this Term. The Attorney General of the United States is again invited to participate. The Attorneys General of the states requiring or permitting segregation in public education will also be permitted to appear as amici curiae upon request to do so by September 15, 1954, and submission of briefs by October 1, 1954.

It is so ordered.

*Together with No. 2, Briggs et al. v. Elliott et al., on appeal from the United States District Court for the Eastern District of South Carolina, argued December 9–10, 1952, reargued December 7–8, 1953; No. 4, Davis et al. v. County School Board of Prince Edward County, Virginia, et al., on appeal from the United States District Court for the Eastern District of Virginia, argued December 10, 1952, reargued December 7–8, 1953, and No. 10, Gebhart et al. v. Belton et al., on certiorari to the Supreme Court of Delaware, argued December 11, 1952, reargued December 9, 1953.

Analyze

1. What Constitutional Amendment guarantees equal educational opportunities to all?
2. What caused this case to be heard by the Supreme Court?
3. What is the effect of segregation on public education?

Explore

1. Since this decision was made more than sixty years ago, do you feel that your education, directly or indirectly, so far reflects the spirit of this decision?
2. In groups, discuss how this case did or did not affect some of the experiences of the essay writers in this chapter?
3. Write about why you feel education in America is better or worse because of the *Brown v. Board of Education* ruling.

Malcolm X
"Learning to Read"

Malcolm X (Malcolm Little) was convicted of robbery in 1946 and served seven years in prison. While there, he educated himself and began to follow the teachings of Elijah Muhammad. During the Civil Rights movement of the 1960s in the United States, he became one of the leading spokespersons for the Black Power movement. He was assassinated in 1965. Our excerpt, in which he describes his self-education, is from his 1965 autobiography.

What are some of the factors that made Malcolm X push for blacks to separate from whites?

It was because of my letters that I happened to stumble upon starting to acquire some kind of a homemade education.

I became increasingly frustrated. At not being able to express what I wanted to convey in letters that I wrote, especially those to Mr. Elijah Muhammad. In the street, I had been the most articulate hustler out there— I had commanded attention when I said something. But now, trying to write simple English, I not only wasn't articulate, I wasn't even functional. How would I sound writing in slang, the way I would *say* it, something such as, "Look, daddy, let me pull your coat about a cat, Elijah Muhammad—"

Many who today hear me somewhere in person, or on television, or those who read something I've said, will think I went to school far beyond the eighth grade. This impression is due entirely to my prison studies.

It had really begun back in the Charlestown Prison, when Bimbi first made me feel envy of his stock of knowledge. Bimbi had always taken charge of any conversations he was in, and I had tried to emulate him. But every book I picked up had few sentences which didn't contain anywhere from one to nearly all of the words that might as well have been in Chinese. When I just skipped those words, of course, I really ended up with little idea of what the book said. So I had come to the Norfolk Prison Colony still going through only book-reading motions. Pretty soon, I would have quit even these motions, unless I had received the motivation that I did.

5   I saw that the best thing I could do was get hold of a dictionary—to study, to learn some words. I was lucky enough to reason also that I should

try to improve my penmanship. It was sad. I couldn't even write in a straight line. It was both ideas together that moved me to request a dictionary along with some tablets and pencils from the Norfolk Prison Colony School.

I spent two days just riffling uncertainly through the dictionary's pages. I'd never realized so many words existed! I didn't know *which* words I needed to learn. Finally, just to start some kind of action, I began copying.

In my slow, painstaking, ragged handwriting, I copied into my tablet everything printed on that first page, down to the punctuation marks.

I believe it took me a day. Then, aloud, I read back, to myself, everything I'd written on the tablet. Over and over, aloud, to myself, I read my own handwriting.

I woke up the next morning, thinking about those words—immensely proud to realize that not only had I written so much at one time, but I'd written words that I never knew were in the world. Moreover, with a little effort, I also could remember what many of these words meant. I reviewed the words whose meanings I didn't remember. Funny thing, from the dictionary first page right now, that "aardvark" springs to my mind. The dictionary had a picture of it, a long-tailed, long-eared, burrowing African mammal, which lives off termites caught by sticking out its tongue as an anteater does for ants.

I was so fascinated that I went on—I copied the dictionary's next page.   10 And the same experience came when I studied that. With every succeeding page, I also learned of people and places and events from history. Actually the dictionary is like a miniature encyclopedia. Finally the dictionary's A section had filled a whole tablet—and I went on into the B's. That was the way I started copying what eventually became the entire dictionary. It went a lot faster after so much practice helped me to pick up handwriting speed. Between what I wrote in my tablet, and writing letters, during the rest of my time in prison I would guess I wrote a million words.

I suppose it was inevitable that as my word-base broadened, I could for the first time pick up a book and read and now begin to understand what the book was saying. Anyone who has read a great deal can imagine the new world that opened. Let me tell you something: from then until I left that prison, in every free moment I had, if I was not reading in the library, I was reading on my bunk. You couldn't have gotten me out of books with a wedge. Between Mr. Muhammad's teachings, my correspondence, my visitors, . . . and my reading of books, months passed without my even thinking about being imprisoned. In fact, up to then, I never had been so truly free in my life.

The Norfolk Prison Colony's library was in the school building. A variety of classes was taught there by instructors who came from such places as Harvard and Boston universities. The weekly debates between inmate teams were also held in the school building. You would be astonished to know how worked up convict debaters and audiences would get over subjects like "Should Babies Be Fed Milk?"

Available on the prison library's shelves were books on just about every general subject. Much of the big private collection that Parkhurst had willed to the prison was still in crates and boxes in the back of the library—thousands of old books. Some of them looked ancient: covers faded, old-time parchment-looking binding. Parkhurst ... seemed to have been principally interested in history and religion. He had the money and the special interest to have a lot of books that you wouldn't have in a general circulation. Any college library would have been lucky to get that collection.

As you can imagine, especially in a prison where there was heavy emphasis on rehabilitation, an inmate was smiled upon if he demonstrated an unusually intense interest in books. There was a sizable number of well-read inmates, especially the popular debaters. Some were said by many to be practically walking encyclopedias. They were almost celebrities. No university would ask any student to devour literature as I did when this new world opened to me, of being able to read and *understand*.

15   I read more in my room than in the library itself. An inmate who was known to read a lot could check out more than the permitted maximum number of books. I preferred reading in the total isolation of my own room.

When I had progressed to really serious reading, every night at about ten P.M. I would be outraged with the "lights out." It always seemed to catch me right in the middle of something engrossing. Fortunately, right outside my door was a corridor light that cast a glow into my room. The glow was enough to read by, once my eyes adjusted to it. So when "lights out" came, I would sit on the floor where I could continue reading in that glow.

At one-hour intervals at night guards paced past every room. Each time I heard the approaching footsteps, I jumped into bed and feigned sleep. And as soon as the guard passed, I got back out of bed onto the floor area of that light-glow, where I would read for another fifty-eight minutes until the guard approached again. That went on until three or four every morning. Three or four hours of sleep a night was enough for me. Often in the years in the streets I had slept less than that.

The teachings of Mr. Muhammad stressed how history had been "whitened"—when white men had written history books, the black man simply had been left out. Mr. Muhammad couldn't have said anything that would have struck me much harder. I had never forgotten how when my class, me and all of those whites, had studied seventh-grade United States history back in Mason, the history of the Negro had been covered in one paragraph, and the teacher had gotten a big laugh with his joke, "Negroes' feet are so big that when they walk, they leave a hole in the ground."

This is one reason why Mr. Muhammad's teachings spread so swiftly all over the United States, among *all* Negroes, whether or not they became followers of Mr. Muhammad. The teachings ring true to every Negro. You can hardly show me a black adult in America—or a white one, for that matter—who knows from the history books anything like the truth about the black man's role. In my own case, once I heard of the "glorious history of the black man," I took special pains to hunt in the library for books that would inform me on details about black history.

I can remember accurately the very first set of books that really 20 impressed me. I have since bought that set of books and I have it at home for my children to read as they grow up. It's called *Wonders of the World*. It's full of pictures of archeological finds, statues that depict, usually, non-European people.

I found books like Will Durant's *Story of Civilization*. I read H. G. Wells' *Outline of History*. *Souls of Black Folk* by W. E. B. Du Bois gave me a glimpse into the black people's history before they came to this country. Carter G. Woodson's *Negro History* opened my eyes about black empires before the black slave was brought to the United States, and the early Negro struggles for freedom.

J. A. Rogers' three volumes of *Sex and Race* told about race-mixing before Christ's time; and Aesop being a black man who told fables; about Egypt's Pharaohs; about the great Coptic Christian Empire; about Ethiopia, the earth's oldest continuous black civilization, as China is the oldest continuous civilization.

Mr. Muhammad's teaching about how the white man had been created led me to *Findings in Genetics,* by Gregor Mendel. (The dictionary's G section was where I had learned what "genetics" meant.) I really studied this book by the Austrian monk. Reading it over and over, especially certain sections, helped me to understand that if you started with a black man, a white man could be produced; but starting with a white man, you never could produce a black man—because the white chromosome is recessive. And since no one disputes that there was but one Original Man, the conclusion is clear.

During the last year or so, in the *New York Times,* Arnold Toynbeell used the word "bleached" in describing the white man. His words were: "White (i.e., bleached) human beings of North European origin . . ." Toynbee also referred to the European geographic area as only a peninsula of Asia. He said there was no such thing as Europe. And if you look at the globe, you will see for yourself that America is only an extension of Asia. (But at the same time Toynbee is among those who have helped to bleach history. He has written that Africa was the only continent that produced no history. He won't write that again. Every day now, the truth is coming to light.)

25   I never will forget how shocked I was when I began reading about slavery's total horror. It made such an impact upon me that it later became one of my favorite subjects when I became a minister of Mr. Muhammad's. The world's most monstrous crime, the sin and the blood on the white man's hands, are almost impossible to believe. Books like the one by Frederick Olmsted opened my eyes to the horrors suffered when the slave was landed in the United States. The European woman, Fanny Kemble, who had married a Southern white slaveowner, described how human beings were degraded. Of course I read *Uncle Tom's Cabin.* In fact, I believe that's the only novel I have ever read since I started serious reading.

Parkhurst's collection also contained some bound pamphlets of the Abolitionist Anti-Slavery Society of New England. I read descriptions of atrocities, saw those illustrations of black slave women tied up and flogged with whips; of black mothers watching their babies being dragged off, never to be seen by their mothers again; of dogs after slaves, and of the fugitive slave catchers, evil white men with whips and clubs and chains and guns. I read about the slave preacher Nat Turner, who put the fear of God into the white slave master. Nat Turner wasn't going around preaching pie-in-the-sky and "non-violent" freedom for the black man. There in Virginia one night in 1831, Nat and seven other slaves started out at his master's home and through the night they went from one plantation "big house" to the next, killing, until by the next morning 57 white people were dead and Nat had about 70 slaves following him. White people, terrified for their lives, fled from their homes, locked themselves up in public buildings, hid in the woods, and some even left the state. A small army of soldiers took two months to catch and hang Nat Turner. Somewhere I have read where Nat Turner's example is said to have inspired John Brown to invade Virginia and attack Harpers Ferry nearly thirty years later, with thirteen white men and five Negroes.

I read Herodotus, "the father of History," or, rather, I read about him. And I read the histories of various nations, which opened my eyes gradually, then wider and wider, to how the whole world's white men had indeed acted like devils, pillaging and raping and bleeding and draining the whole world's non-white people. I remember, for instance, books such as Will Durant's *The Story of Oriental Civilization,* and Mahatma Gandhi's accounts of the struggle to drive the British out of India.

Book after book showed me how the white man had brought upon the world's black, brown, red, and yellow peoples every variety of the suffering of exploitation. I saw how since the sixteenth century, the so-called "Christian trader" white man began to ply the seas in his lust for Asian and African empires, and plunder, and power. I read, I saw, how the white man never has gone among the non-white peoples bearing the Cross in the true manner and spirit of Christ's teachings—meek, humble, and Christlike.

I perceived, as I read, how the collective white man had been actually nothing but a piratical opportunist who used Faustian machinations to make his own Christianity his initial wedge in criminal conquests. First, always "religiously," he branded "heathen" and "pagan" labels upon ancient non-white cultures and civilizations. The stage thus set, he then turned upon his non-white victims his weapons of war.

I read how, entering India—half a *billion* deeply religious brown   30 people—the British white man, by 1759, through promises, trickery, and manipulations, controlled much of India through Great Britain's East India Company. The parasitical British administration kept tentacling out to half of the sub-continent. In 1857, some of the desperate people of India finally mutinied—and, excepting the African slave trade, nowhere has history recorded any more unnecessary bestial and ruthless human carnage than the British suppression of the non-white Indian people.

Over 115 million African blacks—close to the 1930's population of the United States—were murdered or enslaved during the slave trade. And I read how when the slave market was glutted, the cannibalistic white powers of Europe next carved up, as their colonies, the richest areas of the black continent. And Europe's chancelleries for the next century played a chess game of naked exploitation and power from Cape Horn to Cairo.

Ten guards and the warden couldn't have torn me out of those books. Not even Elijah Muhammad could have been more eloquent than those books were in providing indisputable proof that the collective white man had acted like a devil in virtually every contact he had with the world's collective non-white man. I listen today to the radio, and watch television, and read the headlines about the collective white man's fear and tension concerning China. When the white man professes ignorance about why the Chinese hate him so, my mind can't help flashing back to what I read, there in prison, about how the blood forebears of this same white man raped China at a time when China was trusting and helpless. Those original white "Christian traders" sent into China millions of pounds of opium. By 1839, so many of the Chinese were addicts that China's desperate government destroyed twenty thousand chests of opium. The first Opium war was promptly declared by the white man. Imagine! Declaring *war* upon someone who objects to being narcotized! The Chinese were severely beaten, with Chinese-invented gunpowder.

The Treaty of Nanking made China pay the British white man for the destroyed opium; forced open China's major ports to British trade; forced China to abandon Hong Kong; fixed China's import tariffs so low that cheap British articles soon flooded in, maiming China's industrial development.

After a second Opium War, the Tientsin Treaties legalized the ravaging opium trade, legalized a British-French-American control of China's customs. China tried delaying that Treaty's ratification; Peking was looted and burned.

35   "Kill the foreign white devils!" was the 1901 Chinese war cry in the Boxer Rebellion. Losing again, this time the Chinese were driven from Peking's choicest areas. The vicious, arrogant white man put up the famous signs, "Chinese and dogs not allowed."

Red China after World War II closed its doors to the Western white world. Massive Chinese agricultural, scientific, and industrial efforts are described in a book that *Life* magazine recently published. Some observers inside Red China have reported that the world never has known such a hate-white campaign as is now going on in this non-white country where, present birth-rates continuing, in fifty more years Chinese will be half the earth's population. And it seems that some Chinese chickens will soon come home to roost, with China's recent successful nuclear tests.

Let us face reality. We can see in the United Nations a new world order being shaped, along color lines—an alliance among the non-white nations. America's U.N. Ambassador Adlai Stevenson complained not long ago that in the United Nations "a skin game" was being played. He was right. He was facing reality. A "skin game" is being played. But Ambassador Stevenson sounded like Jesse James accusing the marshal of carrying a gun. Because who in the world's history ever has played a worse "skin game" than the white man?

Mr. Muhammad, to whom I was writing daily, had no idea of what a new world had opened up to me through my efforts to document his teachings in books.

When I discovered philosophy, I tried to touch all the landmarks of philosophical development. Gradually, I read most of the old philosophers, Occidental and Oriental. The Oriental philosophers were the ones I came to prefer; finally, my impression was that most Occidental philosophy had largely been borrowed from the Oriental thinkers. Socrates, for instance, traveled in Egypt. Some sources even say that Socrates was initiated into some of the Egyptian mysteries. Obviously Socrates got some of his wisdom among the East's wise men.

I have often reflected upon the new vistas that reading opened to me.   40 I knew right there in prison that reading had changed forever the course of my life. As I see it today, the ability to read awoke inside me some long dormant craving to be mentally alive. I certainly wasn't seeking any degree, the way a college confers a status symbol upon its students. My homemade education gave me, with every additional book that I read, a little bit more sensitivity to the deafness, dumbness, and blindness that was afflicting the black race in America. Not long ago, an English writer telephoned me from London, asking questions. One was, "What's your alma mater?" I told him, "Books." You will never catch me with a free fifteen minutes in which I'm not studying something I feel might be able to help the black man.

Yesterday I spoke in London, and both ways on the plane across the Atlantic I was studying a document about how the United Nations proposes to insure the human rights of the oppressed minorities of the world. The American black man is the world's most shameful case of minority oppression. What makes the black man think of himself as only an internal United States issue is just a catch-phrase, two words, "civil rights." How is the black man going to get "civil rights" before first he wins his *human* rights? If the American black man will start thinking about his *human* rights, and then start thinking of himself as part of one of the world's great peoples, he will see he has a case for the United Nations.

I can't think of a better case! Four hundred years of black blood and sweat invested here in America, and the white man still has the black man begging for what every immigrant fresh off the ship can take for granted the minute he walks down the gangplank.

But I'm digressing. I told the Englishman that my alma mater was books, a good library. Every time I catch a plane, I have with me a book that I want to read—and that's a lot of books these days. If I weren't out here every day battling the white man, I could spend the rest of my life reading, just satisfying my curiosity—because you can hardly mention anything I'm not curious about. I don't think anybody ever got more out of going to prison than I did. In fact, prison enabled me to study far more intensively than I would have if my life had gone differently and I had attended some college. I imagine that one of the biggest troubles with colleges is there are too many distractions, too much panty-raiding, fraternities, and boola-boola and all of that. Where else but in a prison could I have attacked my ignorance by being able to study intensely sometimes as much as fifteen hours a day?

Analyze

1. What motivated Malcolm X to learn to read and write?
2. What pedagogy does he use to increase his vocabulary and penmanship?
3. What does Malcolm X mean when he says from his prison cell that "I never had been so truly free in my life"?

Explore

1. Rodriguez tells us that reading and the scholarly world seemed to be full of alienation and conflict. How does Malcolm X's experience differ from his?
2. We have all doubted and struggled with school and life at times like Malcolm X. Write about some of your experiences of these times, making sure to discover and share what helped you or motivated you to get through your tough stretch.

3. Malcolm X's journey and motivation to self-education is inspirational, considering he was in jail. Make a list of five intellectual things you would like to be better at or learn and the reasons why. Pick one of the items on the list and write an essay on how you are going to become better at it through self-education.

Victor Villanueva
"Spic in English!"

Villanueva has published several influential books in writing, rhetoric, and race studies, among them *Bootstraps: From an American Academic of Color*, *Cross-Talk in Comp Theory: A Reader*, and *Rhetorics of the Americas: 3114 BCE to 2012 CE*, and over sixty-five articles and book chapters. "Spic in English" is a chapter from *Bootstraps* exploring in the schools he attended the ways that he struggled to keep his cultural identity but was regularly labeled or prevented from doing so.

When Villanueva moved from New York to California, the way he spoke and dressed, and foods and things he liked, parts of who he identified himself as, were suddenly the target of ridicule and censorship. Have you ever been the target of ridicule and censorship?

"Spic in English!"

Tension belies the soft calm of muffled brown in the theater-like assembly room at Hamilton. The day had been filled with rumors of Boys High School coming over for an intermural fist fest, a rumble.

OOO-YEA-OH.

An indiscernible chant from outside, like the sounds of spectators at a British or an Italian soccer game. Inside, thick, black garrison belts come off pant loops, are wrapped around fists. Knucks, store-bought brass knuckles, appear from socks. Penny rolls appear, clenched tightly: "Gonna talk cents to them Boys, boys." Blades appear from nowhere.

The clank of brass bars opening metal theater doors. Bright daylight. City buses line the sidewalk. Hamilton doesn't usually get curbside service. Teachers form two flanking walls. No others in sight while eyes adjust. A teacher directs student traffic toward the buses. Silence. The first second.

5   The next second, a scene from a pirate movie. A thickness of fighting, belts whirling, no voices, no shouts, only thuds and grunts. A suit tie is pulled from behind, from fashion accessory to garrote, a slam in the ribs that's felt just above the groin, glasses smashed into the bridge of the nose. Get to the bus. The bus rocks; the hiss of the door; movement; distance from the madness. Spring 1964.

Summer 1964. Looking down from the ninth-floor kitchen window of the projects. Debris flying, cars being overturned, flames and the sounds of sirens. Dad should be home from work. Past midnight, Dad arrives to tell of being caught on Bedford Avenue, bricks and molotov cocktails, lying down on the floorboard of the Corvair till a policeman knocks on the windshield to tell him to get the hell out of there. Riots in Bedford-Stuyvesant and later in Harlem. Mami announces that she will not raise another child in New York. Stela is two. Mami rules, though Dad is ruler.

Dad's cousin (or something) lives in California. November 1964: sad and happy goodbyes to Don Victor, la Comai, Gollo, Papo, and others. Mami, Dad, Stela, Papi, and all possessions in the Corvair, heading across country, to Los Angeles, California.

Events of the trip: a near collision, a first exposure to room service and color television, a waitress charging for water, pronounced *water,* not *wahta.* Scenes of a land that is broad and empty, profound contrast to the crowded cluster that is New York.

California. They park in Compton.

10   It was a cultural vacuum, California. The first Christmas still marks it. Dad's still unemployed, Mom's income barely covers the rent and food; there's a small tree in the living room with toys others wouldn't buy: a doll with only one winking eye, a toy piano without legs, things for Stela. Mom and Dad and Papi forego Christmas. He walks the streets that day—it's sunny and eighty degrees—staring at palm trees. The tropics belonged to Mom and Dad.

Papi was born during a New York blizzard, had passed out from the heat during his one visit to Puerto Rico. Christmas was supposed to be snow and wind, the comforting weight of an overcoat, vapor from nostrils, the smell of steam and the sound of complaining clanks on radiator pipes. Christmas was supposed to be a giant tree in Rockefeller Center, the Central Park folks ice skating below, Gimbel's and Macy's aglow with Christmas tree lights, mechanical elves and reindeer and Santa, giant train sets in the windows. At home, steam and the smells of the big cooking: *pasteles,* Dad making the *carne gisao,* Mami the *masa,* Papi spreading *achiote* on the paper that would be folded into rectangular bundles tied with twine, the bundles boiled. *Turron* for dessert, nougat from Spain. There would be the visit to the *abuela* Doña Teresa or to Tia Fela or to Carlina in Long Island. But this year there were just the immediate four, a forgotten meal, and oatmeal for dessert, and summer in Christmas.

The blacks live in a world separate from him, confined to Watts for the most part, not knowing of portoricans, he figured, not seeing portoricans as somehow the same as they, even when the portorican is white. And he isn't Mexican, what with Mom and Dad's jabs at Mexicans' funny ways with Spanish. And the white kids speak a different language, listen to a music that sounds foreign to his ears—the Beach Boys and Jan and Dean: surfin' safaris and deuce coupes and sloops John D, meaningless.

He tries to be white, kind of, taking the lead of the cultural hybrid in one of the two friends he made in school, Buzz Unruh: hair in the pompadour of the low rider, not the peaked pomp of the white working-class low rider, more the pomp of the Chicano, the Vato, the Pachuco; and Buzz wears Chicano work shirts, Pendletons for status, buttoned all the way not just at the top; Levis instead of starched khakis; modified fenceclimbers, without the high Cuban heels—a white working-class/Chicano mix. Papi, Victor, follows suit. And the dialect of Brooklyn starts to slip with his attempts at social survival during the peer-importance years of adolescence, even though the peers are two. Yet in his room he listens to the Jazz radio station and plays Tito Rodriguez and Pacheco on his portable record player, the suitcase-like machine with detachable box-like speakers; and he reads *Portnoy's Complaint* and *The Godfather,* stories recalling the mixes of New York, a place he is glad to be away from and a place he misses.

His first school in California is Compton Senior High School. The halls don't look much different from Hamilton. The difference is that Compton seems exclusively African American, none of the poor Irish, the Italians, the Puerto Ricans of Hamilton, not even California's Mexicans. He is alone. But he doesn't remain at Compton High long.

15 Mom and Dad move the family to another part of town in order to have him be in a better school district. This is different. Single-story buildings linked by concrete trails and clusters of lockers, a large grassy field where PE classes are conducted, a large parking lot where students—*students*—park their cars and motorcycles and Mopeds. And walking about are boys and girls in baggy short pants and T-shirts, a sea of blond hair and pink faces and blue eyes, assemblies on bleachers facing a basketball court, pep rallies with meaningless rhymes, women in short skirts bouncing about, leading the hyperactive rally, a man in plaid pants among the cheerleaders, himself a cheerleader.

At one assembly, a lone black face speaks to the sea of blond and blue about the time for a "nigro" student-body president, and there is silence and a respectful applause. Blond-and-blue are nicer than the Italian greasers were when we ventured outside the block, but the feeling in the air is somehow no different. No nigro student-body president that year.

He doesn't see the clusters of Mexicans at assemblies. But he does see them around the campus: groups of women in short, tight skirts and black hair teased high, thick black lines encircling large black eyes; the men with toothpicks or matchsticks in the corners of their mouths, thick, shiny black hair combed straight back, dark men dressed in plaid work shirts, white undershirts exposed, khakis with waists worn high, bandannas tied around one leg, shiny pointed shoes. They cluster. And he can feel the bristling when black eyes and blue eyes make contact for too long. And he feels that bristling when he makes eye contact with anyone, blue or black. No "Wazzup?" No "*¿Y que?*" Just loud silences.

First day at Manuel Dominguez Senior High School, a meeting with a counselor. First order of business: a bar of soap and a razor. The first order of business is humiliation. *Que portorro* doesn't have a moustache? His is respectable, neatly trimmed always, never did wear a *chibo,* the little strip of hair from the bottom lip to the chin; never did let the moustache turn into a *chinchow,* the Charlie-Chan like droop below the lipline. He wore his moustache like his father had, like his uncle Diego, like the respectable men of the block, like Zorro. But this is not TV California; it's his new world, and he'll comply. With the now swollen, clean-shaven heavy top lip comes the second order of business, the dress code: shorts must have a pocket, so too must T-shirts, no bare feet—rules for wearing underwear as outerwear, as far as he is concerned. He wears his fence-climbers, pegged pants, white shirt with tabbed collar, a tie, a jacket, his hair combed back. One dresses for school, not because of a code, just because it is school. He is swimming in foreignness. Third order of business: evaluate transcripts.

He knew there would be no college. Hamilton's consolation prize had been architectural drafting. He had the skills, maybe even the talent. Back at Hamilton, he had taken everything he could to prepare him for the job: carpentry and foundry, electrical design, algebra and trig to qualify for strength-of-materials, strength of materials. He mastered the slide rule (which he supplemented with the abacus that John Lee had given him and taught him to use years back). Back in his Bed-Stuy bedroom he had written to Dietz and to Crane and to American Standard, written of his intention to be an architectural draftsman, asked for brochures and drawing templates, and got them. Mom and Dad had given him a fine compass, dividers, a protractor, high-quality triangles, a desk and a T-square, drawing pens, mechanical pencils. There was the promise of a trade on graduation, and the promise that after seven years as an apprentice he could take the AIA test and become an architect.

Dominguez says architectural drafting requires college. But there would   20 be no college. He had resigned himself. The tests had told him so. Dominguez says only so many of all those shop courses can count toward graduation. Strength-of-materials could be a physics course, but to get credit for physics and for the trigonometry there would have to be geometry and a general science prerequisite. Never mind the "A"; there are rules. Physics and trig can't be learned without geometry, can't be understood without the basics. But he had learned and he did understand. No matter. Six months later he's told he won't graduate on schedule. Seems like he hadn't gotten California history his freshman year. It wasn't offered in Brooklyn. So why is he here?

Lockstep and college prep, except that not everyone goes to college. A drafting teacher gives him a special project: design an extension to the school library. He gets building codes, pulls out his templates, recalls his lessons learned at Hamilton, draws a complete set: floor plans, elevations, specs, the works. Gets an "A"—for mechanical drawing, says the report card, not for architectural drawing. No credit, really. Years later, attempting to convert a GED into a diploma (and being denied), he sees the school library's extension. It's remarkably like the one he had designed. No credit and no cash either.

Lockstep, all prearranged, everything on automatic. The geometry teacher recites lectures while staring at the ceiling, never making eye contact. The English teacher requires two-page stories, literally stories, but no reading. History is dates and dead white guys. And PE assumes everyone knows about flag football and decathlons. The block had been basketball, stickball, and king-queen, a kind of handball. The PE teacher shouts, "Go home and get a haircut! And don't come back till you do!" Papi never goes back.

Yet in the short time he was in Dominguez he did manage to make two friends: Buzz Unruh, the tall, lanky, freckle-faced kid who dressed somewhat like the Mexican kids, and Richard Tifft. Tifft had turned to him when he was first introduced to the geometry class and said, "City dude." They were the only kind words, the only acknowledgment, he received in all the introductions in all the classes. Tifft was an Okie, alone, not living in Bell Gardens with the other Okies, a California minority, alone. Later there would be *The Grapes of Wrath*. Later still, there would be the realization that *The Grapes of Wrath* describes the victims of neo-colonialism, the dispossessed because of economics, though blamed on dust. He was taken in by the Tifft household. Tifft's mother was "Ma," his father was "Tifft." He discovered pork fat and beans, taters and fritters. Kind people.

Then the summer of 1965. The Watts riots, flames and looting and shooting on a scale not even imagined at Bed-Stuy. He sits at the Tifft mobile home on the border of Compton and Watts. Flames light up the sky. The sounds of sirens. The sounds of shots fired. Ossie Davis is on the TV saying "Cool it." Tifft, the father, sits with a rifle across his lap. Says, "Might have to kill us some niggers." And somewhere inside, Papi, Victor, is hurt, frightened, confused. He can't let on that something within him is also a nigger.

25   Like many a Latino, I was upset by Richard Rodriguez's autobiography, *Hunger of Memory,* but I did understand, because he brought back so many of the memories of Mom's push for assimilation and the loneliness of the "other" in a foreign place, of California, of how we are not meant to be alone, and the lengths we will go to not to be alone. It wasn't the story that upset me. There were too many parallels to my own. It was the melancholy, the ideological resignation, the way he seemed not to see that biculturalism is as imposed as assimilation. Richard Rodriguez had been through the cauldron and had emerged American he said. And, being American, he

could no longer be Mexican. Yet there is the tension, the hunger, that runs throughout his writing, throughout his story. It is the tension that has others seek him out to discuss his ideas. If Richard Rodriguez were Richard Wilson he'd have no story to tell; if Richard Wilson were describing someone named Rodriguez he wouldn't have the same fame. He remains the other while espousing the same.

Biculturalism does not mean to me an equal ease with two cultures. That is an ideal. Rather, biculturalism means the tensions within, which are caused by being unable to deny the old or the new. Rodriguez struggles at denying the tension, and when he cannot (his hungering memory), he says that is just how it is; it's okay in the long run. I react differently. I resent the tension, that the ideal is not to be realized, that we cannot be the mosaic or the salad bowl. Nor can we be the melting pot, if that were the preference—any more than Richard Rodriguez is allowed to be the American he wishes to be. Rodriguez is not just the writer; he is the Mexican American writer, the writer of the Hispanic experience, whether he cares for the epithets or not, epithets imposed on him even as he denies them—Mexican American, Hispanic. He's still a chili pepper in the pot, not quite melted, like it or not. Rodriguez's mindset is that of the immigrant, attempting to give up "the old country" but minority status is nevertheless ascribed to him.

Even though Rodriguez's success comes to great degree from his arguing the case for assimilation even as his own assimilation is denied him, he is a success. He is, in fact, the noted writer: well-published, anthologized, interviewed by Bill Moyers, an essayist for the *McNeil/Lehrer News Hour*. What he did—what I did in that tension-filled moment in Tifft's mobile home, have done in the years prior and since—is fall back on that painful, confusing strategy that people of color who succeed employ: what Signithia Fordham calls "racelessness." It is the denial of other-cultural affiliation, a denial of the collective, any collective; it is the embracing of America's dominant ideology, the ideology of individualism.

Fordham describes a phenomenon she calls "fictive-kinship" among African Americans and demonstrates how high-achieving African American students distance themselves from that kinship. She describes fictive kinship as the ways in which African Americans assert the collective through particular dress codes, musical styles, other-cultural trappings. In language, the kinship is demonstrated by terms like "brother," "sister," "blood," by the conscious use of Black English. High achievers tend to distance themselves from the cultural trappings and the linguistic codes of those trappings, very often consciously. This is not the same as "passing," an impossibility for those who are not genetically whiter, who are not like Faulkner's octoroon. It is the recognition that for all the talk of black progress, the race has not progressed as far as certain individuals have. Jesse Jackson or Oprah Winfrey are the exceptions, not the rule. It is also the recognition of the school system, a competitive system which measures individual achievement. Racelessness, then, is the decision to go it alone. And it is most clearly marked linguistically, sometimes even by denying that one is choosing to learn to speak white English, by asserting that one is choosing to speak "correct" English, a notion propagated by linguists who eschew the color or even the prestige of the dominant dialect, labelling it as the value-free standard—Standard American English. E. D. Hirsch calls its written form a "grapholect," a consciously contrived, trans-dialectal form of language which serves a normative function in a multidialectal society. It favors no one, he says. But it is clearly closest to the Standard, and the Standard is most like the language of the white middle class.

Choosing to speak the language of the dominant, choosing racelessness, bears a price, however. And that price is alienation—the loss of fictive kinships without being fully adopted by the white community. "Where is your blackness?" from the one community, and "a credit to your race" from the other. "Where is your *raza?*" from the one and (alluding to Richard Rodriguez) "a child of Mexican immigrants" from the other.

30   In a sense, I was pushed into racelessness in California. I had been set up not to establish a fictive kinship with Chicanos. I don't know where Dad learned of dialects, but he did go on about them.

> All this talk about dialects is bullshit. Those Mexicans don't talk *dialects*. They talk their own language, a mishmash of Spanish and Indian. We speak *Castilians* [which he would pronounce cath-til-yano], *real* Spanish, like the kings of Spain.

He wasn't exactly right, historically or linguistically. Both the Mexican's Spanish and the Puerto Rican's really are dialects, neither true to the prestige dialect of four hundred years back. Not only would the Spaniard not pronounce Castilian as he had, but the historical Spanish of the Puerto Rican was Andalusian. Still, his assertion (which he voiced often) shows the degree to which I was taught that the Mexican was not to be regarded as somehow kin to the Puerto Rican, an assertion that the Chicanos and the Vatos made clear at my failed attempts to join the community. *"Mira,"* I'd say, just the way to open a conversation, a phatic device in linguistic jargon. *"¿Mira a que?"* would come the retort, usually accompanied with the flip of eyebrows to a vato brother. *"Oyes,"* they'd say, a phatic device. *"¿Oyes a que?"* I'd say to myself. "Slow down," I'd say when they spoke Spanish. "Slow down," they'd say when I did. And if I spoke of *salsa,* speaking of music, they'd wonder why I was talking about hot sauce. We were different.

"Hispanic" is a convenience created by the Census Bureau. And even as we try to choose our own label, we cannot agree. Some find "Latino" is too much a reference to Latin Americans, different from *mexicanos,* Mexican Americans, Chicanos. None of the terms satisfies the group from northern New Mexico, the actual speakers of something close to Castiliano still. Mexican, Cuban, and Nicaraguan immigrants might have cultural and linguistic similarities, but they also differ. Bilingual Hispanics are not necessarily bilingual in the same languages, not exactly.

He sat in the bleachers at Ebbets Field to watch a Brooklyn Dodgers game. Next to him and his dad sit another portorican boy and his dad. The Giants are up. Bases are loaded, only one out, a batter at plate. The stadium is silent. Suddenly, the black portorican boy next to Papi blurts out, *"¡Mira ese bicho!"* The father barely acknowledges the boy. Papi is shocked. That boy should have been popped in the mouth, at least gotten a scolding. What was that boy looking at anyway? Dad sees the shock on Papi's face, smiles, and explains that for Cubans *un bicho* is a bug, an insect. For the Puerto Rican, the word is a vulgar reference to male genitalia.

Barbara Walters is interviewing Fidel Castro on TV with the help of a translator. She asks Castro to respond to the criticism that he is merely a Russian puppet. Castro gets visibly agitated, angry; his response is long, coming at the translator rapidly. The question is, of course, incendiary. But to fuel the fire, I think, was that the translator had used the word *titere,* literally (in a bilingual dictionary sense), a puppet. For the Cuban and the Puerto Rican, however, the word connotes a smart-alecky kid, a punk.

We Hispanics, Latinos, are a multitude of differences. This is not to argue against bilingual education. Bilingual education, it seems to me, has less to do with language than with a lessening of the chances for alienation, the chance for negating the choice between the collective and racelessness.

I mention our differences to point out how we are the victims of racism in being regarded as all alike, this one thing, Hispanics. And the irony for those who fear what some are calling the "browning of America" is that the facile labeling instigates that browning, though not necessarily in the sense of promoting a brown nationalism. We begin to see ourselves as somehow the same, Latinos or Hispanics or Spanish speakers, even when we no longer speak Spanish; we begin to put aside our differences. We begin to form a fictive kinship.

This is how Fordham describes the historical formation of the fictive-kinship system:

> [T]he system was developed partly in response to two types of mis-treatment from Whites: the economic and instrumental exploitation by Whites during and after slavery, and the historical and continuing tendency by White Americans to treat Black Americans as an undif-ferentiated mass of people, indiscriminately ascribing to them cer-tain inherent strengths and weaknesses . . . Black Americans have generally responded to this mistreatment by inverting the negative stereotypes and assumptions of Whites into positive and functional attributes . . . Thus, Black Americans may have transformed White people's assumptions of Black homogeneity into a collective identity system. (56–57)

Because Hispanic or Latino cultures are varied, our dialects different, our racial mixes many, and because our historical exploitation came by way of different periods of colonialism and neocolonialism, not as stark or singular as slavery, our process of forming a greater fictive-kinship system is slower and somehow less complete than the process undergone by African Americans. Yet we do begin to form a collective bond, united in the collective threat of anti-brown racism. The Spanish cable television network, Univision, for ex-ample, is careful to represent the various Latinos, Hispanics; yet it is the one station, Latino. The portorican transplanted into California soil today would not likely feel the isolation he felt nearly thirty years ago.

Alone, and with no promise for better proffered by the schools, he drops out and goes to work. Like many who are young and uneducated, his first jobs are with the fast-food industry—hamburgers and kraut dogs and chili dogs and tacos and burritos at the local Bun'n'Run. A year earlier, he would have said a *taco* was the heel to a shoe and a *burrito* was a donkey. Now he could put out fifty tacos in less than a minute. Moving up, he becomes a short-order cook. Mom gets him an interview where she works as a key-punch operator for a computerized accounting firm. He maxes a math test and carries himself well with the interviewer, is hired as a checker, looking for keypunch errors when journal balances don't balance. One of the company's computer operators joins the Navy. Victor is sent to the Honeywell computer operations school in Los Angeles, where he learns to operate a Honeywell H-200, a massive machine that holds 16K of memory. And again there is hope for the future.

But it's 1968. General Westmoreland has whispered into President 40 Johnson's ear that the war can be won, given sufficient manpower. This is before the lottery draft system. All eligible nineteen-and-a-half year olds are to be drafted. He's nineteen and a half in 1968.

Fort Ord, California. A thin, short Filipino in a drill sergeant's hat stands before the new recruits:

> Ip you're worried about Bietnam, don't be. Because you're all gonna go anyway and do your job por Uncle Sam. And. Ip you're worried about being killed, don't be. Because you're all such sorry sacks ob shit, you're all going to die anyway.

The words, accent and all, the sun shining on the sergeant standing on the top step to the wooden, two-story barracks, the ice plant peaking through the floorboards on which the sergeant stands, the heat rising visibly from the tar floor, the dropping of the heart like when an elevator begins its too fast descent, the prickly feeling in the face that says blood is rushing away, all are clearer in memory today than this morning's meal.

Victor is told that if he were to reenlist, sign up for an extra year's service, he would be guaranteed training in the field of his choice. The dropout *knew* he would be cannon fodder. He reenlists for personnel specialist school, to become a nice, safe clerk. He had worked in an office and had a way with language. Twenty weeks later, he leaves California for Vietnam. From Long Binh depot to the Central Highlands. They don't need a clerk, so off to a Fire Support Base as a radiotelephone operator—a grunt. Two months later, the company clerk gets malaria, is transferred to Japan. The PFC is sent back to the trains area, the way station between the FSBs and the base camp, where artillery, the MASH, supply, and the company clerks work. Not safe, but a hell of a lot safer.

There isn't much to say about Vietnam. It was and remains somehow unreal no matter how real. Yet, two events mark that year that need mention here. One was the offer to go back to base camp to take the GED exams. The future is abstract enough for a nineteen-year-old, decidedly more so in a war, when mortality becomes all too concrete. I took up the offer because base camp meant ice cream, a steak, and a movie. I did not suffer any test anxiety because I had no future hinging on the test results. Turns out I did well enough to be the equivalent of a high-school graduate. The other event—the greater event—was in finally being back among *portorros,* back among portoricans from the block.

45   And the startling event within that event was when the Japanese American company commander shouted to us (as we huddled in our bunker) that we were in the American Army and that we *would* speak English, even in private. The order was beyond my understanding, especially in its having come from one who was a racial minority, one whose ancestors may have been confined to American concentration camps, whose ancestors had been nearly obliterated from the face of the earth by America only a generation back. Now I see that the order came from one who had succeeded, one who had taken the path of racelessness, one who would impose racelessness on us all.

More than two decades later another Japanese American (Japanese Canadian, really) would impose alienation. He would push for a change in the American constitution that would insist on English. Back then, I thought that what I spoke among my friends should be of little consequence—there was an American war, and I was in it. My loyalty was surely not at issue; I was more loyal, as I saw it, than the white kids who spoke no language other than English but were burning flags. And many years later would think that what I spoke among my friends—what little Spanish I had left— should be of no matter. I was an English professor, more able with English than many, maybe most, of the students who spoke no language other than English. The commander name was Yamashita. The legislator was the late S. I. Hayakawa.

Hayakawa was a Canadian who had come to this country in the 1930s. By the 1940s he had become a leading name in linguistic research. His 1941 *Language in Action* became required reading for most English majors for a couple of decades after. He had been a university president and a United States senator. And he had been the initiator of the English Language Amendment. He had written about how he had been denied an extended stay in America because he was Japanese, even if a native of Canada ("Why the English Language Amendment" 14). Yet he failed to see the racist connotations and ramifications of the drive he initiated. He even went on record with the assertion that Hispanics want a separate Spanish-speaking America. He quoted a handful of the nineteen-sixties Latino fringe ("Official Language" 36–37). So, with John Tanton, a midwestern ophthalmologist, he got the ball rolling. Now there are over seventeen states with English Only laws.

I don't believe that Senator Hayakawa's intent was essentially racist, however, any more than Captain Yamashita's (Hayakawa's alarm over a few Spanish speakers' nationalism notwithstanding). I believe Hayakawa's motives were grounded in a concern for this nation and its people. He believed in the power a command of the English language can wield in this country, the power that a historically English-speaking nation has long enjoyed. Former Senator Huddleston succinctly summed up the belief shared by Hayakawa, and countless others apparently, given the relative success of the English Only movement. Huddleston spoke before a special subcommittee of the Senate Judiciary Committee on English-language legislation:

> For over 200 years, the United States has enjoyed the blessing of one primary language that is spoken and understood by most of its citizens. The previous unquestioned acceptance of the language by immigrants from every linguistic and cultural background has enabled us to come together and prosper as one people. (15)

Prosperity came from the linguistic melt. That makes sense.

But it just isn't true historically. The prosperity, yes, but not quite the acceptance of English. The colonists brought Dutch and some Swedish to the New York-Delaware area, for instance. The Holland Tunnel and Rutgers University remain as reminders. The Huguenots brought French to Louisiana, an officially bilingual state to this day. The Spaniards brought Spanish to Florida, the Southwest, and the West. Germans brought their language to Pennsylvania. Pennsylvania "Dutch" (really Deutsche) remains a distinct dialect, its German influence still present. I have eaten *frankfurters* with *kraut* and mustard since long before *kindergarten*. We are full of German. It is American—not "ethnic," like, say, tacos or Spanish rice or the *barrio*.

Germans did not quietly accept the primacy of English. Those who were 50 in America during the Revolutionary War era were in no hurry to learn

English. They prompted Benjamin Franklin to ask in the spirit of present-day English Only advocates,

> Why should the *Palatine Boors* [Germans] be suffered to swarm onto our Settlements and, by herding together, establish their Language and Manners, to the Exclusion of ours? Why should *Pennsylvania,* founded by the *English,* become a Colony of *Aliens,* who will shortly be so numerous as to Germanize us instead of our Anglifying them? (quoted in Conklin and Lourie 69)

His answer, it turned out, was that those Boors should be suffered because a greater unity could be had in pluralism than in subjugation. The Germans would be necessary allies in a revolution. So, government documents were published in German. After the Revolutionary War, during the drafting of the Constitution, the new nation's designers still decided not to legislate the use of English, despite the perceived threat of a German primacy. The nation builders believed that principles of freedom should include linguistic freedom—even the freedom to speak what my Fathers believed to be an inferior tongue (Heath, "Language Academy").

German became America's semi-official second language, with even some instances of official German. In 1795, Germans petitioned the new congress to have laws published in German as well as English. The petition of the Virginia delegation made it through committee, falling to defeat by only one vote. In the years between 1830 and 1890, 4.5 million more Germans came to the United States. Seven years after the first wave, 1837, Pennsylvania legislated that the public schools be conducted in English and German—legislated that German would have equal status with English. By 1840, Ohio's public schools were bilingual—German-English. Some schools in Minnesota, Maryland, and Indiana were taught exclusively in German (Fallows). Publicly funded German schools existed through much of the nineteenth century (Conklin and Lourie).

The schools did not completely die out until the first world war. Anti-German sentiment produced legislation after legislation forbidding bilingual education in German and English, some forbidding German even in private. The German Americans quieted, assimilated (nearly two hundred years after their first arrival). Their ancestry had made them enemies to many here during the war.

After the first world war the push for "100 percent Americanization" saw bilingual education give way to something like the current teaching of English as a Second Language. Mexican Americans, along with other minorities, were included in a nationwide push at Americanizing the "immigrant," a push with remarkable similarities to the present day. The California Commission on Immigration and Housing, for example, outwardly declared its endorsement of "Americanization propaganda" (Fallows 378). The propaganda campaign evidently worked, given Huddleston's and so many others' belief in a monolingual American past.

Among those being compelled to Americanize were not only Mexicans, but   55
the "new immigrants" as well—the Italians, Yugoslavs, Poles, Rumanians— who were living in ghettos. They were inherently inferior, said the anthropologist Madison Grant and public sentiment. The public believed they were refusing to learn English (Hakuta). Does all this sound familiar?

Intensive English instruction was mandated and instituted. Penalties were imposed on those who spoke other languages. Successful learning of English was gauged by students' abilities to speak like the Anglo middle class. The success of these programs was measured by standardized achievement tests and IQ tests, just like today. These and other criteria determined students' high-school curricula, with racial minorities and immigrants consistently finding their ways into trade-oriented schools—schools like Alexander Hamilton Vocational-Technical High Scnool—rather than college preparatory schools.

By the 1930s, English oral proficiency had become a precondition for immigration. English literacy had become a precondition for voting, a requirement also aimed at Southern Blacks, who were neither immigrants nor bilingual. Language-as-unifier has been used to exclude before.

The argument goes that now the numbers are great; too many can live in Spanish-speaking or Tagalog-speaking or Vietnamese-speaking ghettos, self-contained communities. That may be, but that doesn't mean that parents don't want their children to learn English. Of Latino parents who took part in a 1985 national survey, for instance, 98 percent believed it essential for their children to learn to read and write "perfect" English (Hakuta). Latinos are not in positions of power as a people. That there have been only two Latinos in presidential cabinets in two hundred years (both within the last administration, George Bush's)—only two, despite Latinos having been on this country's soil longer than any other European group—illustrates our relative lack of power. And even if *any* non-English-speaking group had sufficient power to undermine America's English primacy, what profit would there be in it? English is the global *lingua franca*.

The chairman of the PLO sits, traditional headgear wrapped around his head and draped over combat fatigues—the nationalist, one we have sometimes called a terrorist. He speaks to a PBS newsman in English. He assumes the language of the journalist, rather than insist on the pose of the nationalist who regularly draws global attention.

60 PBS television's *The Story of English* notes that the crew of an Air Italia commercial jet, flying over Italian air-space, making a routine local run within Italy, piloted by Italians, speaking to a ground crew which is exclusively Italian, must nevertheless speak in English.

The World Council of Churches has English as its ecumenical language (McCrum, Cran, and MacNeil 20).

English is even the language of the cosmos: Vulcan One's message, representing the people of Earth, approved by the 147 members of the United Nations, is recorded in English (McCrum et al. 19).

Americans attending schools, watching TV, venturing outside their neighborhoods cannot avoid learning English. Even if some did resist, they could not stop the wave of English that would engulf them.

At best, English Only legislation is unnecessary. It provides nothing to foster a faster language-learning rate than people's abilities will allow. English Only laws provide no new schooling. Instead, they are being used to end bilingual programs. Children, in particular, will have to sink or swim. We're told that's how it used to be. But it wasn't. Even the 100 percent Americanization push provided something like ESL.

65 What's worse, "sink or swim" suggests a resignation to let some sink. Too many already do. And when they do, they don't tend to blame a system that fails them; they tend to blame themselves. Those who swim all too often find they have lost sight of their original homelands, that they hunger for the memory. Some neither swim nor sink: alienated from the first culture, not quite a part of the new culture, "tonto in both languages." Better to have two cultures than one, two than none—no matter the tensions. English Only equals sink or swim equals alienation, whether sunk or swimming or lost at sea.

English Only legislation is also racist, sometimes explicitly. I might grant the late Senator Hayakawa high motives, but I cannot grant Hayakawa's partner, co-founder of U.S. English, similar motives. John Tanton was exposed as declaring that he feared a Hispanic takeover, a takeover by fast-breeders faithful to a Roman Church which does not respect the division of church and state (e.g., *The Christian Science Monitor,* 27 Oct. 1988, 5). He had said that America is going to face "the first instance in which those with their pants up are going to get caught with their pants down" (Wingert 22). There is no way to ameliorate these words. They're racist.

Nor is Tanton's an isolated case.

In Massachusetts, a flier from that state's English Only organization warns that unless English Only efforts win support and gain funding, "White children may be taught that they are descendants of European ice people whose lack of skin color identifies them as an inferior race," that bilingual educators will "do away with English and anything European," with students "learn[ing] that Western civilization is a cheap imitation of the true source of world culture, Africa" (Atkins 4). This isn't even limited to anti-Latino sentiment, since Spain, the source of so much of Latino cultures, is still in Europe. In this case, official English legislation has been reduced to black and white.

There's the story from Colorado, in which a restaurant manager fired a waiter for having translated a menu item for a foreign patron.

Or the one from Arizona, in which a parole-board hearing was canceled   70 because the would-be parolee required a translator.

The General Accounting Office has even documented cases of discrimination against workers who speak English with a "foreign" accent, with Latinos being three times as likely to suffer such discrimination as others (Califa).

Some, like Senator Hayakawa, I figure, are no doubt well-intentioned in seeking English Only legislation, but English Only legislation can nevertheless be used to further racism, to invade privacy, to constrain free speech, to deny equal treatment under the law. In short, English Only legislation can be used to violate the First and the Fourteenth Amendments to the Constitution. At bottom, English Only legislation is un-American in the best sense of "American," and too typically American in the worst sense— morally and historically.

Whatever Captain Yamashita's angry invective, we continued to speak in Spanish. Look outside the bunker. See if anyone's around. Speak quietly, nearly in whispers. Speak Spanish. We are Spanish, though not one of us would deny being American.

We were like all the rest of the GIs, nostalgic about "back in the world." "California Dreaming" was probably the most-played song in Vietnam. Our "world" wasn't California; it was *el bloque.* Our world included the portorican Spanglish of the block. The block would not be denied.

We didn't say "back in the world." We and the African Americans talked about "back on the block."

75   Twelve months in Vietnam. Victor returns. Back to the world. But not the block. He's stationed in Stockton, California, an army depot, mainly civilians, with just a handful of military. He marries the woman he had met shortly before entering the army. Marriage is a desperate attempt at continuity, picking up where normalcy had been disrupted by the bizarre. That marriage won't last long. Apart from having to wear a uniform during the days, having to get a haircut more often than he'd like, his life is good in central California, even affluent by his standards. His pay is good; he lives in large family quarters, enjoys the especially low cost of foods at the Commissary, the low cost of civilian medical care. His is an administrative job among civilians. The advantages of the military, without most of the drawbacks. And he and his wife are soon to have a baby. And during the three years he's been in the service the computer field has undergone a boom, computer jobs being filled by college graduates. But he's just a GED. He reenlists.

Analyze

1. In what type of car did the Villanuevas drive to California?
2. What were the dishes that Villanueva's father and mother made at Christmas time?
3. What were the names of the schools Villanueva attended in New York and California?

Explore

1. When Villanueva describes the dress of the kids in California compared to his own, how does their clothing serve as a means to both separate them and make them individual? In an essay describe and categorize the way the groups around you dress; include yourself in this description. Make sure you discuss how clothing is one way we create an individual identity and a group one.
2. Villanueva talks about "racelessness" as "the denial of other-cultural affiliation, a denial of the collective, any collective; it is the embracing of America's dominant ideology, the ideology of individualism." He goes on to discuss "fictive-kinship" among African Americans. He describes fictive-kinship as "how high-achieving African American students distance themselves from that kinship," yet they also "assert the collective

through particular dress codes, musical styles, other-cultural trappings." Discuss what this means using the essays we have read thus far and talk about how, perhaps, all races practice fictive-kinship. Alternatively, create a poster or PowerPoint showing your answer to this task.

3. At one point Villanueva describes how he tried to mix with the Hispanics in California by speaking Spanish with them. He realized, however, the versions they spoke and the accents they each had did not serve to create a common identity; as he says, "We were different." Discuss why you think it was just language that separated him with the Hispanics, or why you believe there were other reasons.

Richard Rodriguez
"Achievement of Desire"

In addition to working as a teacher, Rodriguez has published as a journalist in *Time*, *Mother Jones*, and *Harpers*. His book, *Days of Obligation: An Argument with My Mexican Father*, was nominated for the Pulitzer Prize, and his other books have been highly successful, such as *Hunger of Memory: The Education of Richard Rodriguez*, *Mexico's Children*, and *Brown: The Last Discovery of America*. *Achievement of Desire* derives from Rodriguez's controversial autobiography, *Hunger of Memory*. Some of the Chicano community felt it positively showed the challenges they face living in two cultures, while others denounced it because it seemed to cast blame on Mexican Americans for the problems they have assimilating in American culture.

Do you agree with Rodriguez that we give up part of who we are as we become more and more educated?

I stand in the ghetto classroom—"the guest speaker"—attempting to lecture on the mystery of the sounds of our words to rows of diffident students. "Don't you hear it? Listen! The music of our words. '*Sumer* is *i-cumen in.* . . .' And songs on the car radio. We need Aretha Franklin's voice to fill plain words with music—her life." In the face of their empty stares, I try to create an enthusiasm. But the girls in the back row turn to watch some boy passing outside. There are flutters of smiles, waves. And someone's mouth elongates heavy, silent words through the barrier of glass. Silent words—the lips straining to shape each voiceless syllable: *"Meet meee late errr."* By the door, the instructor smiles at me, apparently hoping that I will be able to spark some enthusiasm in the class. But only one student seems to be listening. A girl, maybe fourteen. In this gray room her eyes shine with ambition. She keeps nodding and nodding at all that I say; she even takes notes. And each time I ask a question, she jerks up and down in her desk like a marionette, while her hand waves over the bowed heads of her classmates. It is myself (as a boy) I see as she faces me now (a man in my thirties).

The boy who first entered a classroom barely able to speak English, twenty years later concluded his studies in the stately quiet of the reading room in the British Museum. Thus with one sentence I can summarize my academic career. It will be harder to summarize what sort of life connects the boy to the man.

With every award, each graduation from one level of education to the next, people I'd meet would congratulate me. Their refrain always the same: "Your parents must be very proud." Sometimes then they'd ask me how I managed it—my "success." (How?) After a while, I had several quick answers to give in reply. I'd admit, for one thing, that I went to an excellent grammar school. (My earliest teachers, the nuns, made my success their ambition.) And my brother and both my sisters were very good students. (They often brought home the shiny school trophies I came to want.) And my mother and father always encouraged me. (At every graduation they were behind the stunning flash of the camera when I turned to look at the crowd.)

As important as these factors were, however, they account inadequately for my academic advance. Nor do they suggest what an odd success I managed. For although I was a very good student, I was also a very bad student. I was a "scholarship boy," a certain kind of scholarship boy. Always successful, I was always unconfident. Exhilarated by my progress. Sad. I became the prized student—anxious and eager to learn. Too eager, too anxious—an imitative and unoriginal pupil. My brother and two sisters enjoyed the advantages I did, and they grew to be as successful as I, but none of them ever seemed so anxious about their schooling. A second-grade student, I was the one who came home and corrected the "simple" grammatical mistakes of our parents. ("Two negatives make a positive.") Proudly I announced—to my family's startled silence— that a teacher had said I was losing all trace of a Spanish accent. I was oddly annoyed when I was unable to get parental help with a homework assignment.

The night my father tried to help me with an arithmetic exercise, he kept reading the instructions, each time more deliberately, until I pried the textbook out of his hands, saying, "I'll try to figure it out some more by myself."

When I reached the third grade, I outgrew such behavior. I became more   5 tactful, careful to keep separate the two very different worlds of my day. But then, with ever-increasing intensity, I devoted myself to my studies. I became bookish, puzzling to all my family. Ambition set me apart. When my brother saw me struggling home with stacks of library books, he would laugh, shouting: "Hey, Four Eyes!" My father opened a closet one day and was startled to find me inside, reading a novel. My mother would find me reading when I was supposed to be asleep or helping around the house or playing outside. In a voice angry or worried or just curious, she'd ask: "What do you see in your books?" It became the family's joke. When I was called and wouldn't reply, someone would say I must be hiding under my bed with a book.

(How did I manage my success?)

What I am about to say to you has taken me more than twenty years to admit: *A primary reason for my success in the classroom was that I couldn't forget that schooling was changing me and separating me from the life I enjoyed before becoming a student.* That simple realization! For years I never spoke to anyone about it. Never mentioned a thing to my family or my teachers or classmates. From a very early age, I understood enough, just enough about my classroom experiences to keep what I knew repressed, hidden beneath layers of embarrassment. Not until my last months as a graduate student, nearly thirty years old, was it possible for me to think much about the reasons for my academic success. Only then. At the end of my schooling, I needed to determine how far I had moved from my past. The adult finally confronted, and now must publicly say, what the child shuddered from knowing and could never admit to himself or to those many faces that smiled at his every success. ("Your parents must be very proud. . . .")

At the end, in the British Museum (too distracted to finish my dissertation) for weeks I read, speed-read, books by modern educational theorists, only to find infrequent and slight mention of students like me. (Much more is written about the more typical case, the lower-class student who barely is helped by his schooling.) Then one day, leafing through Richard Hoggart's *The Uses of Literacy,* I found, in his description of the scholarship boy, myself. For the first time I realized that there were other students like me, and so I was able to frame the meaning of my academic success, its consequent price—the loss.

Hoggart's description is distinguished, at least initially, by deep understanding. What he grasps very well is that the scholarship boy must move between environments, his home and the classroom, which are at cultural extremes, opposed. With his family, the boy has the intense pleasure of intimacy, the family's consolation in feeling public alienation. Lavish emotions texture home life. Then, at school, the instruction bids him to trust lonely reason primarily. Immediate needs set the pace of his parents' lives. From his mother and father the boy learns to trust spontaneity and nonrational ways of knowing. Then, at school, there is mental calm. Teachers emphasize the value of a reflectiveness that opens a space between thinking and immediate action.

10   Years of schooling must pass before the boy will be able to sketch the cultural differences in his day as abstractly as this. But he senses those differences early. Perhaps as early as the night he brings home an assignment from school and finds the house too noisy for study.

> He has to be more and more alone, if he is going to "get on." He will have, probably unconsciously, to oppose the ethos of the hearth, the intense gregariousness of the working-class family group. Since everything centres upon the living-room, there is unlikely to be a room of his own; the bedrooms are cold and inhospitable, and to warm them or the front room, if there is one, would not only be expensive, but would require an imaginative leap—out of the tradition— which most families are not capable of making. There is a corner of the living-room table. On the other side Mother is ironing, the wireless is on, someone is singing a snatch of song or Father says intermittently whatever comes into his head. The boy has to cut himself off mentally, so as to do his homework, as well as he can.

The next day, the lesson is as apparent at school. There are even rows of desks. Discussion is ordered. The boy must rehearse his thoughts and raise his hand before speaking out in a loud voice to an audience of classmates. And there is time enough, and silence, to think about ideas (big ideas) never considered at home by his parents.

Not for the working-class child alone is adjustment to the classroom difficult. Good schooling requires that any student alter early childhood habits.

But the working-class child is usually least prepared for the change. And, unlike many middle-class children, he goes home and sees in his parents a way of life not only different but starkly opposed to that of the classroom. (He enters the house and hears his parents talking in ways his teachers discourage.)

Without extraordinary determination and the great assistance of others at home and at school, there is little chance for success. Typically most working-class children are barely changed by the classroom. The exception succeeds. The relative few become scholarship students. Of these, Richard Hoggart estimates, most manage a fairly graceful transition. Somehow they learn to live in the two very different worlds of their day. There are some others, however, those Hoggart pejoratively terms "scholarship boys," for whom success comes with special anxiety. Scholarship boy: good student, troubled son. The child is "moderately endowed," intellectually mediocre, Hoggart supposes—though it may be more pertinent to note the special qualities of temperament in the child. High-strung child. Brooding. Sensitive. Haunted by the knowledge that one *chooses* to become a student. (Education is not an inevitable or natural step in growing up.) Here is a child who cannot forget that his academic success distances him from a life he loved, even from his own memory of himself.

Initially, he wavers, balances allegiance. ("The boy is himself [until he 15 reaches, say, the upper forms] very much of *hath* the worlds of home and school. He is enormously obedient to the dictates of the world of school, but emotionally still strongly wants to continue as part of the family circle.") Gradually, necessarily, the balance is lost. The boy needs to spend more and more time studying, each night enclosing himself in the silence permitted and required by intense concentration. He takes his first step toward academic success, away from his family.

From the very first days, through the years following, it will be with his parents—the figures of lost authority, the persons toward whom he feels deepest love—that the change will be most powerfully measured. A separation will unravel between them. Advancing in his studies, the boy notices that his mother and father have not changed as much as he. Rather, when he sees them, they often remind him of the person he once was and the life he earlier shared with them. He realizes what some Romantics also know when they praise the working class for the capacity for human closeness, qualities of passion and spontaneity, that the rest of us experience in like measure only in the earliest part of our youth. For the Romantic, this doesn't make working-class life childish. Working-class life challenges precisely because it is an *adult* way of life.

The scholarship boy reaches a different conclusion. He cannot afford to admire his parents. (How could he and still pursue such a contrary life?) He permits himself embarrassment at their lack of education. And to evade nostalgia for the life he has lost, he concentrates on the benefits education will bestow upon him. He becomes especially ambitious. Without the support of old certainties and consolations, almost mechanically, he assumes the procedures and doctrines of the classroom. The kind of allegiance the young student might have given his mother and father only days earlier, he transfers to the teacher, the new figure of authority. "[The scholarship boy] tends to make a father-figure of his [teacher]," Hoggart observes.

But Hoggart's calm prose only makes me recall the urgency with which I came to idolize my grammar school teachers. I began by imitating their accents, using their diction, trusting their every direction. The very first facts they dispensed, I grasped with awe. Any book they told me to read, I read—then waited for them to tell me which books I enjoyed. Their every casual opinion I came to adopt and to trumpet when I returned home. I stayed after school "to help"—to get my teacher's undivided attention. It was the nun's encouragement that mattered most to me. (She understood exactly what—my parents never seemed to appraise so well—all my achievements entailed.) Memory gently caressed each word of praise bestowed in the classroom so that compliments teachers paid me years ago come quickly to mind even today.

The enthusiasm I felt in second-grade classes I flaunted before both my parents. The docile, obedient student came home a shrill and precocious son who insisted on correcting and teaching his parents with the remark: "My teacher told us. . . ."

20　　I intended to hurt my mother and father. I was still angry at them for having encouraged me toward classroom English. But gradually this anger was exhausted, replaced by guilt as school grew more and more attractive to me. I grew increasingly successful, a talkative student. My hand was raised in the classroom; I yearned to answer any question. At home, life was less noisy than it had been. (I spoke to classmates and teachers more often each day than to family members.) Quiet at home, I sat with my papers for hours each night. I never forgot that schooling had irretrievably changed my family's life. That knowledge, however, did not weaken ambition. Instead, it strengthened resolve. Those times I remembered the loss of my past with regret. I quickly reminded myself of all the things my teachers could give me. (They could make me an educated man.) I tightened my grip on pencil and books. I evaded nostalgia. Tried hard to forget. But one does not forget by trying to forget. One only remembers. I remembered too well that education had changed my family's life. I would not have become a scholarship boy had I not so often remembered.

Once she was sure that her children knew English, my mother would tell us, "You should keep up your Spanish." Voices playfully groaned in response. *"¡Pochos!,"* my mother would tease. I listened silently.

After a while, I grew more calm at home. I developed tact. A fourth-grade student, I was no longer the show-off in front of my parents. I became a conventionally dutiful son, politely affectionate, cheerful enough, even—for reasons beyond choosing—my father's favorite. And much about my family life was easy then, comfortable, happy in the rhythm of our living together: hearing my father getting ready for work; eating the breakfast my mother had made me; looking up from a novel to hear my brother or one of my sisters playing with friends in the backyard; in winter, coming upon the house all lighted up after dark.

But withheld from my mother and father was any mention of what most mattered to me: the extraordinary experience of first-learning. Late afternoon: in the midst of preparing dinner, my mother would come up behind me while I was trying to read. Her head just over mine, her breath warmly scented with food. "What are you reading?" Or, "Tell me about your new courses." I would barely respond, "Just the usual things, nothing special." (A half smile, then silence. Her head moving back in the silence. Silence! Instead of the flood of intimate sounds that had once flowed smoothly between us, there was this silence.) After dinner, I would rush to a bedroom with papers and books. As often as possible, I resisted parental pleas to "save lights" by coming to the kitchen to work. I kept so much, so often, to myself. Sad. Enthusiastic. Troubled by the excitement of coming upon new ideas. Eager. Fascinated by the promising texture of a brand-new book. I hoarded the pleasures of learning. Alone for hours. Enthralled. Nervous. I rarely looked away from my books—or back on my memories. Nights when relatives visited and the front rooms were warmed by Spanish sounds, I slipped quietly out of the house.

It mattered that education was changing me. It never ceased to matter. My brother and sisters would giggle at our mother's mispronounced words.

They'd correct her gently. My mother laughed girlishly one night, trying not to pronounce sheep as ship. From a distance I listened sullenly. From that distance, pretending not to notice on another occasion, I saw my father looking at the title pages of my library books. That was the scene on my mind when I walked home with a fourth-grade companion and heard him say that his parents read to him every night. (A strange-sounding book—*Winnie the Pooh*.) Immediately, I wanted to know, "What is it like?" My companion, however, thought I wanted to know about the plot of the book. Another day, my mother surprised me by asking for a "nice" book to read. "Something not too hard you think I might like." Carefully I chose one, Willa Cather's *My Antonia*. But when, several weeks later, I happened to see it next to her bed unread except for the first few pages, I was furious and suddenly wanted to cry. I grabbed up the book and took it back to my room and placed it in its place, alphabetically on my shelf.

25   "Your parents must be very proud of you." People began to say that to me about the time I was in sixth grade. To answer affirmatively, I'd smile. Shyly I'd smile, never betraying my sense of the irony: I was not proud of my mother and father. I was embarrassed by their lack of education. It was not that I ever thought they were stupid, though stupidly I took for granted their enormous native intelligence. Simply, what mattered to me was that they were not like my teachers.

But, "Why didn't you tell us about the award?" my mother demanded, her frown weakened by pride. At the grammar school ceremony several weeks after, her eyes were brighter than the trophy I'd won. Pushing back the hair from my forehead, she whispered that I had "shown" the *gringos*. A few minutes later, I heard my father speak to my teacher and felt ashamed of his labored, accented words. Then guilty for the shame. I felt such contrary feelings. (There is no simple roadmap through the heart of the scholarship boy.) My teacher was so soft-spoken and her words were edged sharp and clean. I admired her until it seemed to me that she spoke too carefully. Sensing that she was condescending to them, I became nervous. Resentful. Protective. I tried to move my parents away. "You both must be very proud of Richard," the nun said. They responded quickly. (They were proud.) "We are proud of all our children." Then this afterthought: "They sure didn't get their brains from us." They all laughed. I smiled.

In fourth grade I embarked upon a grandiose reading program. "Give me the names of important books," I would say to startled teachers. They soon found out that I had in mind "adult books." I ignored their suggestion of anything I suspected was written for children. (Not until I was in college, as a result, did I read *Huckleberry Finn* or *Alice's Adventures in Wonderland*.) Instead, I read *The Scarlet Letter* and Franklin's *Autobiography*. And whatever I read I read for extra credit. Each time I finished a book, I reported the achievement to a teacher and basked in the praise my effort earned. Despite my best efforts, however, there seemed to be more and more books I needed to read. At the library I would literally tremble as I came upon whole shelves of books I hadn't read. So I read and I read and I read: *Great Expectations*; all the short stories of Kipling; *The Babe Ruth Story;* the entire first volume of the *Encyclopedia Britannica* (A-ANSTEY); *the Iliad; Moby Dick; Gone with the Wind; The Good Earth; Ramona; Forever Amber; The Lives of the Saints; Crime and Punishment; The Pearl*. . . . Librarians who initially frowned when I checked out the maximum ten books at a time started saving books they thought I might like. Teachers would say to the rest of the class, "I only wish the rest of you took reading as seriously as Richard obviously does."

But at home I would hear my mother wondering, "What do you see in your books?" (Was reading a hobby like her knitting? Was so much reading even healthy for a boy? Was it the sign of "brains"? Or was it just a convenient excuse for not helping around the house on Saturday mornings?) Always, "What do you see. . . ?"

What *did* I see in my books? I had the idea that they were crucial for my academic success, though I couldn't have said exactly how or why. In the sixth grade I simply concluded that what gave a book its value was some major idea or theme it contained. If that core essence could be mined and memorized, I would become learned like my teachers. I decided to record in a notebook the themes of the books that I read. After reading *Robinson Crusoe,* I wrote that its theme was "the value of learning to live by oneself." When I completed *Wuthering Heights,* I noted the danger of "letting emotions get out of control." Rereading these brief moralistic appraisals usually left me disheartened. I couldn't believe that they were really the source of reading's value. But for many more years, they constituted the only means I had of describing to myself the educational value of books.

I entered high school having read hundreds of books. My habit of reading made me a confident speaker and writer of English. Reading also enabled me to sense something of the shape, the major concerns, of Western thought. (I was able to say something about Dante and Descartes and

30

Engels and James Baldwin in my high school term papers.) In these various ways, books brought me academic success as I hoped that they would. But I was not a good reader. Merely bookish, I lacked a point of view when I read. Rather, I read in order to acquire a point of view. I vacuumed books for epigrams, scraps of information, ideas, themes—anything to fill the hollow within me and make me feel educated. When one of my teachers suggested to his drowsy tenth-grade English class that a person could not have a "complicated idea" until he had read at least two thousand books, I heard the remark without detecting either its irony or its very complicated truth. I merely determined to compile a list of all the books I had ever read. Harsh with myself, I included only once a title I might have read several times. (How, after all, could one read a book more than once?) And I included only those books over a hundred pages in length. (Could anything shorter be a book?)

There was yet another high school list I compiled. One day I came across a newspaper article about the retirement of an English professor at a nearby state college. The article was accompanied by a list of the "hundred most important books of Western Civilization." "More than anything else in my life," the professor told the reporter with finality, "these books have made me all that I am." That was the kind of remark I couldn't ignore. I clipped out the list and kept it for the several months it took me to read all of the titles. Most books, of course, I barely understood. While reading Plato's *Republic,* for instance, I needed to keep looking at the book jacket comments to remind myself what the text was about. Nevertheless, with the special patience and superstition of a scholarship boy, I looked at every word of the text. And by the time I reached the last word, relieved, I convinced myself that I had read *The Republic*. In a ceremony of great pride, I solemnly crossed Plato off my list.

. . . The scholarship boy does not straddle, cannot reconcile, the two great opposing cultures of his life. His success is unromantic and plain. He sits in the classroom and offers those sitting beside him no calming reassurance about their own lives. He sits in the seminar room—a man with *Shadow* skin, the son of working-class Mexican immigrant parents. (Addressing the professor at the head of the table, his voice catches with nervousness.) There is no trace of his parents' accent in his speech. Instead he approximates the accents of teachers and classmates. Coming from *him* those sounds seem suddenly odd. Odd too is the effect produced when *he* uses academic jargon—bubbles at the tip of his tongue: "*Tapas* . . . negative capability . . .

vegetation imagery in Shakespearean comedy." He lifts an opinion from Coleridge, takes something else from Frye or Empson or Leavis. He even repeats exactly his professor's earlier comment. All his ideas are clearly borrowed. He seems to have no thought of his own. He chatters while his listeners smile—their look one of disdain.

When he is older and thus when so little of the person he was survives, the scholarship boy makes only too apparent his profound lack of *self*-confidence. This is the conventional assessment that even Richard Hoggart repeats:

> [The scholarship boy] tends to over-stress the importance of examinations, of the piling-up of knowledge and of received opinions. He discovers a technique of apparent learning, of the acquiring of facts rather than of the handling and use of facts. He learns how to receive a purely literate education, one using only a small part of the personality and challenging only a limited area of his being. He begins to see life as a ladder, as a permanent examination with some praise and some further exhortation at each stage. He becomes an expert imbiber and dolerout; his competence will vary, but will rarely be accompanied by genuine enthusiasms. He rarely feels the reality of knowledge, of other men's thoughts and imaginings, on his own pulses. . . . He has something of the blinkered pony about him. . . .

But this is criticism more accurate than fair. The scholarship boy is a very   35 bad student. He is the great mimic; a collector of thoughts, not a thinker; the very last person in class who ever feels obliged to have an opinion of his own. In large part, however, the reason he is such a bad student is because he realizes more often and more acutely than most other students—than Hoggart himself—that education requires radical self-reformation. As a very young boy, regarding his parents, as he struggles with an early homework assignment, he knows this too well. That is why he lacks self-assurance. He does not forget that the classroom is responsible for remaking him. He relies on his teacher, depends on all that he hears in the classroom and reads in his books. He becomes in every obvious way the worst student, a dummy mouthing the opinions of others. But he would not be so bad—nor would he become so successful, a *scholarship* boy—if he did not accurately perceive that the best synonym for primary "education" is "imitation."

Like me, Hoggart's imagined scholarship boy spends most of his years in the classroom afraid to long for his past. Only at the very end of his schooling does the boy-man become nostalgic. In this sudden change of heart, Richard Hoggart notes:

> He longs for the membership he lost, "he pines for some Nameless Eden where he never was." The nostalgia is the stronger and the more ambiguous because he is really "in quest of his own absconded self yet scared to find it." He both wants to go back and yet thinks he has gone beyond his class, feels himself weighted with knowledge of his own and their situation, which hereafter forbids him the simpler pleasures of his father and mother....

According to Hoggart, the scholarship boy grows nostalgic because he remains the uncertain scholar, bright enough to have moved from his past, yet unable to feel easy, a part of a community of academics.

This analysis, however, only partially suggests what happened to me in my last years as a graduate student. When I traveled to London to write a dissertation on English Renaissance literature, I was finally confident of membership in a "community of scholars." But the pleasure that confidence gave me faded rapidly. After only two or three months in the reading room of the British Museum, it became clear that I had joined a lonely community. Around me each day were dour faces eclipsed by large piles of books. There were the regulars, like the old couple who arrived every morning, each holding a loop of the shopping bag which contained all their notes. And there was the historian who chattered madly to herself. ("Oh dear! Oh! Now, what's this? What? Oh, my!") There were also the faces of young men and women worn by long study. And everywhere eyes turned away the moment our glance accidentally met. Some persons I sat beside day after day, yet we passed silently at the end of the day, strangers. Still, we were united by a common respect for the written word and for scholarship. We did form a union, though one in which we remained distant from one another.

40   More profound and unsettling was the bond I recognized with those writers whose books I consulted. Whenever I opened a text that hadn't been used for years, I realized that my special interests and skills united me to a mere handful of academics. We formed an exclusive—eccentric!—society, separated from others who would never care or be able to share our concerns. (The pages I turned were stiff like layers of dead skin.) I began to wonder: Who, beside my dissertation director and a few faculty members, would ever read what I wrote? and: Was my dissertation much more than

an act of social withdrawal? These questions went unanswered in the silence of the Museum reading room. They remained to trouble me after I'd leave the library each afternoon and feel myself shy—unsteady, speaking simple sentences at the grocer's or the butcher's on my way back to my [apartment].

Meanwhile my file cards accumulated. A professional, I knew exactly how to search a book for pertinent information. I could quickly assess and summarize the usability of the many books I consulted. But whenever I started to write, I knew too much (and not enough) to be able to write anything but sentences that were overly cautious, timid, strained brittle under the heavy weight of footnotes and qualifications. I seemed unable to dare a passionate statement. I felt drawn by professionalism to the edge of sterility, capable of no more than pedantic, lifeless, unassailable prose.

Then nostalgia began.

After years spent unwilling to admit its attractions, I gestured nostalgically toward the past. I yearned for that time when I had not been so alone. I became impatient with books. I wanted experience more immediate. I feared the library's silence. I silently scorned the gray, timid faces around me. I grew to hate the growing pages of my dissertation on genre and Renaissance literature. (In my mind I heard relatives laughing as they tried to make sense of its title.) I wanted something—I couldn't say exactly what. I told myself that I wanted a more passionate life. And a life less thoughtful. And above all, I wanted to be less alone. One day I heard some Spanish academics whispering back and forth to each other, and their sounds seemed ghostly voices recalling my life. Yearning became preoccupation then. Boyhood memories beckoned, flooded my mind. (Laughing intimate voices. Bounding up the front steps of the porch. A sudden embrace inside the door.)

For weeks after, I turned to books by educational experts. I needed to learn how far I had moved from my past—to determine how fast I would be able to recover something of it once again. But I found little. Only a chapter in a book by Richard Hoggart . . . I left the reading room and the circle of faces.

I came home. After the year in England, I spent three summer months 45 living with my mother and father, relieved by how easy it was to be home. It no longer seemed very important to me that we had little to say. I felt easy sitting and eating and walking with them. I watched them, nevertheless, looking for evidence of those elastic, sturdy strands that bind generations in a web of inheritance. I thought as I watched my mother all night: of course a friend had been right when she told me that I gestured and laughed just like my mother. Another time I saw for myself: my father's eyes were much like my own, constantly watchful.

But after the early relief, this return, came suspicion, nagging until I realized that I had not neatly sidestepped the impact of schooling. My desire to do so was precisely the measure of how much I remained an academic. *Negatively* (for that is how this idea first occurred to me): my need to think so much and so abstractly about my parents and our relationship was in itself an indication of my long education. My father and mother did not pass their time thinking about the cultural meanings of their experience. It was I who described their daily lives with airy ideas. And yet, *positively:* the ability to consider experience so abstractly allowed me to shape into desire what would otherwise have remained indefinite, meaningless longing in the British Museum. If, because of my schooling, I had grown culturally separated from my parents, my education finally had given me ways of speaking and caring about that fact.

My best teachers in college and graduate school, years before, had tried to prepare me for this conclusion, I think, when they discussed texts of aristocratic pastoral literature. Faithfully, I wrote down all that they said. I memorized it: "The praise of the unlettered by the highly educated is one of the primary themes of 'elitist' literature." But, "the importance of the praise given the unsolitary, richly passionate and spontaneous life is that it simultaneously reflects the value of a reflective life." I heard it all. But there was no way for any of it to mean very much to me. I was a scholarship boy at the time, busily laddering my way up the rungs of education. To pass an examination, I copied down exactly what my teachers told me. It would require many more years of schooling (an inevitable miseducation) in which I came to trust the silence of reading and the habit of abstracting from immediate experience—moving away from a life of closeness and immediacy I remembered with my parents, growing older—before I turned unafraid to desire the past, and thereby achieved what had eluded me for so long—the end of education.

Analyze

1. What type of family does Rodriguez come from?
2. What are some of the conflicts he feels between school and home?
3. What is a scholarship boy? Do you think we all fit this model to some extent? Explain.

Explore

1. In groups, discuss whether you have noticed any changes in your interactions with friends who have continued in school as opposed to those
   who have not. Compare and contrast the results of the changes and
   share why you believe this took place.
2. Whether you have moved away to go to school or are still home,
   explore how your interactions at home have changed since you have
   been in school. How do you see your parents? How do they treat you?
   Ask them to write down or talk about any changes they have seen in
   you. Write an essay that balances the two views, your parents' view
   about you, and yours about them. Alternatively, create a comic book
   showing the changes and differences.
3. Write a professional letter to Rodriguez giving him advice on how to
   balance what he calls the "scholarship boy" and the idea of "the end of
   education" that he expresses at the end of his essay.

Cathy Davidson
"Project Classroom Makeover"

Davidson has published more than twenty books, including *Closing: The Life
and Death of an American Factory, The Future of Thinking: Learning Institu-
tions in a Digital Age,* and *Now You See It: How Technology and Brain Science
Will Transform Schools and Business for the 21st Century.* She is the Ruth F.
DeVarney Professor of English and John Hope Franklin Humanities Institute
Professor of Interdisciplinary Studies at Duke University, and cofounder of
Duke's Humanities, Arts, Science, and Technology Advanced Collaboratory.
President Obama appointed her in 2011 to the National Council on the
Humanities, and in 2012 she was corecipient of an Educators of the Year
award from the World Technology Network. In this excerpt from *Now You See
It,* Davidson argues that the pedagogy that schools use is antiquated for a
digitally savvy twenty-first-century student body and workforce.

What are some ways that you would recommend that schools could integrate creativity into all the majors?

Do you remember the classic story by Washington Irving, "The Legend of Sleepy Hollow"? It was written in 1820 and features a parody of the pompous schoolmaster in the form of Ichabod Crane, a homely, gawky, and self-satisfied pedant who is confident in his role as a dispenser of knowledge. He knows what does and does not constitute knowledge worth having and is equally sure that students must be drilled in that knowledge and tested to make sure they measure up. If you blindfolded Ichabod Crane, spun him around, and set him down in a twenty-first-century classroom, he would be baffled by electricity, dumbfounded by moving images, confused by the computers and cell phones, but he'd know exactly where to stand, and he'd know exactly where he stood.

It's shocking to think of how much the world has changed since the horse-and-buggy days of Sleepy Hollow and how little has changed within the traditional classroom in America. On March 10, 2010, the National Governors Association and the Council of Chief State School Officers even called for "sweeping new school standards that could lead to students across the country using the same math and English textbooks and taking the same tests, replacing a patchwork of state and local systems in an attempt to raise student achievement nationwide." Ichabod Crane lives!

What in the world is going on? In the past in America, times of enormous innovation in the rest of society, including in technology and in industry, have also been times of tremendous innovation in education. What has happened to us? Rather than thinking of ways we can be preparing our students for their future, we seem determined to prepare them for our past.

Literally. The current passion for national standards is reminiscent of the conversations on education at our country's beginnings, back in 1787, the year the U.S. Constitution was adopted. Technology was changing the world then, too. At the time of the signing of the Constitution, the new invention of steam-powered presses, coupled with the invention of machine-made ink and paper, made for mass printing of cheap books and newspapers, putting print into the hands of middle-class readers for the first time in human history. The new institution of the circulating library made books available even to the working poor. Books proliferated; newspapers sprang up everywhere. And that's when a cry for standards and public education was born in America, in response to a new democratic government that needed informed citizens and new technologies of print that made books and newspapers widely available.

Thomas Jefferson himself advocated that America had to launch a "cru- 5 sade against ignorance" if the nation was to survive as an independent representative democracy. By 1791, when the Bill of Rights was added to the U.S. Constitution, seven states were making provisions for public education. There was not yet anything like an "educational system" in the United States, though. Education was attended to unevenly by local, regional, state, and private institutions, some secular, some sectarian, an inheritance that continues to this day in the form of state-controlled educational policy, local and regional school boards, and other decentralized means of oversight.

Horace Mann, whose name can be found over the entrance of many public schools in America, was the first great champion of national educational reform. The son of a farmer of limited means, Mann clawed his way to an education, earning money by braiding straw to pay the local tuitions for the elementary schools he attended for only six weeks at a time, leaving the rest of his time free to help with family farming operations. He enrolled at Brown University at age twenty, graduated in three years as valedictorian of the class of 1819, and dedicated himself to the creation of the "common schools," which after around 1840 became the predecessor of a free, publicly supported education system.

The common schools were scheduled around the agricultural year so farm kids could attend too. The schools were open to both boys and girls, regardless of class, although several states explicitly forbade the attendance of nonwhite children. The schools were locally controlled, with the kind of local politics governing curriculum and textbook assignments then that we see now in the state-by-state regulation of education, even after our "national educational policy" has been adopted.

Mandatory, compulsory public schooling developed over the course of the last half of the nineteenth century and got its full wind at the turn into the twentieth century as part of America's process of industrialization. Public education was seen as the most efficient way to train potential workers for labor in the newly urbanized factories. Teaching them control, socializing them for the mechanized, routinized labor of the factory was all part of the educational imperative of the day. Whether meant to calm the supposedly unruly immigrant populace coming to American shores or to urbanize farmers freshly arriving in the city, education was designed to train unskilled workers to new tasks that required a special, dedicated form of attention. School was thought to be the right training ground for discipline and uniformity. Kids started attending school at the same age, passed through a carefully graduated system, and were tested systematically on a standardized curriculum, with subjects that were taught in time blocks throughout the day. In ways large and small, the process mimicked the forms of specialized labor on the assembly line, as well as the divisions of labor (from the CEO down to the manual laborers) in the factory itself.

Many features now common in twenty-first-century public education began as an accommodation to the new industrial model of the world ushered in during the last part of the nineteenth century. With machines that needed to run on schedule and an assembly line that required human precision and efficiency, schools began to place a great emphasis on time and timeliness. Curriculum, too, was directed toward focusing on a task, including the mastery of a specified syllabus of required learning. "Efficiency" was the byword of the day, in the world of work and in the world of school. Learning to pay attention as directed—through rote memorization and mastery of facts—was important, and schools even developed forms of rapid-fire question-and-answer, such as the spelling bee or the math bee. This was a new skill, different from the elite models of question-and-answer based on the Socratic method; the agrarian model of problem solving, in which one is responsible for spotting a problem and solving it (whether a wilted corn tassel or an injured horse); and the apprenticeship model of the guild wherein one learned a craft by imitating the skills of a master. An assembly line is far more regular and regulated. One person's tardiness, no matter how good the excuse, can destroy everyone else's productivity on the line. Mandatory and compulsory schooling for children was seen as a way of teaching basic knowledge—including the basic knowledge of tasks, obedience, hierarchy, and schedules. The school bell became a symbol of public education in the industrial era.

10   So did specialization. With the advent of the assembly line, work became segmented. A worker didn't perform a whole job but one discrete task and then passed the job on to the next person and the next and so forth down the assembly line. The ideal of labor efficiency displaced the ideal of artisanship, with increased attention paid to the speed and accuracy of one kind of contribution to a larger industrial process. Focused attention to a task became the ideal form of attention, so different from, for example, the farmer on his horse scanning his land for anything that might look out of place or simply in need of care.

By 1900, state and regional schools were becoming the norm, replacing locally managed ones, and by 1918, every state had passed laws mandating children to attend elementary school or more. A concession was made to Catholics in that they could create a separate, parochial school system that would also meet these state regulations, another legacy that comes down to the present in the form of "faith-based schools."

During the first six decades of the twentieth century, as America ascended to the position of a world power, the rhetoric of education followed suit, with an increasing emphasis on producing leaders. While the nineteenth-century common schools had focused on elementary education, the twentieth-century focus was increasingly on the institution of high school, including improving graduation rates. In 1900, approximately 15 percent of the U.S. population received a high school diploma, a number that increased to around 50 percent by 1950.

After World War II, there was a rapid expansion of both high schools and higher education, invigorated after 1957 when the Russians surprised the world by launching *Sputnik,* the first man-made object ever to orbit the earth. As America competed against Russian science in the Cold War, policy makers placed more and more emphasis on educational attainment. Many economists argue that America's economic growth through the 1960s was fueled by this educational expansion.

Robert Schwartz, dean of the Harvard Graduate School of Education, notes that since the last quarter of the twentieth century, the pattern of educational expansion that has characterized the United States from the Revolutionary War forward has changed. Since 1975, American educational attainment has leveled off or even dropped while there has been a dramatic increase in the number of jobs requiring exploratory, creative problem solving typically encouraged by postsecondary education. We are seeing the first signs that our education system is slipping in comparison to our needs.

The current high school graduation rate is roughly the same as it was in 15 1975, approximately 75 percent. Our graduation rate from four-year colleges is 28 percent, also roughly the same as it was thirty-five years ago. That this has even remained consistent in the face of all that has changed in the last thirty-five years is remarkable enough, a credit to both the drive and quality of American students and the patchwork, piecemeal reforms we've used to hold the system together. Yet while we've been holding steady, other countries have made rapid gains. Whereas in the 1960s we ranked first in the proportion of adults with high school degrees, we now rank thirteenth on the list of the thirty countries surveyed by the Organisation for Economic Co-operation and Development (OECD), an organization that coordinates statistics from market-based democracies to promote growth. By contrast, South Korea has moved from twenty-seventh place on that list to our old number one spot.

Most troubling is what happened from 1995 to 2005. During this one decade, the United States dropped from second to fifteenth place in college completion rates among OECD nations. For the wealthiest and most powerful nation on earth to rank fifteenth is nothing short of a national disgrace. This is especially the case, given that our system of education *presumes* college preparation is the ideal, even in environments where most kids are not going on to college. By that standard, we are failing.

It's not that we cared about education before 1975 but don't today. Our heart is not the problem. Look at the numbers. The Swiss are the only people on earth who spend more per child on public education than Americans. According to OECD, we spend over $11,000 per year per child on public education. That's more than double the rate of South Korea. Education spending accounts for more than 7 percent of our GDP. However, the OECD statistics show that our graduation rates now are roughly on a par with those of Turkey and Mexico, not nations to which we like to compare ourselves by other indicators of our power or success.

It is little wonder that educators and parents are constantly reacting to the comparative, global numbers with ever more strident calls for standards. The problem, however, is the confusion of "high standards" with "standardization." Our national educational policy depends on standardized tests, but it is not at all clear that preparing students to achieve high test scores is equivalent to setting a high standard for what and how kids should know and learn.

The real issue isn't that our schools are too challenging. It's the opposite. Among the top quartile of high school students, the most frequent complaint and cause of disaffection from schooling is boredom and lack of rigor. That also happens to be true among the lowest group, for whom low expectations lead to low motivation. Kids aren't failing because school is too hard but because it doesn't interest them. It doesn't capture their attention.

20   Relevance has been proved to be a crucial factor for keeping students in high school, especially mid- and lower-level students. Tie what kids learn in school to what they can use in their homes, their families, and their neighborhood— and vice versa—and not surprisingly, that relevance kicks their likelihood of staying in school up a few notches. Because in the United States (but not in many countries with higher college attendance), going to college requires money for tuition, our emphasis on college as the grail of secondary education

only rubs in its inaccessibility (its irrelevance) to lower-income kids—a fact that contributes to high school dropouts. Finally, for all groups, and especially for students in the lowest-achieving group, relationships with teachers and counselors who believe in them and support them (often against peer, familial, or cultural pressure) is a determining factor in remaining in school. These key factors for educational success—rigor, relevance, and relationships—have been dubbed the new three *Rs,* with student-teacher ratio being particularly important. Small class size has been proved to be one of the single most significant factors in kids' staying in and succeeding in school. Twenty seems to be the magic number. Even on a neurological level, brain researchers have shown that kids improve with directed, special attention to their own skills and interests, the opposite of our move toward standardization.

The biggest problem we face now is the increasing mismatch between traditional curricular standards of content-based instruction and the new forms of thinking required by our digital, distributed workplace. At any level—blue collar or white collar—those jobs requiring "routine thinking skills" are increasingly performed by machine or outsourced to nations with a lower standard of living than the United States. Yet virtually all of contemporary American education is still based on the outmoded model of college prep that prepares students for middle management and factory jobs that, because of global rearrangements in labor markets, in large part no longer exist.

We've all seen industrial jobs for manual laborers dwindle in the United States and other First World economies, either taken over by machines or outsourced abroad to workers who are unprotected by unions or fair labor laws. The same is now the case for routinized white-collar office jobs. In exploitative "digital sweatshops" all around the world, workers at minimal wages can do everything from preparing your tax return to playing your online strategy games for you, so your avatar can be staging raids while you are on the trading floor or in your executive office on Wall Street.

To be prepared for jobs that have a real future in the digital economy, one needs an emphasis on creative thinking, at all levels. By this I mean the kind of thinking that cannot be computerized and automated. This creative thinking requires attention to surprise, anomaly, difference, and disruption, and an ability to switch focus, depending on what individual, unpredictable problems might arise. Perhaps surprisingly, these noncomputational jobs, impervious to automation, occur at all levels across the blue-collar and white-collar spectrum. Many of these jobs require highly specialized and dexterous problem-solving abilities or interpersonal skills—but do not require a college degree.

We were criticized for the iPod experiment. Many treated it as if it were an extravagance, superfluous to real learning and real education. But the iPod experiment exemplifies a form of inquiry-based problem solving wherein solutions are not known in advance and cannot be more successfully outsourced to either a computer or to a Third World laborer who performs repetitive tasks over and over in horrific conditions at minimal wages. The new global economics of work (whatever one thinks about it politically) is not likely to change, and so we must. And that change begins with schooling. Learning to think in multiple ways, with multiple partners, with a dexterity that cannot be computerized or outsourced, is no longer a luxury but a necessity. Given the altered shape of global labor, the seemingly daring iPod experiment turns out actually to be, in the long run, a highly pragmatic educational model.

25   Part of our failure rate in contemporary education can be blamed on the one-size-fits-all model of standards that evolved over the course of the twentieth century; as we narrow the spectrum of skills that we test in schools, more and more kids who have skills outside that spectrum will be labeled as failures. As what counts as learning is increasingly standardized and limited, increasing numbers of students learn in ways that are not measured by those standards. This is the lesson of attention blindness yet again: If you measure narrowly, you see results just as narrowly. In other words, the more standardized our assessment, the more kids fail. Their failure is then diagnosed as a learning disability or a disorder. But they are failing when assessed by a standard that has almost nothing to do with how they learn online or—more important—what skills they need in a digital age.

The mismatch is just wrong. It's as if we're still turning out assembly-line kids on an assembly-line model in an infinitely more varied and variable customizing, remixed, washable, user-generated, crowdsourced world. As long as we define their success by a unified set of standards, we will continue to miss their gifts, we will not challenge their skills, and, in the end, we will lose them from our schools just as, implicitly, we have lost interest in them.

We need far more inquiry-based opportunities for our kids. It doesn't have to be as expensive or as radical as the iPod experiment. The world is full of problems to solve that cost little except imagination, relevant learning, and careful guidance by a teacher with the wisdom to *not control* every outcome or to think that the best way to measure is by keeping each kid on the same page of the same book at the same time.

I recently visited a middle school where one girl with green- and blue-striped hair, creatively and eccentrically dyed, sat against the wall, remote from the other kids, as drawn into herself as she could possibly be without disappearing, looking for all the world like the kid who will never hear anything. When I, a stranger, came into the classroom, some of the other kids fussed over my unexpected appearance there, and my *difference:* One girl admired my purple leather jacket, another asked if I was an artist, because I was wearing a black turtleneck and skinny black pants. One boy asked about the image of an electric fan on my long, illustrated scarf from South Africa, and a waggish little boy hummed, with perfect pitch, "Who's That Lady?" when he saw me in his classroom. When I asked how in the world a twelve-year-old knew the Isley Brothers, he said snappily, "The Swiffer commercial." There was a lot of buzz in the class about the visitor, in other words. The green-haired girl in the corner slowly shifted her gaze in my direction, gave the smallest upward movement at the corner of her lips before returning to her frown and letting her eyes move back to outer space again, away from the strange visitor, determinedly *not there.*

I thought of a blog post I'd read earlier that week by the prolific business writer Seth Godin, creator of the popular user-generated community Web site Squidoo. Godin's post was called "What You Can Learn from a Lousy Teacher," and his list of what you can learn from the teacher you cannot please included: "Grades are an illusion, your passion and insight are reality; your work is worth more than mere congruence to an answer key; persistence in the face of a skeptical authority figure is a powerful ability; fitting in is a short-term strategy, standing out pays off in the long run; and if you care enough about work to be criticized, you've learned enough for today." This remote young woman against the wall didn't look defeated by school. There was something *resolute* in her. I could sense that she had, somehow, taken in intuitively the kinds of lessons Godin was preaching, even if it would take her another decade to fully realize what, in her body language, she was already showing she'd absorbed.

She stayed that way, barely making eye contact with the teacher or any 30 other students, until drawings begun during the previous class were handed around to be worked on again. The transformation I witnessed then was so rapid and thorough that I thought of what Pygmalion must have seen the first time his statue came to life. She went from being still, glassy-eyed, self-contained, and entirely not-present to a concentrated, focused, dedicated bundle of intensity. She still didn't interact with the other kids, but all eyes were on her as she began her day's work on a highly detailed line drawing she was executing. Unlike the bustle at the other tables in the room, there was a silence around her, with the kids practically tiptoeing into the circle of her aura to watch, not speaking to her or to one another, then moving away. I was dying to see her drawing but even more interested in the compact energy she'd created around herself and the other kids, generated from the passion of her drawing. Rather than interrupt that magic, I moved away.

Later in the day, I saw her waiting for her ride home, in the homeroom period at the end of the day, and again the sullen remoteness of I-am-not-here returned. After all the kids had gone, I asked her teacher to tell me about her. She'd been diagnosed as profoundly learning disabled, with attention deficit disorder. Her parents sent her to this magnet arts school after she had failed elsewhere. At home, the only thing she seemed to enjoy doing was doodling, but her elementary school had laid off its art teachers, sacrificed to educational cutbacks and the fact that, in our standardized forms of testing, there is no EOG (end-of-grade exam) for art. Art is therefore an add-on that many public schools cannot afford. It was only at the new school that her skills as an artist were recognized. She quickly went from the class failure to the class artist. She mastered the editing tools on the class computer and transferred her imagination and creativity there, too, much to the admiration of her classmates.

I think again about what learning disabilities signify for kids today. In the *Diagnostic and Statistical Manual of Mental Disorders* (the infamous DSM), attention deficit disorder is characterized by distractibility, frequent switching from one activity to another, boredom with a task after just a brief time trying to execute it, and difficulty organizing and completing a task or in focusing on a task in which one is not interested. That last phrase is key. ADD almost never applies to *all* activities, only those in which the child is not interested. This isn't a disability (a fixed biological or cognitive condition) but a disposition (susceptible to change depending on the environment). Keep the kids interested and ADD goes away.

The girl with the green hair has special skills that show up nowhere on her compulsory EOG state tests, on which she continues to score poorly. "Your work is worth more than mere congruence to an answer key." This girl's talents don't count on those tests, and yet she has a special and valued ability that cannot be replaced by a computer program. The problem is that her fate is to a large extent controlled by her performance on the EOG tests, and unless the adults in her life—teachers and parents—are resolute in shepherding her along a path where her talents are valued, they may ultimately wind up undeveloped.

I identified with this girl. When I was in school, my talents had been math and writing, and there was a teacher, Miss Schmidt, who saw those gifts, despite my abysmal test scores, despite the fact that we had to memorize the preamble to the Constitution and the Gettysburg Address to graduate from eighth grade and I just couldn't. I tried and failed over and over many times, staying after school, trying to say it out loud and failing again. Miss Schmidt was feeling certain that I wasn't really trying but just being "obstinate." Then, during one of our painful after-class sessions, she had a hunch. She offered me the opportunity to write an essay instead, one essay about each brief text I was failing to memorize. I stayed up all night working on this and returned the next day with my project. My scrawl filled every page in a small spiral binder—*two hundred* pages.

I remember her eyes widening as she took this smudgy, worn binder 35
from my hand. She looked through it in disbelief and bewilderment as she turned over pages and pages of my barely readable handwriting. There were even footnotes. "You still don't have them memorized, do you?" Miss Schmidt asked. I shook my head. After a moment, she got out the special state certification and, beside my name, put the check mark I needed to graduate from middle school. I'd passed.

Sometimes you learn from the good teachers too. It's not easy to be a good teacher all the time. The girl with the green hair was lucky to find one who honored her talent. Before I left his classroom, I told him, if he thought it appropriate, to let the girl know that the visitor, that professor from Duke University, had noticed her beautiful artwork and admired it. I told him, if he thought it appropriate, to let the girl know that, when the visitor was her age, her hair was purple.

Analyze

1. What is Ichabod Crane's occupation?
2. Who said we had to "launch a crusade against ignorance"?
3. What is the number one complaint about education made by the top quartile of high school graduates?

Explore

1. Davidson stresses that making school relevant, in our schools, families, and neighborhoods, for low and high achievers is what keeps kids in school. Write an essay reflecting on what you believe keeps and will keep kids in school. Include your own experiences as valid examples.

2. Davidson claims that "To be prepared for jobs that have a real future in the digital economy, one needs an emphasis on creative thinking, at all levels. By this I mean the kind of thinking that cannot be computerized and automated. This creative thinking requires attention to surprise, anomaly, difference, and disruption, and an ability to switch focus, depending on what individual, unpredictable problems might arise." If you know your major, look over the required classes you will need to take. Create a PowerPoint listing these classes, in another slide show a list with the classes you would cross out and why, and finally in a last list show your new required classes for your major and explain your choices. Use this quote as your inspiration, that is, what would foment creativity of the type Davidson mentions in your major or career choice?

3. In small groups generate a list of ten problems or things you see as wrong in your town or school. Create a master list from all the lists. Have each group select one item that they will attempt to resolve. Write a description of the problem, why it is a problem, how long it has been a problem, and who it affects. Answer why you believe this problem has gone unresolved, and then propose a solution to your problem.

Forging Connections

1. Villanueva says, "Biculturalism does not mean to me an equal ease with two cultures. That is an ideal. Rather, biculturalism means the tensions within, which are caused by being unable to deny the old or the new." In "Rhode Island", Lahiri also explores the experience Villanueva defines here. Through these two stories and their examples, discuss the tensions to which Villanueva refers.

2. Using the readings from this chapter, write an essay discussing why you are in school, and why you are at the school you are at.

3. Write about how *Brown v. the Board of Education* and *Living with Myths* speak in different ways about the same issues.

Looking Further

1. From the essays we have read across these first three chapters, write about the most important elements you have discovered about your identity—who you are—in light of the three chapters' titles and questions. Write your response in the first person and use references to the readings.

2. Taking into account these first three chapters' focus on name, location, and education, write about a theme that connects all three chapters. In making your connections, make sure to reference essays from each chapter.

3. Using the first three chapters' readings and themes, create a PowerPoint presentation or write an essay arguing how you see the role that identity, literacy, and creativity serve in your life.

4

What Do You Do? Work in America

Many of us have had a job. We have worked, oftentimes several jobs, are in between jobs, are looking for a job, or have hopes and plans for a career job. We spend a good part of our lives preparing for work with schooling, degrees, certifications, and then the actual job hunt. The job hunt involves a lot of preparation. We need to look for ads online and in the newspaper for positions that relate to our skills and degrees. We need to prepare and keep updated our résumés, we need to write carefully crafted job application letters, and we then hope to receive a call or e-mail invitation for an interview. Even if we make it that far, we still have to interview well, and we still are competing against many others. If we do not receive a job offer, we might call into question our sense of our abilities and of who we are. We question what we did wrong, what the job winner did right, or what the other person did that we did not or were unable to do.

On the other hand, when we have a job that we have wanted for a long time and have worked hard to attain, we proudly state: I am an accountant, a lawyer, a banker, a real estate broker, a teacher, and so forth. People will ask us what we do as a means of gauging who we are. Our judgments are based on what people do. When people lose their jobs, they often retain their former positions as a means of defining themselves, preferring to say something like "I was a broker." Jobs become an important component to the definition of who we are.

In this chapter we will consider jobs and work from several different lenses. For our first reading, we start with Smith's interview, "Work, in Six Words," in which he asks listeners to share crafted six-word descriptions that capture their professions. These six-word epithets highlight just how much we associate our jobs and titles with who we are and what our positions are in society. Zaslow, in his essay, "The Most Praised Generation Goes to Work," talks about the current generation's propensity for the need for praise for anything they complete or participate in. He argues that they do not need to be the best or even in the top half; they need praise for just showing up. In "Digital Natives Invade the Workplace," Rainie discusses some of the psychological and intellectual differences that younger workers bring to the workplace. The findings help us understand why digital natives do things differently in the workplace, and, in some cases, even better, though their multitasking can be misconstrued as disinterest.

Our next two essays explore the experiences of minorities in the workforce in America. De Palma's "Fifteen Years on the Bottom Rung" compares the lives of two generations of immigrants in the United States. One, a Greek native who came illegally right after World War II, worked hard, and had many different opportunities, such as easier access to citizenship, which changed his and his family's social and economic status here. The other, an undocumented Mexican immigrant, experiences constant setbacks that stem from not having the right paperwork, despite working as hard as his World War II counterpart. The next by Pulitzer Prize winner Studs Terkel is an excerpt about the work experiences of Stephen Cruz from *American Dreams: Lost and Found*. Unlike De Palma's two workers, Stephen Cruz is a successful Latino, but his story is about a different type of workplace challenge.

Our final three essays take a hard look at perceptions of work and the reality of jobs and wealth in America. In "We Are Not All Created Equal: The Truth about the American Class System," Marche argues that the American Dream—work hard and you will become successful and wealthy—is a myth that needs to be exposed, while Smith's essay surprises us with what 65,000 respondents indicate as "The Happiest and Unhappiest Jobs in America." Last, while Carbado and Gulati focus on the black experience and identity in the U.S. workforce, their story sheds light on how we all are actors at times in our social and professional lives.

The readings in this chapter ask us to explore what we do and what we experience in our workplaces. The stories do not offer simple narratives, such as I am an accountant or I am a waiter; rather, they share ideas that open up notions of how much we associate our jobs with our identities and our dreams and goals for our children and ourselves. The message of the stories in this chapter highlights that the grass is not always greener on the other side, that someone who has a job we would like may experience as many difficulties as we presently face or more, even though they earn more money. Calling to mind the task set by our first essay, which is to sum up our work experiences in six words, it might behoove us to say that the underlying message of the readings in this chapter is as follows: *Life is work, so enjoy it.*

NPR
"Work, in Six Words"

The literacy narrative for this reading comes from NPR's *Talk of the Nation*®. In it, Neal Conan interviews Larry Smith, co-founder of *Smith Magazine*, about his current project, "Work, in Six Words." Through his magazine, he has published several successful books that deal with finding six words to describe subjects ranging from stories of love and life, stories about pregnancy, and even stories about brushes with fame. In this interview, Smith shares some six-liners listeners have shared. For more on this interview in audio and text from National Public Radio, visit http://www.npr.org.

How would you summarize your job, current school experience, or a class of yours in six words?

NEAL CONAN (host): It's Labor Day, a time to celebrate, remember, commiserate about work. It might be tough to sum up an entire career or years of pent-up anger in just six words, but the folks at *Smith Magazine* want you to give it a shot. For a few years now, they've been collecting six-word memoirs from Valentine's Day to brushes with fame to pregnancy. We want to hear your six word memoir about work on this Labor Day. Tell us your lessons learned, why you do what you do, even something about your boss, but boil it down to six words, please. The number: 800-989-8255. E-mail: talk@npr.org. You can also join the conversation on our website. That's at npr.org, click on TALK OF THE NATION. Joining us from our bureau in New York is Larry Smith, cofounder of *Smith Magazine*. Nice to have you back on the program.

LARRY SMITH: Oh, so good to be here, Neal.

CONAN: And one from the website, and it might hit close to home for you: Happiness is being your own boss.

SMITH: Well, that's true. You know, work—it's a tough time right now with people in jobs and the economy, but we saw a lot of really positive things in just six words. From the very specific: dwelled on past—became an anthropologist.

(SOUNDBITE OF LAUGHTER)

5   **SMITH:** . . . to something like: the five patients I'll always remember, which was one of our winners of this contest. And we learned—when I talk to this woman, she was a nurse and it was about learning more from her patients than, you know, I think giving them and how these people really inspired her.

CONAN: What kind of—what volume of response do you get with these contests, in this one in particular?

SMITH: Well, we've done a bunch of six word memoir projects as you've mentioned. And what works for six words is when you tap in to something that people are passionate about, obviously, life, love. We've done six words on coming home from war with veterans groups. But we got about 7,500 responses this summer around a few different topic areas. Why I do what I do, lessons, bosses, and what inspires me to do my very best work.

CONAN: There are a couple of others here from your website: Partied with managers, now I'm unemployed.

SMITH: And perhaps this is a corollary: Never completely disrobe at the office.

(SOUNDBITE OF LAUGHTER)

10   **CONAN:** May have been fed in by the same person at different times.

SMITH: Tough night.

CONAN: Business suits suck. Hawaiian shirts rock.

SMITH: Right and, you know, just six words, but you sort of, you get the whole story right there. Watch your back, cover your butt—a very good six word life lesson. You know, we—the six word project is kind of—it's a compliment to a study this big consulting group, Mercer did. And they did all this data, massive research. They said, all right, what if we added a populist kind of piece of this research and just ask people to place where people are used to selling up their life, their work lives, their love life, their own life in just six words. And I feel like, you know, we're going to make a book, as we always, do of some of our favorites and you can read all the management books in the world and, you know, some of them are great. But I kind of feel there's just a lot to learn about the workplace in just six words.

> "Watch your back, cover your butt—a very good six word life lesson."

CONAN: I remember books like, you know, *The 60 Second Manager* and that sort of stuff. You can—the best of these are very lyrical and tell great stories. Yeah, sure, the worst ones are like bumper stickers, but the best are really good.

SMITH: Yeah, they are really good. And, you know, we really believe at *Smith Magazine* that if you ask regular people and most of these people, you know, I call them and I say, they, you won. You know, you won one of the prizes and they say, oh, my God. I'm not a writer. And my point is, no, in fact, you are a writer. And when you write something like, you know, who doesn't love the payroll lady, and I call up Mindy in Portland to say you're a winner and she's a payroll lady. You know, it's so fun.

(SOUNDBITE OF LAUGHTER)

CONAN: Here is one that we've gotten just in this hour. This from Martha in Hoboken: Grandpa drove horses, I massage websites.

SMITH: And, yeah, you see in two generations the whole arc. And a lot of people, I mean, across all the six word memoir projects, they talk about their parents, of course, the influence, but their grandparents. And I think it's because in some sense, like, lessons sometimes skip a generation, you know, one of my own six word memoirs on the work life is in fact about my dad and its lesson which was: dad said do one thing well. As it turns out, when I finally started listening to him and really focused on the six words, they're really started working out.

CONAN: Let's see if we could get some callers in on the conversation. We're asking for your six word memoirs on work. Larry Smith of *Smith Magazine* is with us.

SMITH: As it turns out, when I finally started listening to him and really focus on the six words, it really started working out.

15

20   **CONAN:** Let's see if we can get some callers in on the conversation. We're asking for your six-word memoirs on work. Larry Smith of *Smith Magazine* is with us. 800-989-8255. E-mail us: talk@npr.org. And let's start with Ron, and Ron is with us from Denver.

RON: Hello, there.

CONAN: Hi, there. What's your six word memoir on work?

RON: Air traffic control: excitement not good.

(SOUNDBITE OF LAUGHTER)

25   **CONAN:** Is there a punctuation mark there, a dash or a colon?

RON: Yeah, I want to see a comma in between there.

CONAN: A comma. OK.

SMITH: I was feeling a semicolon.

CONAN: Semicolon? OK. Do you . . .

30   **RON:** Yeah, that'll work.

CONAN: All right. Ron, I think that's a motto. Are you an air-traffic controller?

RON: Yes, I am. I just left work. I'm on my way home.

CONAN: Drive carefully, because another place where excitement is not good is on the drive home.

RON: I've got hands-free Bluetooth.

35   **CONAN:** OK. Thanks very much for the call.

SMITH: That's a T-shirt waiting to happen.

CONAN: That's a T-shirt waiting to happen. Here's an e-mail from Bill in Branford, Connecticut: muscles flex—home, bridges, nations rise. I like that. That's . . .

SMITH: That's like the story of America here on Labor Day, isn't it?

CONAN: On Labor Day, you can—you can see that sweaty 1930s poster coming to life.

40   **SMITH:** Absolutely. What's that great painter who does all those great—those rebuilding—Thomas Harding—I can't remember. But, yeah, it's a bit—and, you know, the thing is, we see things about—we see something like have a passion for flawless formatting, right? And so that's someone who's probably doing Excel all day, right, or copy editing. And then you have people working with their hands, building this nation. Whether it's metaphorical or, in fact, quite specific, it's a version of the work life. And it makes—we can really get the image we love in a great way.

CONAN: Do you get persnickety? For example, on one of your websites is: Beware the ears of the water cooler.

SMITH: I'll tell you, there were many themes, and one theme is about food and co-workers, such as: Butter up the HR department with chocolate. But there were a lot of six word memoirs about the water cooler and office gossip and, you know, sort of, like warnings, which is one—you know, one of my favorites was: Somebody at work reads your blog.

(SOUNDBITE OF LAUGHTER)

SMITH: Very modern six words about work. And, you know, if you're graduating college right now, like, heed those six words, because somebody at work does read your blog, and probably your Facebook page.

CONAN: Let's go next to Nabil(ph), Nabil with us from Utica, in New York.

NABIL: Hi. How's it going? Mine's actually short and very interpretive. It's: What matters is what we do.

CONAN: What matters—that's . . .

NABIL: What matters is what we do.

CONAN: I think that—that's another T-shirt waiting to happen.

(SOUNDBITE OF LAUGHTER)

SMITH: And some of the six word memoirs, like that one, are very much, you know, like life-work mottos. Tell me I can't, I will. And it, you know, it is more general. But—and really, I mean, you feel a little bit of reminder of what work was supposed to be, some of the lessons you may have gotten along the way and forgotten.

CONAN: Or practical advice. And Nabil, thanks very much for the call. This is from Daniel in Cincinnati: Take care of the regular customers. That could be posted everywhere in a workspace.

SMITH: Absolutely, whether your customer is, in fact, the U.S. government, or someone you're making Excel spreadsheet for.

CONAN: Let's go next to Crystal(ph), and Crystal with us from Fresno.

CRYSTAL: Yes. Mine is, not—I'm not just a sky waitress.

(SOUNDBITE OF LAUGHTER)

CONAN: I take it you are an air hostess.

CRYSTAL: I am.

CONAN: And you are treated like a waitress a lot, I guess?

CRYSTAL: Oh, boy, yeah. They're amazed when I tell them I used to do caviar in first class. They just laugh, and they just demand. And they don't realize we're trying our best, but we don't have 7-11 upstairs.

(SOUNDBITE OF LAUGHTER)

CONAN: And have people become more obstreperous in these days of evermore crowded flights?

CRYSTAL: Well, I don't blame them. The seats do seem to be getting smaller. Maybe 'm just getting wider, but I—they are a little short with us. But—and the good majority, they understand, and they're kind. But you hear one person (technical difficulties) flying, and they comment on how we're just sky waitresses. So they don't realize we went school and we chose—some of us chose this path, even after graduating from college, because we wanted to see the world.

60   CONAN: Crystal, thanks very much for the call. We appreciate it, and we appreciate the flight attendants who we encounter on our flights.

CRYSTAL: Oh, thank you so much.

CONAN: Appreciate that. Do you find that most people, Larry Smith, write in about their own profession?

SMITH: Well, they do both. I mean, so, Molly Ringwald, the actress, wrote a six word memoir unintentionally about work a while ago, and she says: Acting is not all I am. In a sense, it's not unlike—she's saying something different than being a sky waitress, right? But also, I—when I first heard that, I thought what the caller was saying was, you know, I—there are a lot of parts of me. I'm not just working on an airplane in the sky, but I have many multi-facets. But—so people did both. They were very general and very specific. You know, dwelled on past, became an anthropologist. That's pretty interesting, saying something about their personality and what direction they decided to go into.

CONAN: This, I think, from somebody who's probably in the profession referred to in the six word memoir: Law librarian? No one said interesting.

65   SMITH: Exactly. And then you get something like: Auditor, reality check of report cards. And they've just put it, you know, the—what—you don't—they've just kind of updated the idea of what is an auditor all the way back from grade school.

CONAN: We're talking with Larry Smith, cofounder of *Smith Magazine*, which, this summer, ran a contest on six word memoirs on work. 800-989-8255. If you'd like to participate, email us: talk@npr.org. And, well, like so many, this from a listener: Feel lucky to be working today. I can say that, too. You're listening to TALK OF THE NATION, coming to you from NPR News. And let's go next to—this is Jeff, and Jeff with us from DeKalb, Illinois.

JEFF: Yes. Hey. How are you doing?

CONAN: I'm good.

JEFF: Oh, glad to hear it. Mine—you see, I'm actually—I do a lot of temporary, part-time jobs, and so my resume is full of them. And mine is: I get better with each one.

(SOUNDBITE OF LAUGHTER)

70   CONAN: Temporary jobs. That's a—is that a career path all of its own?

JEFF: Oh, no. It's not. I'm—well, I'm a communications major, and I've been graduated for about three years, looking for a full-time job in radio, and two of my jobs are at radio stations. I've been an announcer at a speedway at our local speed track for stock-car racing. I've been a substitute teacher. I work in a factory now, packing plastic blisters that everybody hurts themselves trying to open. So, yeah, I've just kind of spanned out to all kinds of things, but still looking for that really genuinely golden job that I've been looking for, you know?

CONAN: But a couple of jobs in radio. I have to ask: Where did you spend all the money?

(SOUNDBITE OF LAUGHTER)

JEFF: Oh, yes. Well, one of them is—one of them's public radio, and one of them's just a local AM station, you know? So there you go.

(SOUNDBITE OF LAUGHTER)

CONAN: Jeff, good luck, and I hope you get out of the plastic bubble business real soon.

JEFF: Oh, thank you so much, Neal.   75

CONAN: Appreciate it.

SMITH: Well, you know, Jeff really points to a trend we saw, and I think (unintelligible) saw, as well, which is that, you know, the freelance culture, self-employed culture it's much bigger, I think, both by necessity and by design. People don't think about in the same way as our parents or grandparents did about one job, one career. And so one of my favorites is freelancer: always employee of the month.

(SOUNDBITE OF LAUGHTER)

CONAN: This is from Nurse Barb: Too tired to care, care anyway.

SMITH: Right. And that's that little bit of inspiration. So it's like: My job helps find the cure. You know, we don't know what nurse does. We don't know what that person finding the cure is, but they're getting up and they're just going, doing their job.

CONAN: And then there's the people who have a little attitude. This from a caller, labor: not just for babies anymore.   80

(SOUNDBITE OF LAUGHTER)

SMITH: Very nice for Labor Day.

CONAN: Let's go next to Rolfe, Rolfe with us from Apple Valley in Minnesota.

ROLFE: Academe marking territory, make ivory towers.

(SOUNDBITE OF LAUGHTER)

CONAN: Are you a toiler in the groves of academe?

ROLFE: I'm an adjunct professor at two places where I really love to work   85
and love the people, but I have seen some very awful territorial stuff that has nothing to do with idealism of teaching students and all that. And I think those are some of the worst things in academia. There are some wonderful things there, but I think the towers were originally shiny white, then something turned them a little ivory, off-colored.

CONAN: A little ecru stain there. Yes. OK. Rolfe, thanks very much for the call—phone call.

ROLFE: OK.

CONAN: Let's see if we go next to—this is Joe, Joe with us from Phoenix.

JOE: Yes.

90 **CONAN:** Go ahead. What's your six word memoir on work?

JOE: Wonderful vacation from home every day.

SMITH: You must have children.

JOE: I love my job, and sometimes it's easier to come to work than it is to be at home with my kids.

CONAN: And what do you do for a living, Joe?

95 **JOE:** I put peanuts on an airplane.

CONAN: You put peanuts on an airplane?

JOE: I stock planes for a great airline.

CONAN: And I, you know, I used to get so confused between, you know, having to choose between the lobster and the fillet. I'm glad now I just have peanuts to . . .

JOE: All I can say is at least you still get peanuts from us.

100 **CONAN:** OK.

SMITH: I just wrote you a six word memoir: I get high working for peanuts.

(SOUNDBITE OF LAUGHTER)

JOE: That's a good T-shirt. I could use that.

CONAN: A good T-shirt.

SMITH: I could go onto the T-shirt business.

105 **CONAN:** And I think the airline you may work for, Joe, they like T-shirts there.

JOE: They do, very much.

CONAN: Talk to you later. Bye-bye.

JOE: Thanks.

CONAN: This from Eugene: Never work, do what you love. Well, there's one of those affirmational ones. And this one from Leslie in St. Louis: Used to work; now I sing.

110 **SMITH:** You see—you also see a trend of people going from profession to passion. And when it works out, it's, you know, it's the best of both worlds. So there's one I really liked, amateur chocolatier: making life little sweeter.

CONAN: That's nice, too. That's nice, too. Let's see if we can go next to John, John with us from Lansing.

JOHN: Good afternoon. Mine is: My father taught me to work.

CONAN: And what did your father do for a living?

JOHN: Well, my father was the consummate salesman.

115 **CONAN:** The consummate salesman. And how did he teach you?

JOHN: Well, I watched what he did, and I do what he did. And that was get up every day and go to work and be good to people. And as a salesman, his favorite line was—someone would say, I want to buy that car. My father would say, you can buy it. I'm not going to work real hard of selling it to you if he didn't like the particular car or if he knew its history. He had ethics. He was a great man.

CONAN: John, thanks for the—thanks for the story. Appreciate it. And, Larry Smith, just a few seconds left, can you give us the overall winner?

(SOUNDBITE OF MUSIC)

SMITH: Well, we had 12 winners, but one of our all-time favorites is— because I think we're going to have to give this one to Mindy: Who doesn't love the payroll lady?

CONAN: OK. We'll go out with this one from Laura in Cincinnati: Everyone happy? Don't drink the Kool-Aid. Larry Smith, thanks very much for your time, as always.

SMITH: It's been great talking six with you, Neal.   120

CONAN: Larry Smith, co-founder of *Smith Magazine*. Tomorrow, Philip Schultz: One way or another, his life has always been defined by a constant struggle with words. We'll talk to him about "My Dyslexia." Join us for that. I'm Neal Conan. It's the TALK OF THE NATION, from NPR News.

Analyze

1. In six words describe your job.
2. In six words describe your major.
3. In six words describe your class.

Explore

1. What effect does summing up your job in six words have, and what are some of the choices you have to make when trying to say something in six words?

2. In six words and six images, write your epitaph on a tombstone made of cardboard. Share these in class and discuss the choices you made in creating your own tombstone epitaph. What do you want to be re-membered by?

3. Write one six-liner for each of the first four chapters of *Identity: A Reader for Writers* that shows the role that identity serves for each theme.

Jeffery Zaslow
"The Most Praised Generation
Goes to Work"

Jeffery Zaslow wrote for the *Wall Street Journal* for four years and for the *Chicago Sun-Times* until his death. His well-known column, *All That Zazz*, at the *Chicago Sun-Times*, replaced Ann Landers's advice column. Zaslow won the column in a contest that he entered, coincidentally, so that he could write an article about the selection process. He published several successful books, such as *The Last Lecture* and *The Girls from Ames*. In this essay he argues that the current generation grew up receiving praise for everything and anything it did, no matter how mundane or average. As a result, it expects the same in the workplace.

Do you agree with Zaslow that our society has gone overboard in making everyone a winner, even just for participating in an event?

You, You, You—you really are special, you are! You've got everything going for you. You're attractive, witty, brilliant. "Gifted" is the word that comes to mind.

Childhood in recent decades has been defined by such stroking—by parents who see their job as building self-esteem, by soccer coaches who give every player a trophy, by schools that used to name one "student of the month" and these days name 40.

Now, as this greatest generation grows up, the culture of praise is reaching deeply into the adult world. Bosses, professors and mates are feeling the need to lavish praise on young adults, particularly twentysomethings, or else see them wither under an unfamiliar compliment deficit.

Employers are dishing out kudos to workers for little more than showing up. Corporations including Lands' End and Bank of America are hiring consultants to teach managers how to compliment employees using email, prize packages and public displays of appreciation. The 1,000-employee Scooter Store Inc., a power-wheelchair and scooter firm in New Braunfels, Texas, has a staff "celebrations assistant" whose job it is to throw confetti—25 pounds a week—at employees. She also passes out 100 to 500 celebratory helium balloons a week. The Container Store Inc. estimates that one of its 4,000 employees receives praise every 20 seconds, through such efforts as its "Celebration Voice Mailboxes."

Certainly, there are benefits to building confidence and showing attention. But some researchers suggest that inappropriate kudos are turning too many adults into narcissistic praise-junkies. The upshot: A lot of today's young adults feel insecure if they're not regularly complimented.

America's praise fixation has economic, labor and social ramifications. Adults who were overpraised as children are apt to be narcissistic at work and in personal relationships, says Jean Twenge, a psychology professor at San Diego State University. Narcissists aren't good at basking in other people's glory, which makes for problematic marriages and work relationships, she says.

Her research suggests that young adults today are more self-centered than previous generations. For a multi-university study released this year, 16,475 college students took the standardized narcissistic personality inventory, responding to such statements as "I think I am a special person." Students' scores have risen steadily since the test was first offered in 1982. The average college student in 2006 was 30% more narcissistic than the average student in 1982.

Praise Inflation

Employers say the praise culture can help them with job retention, and marriage counselors say couples often benefit by keeping praise a constant part of their interactions. But in the process, people's positive traits can be exaggerated until the words feel meaningless. "There's a runaway inflation of everyday speech," warns Linda Sapadin, a psychologist in Valley Stream, N.Y. These days, she says, it's an insult unless you describe a pretty girl as "drop-dead gorgeous" or a smart person as "a genius." "And no one wants to be told they live in a nice house," says Dr. Sapadin. " 'Nice' was once sufficient. That was a good word. Now it's a put-down."

The Gottman Institute, a relationship-research and training firm in Seattle, tells clients that a key to marital happiness is if couples make at least five times as many positive statements to and about each other as negative ones. Meanwhile, products are being marketed to help families make praise a part of their daily routines. For $32.95, families can buy the "You Are Special Today Red Plate," and then select one worthy person each meal to eat off the dish.

10   But many young married people today, who grew up being told regularly that they were special, can end up distrusting compliments from their spouses. Judy Neary, a relationship therapist in Alexandria, Va., says it's common for her clients to say things like: "I tell her she's beautiful all the time, and she doesn't believe it." Ms. Neary suspects: "There's a lot of insecurity, with people wondering, 'Is it really true?'"

"Young married people who've been very praised in their childhoods, particularly, need praise to both their child side and their adult side," adds Dolores Walker, a psychotherapist and attorney specializing in divorce mediation in New York.

Employers are finding ways to adjust. Sure, there are still plenty of surly managers who offer little or no positive feedback, but many withholders are now joining America's praise parade to hold on to young workers. They're being taught by employee-retention consultants such as Mark Holmes, who encourages employers to give away baseball bats with engravings ("Thanks for a home-run job") or to write notes to employees' kids ("Thanks for letting dad work here. He's terrific!").

Bob Nelson, billed as "the Guru of Thank You," counsels 80 to 100 companies a year on praise issues. He has done presentations for managers of companies such as Walt Disney Co. and Hallmark Cards Inc., explaining how different generations have different expectations. As he sees it, those over age 60 tend to like formal awards, presented publicly. But they're more laid back about needing praise, and more apt to say: "Yes, I get recognition every week. It's called a paycheck." Baby boomers, Mr. Nelson finds, often prefer being praised with more self-indulgent treats such as free massages for women and high-tech gadgets for men.

Workers under 40, he says, require far more stroking. They often like "trendy, name-brand merchandise" as rewards, but they also want near-constant feedback. "It's not enough to give praise only when they're exceptional, because for years they've been getting praise just for showing up," he says.

15   Mr. Nelson advises bosses: If a young worker has been chronically late for work and then starts arriving on time, commend him. "You need to recognize improvement. That might seem silly to older generations, but today, you have to do these things to get the performances you want," he says. Casey Priest, marketing vice president for Container Store, agrees. "When you set an expectation and an employee starts to meet it, absolutely praise them for it," she says.

Sixty-year-old David Foster, a partner at Washington, D.C., law firm Miller & Chevalier, is making greater efforts to compliment young associates—to tell them they're talented, hard-working and valued. It's not a natural impulse for him. When he was a young lawyer, he says, "If you weren't getting yelled at, you felt like that was praise."

But at a retreat a couple of years ago, the firm's 120 lawyers reached an understanding. Younger associates complained that they were frustrated; after working hard on a brief and handing it in, they'd receive no praise. The partners promised to improve "intergenerational communication." Mr. Foster says he feels for younger associates, given their upbringings. "When they're not getting feedback, it makes them very nervous."

Modern Pressures

Some younger lawyers are able to articulate the dynamics behind this. "When we were young, we were motivated by being told we could do anything if we believed in ourselves. So we respond well to positive feedback," explains 34-year-old Karin Crump, president of the 25,000-member Texas Young Lawyers Association.

Scott Atwood, president-elect of the Young Lawyers Division of the Florida Bar, argues that the yearning for positive input from superiors is more likely due to heightened pressure to perform in today's demanding firms. "It has created a culture where you have to have instant feedback or you'll fail," he says.

In fact, throughout history, younger generations have wanted praise 20 from their elders. As Napoleon said: "A soldier will fight long and hard for a bit of colored ribbon." But when it comes to praise today, "Gen X-ers and Gen Y-ers don't just say they want it. They are also saying they require it," says Chip Toth, an executive coach based in Denver. How do young workers say they're not getting enough? "They leave," says Mr. Toth.

Many companies are proud of their creative praise programs. Since 2004, the 4,100-employee Bronson Healthcare Group in Kalamazoo, Mich., has required all of its managers to write at least 48 thank-you or praise notes to underlings every year.

Universal Studios Orlando, with 13,000 employees, has a program in which managers give out "Applause Notes," praising employees for work well done. Universal workers can also give each other peer-to-peer "S.A.Y.

It!" cards, which stand for "Someone Appreciates You!" The notes are redeemed for free movie tickets or other gifts.

Bank of America has several formal rewards programs for its 200,000 employees, allowing those who receive praise to select from 2,000 gifts. "We also encourage managers to start every meeting with informal recognition," says Kevin Cronin, senior vice president of recognition and rewards. The company strives to be sensitive. When new employees are hired, managers are instructed to get a sense of how they like to be praised. "Some prefer it in public, some like it one-on-one in an office," says Mr. Cronin.

No More Red Pens

Some young adults are consciously calibrating their dependence on praise. In New York, Web-developer Mia Eaton, 32, admits that she loves being complimented. But she feels like she's living on the border between a twentysomething generation that requires overpraise and a thirtysomething generation that is less addicted to it. She recalls the pre-Paris Hilton, pre-reality-TV era, when people were famous—and applauded— for their achievements, she says. When she tries to explain this to younger colleagues, "they don't get it. I feel like I'm hurting their feelings because they don't understand the difference."

25   Young adults aren't always eager for clear-eyed feedback after getting mostly "atta-boys" and "atta-girls" all their lives, says John Sloop, a professor of rhetorical and cultural studies at Vanderbilt University. Another issue: To win tenure, professors often need to receive positive evaluations from students. So if professors want students to like them, "to a large extent, critical comments [of students] have to be couched in praise," Prof. Sloop says. He has attended seminars designed to help professors learn techniques of supportive criticism. "We were told to throw away our red pens so we don't intimidate students."

At the Wharton School of the University of Pennsylvania, marketing consultant Steve Smolinsky teaches students in their late 20s who've left the corporate world to get M.B.A. degrees. He and his colleagues feel handcuffed by the language of self-esteem, he says. "You have to tell students, 'It's not as good as you can do. You're really smart, and can do better.'"

Mr. Smolinsky enjoys giving praise when it's warranted, he says, "but there needs to be a flip side. When people are lousy, they need to be told that." He notices that his students often disregard his harsher comments. "They'll say, 'Yeah, well . . .' I don't believe they really hear it."

In the end, ego-stroking may feel good, but it doesn't lead to happiness, says Prof. Twenge, the narcissism researcher, who has written a book titled *Generation Me: Why Today's Young Americans Are More Confident, Assertive, Entitled—and More Miserable Than Ever Before.* She would like to declare a moratorium on "meaningless, baseless praise," which often starts in nursery school. She is unimpressed with self-esteem preschool ditties, such as the one set to the tune of "Frère Jacques": "I am special/ I am special/ Look at me . . ."

For now, companies like the Scooter Store continue handing out the helium balloons. Katie Lynch, 22, is the firm's "celebrations assistant," charged with throwing confetti, filling balloons and showing up at employees' desks to offer high-fives. "They all love it," she says, especially younger workers who "seem to need that pat on the back. They don't want to go unnoticed."

Ms. Lynch also has an urge to be praised. At the end of a long, hard day   30 of celebrating others, she says she appreciates when her manager, Burton De La Garza, gives her a high-five or compliments her with a cellphone text message.

"I'll just text her a quick note—'you were phenomenal today,'" says Mr. De La Garza, "She thrives on that. We wanted to find what works for her, because she's completely averse to confetti."

Analyze

1. What types of praise does the author mention, and why do you think so much praise is doled out in just about every social setting?
2. What does "Narcissists aren't good at basking in other people's glory" suggest?
3. In small groups, create a list of what Professor Twenge calls "meaningless, baseless praise."

Explore

1. Explore the pros and cons of doling out praise for almost everything by making a list or collection. Once you have a list, write a letter to a teacher, coach, or someone you select who needs to know why this is or is not a good practice.

2. Write an essay in the style of Zaslow's, but one that argues that we need to scold and ridicule in order to toughen up for what real life in both school and the workplace will be like.

3. Write a letter to Zaslow telling him why so much praise is okay. You might want to make the point that we will almost inevitably receive criticism for many things that we do, so it is helpful to get praise when we can.

Lee Rainie
"Digital Natives Invade the Workplace"

Rainie is the director of the Pew Internet and American Life Project, a non-profit, nonpartisan group that studies the social impact of the Internet, and which has completed and published more than 350 reports examining online activities and the role of the Internet in our lives. He is author and coauthor of several books on the same subject. In this essay the author reports on the types of and amounts of digital experience current generations possess when they hit the workforce.

How do you fit the workplace digital profile characterized in the article?

Young people may be newcomers to the world of work, but it's their bosses who are immigrants into the digital world.

As consultant Marc Prensky calculates it, the life arc of a typical 21-year-old entering the workforce today has, on average, included 5,000 hours of video game playing, exchange of 250,000 emails, instant messages, and phone text messages, 10,000 hours of cell phone use. To that you can add 3,500 hours of time online.

Our work at the Pew Internet Project shows that an American teen is more likely than her parents to own a digital music player like an iPod, to have posted writing, pictures or video on the internet, to have created a blog or profile on a social networking web site like MySpace, to have downloaded digital content such as songs, games, movies, or software, to have shared a remix or "mashup" creation with friends, and to have snapped a photo or video with a cell phone.

"Today's younger workers are not 'little uses,'" argues Prensky, an educator, gaming expert, author of *Don't Bother Me, Mom—I'm Learning.* "Their preference is for sharing, staying connected, instantaneity, multi-tasking, assembling random information into patterns, and using technology in new ways. Their challenge to the established way of doing things in the business world has already started."

Those challenges often flow from young workers' embrace of technolo-   5 gies that have grown up with them. Today's 21-year-old was born in 1985— 10 years after the first consumer computers went on sale and the same year that the breakthrough "third generation" video game, Nintendo's "Super Mario Brothers," first went to market. When this young worker was a tod-dler, the basic format of instant messaging was developed. And at the time this young worker entered kindergarten in 1990, Tim Berners-Lee wrote a computer program called the World Wide Web. Upon entering middle school, our worker might have organized his schedule with a gadget called a Palm Pilot (first shipped in 1996). And at the dawn of high school for our worker in 1999, Sean Fanning created the Napster file-sharing service. When the worker graduated from high school four years later, his gifts might have included an iPod (patented in 2002) and a camera phone (first shipped in early 2003).

Our worker's college career saw the rise of blogs (already two-years-old in 2000), RSS feeds (coded in 2000), Wikipedia (2001), social network sites (Friendster was launched in 2002), tagging (Del.icio.us was created in 2003), free online phone calling (Skype software was made available in 2003), podcasts (term coined in 2004), and the video explosion that has occurred as broadband internet connections become the norm in house-holds (YouTube went live in 2005).

Now, we have a reversal of the normal situation, where young people migrate into a workplace manned by seasoned natives. Instead, in this digitalized age, this 21-year-old and his peers are showing up in human resources offices as digital natives in a workplace world dominated by digital immigrants—that is, elders who often feel less at ease with new technologies.

How different are they? How different are they? David Cintz, 22, and a student at California State University, Chico, says his father is a highly accomplished technologist who worked for years at Hewlett- Packard, but father and son treat technology differently. "He can kick my butt on programming, but I'm the one who works all the time with two monitors on, listening to an internet radio station, with multiple IM screens on, or having online phone conversations simultaneously," notes the younger Cintz. "I'm the one living in the digital world, plugged into more devices. For him, it's work. For me, it's lifestyle."

Several years ago when she was interviewing a 17-year old girl named LaShonda for a project about the future of work, Rebecca Ryan, founder of a hip consulting firm named Next Generation Consulting, noted the difference between digital natives and their digital immigrant elders. In an email, she explains:

10   "We were at a food court in a mall outside Seattle. While I was interviewing her, she was IM'ing, had her PDA on, her cell phone, the whole thing. . . . I was so put off. I thought, 'She's not paying attention!' And so I asked her, 'LaShonda, what do you think will be the impact of technology on the future of work?' She looked me in the eye and asked, 'What do you mean by technology?' I looked at all of her gadgets on the table and said, 'Like this stuff!' She said, 'This is only technology for people who weren't raised with it.' Whoa. The point that came home to rest for me is that for LaShonda, IM'ing and texting are like breathing. Fish don't know they're in water. LaShonda didn't consider her gadgets technology."

This generational difference will inevitably pose challenges and create opportunities for the firms that hire them because natives have experiences and values that are different from digital immigrants. Herewith, five new realities of the digital natives' lives that should be understood by their new employers:

Reality 1—They Are Video Gamers and That Gives Them Different Expectations about How to Learn, Work, and Pursue Careers

A host of experts have affirmed that today's young workers have internalized the new realities of work. "In contrast to a generation ago, job entrants now do not expect lifetime employment from a single employer; they do not expect a full menu of paid corporate benefits; they do not relish jobs in hierarchical bureaucracies," argues Edward Lawler, Director of the Center for Effective Organizations at the University of Southern California, and co-author of the forthcoming book, *The New American Workplace*. "To them, the word 'career' is plural."

These attitudes clearly reflect the larger realities of the changing nature of work. Yet there is also some evidence that the ethos of video gaming plays a role. Studies at the Pew Internet & American Life Project show that virtually all college students play video, computer or internet games and 73% of teens do so. John Beck and Mitchell Wade argue in their book, *Got Game: How the Gamer Generation Is Reshaping Business Forever,* that games are the "training program" for young workers that helps form their attitudes about the way the work-world operates—a world full of data-streams, where analysis and decisions come at twitch speed, where failure at first is the norm, where the game player is the hero, and where learning takes place informally.

For companies, this puts a premium on designing engaging work that   15 allows workers to make a clear contribution and be rewarded for same. If "organization man" has become "gaming man," then the importance of worker morale is elevated—as is the value of basing work on completed tasks, rather than other measures of work effort such as hours on the job. "Give them projects to complete and then stand out of the way," argues James Ware, who helps run Future of Work, an organization for facilities, information technology, and human resources professionals based in Prescott, Arizona. "These kids quit when they are frustrated trying to finish an effort that will 'get them to the next level.' "

Reality 2—They Are Technologically Literate, but That Does Not Necessarily Make Them Media Literate

Our research has found consistently that the dominant metaphor for the internet in users' minds is a vast encyclopedia—more than it is a playground, a commercial mall, a civic commons, a kaffee klatch, or a peep show. This is especially true for younger users, who have grown up relying on it to complete school assignments, perhaps too often clipping and pasting material from websites into term papers. Sandra Gisin, who oversees knowledge and information management at reinsurance giant Swiss Re, says her colleagues marvel at the speed with which younger workers communicate and gather information. Still, she has had enough bad experiences with credulous younger workers accepting information from the top link on a Google search result that she says the firm will begin new training programs next year to teach workers how to evaluate information and to stress that "not all the best information is free."

Dow Jones news organizations have similar worries. They have created programs for journalism educators and reporters-in-training to drive home the point that journalists should not rely on Web sources without checking its origin and confirming it in other ways. "We drive home the point that it's not good enough to say, 'I read it on the internet,' without taking other steps to verify it," notes Clare Hart, Executive Vice President of Dow Jones and President of the Enterprise Media Group.

At the same time, younger workers' comfort with online tools can be a boon to marketing departments. Hart, 45, says younger workers on the staff "convinced us Baby Boomers" to put more information from Dow Jones conference presentations online and to create podcasts of the best of them. Since then, email offering podcasts gets opened about 20% more frequently than traditional marketing email.

20 **Reality 3—They Are Content Creators and That Shapes Their Notions about Privacy and Property**

More than half of American teenagers have created a blog, posted an artistic or written creation online, helped build a website, created an online profile, or uploaded photos and videos to a website. They think of the internet as a place where they can express their passions, play out their identities, and gather up the raw material they use for their creations.

So, why shouldn't young employees think it clever and fun to post on their blogs pictures of Apple computers being delivered to the loading bay at Microsoft headquarters? That is what Michael Hanscom, a temp employee for a Microsoft vendor, did and was quickly fired for violating the company's non-disclosure rules. An even more benign episode ended the same way when Bill Poon, a database marketing manager for Collectors Universe, a sports memorabilia authenticating company in Los Angeles, posted a photo of his department's president on his MySpace profile. Poon also filed a few comments poking fun at the firm's dress code and cubicle culture and was axed based on the company's concerns about "identity theft."

In the many-to-many broadcast environment of the internet, the prospects for data hemorrhage from companies have grown exponentially. The rise of consumer-creations online also means that outsiders have all manner of ways to record and report on the behavior of employees—as AOL discovered recently when a customer recorded and posted a frustrating telephone encounter with a customer service representative who refused his request to change his service plan and persistently pressed him with other options.

Clearly, firms need to create policies about how internal bloggers should treat company information, what kinds of intellectual property need to be protected, and basic norms of behavior that should guide people who want to create online material.

Reality 4—They Are Product and People Rankers and That Informs Their Notions of Propriety

25

This is the wisdom-of-crowds generation that grew up rating peers' physical attributes (amihotornot.com), pop culture creations (metacritic.com reviews), teachers' style and grading practices (ratemyprofessors.com), products and services (epinions.com), and even weddings (bridezilla.com). No surprise, then, that there are websites drawing decent traffic for people to rate their bosses, their clients, and their customers. The tone of online commentary is often flame-oriented, racy, and retaliatory. This, too, is the generation that has given rise to cyber-bullying.

So, organizations might ponder adding a new clause or two to the policy manual about online etiquette inside and outside the workplace. "Most companies have policies in place against harassment based on things like sex, race, and ethnicity," says Lynn Karoly, an economist at the RAND Corporation who has studied the 21st Century workplace. "But we should probably create new categories of policies to handle unacceptable online behaviors where liability might emerge."

Reality 5—They Are Multi-Taskers Often Living in a State of "Continusous Partial Attention" and That Means the Boundary Between Work and Leisure Is Quite Permeable

The ubiquity of gadgets and media allows younger workers to toggle back and forth quickly between tasks for work and chatter with their friends, research for projects and diversions on their screens. Many marvel at their capacity to juggle multiple tasks at once. An even sharper insight comes from Linda Stone, a technology consultant, who has noted that many technophiles function in a condition she calls "continuous partial attention," where they are scanning all available data sources for the optimum inputs.

Those who operate in such a state are not as productive as those who stay on task. They also do not make distinctions between the zones of work and leisure, consumer and producer, education and entertainment. "Their worlds bleed together," argues Charles Grantham, another principal at Future of Work. "It is pretty useless to try to draw borders around different

30

spheres of life for them. It's better to let them shift among them at their own choosing as long as the work gets done."

Rebecca Ryan of Next Generation Consulting says she has recently gained a new appreciation for young workers' capacity to multi-task even when it seems rude and inattentive. In an email, she explained:

"We currently have an intern who's working on several critical projects. She's brilliant and a great fit for our team. At meetings, she's online the whole time. At first, I was totally put off by this—Why isn't she looking me in the eye? But then I realized that our 'to do' lists were a LOT shorter after these meetings because she would locate the information we needed in real time, which eliminated the need for a lot of follow-up work. So, something that I initially perceived as 'poor manners' on her part actually ended up being a great efficiency in our team meetings."

Again, companies would be wise to spell out their tolerance levels for the amount of personal activity workers are allowed on the clock and their expectations about the availability of workers outside the office and after hours.

Many firms see no option but to embrace the world of digital natives. Agilent Technologies, a top global measurement company, began early this year to distribute iPod Nanos to new employees hired from U.S. college campuses. The Nanos were preloaded with podcasts describing each of the benefits offered by the company, such as the 401(k) retirement plan and options for health insurance. "The college kids loved getting the benefit overviews preloaded on the iPod, while our older workers often preferred to read about these things on our web site," notes human resources manager Cathy Taylor. "There are different generational learning styles."

35   Still, the ethic of podcasting information has now begun to spread through the company and some of those older workers have caught the bug, too. For a recent retirement party, staffers from Agilent's far-flung offices collaborated on a podcast for the retiree. "You Raise Me Up" by Andrea Bocelli was dubbed over the voiced well wishes and the podcast was played over a WebEx teleconference. "It was a first for a virtual retirement party," enthuses Taylor. "We'll be doing it again."

Analyze

1. Of the digital items that the average teen has used (listed in paragraph two), how many have you used? Have you used any additional items?

2. YouTube went live in 2005. When did you first use it and for what purposes? How do you use it now?
3. What role does video gaming play in shaping views toward the workplace?

Explore

1. The article discusses five ways that digital natives behave differently in the workplace. Write an essay discussing how these are strengths, not weaknesses. Include other ways that digital natives bring different skills to the workplace. As an alternative assignment create a comic or a collage to show this.
2. Write an essay (include visuals if relevant) describing the type of workplace you would like and how you would bring many or more of the skills discussed in this article to that workplace. Make it clear that the digital native skills are, in some cases, better, and why, in other cases, just different.
3. Discuss the skills that digital natives bring to the workplace. Convey your ideas in a tweet (140 characters), a text, and a one-page memo. When finished, compare and contrast the three forms and determine the strengths and weaknesses of each.

Anthony De Palma
"Fifteen Years on the Bottom Rung"

Anthony DePalma worked for 22 years with *The New York Times* as a reporter and foreign correspondent. While with the *Times*, he wrote several of their Pulitzer Prize–winning "Portraits of Grief." In 2007 he was an Emmy finalist for "Toxic Legacy," and in 2009 he won the Maria Moors Cabot Prize for distinguished international reporting. He is also the author of several successful books. In this essay he shows how many immigrants still come to this country with the goal of getting ahead financially and socially, but how the opportunities have changed for the worst.

How would you feel if you were stuck on the bottom rung?

In the dark before dawn, when Madison Avenue was all but deserted and its pricey boutiques were still locked up tight, several Mexicans slipped quietly into 3 Guys, a restaurant that the Zagat guide once called "the most expensive coffee shop in New York."

For the next 10 hours they would fry eggs, grill burgers, pour coffee and wash dishes for a stream of customers from the Upper East Side of Manhattan. By 7:35 a.m., Eliot Spitzer, attorney general of New York, was holding a power breakfast back near the polished granite counter. In the same burgundy booth a few hours later, Michael A. Wiener, co-founder of the multibillion-dollar Infinity Broadcasting, grabbed a bite with his wife, Zena. Just the day before, Uma Thurman slipped in for a quiet lunch with her children, but the paparazzi found her and she left.

More Mexicans filed in to begin their shifts throughout the morning, and by the time John Zannikos, one of the restaurant's three Greek owners, drove in from the North Jersey suburbs to work the lunch crowd, Madison Avenue was buzzing. So was 3 Guys.

"You got to wait a little bit," Mr. Zannikos said to a pride of elegant women who had spent the morning at the Whitney Museum of American Art, across Madison Avenue at 75th Street. For an illiterate immigrant who came to New York years ago with nothing but $100 in his pocket and a willingness to work etched on his heart, could any words have been sweeter to say?

5   With its wealthy clientele, middle-class owners and low-income work force, 3 Guys is a template of the class divisions in America. But it is also the setting for two starkly different tales about breaching those divides.

The familiar story is Mr. Zannikos's. For him, the restaurant—don't dare call it a diner—with its $20 salads and elegant décor represents the American promise of upward mobility, one that has been fulfilled countless times for generations of hard-working immigrants.

But for Juan Manuel Peralta, a 34-year-old illegal immigrant who worked there for five years until he was fired last May, and for many of the other illegal Mexican immigrants in the back, restaurant work today is more like a dead end. They are finding the American dream of moving up far more elusive than it was for Mr. Zannikos. Despite his efforts to help them, they risk becoming stuck in a permanent underclass of the poor, the unskilled and the uneducated.

That is not to suggest that the nearly five million Mexicans who, like Mr. Peralta, are living in the United States illegally will never emerge from the shadows. Many have, and undoubtedly many more will. But the sheer size of the influx—over 400,000 a year, with no end in sight—creates a problem all its own. It means there is an ever-growing pool of interchangeable workers, many of them shunting from one low-paying job to another. If one moves on, another one—or maybe two or three—is there to take his place.

Although Mr. Peralta arrived in New York almost 40 years after Mr. Zannikos, the two share a remarkably similar beginning. They came at the same age to the same section of New York City, without legal papers or more than a few words of English. Each dreamed of a better life. But monumental changes in the economy and in attitudes toward immigrants have made it far less likely that Mr. Peralta and his children will experience the same upward mobility as Mr. Zannikos and his family.

Of course, there is a chance that Mr. Peralta may yet take his place   10 among the Mexican-Americans who have succeeded here. He realizes that he will probably not do as well as the few who have risen to high office or who were able to buy the vineyards where their grandfathers once picked grapes. But he still dreams that his children will someday join the millions who have lost their accents, gotten good educations and firmly achieved the American dream.

Political scientists are divided over whether the 25 million people of Mexican ancestry in the United States represent an exception to the classic immigrant success story. Some, like John H. Mollenkopf at the City University of New York, are convinced that Mexicans will eventually do as well as the Greeks, Italians and other Europeans of the last century who were usually well assimilated after two or three generations. Others, including Mexican-Americans like Rodolfo O. de la Garza, a professor at Columbia, have done studies showing that Mexican-Americans face so many obstacles that even the fourth generation trails other Americans in education, home ownership and household income.

The situation is even worse for the millions more who have illegally entered the United States since 1990. Spread out in scores of cities far beyond the Southwest, they find jobs plentiful but advancement difficult. President Vicente Fox of Mexico was forced to apologize this month for declaring publicly what many Mexicans say they feel, that the illegal immigrants "are doing the work that not even blacks want to do in the United States." Resentment and race subtly stand in their way, as does a lingering attachment to Mexico, which is so close that many immigrants do not put down deep roots here. They say they plan to stay only long enough to make some money and then go back home. Few ever do.

But the biggest obstacle is their illegal status. With few routes open to become legal, they remain, like Mr. Peralta, without rights, without security and without a clear path to a better future.

"It's worrisome," said Richard Alba, a sociologist at the State University of New York, Albany, who studies the assimilation and class mobility of contemporary immigrants, "and I don't see much reason to believe this will change."

15   Little has changed for Mr. Peralta, a cook who has worked at menial jobs in the United States for the last 15 years. Though he makes more than he ever dreamed of in Mexico, his life is anything but middle class and setbacks are routine. Still, he has not given up hope. Querer es poder, he sometimes says: Want something badly enough and you will get it.

But desire may not be enough anymore. That is what concerns Arturo Sarukhan, Mexico's consul general in New York. Mr. Sarukhan recently took an urgent call from New York's police commissioner about an increase in gang activity among young Mexican men, a sign that they were moving into the underside of American life. Of all immigrants in New York City, officials say, Mexicans are the poorest, least educated and least likely to speak English.

The failure or success of this generation of Mexicans in the United States will determine the place that Mexicans will hold here in years to come, Mr. Sarukhan said, and the outlook is not encouraging.

"They will be better off than they could ever have been in Mexico," he said, "but I don't think that's going to be enough to prevent them from becoming an underclass in New York."

Different Results

There is a break in the middle of the day at 3 Guys, after the lunchtime limousines leave and before the private schools let out. That was when Mr. Zannikos asked the Mexican cook who replaced Mr. Peralta to prepare some lunch for him. Then Mr. Zannikos carried the chicken breast on pita to the last table in the restaurant.

20   "My life story is a good story, a lot of success," he said, his accent still heavy. He was just a teenager when he left the Greek island of Chios, a few miles off the coast of Turkey. World War II had just ended, and Greece was in ruins. "There was only rich and poor, that's it," Mr. Zannikos said. "There

was no middle class like you have here." He is 70 now, with short gray hair and soft eyes that can water at a mention of the past.

Because of the war, he said, he never got past the second grade, never learned to read or write. He signed on as a merchant seaman, and in 1953, when he was 19, his ship docked at Norfolk, Va. He went ashore one Saturday with no intention of ever returning to Greece. He left behind everything, including his travel documents. All he had in his pockets was $100 and the address of his mother's cousin in the Jackson Heights-Corona section of Queens.

Almost four decades later, Mr. Peralta underwent a similar rite of passage out of Mexico. He had finished the eighth grade in the poor southern state of Guerrero and saw nothing in his future there but fixing flat tires. His father, Inocencio, had once dreamed of going to the United States, but never had the money. In 1990, he borrowed enough to give his first-born son a chance.

Mr. Peralta was 19 when he boarded a smoky bus that carried him through the deserted hills of Guerrero and kept going until it reached the edge of Mexico. With eight other Mexicans he did not know, he crawled through a sewer tunnel that started in Tijuana and ended on the other side of the border, in what Mexicans call el Norte.

He had carried no documents, no photographs and no money, except what his father gave him to pay his shifty guide and to buy an airline ticket to New York. Deep in a pocket was the address of an uncle in the same section of Queens where Mr. Zannikos had gotten his start. By 1990, the area had gone from largely Greek to mostly Latino.

Starting over in the same working-class neighborhood, Mr. Peralta and   25 Mr. Zannikos quickly learned that New York was full of opportunities and obstacles, often in equal measure.

On his first day there, Mr. Zannikos, scared and feeling lost, found the building he was looking for, but his mother's cousin had moved. He had no idea what to do until a Greek man passed by. Walk five blocks to the Deluxe Diner, the man said. He did.

The diner was full of Greek housepainters, including one who knew Mr. Zannikos's father. On the spot, they offered him a job painting closets, where his mistakes would be hidden. He painted until the weather turned cold. Another Greek hired him as a dishwasher at his coffee shop in the Bronx.

It was not easy, but Mr. Zannikos worked his way up to short-order cook, learning English as he went along. In 1956, immigration officials raided the coffee shop. He was deported, but after a short while he managed to sneak back into the country. Three years later he married a Puerto Rican from the Bronx. The marriage lasted only a year, but it put him on the road to becoming a citizen. Now he could buy his own restaurant, a greasy spoon in the South Bronx that catered to a late-night clientele of prostitutes and undercover police officers.

Since then, he has bought and sold more than a dozen New York diners, but none have been more successful than the original 3 Guys, which opened in 1978. He and his partners own two other restaurants with the same name farther up Madison Avenue, but they have never replicated the high-end appeal of the original.

30   "When employees come in I teach them, 'Hey, this is a different neighborhood,'" Mr. Zannikos said. What may be standard in some other diners is not tolerated here. There are no Greek flags or tourism posters. There is no television or twirling tower of cakes with cream pompadours. Waiters are forbidden to chew gum. No customer is ever called "Honey."

"They know their place and I know my place," Mr. Zannikos said of his customers. "It's as simple as that."

His place in society now is a far cry from his days in the Bronx. He and his second wife, June, live in Wyckoff, a New Jersey suburb where he pampers fig trees and dutifully looks after a bird feeder shaped like the Parthenon. They own a condominium in Florida. His three children all went far beyond his second-grade education, finishing high school or attending college.

They have all done well, as has Mr. Zannikos, who says he makes about $130,000 a year. He says he is not sensitive to class distinctions, but he admits he was bothered when some people mistook him for the caterer at fund-raising dinners for the local Greek church he helped build.

All in all, he thinks immigrants today have a better chance of moving up the class ladder than he did 50 years ago.

35   "At that time, no bank would give us any money, but today they give you credit cards in the mail," he said. "New York still gives you more opportunity that any other place. If you want to do things, you will."

He says he has done well, and he is content with his station in life. "I'm in the middle and I'm happy."

A Divisive Issue

Mr. Peralta cannot guess what class Mr. Zannikos belongs to. But he is certain that it is much tougher for an immigrant to get ahead today than 50 years ago. And he has no doubt about his own class.

"La pobreza," he says. "Poverty."

It was not what he expected when he boarded the bus to the border, but it did not take long for him to realize that success in the United States required more than hard work. "A lot of it has to do with luck," he said during a lunch break on a stoop around the corner from the Queens diner where he went to work after 3 Guys.

"People come here, and in no more than a year or two they can buy their   40 own house and have a car," Mr. Peralta said. "Me, I've been here 15 years, and if I die tomorrow, there wouldn't even be enough money to bury me."

In 1990, Mr. Peralta was in the vanguard of Mexican immigrants who bypassed the traditional barrios in border states to work in far-flung cities like Denver and New York. The 2000 census counted 186,872 Mexicans in New York, triple the 1990 figure, and there are undoubtedly many more today. The Mexican consulate, which serves the metropolitan region, has issued more than 500,000 ID cards just since 2001.

Fifty years ago, illegal immigration was a minor problem. Now it is a divisive national issue, pitting those who welcome cheap labor against those with concerns about border security and the cost of providing social services. Though newly arrived Mexicans often work in industries that rely on cheap labor, like restaurants and construction, they rarely organize. Most are desperate to stay out of sight.

Mr. Peralta hooked up with his uncle the morning he arrived in New York. He did not work for weeks until the bakery where the uncle worked had an opening, a part-time job making muffins. He took it, though he didn't know muffins from crumb cake. When he saw that he would not make enough to repay his father, he took a second job making night deliveries for a Manhattan diner. By the end of his first day he was so lost he had to spend all his tip money on a cab ride home.

He quit the diner, but working there even briefly opened his eyes to how easy it could be to make money in New York. Diners were everywhere, and so were jobs making deliveries, washing dishes or busing tables. In six months, Mr. Peralta had paid back the money his father gave him. He bounced from job to job and in 1995, eager to show off his newfound success, he went back to Mexico with his pockets full of money, and he married. He was 25 then, the same age at which Mr. Zannikos married. But the similarities end there.

45   When Mr. Zannikos jumped ship, he left Greece behind for good. Though he himself had no documents, the compatriots he encountered on his first days were here legally, like most other Greek immigrants, and could help him. Greeks had never come to the United States in large numbers—the 2000 census counted only 29,805 New Yorkers born in Greece—but they tended to settle in just a few areas, like the Astoria section of Queens, which became cohesive communities ready to help new arrivals.

Mr. Peralta, like many other Mexicans, is trying to make it on his own and has never severed his emotional or financial ties to home. After five years in New York's Latino community, he spoke little English and owned little more than the clothes on his back. He decided to return to Huamuxtitlán (pronounced wa-moosh-teet-LAHN), the dusty village beneath a flat-topped mountain where he was born.

"People thought that since I was coming back from el Norte, I would be so rich that I could spread money around," he said. Still, he felt privileged: his New York wages dwarfed the $1,000 a year he might have made in Mexico.

He met a shy, pretty girl named Matilde in Huamuxtitlán, married her and returned with her to New York, again illegally, all in a matter of weeks. Their first child was born in 1996. Mr. Peralta soon found that supporting a family made it harder to save money. Then, in 1999, he got the job at 3 Guys.

"Barba Yanni helped me learn how to prepare things the way customers like them," Mr. Peralta said, referring to Mr. Zannikos with a Greek title of respect that means Uncle John.

50   The restaurant became his school. He learned how to sauté a fish so that it looked like a work of art. The three partners lent him money and said they would help him get immigration documents. The pay was good.

But there were tensions with the other workers. Instead of hanging their orders on a rack, the waiters shouted them out, in Greek, Spanish and a kind of fractured English. Sometimes Mr. Peralta did not understand, and they argued. Soon he was known as a hothead.

Still, he worked hard, and every night he returned to his growing family. Matilde, now 27, cleaned houses until the second child, Heidi, was born three years ago. Now she tries to sell Mary Kay products to other mothers at Public School 12, which their son, Antony, 8, attends.

Most weeks, Mr. Peralta could make as much as $600. Over the course of a year that could come to over $30,000, enough to approach the lower middle class. But the life he leads is far from that and uncertainty hovers over everything about his life, starting with his paycheck.

To earn $600, he has to work at least 10 hours a day, six days a week, and that does not happen every week. Sometimes he is paid overtime for the extra hours, sometimes not. And, as he found out in May, he can be fired at any time and bring in nothing, not even unemployment, until he lands another job. In 2004, he made about $24,000.

Because he is here illegally, Mr. Peralta can easily be exploited. He cannot file a complaint against his landlord for charging him $500 a month for a 9-foot-by-9-foot room in a Queens apartment that he shares with nine other Mexicans in three families who pay the remainder of the $2,000-a-month rent. All 13 share one bathroom, and the established pecking order means the Peraltas rarely get to use the kitchen. Eating out can be expensive.

Because they were born in New York, Mr. Peralta's children are United States citizens, and their health care is generally covered by Medicaid. But he has to pay out of his pocket whenever he or his wife sees a doctor. And forget about going to the dentist.

As many other Mexicans do, he wires money home, and it costs him $7 for every $100 he sends. When his uncle, his nephew and his sister asked him for money, he was expected to lend it. No one has paid him back. He has middle-class ornaments, like a cellphone and a DVD player, but no driver's license or Social Security card.

He is the first to admit that he has vices that have held him back; nothing criminal, but he tends to lose his temper and there are nights when he likes to have a drink or two. His greatest weakness is instant lottery tickets, what he calls "los scratch," and he sheepishly confesses that he can squander as much as $75 a week on them. It is a way of preserving hope, he said. Once he won $100. He bought a blender.

Years ago, he and Matilde were so confident they would make it in America that when their son was born they used the American spelling of his name, Anthony, figuring it would help pave his passage into the mainstream. But even that effort failed.

60   "Look at this," his wife said one afternoon as she sat on the floor of their room near a picture of the Virgin of Guadalupe. Mr. Peralta sat on a small plastic stool in the doorway, listening. His mattress was stacked against the wall. A roll of toilet paper was stashed nearby because they dared not leave it in the shared bathroom for someone else to use.

She took her pocketbook and pulled out a clear plastic case holding her son's baptismal certificate, on which his name is spelled with an "H." But then she unfolded his birth certificate, where the "H" is missing.

"The teachers won't teach him to spell his name the right way until the certificate is legally changed," she said. "But how can we do that if we're not legal?"

Progress, but Not Success

An elevated subway train thundered overhead, making the afternoon light along Roosevelt Avenue blink like a failing fluorescent bulb. Mr. Peralta's daughter and son grabbed his fat hands as they ran some errands. He had just finished a 10-hour shift, eggs over easy and cheeseburgers since 5 a.m. It had been especially hard to stand the monotony that day. He kept thinking about what was going on in Mexico, where it was the feast day of Our Lady of the Rosary. And, oh, what a feast there was— sweets and handmade tamales, a parade, even a bullfight. At night, fireworks, bursting loud and bright against the green folds of the mountains. Paid for, in part, by the money he sends home.

But instead of partying, he was walking his children to the Arab supermarket on Roosevelt Avenue to buy packages of chicken and spare ribs, and hoping to get to use the kitchen. And though he knew better, he grabbed a package of pink and white marshmallows for the children. He needed to buy tortillas, too, but not there. A Korean convenience store a few blocks away sells La Maizteca tortillas, made in New York.

65   The swirl of immigrants in Mr. Peralta's neighborhood is part of the fabric of New York, just as it was in 1953, when Mr. Zannikos arrived. But most immigrants then were Europeans, and though they spoke different languages, their Caucasian features helped them blend into New York's middle class.

Experts remain divided over whether Mexicans can follow the same route. Samuel P. Huntington, a Harvard professor of government, takes the extreme view that Mexicans will not assimilate and that the separate culture they are developing threatens the United States.

Most others believe that recent Mexican immigrants will eventually take their place in society, and perhaps someday muster political clout commensurate with their numbers, though significant impediments are slowing their progress. Francisco Rivera-Batiz, a Columbia University economics professor, says that prejudice remains a problem, that factory jobs have all but disappeared, and that there is a growing gap between the educational demands of the economy and the limited schooling that the newest Mexicans have when they arrive.

But the biggest obstacle by far, and the one that separates newly arrived Mexicans from Greeks, Italians and most other immigrants—including earlier generations of Mexicans—is their illegal status. Professor Rivera-Batiz studied what happened to illegal Mexican immigrants who became legal after the last national amnesty in 1986. Within a few years, their incomes rose 20 percent and their English improved greatly.

"Legalization," he said, "helped them tremendously."

Although the Bush administration is again talking about legalizing some Mexicans with a guest worker program, there is opposition to another amnesty, and the number of Mexicans illegally living in the United States continues to soar. Desperate to get their papers any way they can, many turn to shady storefront legal offices. Like Mr. Peralta, they sign on to illusory schemes that cost hundreds of dollars but almost never produce the promised green cards.   70

Until the 1980's, Mexican immigration was largely seasonal and mostly limited to agricultural workers. But then economic chaos in Mexico sent a flood of immigrants northward, many of them poorly educated farmers from the impoverished countryside. Tighter security on the border made it harder for Mexicans to move back and forth in the traditional way, so they tended to stay here, searching for low-paying unskilled jobs and concentrating in barrios where Spanish, constantly replenished, never loses its immediacy.

"Cuidado!" Mr. Peralta shouted when Antony carelessly stepped into Roosevelt Avenue without looking. Although the boy is taught in English at school, he rarely uses anything but Spanish at home.

Even now, after 15 years in New York, Mr. Peralta speaks little English. He tried English classes once, but could not get his mind to accept the new sounds. So he dropped it, and has stuck with only Spanish, which he concedes is "the language of busboys" in New York. But as long as he stays in his neighborhood, it is all he needs.

It was late afternoon by the time Mr. Peralta and his children headed home. The run-down house, the overheated room, the stacked mattress and the hoarded toilet paper—all remind him how far he would have to go to achieve a success like Mr. Zannikos's.

75   Still, he says, he has done far better than he could ever have done in Mexico. He realizes that the money he sends to his family there is not enough to satisfy his father, who built stairs for a second floor of his house made of concrete blocks in Huamuxtitlán, even though there is no second floor. He believes Manuel has made it big in New York and he is waiting for money from America to complete the upstairs.

Manuel has never told him the truth about his life up north. He said his father's images of America came from another era. The older man does not know how tough it is to be a Mexican immigrant in the United States now, tougher than any young man who ever left Huamuxtitlán would admit. Everything built up over 15 years here can come apart as easily as an adobe house in an earthquake. And then it is time to start over, again.

A Conflict Erupts

It was the end of another busy lunch at 3 Guys in late spring 2003. Mr. Peralta made himself a turkey sandwich and took a seat at a rear table. The Mexican countermen, dishwashers and busboys also started their breaks, while the Greek waiters took care of the last few diners.

It is not clear how the argument started. But a cross word passed between a Greek waiter and a Mexican busboy. Voices were raised. The waiter swung at the busboy, catching him behind the ear. Mr. Peralta froze. So did the other Mexicans.

Even from the front of the restaurant, where he was watching the cash register, Mr. Zannikos realized something was wrong and rushed back to break it up. "I stood between them, held one and pushed the other away," he said. "I told them: 'You don't do that here. Never do that here.'"

80   Mr. Zannikos said he did not care who started it. He ordered both the busboy and the waiter, a partner's nephew, to get out.

But several Mexicans, including Mr. Peralta, said that they saw Mr. Zannikos grab the busboy by the head and that they believed he would have hit him if another Mexican had not stepped between them. That infuriated them because they felt he had sided with the Greek without knowing who was at fault.

Mr. Zannikos said that was not true, but in the end it did not matter. The easygoing atmosphere at the restaurant changed. "Everybody was a little cool," Mr. Zannikos recalled.

What he did not know then was that the Mexicans had reached out to the Restaurant Opportunities Center, a workers' rights group. Eventually six of them, including Mr. Peralta, cooperated with the group. He did so reluctantly, he said, because he was afraid that if the owners found out, they would no longer help him get his immigration papers. The labor group promised that the owners would never know.

The owners saw it as an effort to shake them down, but for the Mexicans it became a class struggle pitting powerless workers against hard-hearted owners.

Their grievances went beyond the scuffle. They complained that with 85 just one exception, only Greeks became waiters at 3 Guys. They challenged the sole Mexican waiter, Salomon Paniagua, a former Mexican army officer who, everyone agreed, looked Greek, to stand with them.

But on the day the labor group picketed the restaurant, Mr. Paniagua refused to put down his order pad. A handful of demonstrators carried signs on Madison Avenue for a short while before Mr. Zannikos and his partners reluctantly agreed to settle.

Mr. Zannikos said he felt betrayed. "When I see these guys, I see myself when I started, and I always try to help them," he said. "I didn't do anything wrong."

The busboy and the Mexican who intervened were paid several thousand dollars and the owners promised to promote a current Mexican employee to waiter within a month. But that did not end the turmoil.

Fearing that the other Mexicans might try to get back at him, Mr. Paniagua decided to strike out on his own. After asking Mr. Zannikos for advice, he bought a one-third share of a Greek diner in Jamaica, Queens. He said he put it in his father's name because the older man had become a legal resident after the 1986 amnesty.

After Mr. Paniagua left, 3 Guys went without a single Mexican waiter 90 for 10 months, despite the terms of the settlement. In March, an eager Mexican busboy with a heavy accent who had worked there for four years got a chance to wear a waiter's tie.

Mr. Peralta ended up having to leave 3 Guys around the same time as Mr. Paniagua. Mr. Zannikos's partners suspected he had sided with the labor group, he said, and started to criticize his work unfairly. Then they cut back his schedule to five days a week. After he hurt his ankle playing soccer, they told him to go home until he was better. When Mr. Peralta came back to work about two weeks later, he was fired.

Mr. Zannikos confirms part of the account but says the firing had nothing to do with the scuffle or the ensuing dispute. "If he was good, believe me, he wouldn't get fired," he said of Mr. Peralta.

Mr. Peralta shrugged when told what Mr. Zannikos said. "I know my own work and I know what I can do," he said. "There are a lot of restaurants in New York, and a lot of workers."

When 3 Guys fired Mr. Peralta, another Mexican replaced him, just as Mr. Peralta replaced a Mexican at the Greek diner in Queens where he went to work next.

This time, though, there was no Madison Avenue address, no elaborate menu of New Zealand mussels or designer mushrooms. In the Queens diner a bowl of soup with a buttered roll cost $2, all day. If he fried burgers and scraped fat off the big grill for 10 hours a day, six days a week, he might earn about as much as he did on Madison Avenue, at least for a week.

95   His schedule kept changing. Sometimes he worked the lunch and dinner shift, and by the end of the night he was worn out, especially since he often found himself arguing with the Greek owner. But he did not look forward to going home. So after the night manager lowered the security gate, Mr. Peralta would wander the streets.

One of those nights he stopped at a phone center off Roosevelt Avenue to call his mother. "Everything's O.K.," he told her. He asked how she had spent the last $100 he sent, and whether she needed anything else. There is always need in Huamuxtitlán.

Still restless, he went to the Scorpion, a shot-and-beer joint open till 4 a.m. He sat at the long bar nursing vodkas with cranberry juice, glancing at the soccer match on TV and the busty Brazilian bartender who spoke only a little Spanish. When it was nearly 11 p.m., he called it a night.

Back home, he quietly opened the door to his room. The lights were off, the television murmuring. His family was asleep in the bunk bed that the store had now threatened to repossess. Antony was curled up on the top, Matilde and Heidi cuddled in the bottom. Mr. Peralta moved the plastic stool out of the way and dropped his mattress to the floor.

The children did not stir. His wife's eyes fluttered, but she said nothing. Mr. Peralta looked over his family, his home.

"This," he said, "is my life in New York."   100

Not the life he imagined, but his life. In early March, just after Heidi's third birthday, he quit his job at the Queens diner after yet another heated argument with the owner. In his mind, preserving his dignity is one of the few liberties he has left.

"I'll get another job," he said while baby-sitting Heidi at home a few days later. The rent is already paid till the end of the month and he has friends, he said. People know him. To him, jobs are interchangeable—just as he is to the jobs. If he cannot find work as a grillman, he will bus tables. Or wash dishes. If not at one diner, then at another.

"It's all the same," he said.

It took about three weeks, but Mr. Peralta did find a new job as a grillman at another Greek diner in a different part of New York. His salary is roughly the same, the menu is roughly the same (one new item, Greek burritos, was a natural), and he sees his chance for a better future as being roughly the same as it has been since he got to America.

A Long Day Closes

It was now dark again outside 3 Guys. About 9 p.m. Mr. Zannikos asked   105
his Mexican cook for a small salmon steak, a little rare. It had been another busy 10-hour day for him, but a good one. Receipts from the morning alone exceeded what he needed to take in every day just to cover the $23,000 a month rent.

He finished the salmon quickly, left final instructions with the lone Greek waiter still on duty and said good night to everyone else. He put on his light tan corduroy jacket and the baseball cap he picked up in Florida.

"Night," he said to the lone table of diners.

Outside, as Mr. Zannikos walked slowly down Madison Avenue, a self-made man comfortable with his own hard-won success, the bulkhead doors in front of 3 Guys clanked open. Faint voices speaking Spanish came from below. A young Mexican who started his shift 10 hours earlier climbed out with a bag of garbage and heaved it onto the sidewalk. New Zealand mussel shells. Uneaten bits of portobello mushrooms. The fine grounds of decaf cappuccino.

One black plastic bag after another came out until Madison Avenue in front of 3 Guys was piled high with trash.

110   "Hurry up!" the young man shouted to the other Mexicans. "I want to go home, too."

Analyze

1. What does the author mean when he says 3 Guys is a "template of the class divisions in America"?
2. What are the similarities and differences between Mr. Zannikos's and Mr. Peralta's immigration experiences and stories?
3. What keeps Mexican immigrants from finding good jobs and making it to the middle class?

Explore

1. In Chapter 2, Buchannan quotes Harvard professor Samuel P. Huntington: "Mexicans will not assimilate and . . . the separate culture they are developing threatens the United States." Compare this essay with Buchanan's or another essay that you have read. Write an essay showing what your researched view is.
2. Our identities are affected by what we feel we deserve or have earned. If we do not receive equal opportunities compared to what we believe others have received, we feel downtrodden. Compare Peralta's experiences with any of the other readings in *Identity: A Reader for Writers* (or elsewhere such as a movie, article, etc.). How do these experiences serve to create an identity for us, and even for our race?
3. Mr. Peralta struggles to achieve the American Dream. Do you know anyone with a similar story of struggle, who just cannot seem to make it? What are the factors that prevent this person from moving to another social and economic level? If you can, interview this person and then write a story about his or her experiences.

Studs Terkel
"Stephen Cruz"

Studs Terkel was well known on many fronts, but he was best known as an author of oral histories of common Americans, from which he published many books, including *Working, Division Street,* and *Hard Times.* This excerpt is an example of one of his oral histories focused on working life in America. In this piece we learn about the negative effects workplace racial profiling can have.

How do you feel about this Mexican-American worker's experiences? Do you feel we all need to modify our definitions and notions of what success means?

*H*e is thirty-nine.
    "The family came in stages from Mexico. Your grandparents usually came first, did a little work, found little roots, put together a few bucks, and brought the family in, one at a time. Those were the days when controls at the border didn't exist as they do now."

You just tried very hard to be whatever it is the system wanted of you. I was a good student and, as small as I was, a pretty good athlete. I was well liked, I thought. We were fairly affluent, but we lived down where all the trashy whites were. It was the only housing we could get. As kids, we never understood why. We did everything right. We didn't have those Mexican accents, we were never on welfare. Dad wouldn't be on welfare to save his soul. He woulda died first. He worked during the depression. He carries that pride with him, even today.

Of the five children, I'm the only one who really got into the business world. We learned quickly that you have to look for opportunities and add things up very quickly. I was in liberal arts, but as soon as Sputnik went up, well, golly, hell, we knew where the bucks were. I went right over to the registrar's office and signed up for engineering. I got my degree in '62. If you had a master's in business as well, they were just paying all kinds of bucks. So that's what I did. Sure enough, the market was super. I had fourteen job offers. I could have had a hundred if I wanted to look around.

5   I never once associated these offers with my being a minority. I was
aware of the Civil Rights Act of 1964, but I was still self-confident enough
to feel they wanted me because of my abilities. Looking back, the reason
I got more offers than the other guys was because of the government edict.
And I thought it was because I was so goddamned brilliant (Laughs). In
1962, I didn't get as many offers as those who were less qualified. You have
a tendency to blame the job market. You just don't want to face the issue of
discrimination.

I went to work with Procter & Gamble. After about two years, they told
me I was one of the best supervisors they ever had and they were gonna
promote me. Okay, I went into personnel. Again, I thought it was because
I was such a brilliant guy. Now I started getting wise to the ways of the
American Dream. My office was glass-enclosed, while all the other offices
were enclosed so you couldn't see into them. I was the visible man.

They made sure I interviewed most of the people that came in. I just
didn't really think there was anything wrong until we got a new plant
manager, a southerner. I received instructions from him on how I should
interview blacks. Just check and see if they smell, okay? That was the beginning of my training program. I started asking: Why weren't we hiring more
minorities? I realized I was the only one in a management position.

I guess as a Mexican I was more acceptable because I wasn't really black.
I was a good compromise. I was visibly good. I hired a black secretary, which
was *verboten*. When I came back from my vacation, she was gone. My boss
fired her while I was away. I asked why and never got a good reason.

Until then, I never questioned the American Dream. I was convinced
if you worked hard, you could make it. I never considered myself different.
That was the trouble. We had been discriminated against a lot, but I never
associated it with society. I considered it an individual matter. Bad people,
my mother used to say. In '68 I began to question.

10   I was doing fine. My very first year out of college, I was making twelve
thousand dollars. I left Procter & Gamble because I really saw no opportunity. They were content to leave me visible, but my thoughts were not really
solicited. I may have overreacted a bit, with the plant manager's attitude,
but I felt there's no way a Mexican could get ahead here.

I went to work for Blue Cross. It's 1969. The Great Society is in full
swing. Those who never thought of being minorities before are being
turned on. Consciousness raising is going on. Black programs are popping
up in universities. Cultural identity and all that. But what about the one

issue in this country: economics? There were very few management jobs for minorities, especially blacks.

The stereotypes popped up again. If you're Oriental, you're real good in mathematics. If you're Mexican, you're a happy guy to have around, pleasant but emotional. Mexicans are either sleeping or laughing all the time. Life is just one big happy kind of event. *Mañana.* Good to have as part of the management team, as long as you weren't allowed to make decisions.

I was thinking there were two possibilities why minorities were not making it in business. One was deep, ingrained racism. But there was still the possibility that they were simply a bunch of bad managers who just couldn't cut it. You see, until now I believed everything I was taught about the dream: The American businessman is omnipotent and fair. If we could show these turkeys there's money to be made in hiring minorities, these businessmen—good managers, good decision makers—would respond. I naïvely thought American businessmen gave a damn about society, that given a choice they would do the right thing. I had that faith.

I was hungry for learning about decision-making criteria. I was still too far away from top management to see exactly how they were working. I needed to learn more. Hey, just learn more and you'll make it. That part of the dream hadn't left me yet. I was still clinging to the notion of work your ass off, learn more than anybody else, and you'll get in that sphere.

During my fifth year at Blue Cross, I discovered another flaw in the American Dream. Minorities are as bad to other minorities as whites are to minorities. The strongest weapon the white manager had is the old divide and conquer routine. My mistake was thinking we were all at the same level of consciousness.

I had attempted to bring together some blacks with the other minorities. There weren't too many of them anyway. The Orientals never really got involved. The blacks misunderstood what I was presenting, perhaps I said it badly. They were on the cultural kick: a manager should be crucified for saying "Negro" instead of "black." I said as long as the Negro or the black gets the job, it doesn't mean a damn what he's called. We got into a huge hassle. Management, of course, merely smiled. The whole struggle fell flat on its face. It crumpled from divisiveness. So I learned another lesson. People have their own agenda. It doesn't matter what group you're with, there is a tendency to put the other guy down regardless.

The American Dream began to look so damn complicated, I began to think: Hell, if I wanted, I could just back away and reap the harvest myself.

¹⁵

By this time, I'm up to twenty-five thousand dollars a year. It's beginning to look good, and a lot of people are beginning to look good. And they're saying: "Hey, the American Dream, you got it. Why don't you lay off?" I wasn't falling in line.

My bosses were telling me I had all the "ingredients" for top management. All that was required was to "get to know our business." This term comes up all the time. If I could just warn all minorities and women whenever you hear "get to know our business," they're really saying "fall in line." Stay within that fence, and glory can be yours. I left Blue Cross disillusioned. They offered me a director's job at thirty thousand dollars before I quit.

All I had to do was behave myself. I had the "ingredients" of being the Chicano, the equivalent of the good nigger. I was smart. I could articulate well. People didn't know by my speech patterns that I was of Mexican heritage. Some tell me I don't look Mexican, that I have a certain amount of Italian, Lebanese, or who knows. (Laughs.)

20   One could easily say: "Hey, what's your bitch? The American Dream has treated you beautifully. So just knock it off and quit this crap you're spreading around." It was a real problem. Every time I turned around, America seemed to be treating me very well.

Hell, I even thought of dropping out, the hell with it. Maybe get a job in a factory. But what happened? Offers kept coming in. I just said to myself: God, isn't this silly? You might as well take the bucks and continue looking for the answer. So I did that. But each time I took the money, the conflict in me got more intense, not less.

Wow, I'm up to thirty-five thousand a year. This is a savings and loan business. I have faith in the executive director. He was the kind of guy I was looking for in top management: understanding, humane, also looking for the formula. Until he was up for consideration as executive V.P. of the entire organization. All of a sudden everything changed. It wasn't until I saw this guy flip-flop that I realized how powerful vested interests are. Suddenly he's saying: "Don't rock the boat. Keep a low profile. Get in line." Another disappointment.

Subsequently, I went to work for a consulting firm. I said to myself: Okay, I've got to get close to the executive mind. I need to know how they work. Wow, a consulting firm.

Consulting firms are saving a lot of American businessmen. They're doing it in ways that defy the whole notion of capitalism. They're not allowing these businesses to fail. Lockheed was successful in getting U.S. funding guarantees because of the efforts of consulting firms working on their behalf, helping them look better. In this kind of work, you don't find minorities. You've got to be a proven success in business before you get there.

The American dream, I see now, is governed not by education, opportunity, and hard work, but by power and fear. The higher up in the organization you go, the more you have to lose. The dream is *not losing*. This is the notion pervading American today: Don't lose. 25

When I left the consulting business, I was making fifty-five thousand dollars a year. My last performance appraisal was: You can go a long way in this business, you can be a partner, but you gotta know our business. It came up again. At this point, I was incapable of being disillusioned any more. How easy it is to be swallowed up by the same set of values that governs the top guy. I was becoming that way. I was becoming concerned about losing that fifty grand or so a year. So I asked other minorities who had it made. I'd go up and ask 'em: "Look, do you owe anything to others?" the answer was: "We owe nothing to anybody." They drew from the civil rights movement but felt no debt. They've quickly forgotten how it happened. It's like I was when I first got out of college. Hey, it's really me, I'm great. I'm as angry with these guys as I am with the top guys.

Right now, it's confused. I've had fifteen years in the business world as "a success." Many Anglos would be envious of my progress. Fifty thousand dollars a year puts you in the one or two top percent of all Americans. Plus my wife making another thirty thousand. We had lots of money. When I gave it up, my cohorts looked at me not just as strange, but as something of a traitor. "You're screwing it up for all of us. You're part of our union, we're the elite, we should govern. What the hell are you doing?" So now I'm looked at suspiciously by my peer group as well.

I'm teaching at the University of Wisconsin at Platteville. It's nice. My colleagues tell me what's on their minds. I got a farm next-door to Platteville. With farm prices being what they are (laughs), it's a losing proposition. But with university work and what money we've saved, we're going to be all right.

The American Dream is getting more elusive. The dream is being governed by a few people's notion of what the dream is. Sometimes I feel it's a small group of financiers that gets together once a year and decides all the world's issues.

30   It's getting so big. The small-business venture is not there anymore. Business has become too big to influence. It can't be changed internally. A counterpower is needed.

Analyze

1. What kind of degree did Cruz get and why?
2. What types of discrimination does Cruz feel he has experienced?
3. What did Cruz do that was *verboten?*

Explore

1. In several of the essays in this chapter the writers are looking for a version of the American Dream. Some "make it," and some are still trying. Write a letter to Cruz telling him two of the other stories from this chapter (or if you know of another include it) so that he will see that others have had his challenges and have learned to cope with them.

2. Interview someone who is in a position that you would like to have when you are done with your degree. Find out what they experienced on their path toward that position and how they feel now that they are there. See whether they experienced any of the types of discrimination that Cruz experienced. Write up your results in the form of a story like Terkel did with Cruz.

3. Many people dream of the successes that Cruz had in his career. Of course, he has had challenges and issues that have tapered the effect of his successes. Write an essay about what Cruz's concerns are and suggest what might be done to eliminate some of these concerns in the future, or produce a PowerPoint telling of the negative effects of job profiling. Your audience is a room full of corporate human resources employees.

Stephen Marche
"We Are Not All Created Equal: The Truth about the American Class System"

Marche is a novelist and mainstream writer. His first novel, *Raymond and Hannah*, was published in 2005, and his second, *Shining at the Bottom of the Sea*, in 2007. His *Esquire* monthly column, "A Thousand Words about Our Culture," was a finalist for columns and commentary award by the American Society of Magazine Editors. His articles can also be read in the *New York Times* and the *Atlantic*. We Are Not All Created Equal argues that some of the old factors that determined wealth, such as race and gender, are now clearly determined by class.

Marche's argument is a sobering one. Was his intent to merely inform us, make us angry, wake us up from our delusion of the American Dream, or something else?

There are some truths so hard to face, so ugly and so at odds with how we imagine the world should be, that nobody can accept them. Here's one: It is obvious that a class system has arrived in America—a recent study of the thirty-four countries in the Organization for Economic Cooperation and Development found that only Italy and Great Britain have less social mobility. But nobody wants to admit: If your daddy was rich, you're gonna stay rich, and if your daddy was poor, you're gonna stay poor. Every instinct in the American gut, every institution, every national symbol, runs on the idea that anybody can make it; the only limits are your own limits. Which is an amazing idea, a gift to the world—just no longer true. Culturally, and in their daily lives, Americans continue to glide through a ghostly land of opportunity they can't bear to tell themselves isn't real. It's the most dangerous lie the country tells itself.

More than anything else, class now determines Americans' fates. The old inequalities—racism, sexism, homophobia—are increasingly antiquated. Women are threatening to overwhelm men in the workplace, and the utter collapse of the black lower middle class in the age of Obama—a catastrophe for the African-American community—has little to do with prejudice and everything to do with brute economics. Who wins and who loses has become simplified, purified: those who own and those who don't. Meanwhile Great Britain, the source of the class system, has returned, plain and simple, to its old aristocratic masters. Reverting to type, the overlords and the underclass seem little removed from their eighteenth-century predecessors. The overlords preach shared sacrifice from their palaces and the underclass riots and the middle classes quietly judge. Everybody knows where he stands.

Not in America. In the United States, the emerging aristocracy remains staunchly convinced that it is not an aristocracy, that it's the result of hard work and talent. The permanent working poor refuse to accept that their poverty is permanent. The class system is clandestine. And yet the most cherished dreams are the hardest to awaken from. The best-made shows on television now—some of the most beautifully shot, most beautifully articulated television shows ever made—capture in achingly precise detail the era that economists call the Great Compression, that shimmering, virtuous period before the 1970s when the middle class swelled so much that it came to believe it could never stop swelling—the original dangerous illusion. *Pan Am* is an unlikely parable of American fluidity. Being stuck in a tube in the air, serving coffee, and having your ass grabbed achieves glamour by virtue of the characters' ease of movement. Don Draper is a new Gatsby—he transforms himself from penniless vet to salesclerk to partner in an ad firm. Meanwhile, in Sitcomland, *Modern Family* has replaced working-class heroes like Homer Simpson and Ralph Kramden with the top 1 percent, and yet everyone, including the audience, seems to accept them as representative.

Meaningful, substantive approaches to class are going to have to come from elsewhere. This month, the second season of *Downton Abbey* returns to PBS, and we may as well all have a look, because if we are going to have a European-style class system, we better begin to import their values. The scenery is extremely lovely. The arrangements are very cozy. British aristocrats always look like they're daring the world to line them all up against a wall and erase the entire parasitical group of them, but at Downton, at least, the ruling class is somewhat aware of the arbitrary nature of its status. The American ruling class could learn from their humility. At Downton Abbey, where everyone has a place, at least the boy who cleans the boots and knives isn't a bad person because his job.

Herman Cain's comment in a recent interview on the Occupy Wall 5
Street movement, which is by no means an uncommon opinion, was this:
"If you're not rich, blame yourself." The old Calvinist strain that connects
prosperity to divine election runs deep. Work hard and stay late and you get
to be a banker or doctor; drop out of high school or start using drugs and
you'll end up at McDonald's. Even among liberals, the new trend toward
behavioral economics demonstrates how poor people fare worse on tests
requiring self-control, how their personal weaknesses create cycles of poverty. You don't have to be on talk radio to believe that the poor must be
doing something wrong.

The Great Outcry that has filled the country with inchoate rage is the
bloody mess of this fundamental belief in the justice of American outcomes
crashing headfirst into the new reality. The majority of new college grads in
the United States today are either unemployed or working jobs that don't
require a degree. Roughly 85 percent of them moved back home in 2011,
where they sit on an average debt of $27,200. The youth unemployment rate
in general is 18.1 percent. Are these all bad people? None of us—not
Generation Y, not Generation X, and certainly not the Boomers—have
ever faced anything like it. The Tea Partiers blame the government. The
Occupiers blame the financial industry. Both are really mourning the arrival
of a new social order, one not defined by opportunity but by preexisting
structures of wealth. At least the ranters are mourning. Those who are not
screaming or in drum circles mostly pretend that the change isn't happening.

Post-hope, it is hard to imagine even any temporary regression back to
the days of the swelling American middle class. The forces of inequality are
simply too powerful and the forces against inequality too weak. But at least
we can end the hypocrisy. In ten years, the next generation will no longer
have the faintest illusion that the United States is a country with equality
of opportunity. The least they're entitled to is some honesty about why.

Analyze

1. What two countries have less social mobility than the United States?
2. What percent of college graduates moved back home in 2011, and
   what is their average debt?
3. What are three of the television shows Marche mentions and how does
   he use them as examples?

Explore

1. Marche says, "In the United States, the emerging aristocracy remains staunchly convinced that it is not an aristocracy, that it's the result of hard work and talent. The permanent working poor refuse to accept that their poverty is permanent. The class system is clandestine." Create a comic that develops this argument.

2. In groups pick a few TV shows you watch or a couple recent movies and create a taxonomy of how rich and poor people are characterized, in the ways they behave and how they got where they are (rich or poor). Once done with the taxonomy, survey the class to see if they feel the characters from the classes reflect how they see them, that is, as representative.

3. Marche's argument is that if we are born rich, we stay that way, and if born poor, we remain this way. Write a researched essay in which you agree or disagree with him.

Jacquelyn Smith
"The Happiest and Unhappiest Jobs in America"

As a writer for Forbes since 2010, Smith started by covering the stock market but, the same year, she switched to focusing on careers and jobs, which she says is when people were "vigorously hunting for jobs or desperately trying to hold on to the ones they have." In this article Smith, who draws her findings from a Careerbliss.com study analyzing 65,000 workers, arrived at some interesting findings about who is happy and unhappy in their workplace.

Before you read the essay, what do you think makes a happy and unhappy job?

You probably don't think of construction managers, sales representatives, or quality assurance engineer as the most cheerful employees. But as it turns out, they are. These are three of the happiest careers in America, according to online jobs site Careerbliss.com.

CareerBliss compiled a list of the 10 happiest jobs based on analysis from more than 65,000 employee-generated reviews in 2012. Employees all over the country were asked to evaluate ten factors that affect workplace happiness. Those include one's relationship with the boss and co-workers, work environment, job resources, compensation, growth opportunities, company culture, company reputation, daily tasks, and control over the work one does on a daily basis.

They evaluated each factor on a five-point scale and also indicated how important it was to their overall happiness. The numbers were combined to find an average rating of overall employee happiness for each respondent, and then sorted by job title to find which occupations had the happiest workers. A minimum of 50 employee reviews was required to be considered for CareerBliss' 10 Happiest Jobs in America, and executive level jobs, like chief executive, were excluded from the study.

"It is vital to understand how employees in these positions feel about their work environment," says Heidi Golledge, chief executive of Career-Bliss. "Whether you are someone looking to transition into one of these careers, or are currently in one of these jobs, this can help arm you with the information needed to truly understand the rewards and challenges. In addition, any employer managing people in these types of positions can gauge how their employees may feel, and can adjust elements to help create happier work environments."

The happiest employees of all aren't kindergarten teachers or veterinarians. They're real estate agents. Professionals with this job title are typically responsible for renting, buying, or selling property for clients. According to the BLS, they study property listings, interview prospective clients, accompany clients to property site, discuss conditions of sale, and draw up real estate contracts. They make about $51,170 per year, on average—but top earning real estate agents rake in over $92,000. 5

With an index score of 4.26, real estate agents said they are more than satisfied with the control they have over the work they do on a daily basis. They're also fairly content with their bosses.

"Real estate agents have definitely weathered quite a financial storm over the past few years but right now rates are between 2% and 3% and inventory is low, making it a real estate agents dream as new homes hit the market and are getting multiple offers in the first week," Golledge says. "Right now, it is a seller's market so the real estate agent's cost of advertising and marketing is very low and commissions are high. Happy times."

The second most blissful job is senior quality assurance engineer, which earned an index score of 4.23. Professionals with this job title are typically involved in the entire software development process to ensure the quality of the final product. This can include processes such as requirements gathering and documentation, source code control, code review, change management, configuration management, release management, and the actual testing of the software, explains Matt Miller, chief technology officer at CareerBliss.

These professionals "typically make between $85,000 and $100,000 a year in salary and are the gatekeepers for releasing high quality software products," Miller adds. Organizations generally will not allow software to be released until it has been fully tested and approved by their software quality assurance group, he adds.

10   Golledge says the job requires long hours and intense demands— however, senior quality assurance engineers feel rewarded at work, "as they are typically the last stop before software goes live and correctly feel that they are an integral part of the job being done at the company."

Senior sales representative is the third happiest job in America, according to CareerBliss data. The profession scored a 4.19. Employees in this job are most content with the amount of control they have over the work they do, and their daily tasks.

"Being able to control what you do and how much money you make are key happiness factors," Golledge explains. "Sales jobs can often be flexible and provide a rewarding environment, where pay structure is based off of results. For many in this field who receive bonuses and/or commission compensation for positive results can actually boost overall happiness as seen in our most recent data. Even more important is the work that they are doing. The economy is improving to make sales success achievable and closing a deal is always a positive motivator for extroverts who choose sales careers."

Construction superintendent and senior application developer round out the top five happiest jobs in America, with index scores of 4.10 and 4.08, respectively.

Using the same methodology, CareerBliss also compiled a gloomier list: The Unhappiest Jobs in America.

If you happen to be a customer service associate, marketing coordinator or legal assistant and you're constantly down in the dumps—you're not alone. 15

These are three of the nation's unhappiest professions, according to CareerBliss.

But associate attorney is the unhappiest of all, with an index score of 2.89 out of 5.

"Associate attorneys stated they felt most unhappy with their company culture," Golledge says. "In many cases, law firms are conducted in a structured environment that is heavily centered on billable hours. It may take several years for an associate attorney to rise to the rank of partner. People in this position rated the way they work and the rewards they receive lower than any other industry."

The second and third unhappiest jobs are customer service associate and clerk. They earned scores of 3.16 and 3.18, respectively. People in both of these jobs cite growth opportunities and workplace culture as the two things they are most dissatisfied with.

"The lack of growth opportunities was a huge factor for customer service associates," Golledge says. "For many people in this position, not having a clear path to their next position within their current company impacted their overall happiness." 20

Surprises on this year's list: Teachers and nurses.

"[We have] found through our research that teachers appear to be quite happy with their work and their co-workers. However, the rewards for their work, lack of support, and lack of opportunities to be promoted counteract many of the good parts of the job," she says. "Nurses, on the other hand, have more issues with the culture of their workplaces, the people they work with, and the person they work for. The factors driving the unhappiness tell different stories for these two jobs."

Analyze

1. What is the salary range of real estate agents?
2. What do senior quality assurance engineers do?
3. What is the unhappiest job and what makes it so low?

Explore

1. Smith says that "being able to control what you do and how much money you make are key happiness factors." Write an essay about the career you have chosen and why. Discuss where it fits the happiness and unhappiness factors discussed in the article. If possible, interview someone from your chosen career to see what their views are in these categories.

2. Write an essay exploring how jobs are a significant part of our identity, keeping in mind the happiness and unhappiness factors, but also how we feel when people ask us, What do you do? And how we feel when people tell us what they do. How do we respond when someone has a prestigious job, or a less glamorous one, and what makes them so?

3. In groups assigned by your instructor, create a survey measuring the happiest and unhappiest majors on your campus. Compile your results, and, in an article like Smith's present your findings.

Devon W. Carbado and Miti Gulati
"Working Identity"

Carbado is a law professor at UCLA. He is the recipient of the Law School's Rutter Award for Excellence in Teaching, the Eby Award for the Art of Teaching, and the inaugural recipient of the Fletcher Foundation Fellowship, awarded to scholars whose work supports the goals of *Brown v. Board of Education*. He is coeditor of *Race Law Stories* and is coauthor of *Acting White? Rethinking Race in Post-Racial America*. Gulati is a law professor at Duke University. He has authored articles in journals such as the *Tulane Law Review*, the *University of Missouri Law Review*, the *Maine Law Review*, *Law and Contemporary Problems*, *Law and Social Inquiry*, *European Business Organization Law Review*, and *International Review of Law & Economics*. He is coauthor of two books, *The 3 1/2 Minute Transaction: Boilerplate and the Limits of Contract Design*, and *Acting White? Rethinking Race in Post-Racial America*. In our reading from *Acting White?* the authors argue blacks play secondary roles in a play—their workplaces/school admissions, politics—to avoid social hardships and to gain something from it.

From the readings from this chapter, do you think any of the writers' experiences fit what Carbado and Gulati describe?

Being an African American in a predominantly white institution is like being an actor on stage. There are roles one has to perform, storylines one is expected to follow, and dramas and subplots one should avoid at all cost. Being an African American in a predominantly white institution is like playing a small but visible part in a racially specific script. The main characters are white. There are one or two blacks in supporting roles. Survival is always in question. The central conflict is to demonstrate that one is black enough from the perspective of the supporting cast and white enough from the perspective of the main characters. The "double bind" racial performance is hard and risky. Failure is always just around the corner. And there is no acting school in which to enroll to rehearse the part.

Yet, blacks working in white institutions act out versions of this "double bind" racial performance every day. It is part of a broader phenomenon that we call "Working Identity." Working Identity is constituted by a range of racially associated ways of being, including how one dresses, speaks, styles one's hair; one's professional and social affiliations; who one marries or dates; one's politics and views about race; where one lives; and so on and so forth. The foregoing function as a set of racial criteria people can employ to ascertain not simply whether a person is black in terms of how she looks but whether that person is black in terms of how she is perceived to act. In this sense, Working Identity refers both to the perceived choices people make about their self-presentation (the racially associated ways of being listed above) and to the perceived identity that emerges from those choices (how black we determine a person to be).

Paying attention to Working Identity is important. Few institutions today refuse to hire any African Americans. Law expressly prohibits that form of discrimination and society frowns upon it. Indeed, most institutions profess a commitment to diversity, so much so that "diversity is good for business" is now a standard corporate slogan. Companies that invoke that mantra will have at least one black face on the company brochure or website. Moreover, employers want to think of themselves as "colorblind." That perception is hard to sell if all the employees are white. Finally, to the extent that there are some blacks in the workplace, the employer can use them as a shield against charges of racism or racial insensitivity: "How can you say we are racist. Obviously, we wouldn't adopt a policy that would hurt our African American colleagues."

The reality today, therefore, is that most firms want to hire *some* African Americans. The question is, which ones? Working Identity provides a basis upon which they can do so. Employers can screen their application pool for African Americans with palatable Working Identities. These African Americans are not "too black"—which is to say, they are not racially salient as African Americans. Some of them might even be "but for" African Americans—"but for" the fact that they look black, they are otherwise indistinguishable from whites. From an employer's perspective, this subgroup of African Americans is racially comfortable in part because they negate rather than activate racial stereotypes. More generally, the employer's surmise is that these "good blacks" will think of themselves as people first and black people second (or third or fourth); they will neither "play the race card" nor generate racial antagonism or tensions in the workplace; they will not let white people feel guilty about being white; and they will work hard to assimilate themselves into the firm's culture. The screening of African Americans along these lines enables the employer to extract a diversity profit from its African American employees without incurring the cost of racial salience. The employer's investment strategy is to hire enough African Americans to obtain a diversity benefit without incurring the institutional costs of managing racial salience.

5   At least ten implications flow from what we have just said.

1. Discrimination is not only an inter-group phenomenon, it is also an intra-group phenomenon. We should care both about employers preferring whites over blacks (an inter-group discrimination problem) and about employers preferring racially palatable blacks over racially salient ones (an intra-group discrimination problem).

2. The existence of intra-group discrimination creates an incentive for African Americans to work their identities to signal to employers that they are racially palatable. They will want to cover up their racial salience to avoid being screened out of the application pool.

3. Signaling continues well after the employee is hired. The employee understands that she is still black on stage; that her employer is watching her racial performance with respect to promotion and pay increases. Accordingly, she becomes attuned to the roles her Working Identity performs. She will want the employer to experience her Working Identity as a diversity profit, not a racial deficit.

4. Working Identity requires time, effort, and energy—it is work, "shadow work." The phenomenon is part of an underground racial economy in which everyone participates and to which almost everyone simultaneously turns a blind eye.

5. Working Identity is not limited to the workplace. Admissions officers 10 can screen applicants based on their Working Identity. Police officers can stop, search, and arrest people based on Working Identity. The American public can vote for politicians based on their Working Identity. Here, too, there are incentives for the actor—to work her identity to gain admissions to universities, to avoid unfriendly interactions with the police, and to gain political office.

6. Working Identity is costly. It can cause people to compromise their sense of self; to lose themselves in their racial performance; to deny who they are; and to distance themselves from other members of their racial group. Plus, the strategy is risky. Staying at work late to negate the stereotype that one is lazy, for example, can confirm the stereotype that one is incompetent, unable to get work done within normal work hours.

7. Working Identity raises difficult questions for law. One can argue that discrimination based on Working Identity is not racial discrimination at all. Arguably, it is discrimination based on behavior or culture rather than race. Therefore, perhaps the law should not intervene. And even assuming that this form of discrimination is racial discrimination, it still might be a bad idea for the law to get involved. Do we really want judges deciding whether a person is or isn't "acting white" or "acting black"—and the degree to which they might be doing so? It is difficult to figure out what role, if any, law should play.

8. Working Identity transcends the African American experience. Everyone works their identity. Everyone feels the pressure to fit in, including white, heterosexual men. But the existence of negative racial stereotypes increases those pressures and makes the work of fitting in harder and more time consuming. African Americans are not the only racial minority that experiences this difficulty, though our focus in the book is primarily on this group.

9. Nor is race the only social category with a Working Identity dimension. Women work their identities as feminine or not. Men are expected to act like men. Gays and lesbians are viewed along a continuum of acting straight or not. Racial performance is but part of a broader Working Identity phenomenon.

10. We all have a Working Identity whether we want to or not. Working 15 Identity does not turn on the intentional, strategic behavior of the actor.

Analyze

1. How do Carbado and Gulati define "working identity"?
2. How does working identity play a role in hiring in America?
3. What do Carbado and Gulati mean when they say employers want to hire blacks who look black but are indistinguishable from whites?

Explore

1. The authors present black employees as having to perform secondary roles in a play (their workplace). From the ten points Carbado and Gulati list, write an essay supporting or disagreeing with their argument.
2. Write an essay drawing from Carbado and Gulati's arguments about another race in America that also has the same challenges. You can draw from personal experience, from the essays in our book, or from experiences you have heard others talk about.
3. In point 5 Carbado and Gulati talk about the ways black Americans work their identity to avoid certain social hardships and to exact some sort of gain (e.g., college admissions, politics, etc.). In point 8 they say we all work our identity to fit in. How do the people in this chapter work their identity to fit in and why is this so common?

Forging Connections

1. Write a six-word description for each of the readings in this chapter.
2. When it comes to work, the American Dream is a myth that is ingrained in our lives, native born and immigrant alike, from birth to death. Write an essay exploring this myth: discuss whether it still exists, and if so for whom, and why it has worked for some and not for others.
3. In a collaborative group, focus on 3–4 types of jobs, ranging from low-wage to high-wage. Locate one person from each of these job types and interview them. Create one questionnaire that you will use for these interviews. If you can, record and take notes of the interviews so you can capture everything the interviewee says. Write an essay about your findings and how they relate to the forms of work and identity in this chapter.

Looking Further

1. Do our names and other identity-forming aspects of our lives affect the opportunities we have? How so?
2. Explore how last names, cultural identity, places of nationality, and education affect where we work and what our economic identity is in the context of this chapter's themes.
3. Apply the concept of working identity from this chapter to 3–5 movie or TV series characters with which you are familiar. Write an essay arguing how they do or do not fit the concept.

Whom Do You Love? Romance & Relationships in America

5

Have you ever been really, really in love? Have you ever broken up with someone or been left on the curb, or asked in a friendly way during a breakup to still be friends? By now, you might think people would know more about what makes us tick when it comes to love and relationships; as it has panned out, though, it seems that while we are pretty good at falling in love, we're less adept at maintaining it.

According to the *Oxford English Dictionary*, love is:

> A feeling or disposition of deep affection or fondness for someone, typically arising from a recognition of attractive qualities, from natural affinity, or from sympathy and manifesting itself in concern for the other's welfare and pleasure in his or her presence (distinguished

from sexual love at sense 4a); great liking, strong emotional attachment; (similarly) a feeling or disposition of benevolent attachment experienced towards a group or category of people, and (by extension) towards one's country or another impersonal object of affection. (OED Online)

It's possible that some of us might see some of our own experiences in this definition, but the fact remains that we each have details and experiences that are unique to our relationships. So while the dictionary may provide one definition of the word "love," a better way to understand the topic as a whole is to see how it has been discussed and defined through relationships in a variety of ways, beyond the dictionary definition.

Our readings in Chapter 5 explore several facets important to understanding the complexities of relationships, behavior, and personalities. We start with our transcription of Feldman's talk, "Finding the 'Liar' in All of Us." In any interaction we have with others, from unknown to intimate partner, we all lie. The next few readings bring in sex, cheating, and the effects these have on our notions of love. In DiFalco's "Internet Cheating: In the Clicks of a Mouse, a Betrayal," the author discovers her husband's use of the Internet to have affairs with other women. Tannen, in "Sex, Lies, and Conversation," explores relationships, especially the differences between how men and women communicate, to help explain why couples do not communicate well or stop communicating altogether, which she says usually signifies that love is lost. Why is being aware of the degree of our lies important to our long-term relationships? We look to classical philosophy to answer the ageless question: What is love? Our excerpt comes from Plato's *Phaedrus* and is in the form of a dialogue between Phaedrus and Socrates. Shifting to a humorous reflection on how we do and do not think about sex, Shawn's "Is Sex Interesting?" asks us to think about the role sex plays in romance and how, perhaps, we attribute too much to it.

Our last three essays explore notions of love from distinct angles. Chen looks at the myth of the stable traditional family (man and woman) as the foundation for future stability in all facets of life in "Farewell, June Cleaver: 'Non-Traditional Families' and Economic Opportunity," and in "Sibling Rivalry Grows Up," Bernstein explores the love-hate relationships we often have with our siblings and how it is a psychological condition rarely talked about and typically left unresolved. Our final reading is "Anthem," Kapur's poem immersing us in a gritty hymn of love to her country.

By reading, discussing, and writing about love from so many angles, we come to understand that, as much as we analyze the matter, it still has a mysterious effect on us, and it is a feeling that affects us all in many different, yet significant, ways. Part of what we learn is that various forms of love have been important for humanity from time immemorial, since before we were even able to record our thoughts about it. One thing we do know is that a large part of our lives and who we are is spent on our beginning, working out, or ending relationships. As we explore here, we have many types of love that are the core of how we define ourselves.

Robert Feldman
"Finding the 'Liar' in All of Us"

In this reading, National Public Radio interviews an expert on lying. Feldman, professor of psychology and associate dean in the College of Social and Behavioral Sciences at the University of Massachusetts, has studied lying for over 25 years and finds that when we are aware of our own dishonesty we tend to distrust others even more than usual. Our "little white lies" set the stage for more dishonesty, creating a whole "culture of lies." For more on this interview in audio and text from National Public Radio, visit http://www.npr.org.

How often do you think you lie in a day and are lied to? Do you agree or disagree with Feldman on why, as his title suggests, we all have a part of us that regularly lies?

NEAL CONAN, host:
This is TALK OF THE NATION.
I'm Neal Conan in Washington.

> "Sometime earlier today, somebody almost certainly told you a lie."

Sometime earlier today, somebody almost certainly told you a lie. If you chatted with a stranger on the bus for 10 minutes, research suggests you probably heard three. And the odds are not better if you were talking with a co-worker or with your spouse. And again, according to research, you almost certainly believed everyone.

Psychologist Robert Feldman concludes that we live among a web of liars—
yes, a few greedy businessmen and con artists, but much more often our
friends, family colleagues and, yes, ourselves. He believes that humans are
programmed to lie and programmed to believe them. Today: our duplici-
tous nature and the liars in our lives.

Later in the hour, Dawn Turner Trice questions honesty and interracial relationships. But first, when was the last time somebody lied to you? Give us a
call: 800-989-8255. E-mail: talk@npr.org. And you can join the conversation on our Web site. That's at npr.org. Click on **TALK OF THE NATION**.

5   Robert Feldman's new book is the *The Liar in Your Life*. He's associate
dean at the College of Social and Behavioral Sciences at the University of
Massachusetts, Amherst, and joins us from our member station there,
WFCR. Nice to have you on the program today.

Professor ROBERT FELDMAN (Associate Dean, College of Social and
Behavioral Sciences): Glad to be here, Neal.

CONAN: And when was the last time somebody told you a lie?

Prof. FELDMAN: Oh, probably about five minutes ago . . .

(SOUNDBITE OF LAUGHTER)

10   Prof. FELDMAN: . . . when they—I think I was told I was looking good
and ready to go.

CONAN: And quite possibly, you were. But nevertheless, these are sort of
the lies that we use as social lubricant, if you will.

Prof. FELDMAN: Exactly, exactly. These are part and parcel of everyday
social interaction. When we're with our friends, when we're with people
we're just meeting for the first time, even when we're with our spouses and
loved ones, the lies are thick and furious.

CONAN: And you say a lot of people—these are little white lies.
Nevertheless, you say, they come with a price attached.

Prof. FELDMAN: The little white lies do matter. In part, it's because
these lies can very easily lead to other lies and bigger lies. And the other
thing is it leads to a kind of lack of authenticity in our everyday life. We
don't really know where we stand. We don't really ever get a good sense of
who we are and what our strengths and weaknesses are as people if people
are constantly not telling us the truth.

15   CONAN: Even in those little daily interactions—I must say I grew up in
New York and was quite accustomed to surly people on the streets who
made no bones about telling me their opinion about anything, and then
moving to Washington, D.C., where the normal reaction was have a nice
day and what a pleasure. And I found that, well, disingenuous.

Prof. FELDMAN: And also kind of refreshing, because it is more
pleasant to be in a world in which people are nice and telling us the kinds

of things that we would like to hear. But the reality is that ultimately, these lies have a price, and there's something to be said for the New York style of truth.

CONAN: Nevertheless, it does make a—put a little more friction in your life . . .

(SOUNDBITE OF LAUGHTER)

CONAN: . . . as it were. And as we go through, though, it's interesting, you say, we are primed to—liars have an advantage over us.

Prof. FELDMAN: Yes. As I talk about in my book, there is a definite liar's advantage. First of all, we're very bad at telling when someone else is lying to us. The nonverbal cues that we often think give away people, in fact, do not give them away. There's no single or even set of nonverbal behaviors that tell us when someone is being deceptive. So most of the time, we have about a 50-50 chance of determining if somebody's telling us the truth. So the liars do have an advantage in that way.

CONAN: And I want to stop you there. Poker players famously can read   20 other people at the table, and they have what are known as tells. The guy is bluffing every time he scratches his nose or something like that.

Prof. FELDMAN: Well, yeah. And some of us are really good at learning those kinds of tells. But one of the things that happens at a poker table is that you eventually learn whether the person is bluffing or not. In every-day life, we don't get that advantage. We don't—we're not able to tell if someone has been lying to us or not most of the time. So we don't have much feedback in terms of whether we are correct in our assumptions about when someone is lying or not to us. There's also a truth bias that we carry around with us that most of us just generally believe that others are telling us the truth. So we're not very good in that sense in determining whether somebody is lying to us.

CONAN: And you suggest . . .

Prof. FELDMAN: And finally, it takes a lot of work to tell—to spend effort, to think about all the time whether someone's being truthful or not truthful. So most of the time, we are more than willing to let the lie slip by us.

CONAN: Now, let's get some callers in on the conversation. We're asking people: When was the last time somebody lied to you? Give us a call: 800-989-8255. E-mail: talk@npr.org. We're talking with Robert Feldman about his book *The Liar in Your Life: The Way to Truthful Relationships*. And Christina is on the line, calling from San Antonio.

CHRISTINA (Caller): Hi.   25

CONAN: Hi, Christina.

CHRISTINA: I'm pregnant, and I think just about every day someone tells me that I look great, which I like. It's very flattering. But don't think it's necessarily true because not only have I gained my weight, which is fine, but I don't sleep very well. So my eyes are puffy. I haven't been able to do my hair colored, so my grays are coming out. And my daughter is four. She looks at me sometimes. I can tell when she thinks, wow, mommy looks really different.

(SOUNDBITE OF LAUGHTER)

CHRISTINA: So . . .

30   **CONAN:** I'm sure you've heard that you're glowing.

CHRISTINA: Yeah, you get that. You're glowing. You're beautiful. You look gorgeous, all that stuff. But I tell you what, even though I know it's not entirely true, it does make me feel good. And tell my girlfriends, keep it coming. Keep on talking. I look great.

(SOUNDBITE OF LAUGHTER)

CONAN: And Robert Feldman, that's part of the reinforcement process.

Prof. FELDMAN: That is part of the reinforcement process where we want those lies to come to us. We want to be told that we do look good. And—I mean, first of all, there may be some people who believe that a pregnant woman does look beautiful, no matter what. And there are other people who are just saying that. But as you say, you enjoy hearing that you look good, even if you don't truly 100 percent believe that you're looking your very best.

35   **CHRISTINA:** Right.

Prof. FELDMAN: And I think this just illustrates one of the facts about lying in everyday life, that very often, we are not only accepting of other people's lies, we embrace them. We want to believe them because they make us feel better about ourselves. They make us think that we look better, that we're smarter, that we're better people. So it makes it very hard to switch back and forth from saying, oh, I want to accept those lies to being in a mode where you actually want to identity the lies that others tell you.

CONAN: Christina, I think you look beautiful.

(SOUNDBITE OF LAUGHTER)

CHRISTINA: Oh, thank you.

40   **Prof. FELDMAN:** Me, too.

(SOUNDBITE OF LAUGHTER)

CONAN: Thanks very much.

CHRISTINA: Have a good day.

CONAN: Bye-bye. Let's go next to Michael, Michael with us from Duluth.

45   **MICHAEL (Caller):** Hello.

CONAN: Hi, Michael.

MICHAEL: Hi. I do want to say that I love pregnant women. I think they do look great.

(SOUNDBITE OF LAUGHTER)

MICHAEL: I don't know, something about them just makes me—I love pregnant women. But my lie is—my favorite lie is when I was in getting knee surgery, and the anesthetist comes in. He gives me a shot, what he said would soften me up. And he tells me that my doctor is the best. He said, this guy is the greatest. And I was just loosened up. I just went, you're lying. I said—and I called him on it, and I could see by the look in his face that he was lying. But the doctor was fine. I mean there was no question about that.

But they want you to go into the surgery and feel like, you know, every-   50
thing's okay. They don't want to you going into there going, oh, my God.
What's going to happen here? They just tell you, this guy is the greatest
and it's wonderful and everything's going to be fine. But anyway, it made
me laugh. That was my funnest—the greatest lie, I think.

CONAN: Interesting. And I'm sure he remembered it was the right knee
and not the left.

MICHAEL: He remembers that it was the right knee and not the left, yes.

(SOUNDBITE OF LAUGHTER)

CONAN: Okay. Michael, thanks very much for the call, appreciate it.

MICHAEL: You're welcome.   55

CONAN: And this goes on to the question of why—well, you've explained to us, Robert Feldman, why we're tending to believe the lies. Why
do we go on and tell them? Because there are a number of interesting motives going on here.

Mr. FELDMAN: Oh, we tell lies because they work, that we—first of all,
people like others who tell them the things that they want to hear. So
there's a social advantage in that way. The other thing that lies can do is
give you an advantage over someone else in a business negotiation. It can
keep the social situation moving a lot more smoothly.

So there are many different kinds of motivations for the lies, and
sometimes people want to make a distinction between white lies and other
kinds of lies but it's my feeling, and as I talk about it in the book, that all
these lies actually do take a toll in social relationships. That in fact these
white lies do add up and there can be a kind of snowball effect where the
white lies, if you're very good at it, and they—work very well in social
settings for you, the white lies can lead to bigger and bigger kinds of lies.
So it really is a kind of slippery slope and very dangerous.

CONAN: You tell the story, in fact, of a—I guess it's now a famous story
of a 31-year-old man who lied his way into Princeton, made up a name,

a whole back-story. And you read this and it just seems ridiculous. This was clearly something that was devised to, well, make him look the best possible—like the best possible candidate Princeton had ever seen.

60   **Mr. FELDMAN:** And not only did he lie his way into Princeton, but he was there for years and no one caught on. And obviously, they have pretty smart people at Princeton but I think this illustrates part of the liar's advantage. Most of the time, we don't delve into people's backgrounds. We do accept that they are the people that they say they are. And so it makes it surprisingly easy for people to get away with their lies.

CONAN: And you don't have to be the golden-tongued con man to get away with this.

Mr. FELDMAN: No, no, not at all. I mean, you just need to be consistent and tell the lie over and over again, and people will tend to believe the lie.

CONAN: And what about those television shows where looking up and to your left absolutely guaranteed you're telling a lie?

Mr. FELDMAN: Doesn't work. The non-verbal behaviors, all the behaviors that people say are related to lies, may be related to lies on one level, but those same non-verbal behaviors may mean something totally different. They may mean you're anxious. They may mean you're unhappy. They may mean something very, very different. So the problem is that when you see these non-verbal behaviors, yes, in fact, it may be related to lying, but it also may be related to all sorts of other emotional states and we're not very good at sorting those out.

65   **CONAN:** Robert Feldman is with us. We're talking about his book, *The Liar in Your Life: The Way To Truthful Relationships.* We'll have more of your calls in just a moment, 800-989-8255. E-mail us, talk@npr.org.

If you've been following the news today, you know that former President Clinton went to North Korea to try to arrange the release of two American journalists who'd been sentenced to, I think, 12 years at hard labor. The Associated Press is reporting that North Korea says those two journalists have been pardoned. Stay tuned to NPR News for the latest on that as it develops.

I'm Neal Conan, it's the TALK OF THE NATION from NPR News.
(SOUNDBITE OF MUSIC)
CONAN: This is TALK OF THE NATION. I'm Neal Conan in Washington. You're a liar, and yes, so am I. Robert Feldman says we all lie all the time, even to ourselves, when we say I feel fine, or I like your dress, the little white lies might help us avoid awkward social moments. Imagine telling a coworker, your hair looks terrible. But all those fibs make us more and more tolerant of deception. That's among the arguments in Robert Feldman's new book. It's titled *The Liar in Your Life.*

He studied the hows and whys of lying for more than 20 years. So   70
when was the last time someone lied to you? 800-989-8255. E-mail is
talk@npr.org, and you can join the conversation on our Web site. That's at
npr.org. Click on TALK OF THE NATION. Let's go next to Gigi(ph),
Gigi with us from Boston. Gigi?

BRANDON (Caller): This is Brandon(ph). I just called in.

CONAN: Oh, all right. I'm sorry, Brandon, go ahead.

BRANDON: Oh, that's great, didn't even get a chance to screen me, but
my question is more—where is the line between accentuating the positive
and actually telling a lie? And you know, for example, I tell my wife every
day that she's beautiful, which is absolutely true, but some days, she's more
beautiful than others and she has more time to do the things that women
do to do those things. So I'm just kind of curious about that.

CONAN: When is it a lie and when is it an exaggeration, Robert
Feldman?

Mr. FELDMAN: Well, there is no fine line here. It's really a matter of   75
gradations. If, in your heart you believe she's beautiful every day, then
you're certainly not lying to her. But it does raise the issue of how we distinguish between different kinds of lies. And ultimately, my position is
that a lie is a lie is a lie, that these lies add up, these lies exact a social toll
from us and that when you are being deceptive, there is a price to be paid.
But in your case, you're talking about something that you believe is true.
So it wouldn't fit my definition of a lie.

CONAN: All right, thanks, Brandon.

BRANDON: Thank you.

CONAN: Bye-bye, and I was pushing the wrong button. This, I think,
is Gigi.

GIGI (Caller): Hello.

CONAN: Hi, you're on the air, Gigi. Go ahead, please.   80

GIGI: So this is very interesting. Just a couple of days ago, I met someone,
and we went and had this great date, and he was telling me all these things
about himself, and I didn't really think one thing or the other. And then
we went to dinner, and I was extremely tired, and so we got the bill, he
took it in his hand. I went to the bathroom. I came out. He went to the
bathroom, and then we walked out.

   And something inside said something is weird, and I said I was really
tired, and I needed to go home, and he kept saying, you know, let's go get
ice cream and trying to duck me in the stores just past the restaurant, and
then we got up a couple blocks later, and there was a bench around the
corner. So we sat down, and then he wanted to walk me back to my car but
across the street. And something inside said it was wrong, and as we're

walking across the street in front of the restaurant, someone comes running out saying, you didn't pay your bill.

And then it turns out he didn't go to law school. He never went to the undergrad he went to. Everything he told me had been a lie.

CONAN: Wow.

85   **GIGI:** It was very interesting, and it was originally gut instinct, but it was him trying to, like, walk me across the street instead of the side of the street my car was on, trying to duck in and, like, maybe grab a cup of coffee afterwards, when I had said I was really tired. I mean, all these things together, it was very interesting. So I called him on it. I mean, I called him right out on it.

Mr. FELDMAN: I suspect this will be your last date with this guy.

(SOUNDBITE OF LAUGHTER)

Mr. FELDMAN: I think you make a very good point, and that is that we do have to listen to our gut, although you may not be 100 percent accurate when you get these feelings, these intuitions. In fact, they can be quite right. And here you have, it sounds like, a fair amount of evidence. It wasn't just one thing or another but several different things that just didn't . . .

GIGI: I called NYU. I called Duke. Nobody could verify him, yeah.

90   **Mr. FELDMAN:** Well, I think it's very good in this kind of situation to look at the evidence. First of all, look at the evidence rationally but also follow those gut feelings.

GIGI: Yeah.

CONAN: And one of the ways—and thanks, Gigi, for the call, and good luck—better luck with your next date. Oh, I'm sorry, Gigi.

GIGI: . . . to trust their gut because I could have been in a really dangerous situation.

CONAN: Oh, well that's exactly what I was going to ask, follow up with Robert Feldman, and that is one of the ways you say is the way toward a more truthful relationship is, in fact, to, well, when in doubt, verify.

95   **Mr. FELDMAN:** Exactly, exactly. I talk about something called active honesty assessment, and what it means is you really have to put in the effort, the thought, into thinking about the people that you're dealing with, particularly those you don't know very well. And think about whether they are telling you what appears to be the truth and whether there's any way to verify it.

I mean, it's hardly very romantic. I'm the first to admit that, but I think in all sorts of situations where you are unsure of somebody else, I think it does make some sense, as you did, to make some calls and find out what, you know, what the truth is.

CONAN: Let's go next to Kelly(ph), Kelly in Denver.

KELLY (Caller): Yes. I had a question about the Internet and . . .

CONAN: Everybody tells the truth on the Internet.

KELLY: Yes, and lying over the Internet. I frequent a parenting message board and I'm thinking of one particular instance where a woman was posting and claimed to have a child who was dying and then died of cancer. And she had gone to the extent of setting up a blog, using pictures and actually ended up being—had posted the story on multiple parenting messaging boards, and eventually just kind of started to ring false to some people who started doing some Googling and found out that she had swiped the pictures from various online accounts and just basically went through and looked through the details and then, you know, tried to confront this woman, you know, made public all these details that didn't add up.

And then, of course, we never hear from that person again. They don't   100
necessarily admit that they lie. They just—suddenly you never hear from them again.

CONAN: It's interesting. There are cases like that, Robert Feldman. The former mayor, I think, of Atlantic City, who made up a story of, well, military honors that he had not earned. He said he'd served in the Green Berets and had never done that. And these things can become quite elaborate.

Mr. FELDMAN: Oh, yeah, they are very elaborate, and it's really paradoxical about the Internet. What I found in my research, and what I talk about in the book, is that we lie more on the Internet than we do face to face. So it's easier for us to lie in e-mail, and it's easier for us to lie in instant messaging than it is in face-to-face conversations, and as we know, it's pretty easy to lie in face-to-face conversations.

The paradox is that, in some ways, using the Internet allows you to identify when someone is lying. So it's both easier to lie on the Internet, and there are—the case that you talk about, I talk about in the book, it's both easier to lie, and people do it and develop false identities. And they're all—we use user names that are not true, but at the same time, the incredible strength of the Internet is that you can use it to find out when some of these instances are not accurate. But it is way too easy for people to be dishonest in using the Web.

CONAN: Kelly, thanks very much.

KELLY: Thank you.   105

CONAN: Bye-bye. Here's an e-mail from Michelle(ph) in Chicago. I think one of my students—I'm a teacher—lied to me. He is seven years old. He has a good imagination, and he has ADHD. He said he caught a spider and gave it a ride in a motorboat. Kids make up a lot of stories, so I don't consider it a true lie, just a flight of fancy. Is this considered a true lie? His only motive seems to have been to get attention.

Mr. FELDMAN: Well, it is a lie if it's not true. And I mean, I think imagination is wonderful, but we also have to teach our kids the value of telling the truth. It's very hard to do that because as—I mean, kids start lying when they're, some as young as two years of age. By three, they begin to lie on a more regular basis. And for parents, it's very hard to teach their children to be honest.

We talk about—we, I think most of us would say that honesty is the best policy, and that's what we teach our children. And we talk about American icons like George Washington, and Abraham Lincoln never told a lie, that sort of thing, but at the same time, we actually teach them to lie. We tell them a friend is coming over and bringing a gift to you. Make sure you tell them that you like it, even if you don't. Please tell them that, that you wanted this gift, or . . .

CONAN: Well, we're teaching them those social rules that make this—make their existence going to be easier a little later on.

110   **Mr. FELDMAN:** It is going to be easier, but it's also a very mixed message. We're telling them that on the one hand, always tell the truth, and on the other hand, well not so much. It's okay to lie in some cases.

We tell them that the telephone rings, and you see it's the boss calling, your boss calling, you say to your kid, oh, tell him that I'm not here. And it's a very difficult message for kids to understand because on the one hand, it's always tell the truth, on the other, well, it's okay to lie in some cases.

CONAN: Let's go next to Dee(ph), Dee with us from Augusta, Georgia.

DEE (Caller): Hi. I have a friend with whom I wasn't able to make contact for several months, and finally when I called her, she told me that her husband had been very ill and was in rehabilitation out of state.

So I believed it. I continued to call and try to check on her, but she would never answer the phone. So I was concerned, but didn't stress over it. Well, the other night, she called me and said I have to come clean to you. He actually left me six months ago and . . .

115   **CONAN:** Whoa.

DEE: . . . and I didn't want anyone to know. No one really knows. And I was, of course—I was horrified because she's such a good friend and I hurt for her because I could have provided comfort during her time of pain.

CONAN: And I—would that come into the category, Robert Feldman, of lies to make us look better?

Prof. FELDMAN: It's lies to make us look better. It's lies to—I mean, in some cases, lies are motivated by just sheer embarrassment. And I think this is one of those cases. But I think the long-term result is going to be that you may never trust this woman in the same way that you did before this incident. And that, of course, is one of the costs of lying.

CONAN: You write specifically—and Dee, thanks very much for the call.

DEE: Sure. 120

CONAN: You write specifically about couples who have been undone by infidelity, yet sometimes, you say those bonds can be reestablished and can be stronger than ever.

Prof. FELDMAN: Well, they can be reestablished, and the marriage ultimately can be strengthened. But it's a relationship that's on different terms, where you have to have real forgiveness on the part of the person who's been cheated on. And there is a realization, I think, that the relationship is not going to be the same as it was before this loss of trust occurred.

And I do write about the ways in which you can try and rebuild trust in a relationship, but it's certainly not easy and it doesn't always work. There are relationships that just cannot be repaired. But if both parties are willing to move on and to accept this—the new reality of the relationship, it is possible to move on.

CONAN: Robert Feldman, the author of *The Liar in Your Life: The Way to Truthful Relationships*. 800-989-8255. E-mail us: talk@npr.org.

You're listening to TALK OF THE NATION from NPR News. 125

An e-mail from Jay: As an attorney, I am constantly amazed by the number of clients who lie to me. This occurs even after having a long and serious talk about the importance of giving me all of the facts as they are and not as the client wishes them to be.

Numerous attorneys are burned every day in depositions or at trial by the unraveling of their clients' lies. Nine times out of 10, the facts could have been successfully dealt with by the attorney if they had only known the truth ahead of time. Why the people engage in this type of self-destructive lying?

Prof. FELDMAN: Well, I think they don't, first of all, understand necessarily the consequences. And sometimes, people fool themselves. It may not be the case that these people are actively lying on any kind of conscious basis, but that they've somehow, in their own mind, created a situation which puts them in a somewhat—more favorable light. And so they really don't even understand what the objective truth of the situation is. It's very easy to convince ourselves of one thing or another and to believe it so much that it becomes our reality.

CONAN: Our subjective reality transformed into an objective reality—at least in our own brains.

130   **Prof. FELDMAN**: Exactly. Exactly.

CONAN: Yeah. Let's go to Laura. Laura's calling from Madison.

LAURA (Caller): Yeah. To be true to myself, I'm a transsexual. To be true to myself, it would seem that I'd lie to everyone else.

CONAN: Hmm.

Prof. FELDMAN: Well, it depends, you know, where you are in the stage of telling other people about it. I think you—it's helpful to move in a direction of being honest with other people, even though there can be some very, very painful moments.

135   **LAURA**: So when—honesty to other people, is that to present myself as who I feel I am?

Prof. FELDMAN: If you're presenting yourself as the person that you believe you are, then you're presenting yourself in an honest way. And I think that is the goal that all of us should have, to present ourselves in as honest and open a way as we possibly can and to show that true person who we are.

CONAN: Laura, is that the case for some of the time?

LAURA: Well, let's say that I—I'm sorry. But for a lack of a better term, let's say that I hook up with a guy. He would feel abused. Do you get where I'm coming from?

CONAN: Yeah. I get your point. Is it a burden to lie?

140   **LAURA**: It's a—oh, it's a huge burden.

CONAN: And so even though this is making, in a way, your life possible, making those immediate situations survivable, it's—there's a penalty you pay for it for telling the lies.

LAURA: And . . .

Prof. FELDMAN: And there's also probably . . .

LAURA: I self-flagellate every day.

145   **(SOUNDBITE OF LAUGHTER)**

Prof. FELDMAN: And there's a penalty involved for being truthful, too, I think, in this . . .

LAURA: Yeah.

Prof. FELDMAN: . . . kind of situation.

CONAN: I think . . .

150   **Prof. FELDMAN**: It's a very hard situation.

CONAN: I think of it's the no-win situation in that regard.

LAURA: And so, what is truth in this case? What is the . . .

CONAN: Well, I think you have to look inside yourself for that, Laura.

LAURA: Hmm.

155   **CONAN**: I'm not sure if those of us who, on the other end of the phone line can help you there.

LAURA: Thank you.

CONAN: Good luck. And Robert Feldman, you end by pointing out in your book that, of course, we have to accept the lies that we tell every day and the ones that we get away with, and, well, the little pangs of conscience that we feel every time we do.

Prof. FELDMAN: We do. We have to look into ourselves, I think, and we have to try to lead as honest a life as we possibly can. I talk about how honesty is not the perfect policy, but it is the best policy. And the more we can strive to be honest—both with other people and to demand honesty from others towards us—the better off we're going to be.

By asking others to tell us the truth—and I think you do have to go out of your way to ask others to be truthful to you—you're going to have a better understanding of who you are and you're going to be—end up leading a more authentic life.

CONAN: And here's an e-mail we got from James in South Bend. Here are a few that I just never believe: This won't hurt a bit. I'm from the government, and I'm here to help. And one that's not quite a lie but always puts me on guard: Trust me. And if James thinks those were original with him, he's lying.

Anyway, Robert Feldman, thank you very much.

160

Prof. FELDMAN: Thank you, Neal. It was good to be here.

CONAN: Robert Feldman is the author of *The Liar in Your Life: The Way to Truthful Relationships*.

When we come back after a short break, we'll be talking about honesty of a different sort. How open are we in interracial relationships? Dawn Turner Trice joins us.

It's the TALK OF THE NATION from NPR News.

Analyze

1. What are common occasions when we lie?
2. What are some of the common little white lies he says people tell?
3. How is infidelity a lie? Can such a lie be overcome?

Explore

1. Feldman says lies "are part and parcel of everyday social interaction. When we're with our friends, when we're with people we're just meeting for the first time, even when we're with our spouses and loved ones, the lies are thick and furious." In the context of a recent social event (e.g., a party, watching a sporting event, or TV show) with friends you

recently met at school, or with your partner, discuss the types and extent of lies you believe you have been told, and why you think they were told to you, or to the contrary the lies you have told and why.

2. One of Feldman's callers, Brandon, asks, "[w]here is the line between accentuating the positive and actually telling a lie? And you know, for example, I tell my wife every day that she's beautiful, which is absolutely true, but some days, she's more beautiful than others and she has more time to do the things that women do to do those things. So I'm just kind of curious about that." Write an essay arguing that such thinking and practice can lead to more serious lies in a relationship, or that such lies lead to a long-lasting one. An option to an essay is a comic showing the above argument.

3. Using the information supplied in this chapter's readings, individually or in groups create a "A Guide to Healthy Lying Relationships" for your classmates.

Teresa DiFalco
"Internet Cheating: In the Clicks of a Mouse, a Betrayal"

DiFalco was a programmer and systems analyst for fifteen years before focusing full time on being a professional writer. She has published in *The New York Times*, *Willamette Week*, *Salem Monthly*, and *McSweeney's*. Here DiFalco shares with us her failing and then failed marriage and her discovery that it is easy to find people on the Internet who are willing to cheat with us.

> How do people who post "partner" ads in places like Craigslist, such as the author's husband (and DiFalco as well), fit into Tannen's and Feldman's observations on the role and effects of lying?

Three years ago I discovered my husband was having an affair with a woman who had answered his ad in the "casual encounters" section of Craigslist. I was a 40-year-old suburban soccer mom and library volunteer.

On a typical day I did freelance work in the mornings, picked the kids up from school, fixed dinner and helped with homework. My husband, a tall executive with a winning smile, came home each night around 6 with kisses all around, often straight from a prearranged encounter.

Looking back, I see the signs I missed. My husband worked an hour away, so most of his life happened far from us. There were financial worries, and we were quietly growing apart. Even so, our family time was nice: we barbecued, hosted dinners for friends, held backyard movie nights. In hindsight it's obvious that things were not what they seemed, but life has a way of moving you along. What I knew was that my husband came home every night. In the moment, I didn't suspect a thing.   Details of my husband's other life arrived in an e-mail from "John Smith," a friend of the woman my husband was seeing. She had confided in him, and for some reason he felt compelled to find and tell me. What followed were the most surreal months of my life. In the dizzying swirl of shock and explanation, anger and tears, and then separation, I became fixated on the world my husband had been living in. And as any victim of adultery obsesses over "the other" in her partner's life, I became increasingly obsessed with the casual encounters world of Craigslist, so much so that I decided to post an ad of my own.

My decision was impulsive. I was sitting on our back patio, listening to the snores of our family dog and laughter from my children. Against this backdrop, my act felt sordid. Three mouse clicks put me into "w4m" (women for men). I hadn't thought it through but managed a serviceable ad on my feet. It read: "Freshly divorced and want my confidence back! I'm 5'10", long sandy blond hair. I'm new at this, a little nervous. I don't know what to put down."

I thought it made me sound innocent but willing. I wasn't divorced yet but thought it sounded sexy to say so. I lied about my name and town but not my height or hair. I didn't post a photo, but it turned out I didn't need to. My first reply came in minutes. It was from Joe and said, simply, "Let's do this!" He knew a nice, clean hot-tub place. Could I meet him in an hour?

A hot-tub place? An hour?   5

Joe's proposal was sudden and unexpected, and to my surprise, it made my heart skip. This was the first amorous offer I had received from someone besides my husband in 12 years. I refreshed my e-mail and a dozen more replies showed up. Within the hour I had more than 100. I was appalled but also flattered. All this attention! Never mind that they were strangers, never mind the poorly shot and often graphic photos they sent of themselves. I had been instantly transformed, from sexual reject to desirable poseur. I had more than 400 replies by the end of the day. How many people were having anonymous sex this way? It seemed like a lot. I began casting sidelong glances at men in the grocery store. How many of them had hooked up that day? What if one had answered my ad? Most of the photos I received were of nude or scantily clad torsos with faces obscured by a camera flash in the mirror, though it seemed many of the men were family types. Craigslist (like AshleyMadison.com and similar services) offered them a quick and anonymous sex fix that didn't interfere with their lives.

Many were too forward for me. I needed some pretense of small talk. But I responded to John, a teacher. He was clothed in his photo, with a friendly smile. We liked similar music, and he thought I was witty. I responded to Chris, too; he seemed sensitive. He was in the middle of a divorce, so I used him as a sounding board for my own angst. Then there was Joe, the man who first replied; he was aggressively flirtatious. Though he was explicit about his intentions, his picture, like John's, was safe for work, and for a while he humored my need for words. After a few e-mail exchanges, I felt as if I knew him. He sent a picture of himself on his boat, and I imagined us riding around on it together. He looked burly, like someone who was handy around the house. I was nuts to be thinking this way. These men weren't wondering if I cooked a good meal. They didn't want me to ride on their boats. This was where you went to arrange sex, plain and simple, and I'd led them to believe I had a similar goal. I was shamelessly misrepresenting myself. Joe talked about his children: he, too, was married. Most of the men were. I told myself I didn't care. They wrote that their wives were either depressed or sick (often fibromyalgia, for some reason). It's very likely what my own husband said about me. I went the furthest with Joe. I don't mean physically, but we exchanged the greatest number of e-mails. Joe wanted a picture. Well, everyone did, but he hounded me. My marriage was essentially over, and in the ugly swirl of it all, what I kept thinking was, My husband left because I wasn't sexy enough. I thought if my soon-to-be ex-husband could send a picture, and if the women who answered his ad could send pictures, then I could, too.

People tend to take their pictures in front of mirrors, because what other option is there? It's an awkward favor to ask of someone. I had a big mirror in my bathroom, but I didn't like my bathroom and spent a ridiculous amount of time staging it before moving on to what to wear. This process (and I can't believe I took it this far) may have been the most humiliating of all. I picked out an old black negligee, my finest. Then, in unflattering light, I stood before my bathroom mirror with cellphone camera in hand and posed.

It was horrible.

I tried to show cheekbones, cleavage and confidence. But when I smiled   10 I looked like a field-trip chaperone in a cheap teddy. When I didn't smile, I looked sad. I spent an hour trying to get one decent shot in which I didn't look absurd. I couldn't get it. I cried. My therapist told me the next week: "Don't be so hard on yourself. You're just not the type."

I didn't, thank God, send Joe a picture. And after I turned down one too many of his invitations, he moved on.

Eventually that's what I did, too. Chris sent periodic e-mails for months. They were sweet at first. His final one was more graphic, and I got the point. I had lied about my intentions and about who I was, and I was disgusted with myself. Regardless of how friendly the men acted, they were strangers who wanted to have sex. They didn't care that I had planted tomatoes in the garden or gone wine tasting with friends. They must have thought I was crazy rattling off the mundane details of my days. And while I liked the attention, I also realized I had lost my mind. These were men who didn't even know what I looked like, or where I lived, or how sweet my children were. It was a depressing experiment. What I had wanted was for my marriage not to have blown apart. What I wanted, sexy or not, was a committed, monogamous man who didn't mind hanging around the house. I didn't close my fake e-mail account, and a few months ago I checked it for the first time in over a year. There were e-mails for mortgage rates and the like, and there was an e-mail from Joe, sent just the previous week. Again, my heart skipped. Will weirdness never end? He was still a stranger, after all: a man who wanted sex in a hot tub, with anyone. And yet, I thought, how sweet of him to remember me. The message was a graphic photo of his midsection, no words. And my address in the "to" line was one of many.

I'm sorry for misleading the men who responded to my ad. Maybe there were moments I thought I was being sincere, despite my fake name and cloudy details. But let's face it: I was using them for my own attention fix. I felt guilty about that, for a time. In the fog of betrayal and divorce, I had lost sight of myself and pretended to be someone I was not. And perhaps that's what my husband had been doing in what I thought was our real life. Pretending to be someone he was not.

Analyze

1. How many replies did DiFalco have at the end of the first day of her posting?
2. What does DiFalco argue are the differences between why men and women go to web sites for sexual encounters?
3. Why does DiFalco fail to follow through with meeting any men who contacted her through the Internet?

Explore

1. Research why so many people use the Internet to find partners (even though they may already have one). As you gather information, keep in mind the role and effect that lies play that both Tannen and Feldman state and see how well they match.
2. Write an argument either warning about or praising why Internet dating sites are good for single or married individuals (pick one).
3. Notice how much of our identity becomes an important part of our relationship with our partner. As DiFalco shows us, we tend to spiral out of control in search of a new identity or to discover pieces of our lost identity when we break up. Create a comic showing the bonds of a loving relationship, a cheating partner (or both), and then the results of that relationship during and after breakup.

Deborah Tannen
"Sex, Lies, and Conversation"

Tannen is a professor at Georgetown University. She has published numerous books and articles about the ways that everyday conversations affect our relationships. Several of her books have been on the *New York Times* best sellers list. Her best-known book, *You Just Don't Understand: Women and Men in Conversation*, was No. 1 for eight months on the *New York Times* best sellers list and has been translated into thirty-one languages. She is also the author of *You Were Always Mom's Favorite!: Sisters in Conversation throughout Their Lives*, a *New York Times* best-seller. She is a frequent guest on television and radio news shows such as *The Colbert Report, 20/20, Good Morning America, The Today Show, The News Hour with Jim Lehrer, Charlie Rose, Oprah, Hardball, Nightline, Morning Edition,* and *All Things Considered.* In this essay Tannen shares some of the communication style differences between men and women and how being aware of them could help save relationships.

If you are a female, why do you want, as Tannen suggests, a conversational partner above everything else? If male, why do you avoid conversing with your partner?

I was addressing a small gathering in a suburban Virginia living room—a women's group that had invited men to join them. Throughout the evening, one man had been particularly talkative, frequently offering ideas and anecdotes, while his wife sat silently beside him on the couch. Toward the end of the evening, I commented that women frequently complain that their husbands don't talk to them. This man quickly concurred. He gestured toward his wife and said, "She's the talker in our family." The room burst into laughter; the man looked puzzled and hurt. "It's true," he explained. "When I come home from work I have nothing to say. If she didn't keep the conversation going, we'd spend the whole evening in silence."

This episode crystallizes the irony that although American men tend to talk more than women in public situations, they often talk less at home. And this pattern is wreaking havoc with marriage.

The pattern was observed by political scientist Andrew Hacker in the late '70s. Sociologist Catherine Kohler Riessman reports in her new book *Divorce Talk* that most of the women she interviewed—but only a few of the men—gave lack of communication as the reason for their divorces. Given the current divorce rate of nearly 50 percent, that amounts to millions of cases in the United States every year—a virtual epidemic of failed conversation.

In my own research, complaints from women about their husbands most often focused not on tangible inequities such as having given up the chance for a career to accompany a husband to his, or doing far more than their share of daily life-support work like cleaning, cooking, social arrangements and errands. Instead, they focused on communication: "He doesn't listen to me," "He doesn't talk to me." I found, as Hacker observed years before, that most wives want their husbands to be, first and foremost, conversational partners, but few husbands share this expectation of their wives.

5   In short, the image that best represents the current crisis is the stereotypical cartoon scene of a man sitting at the breakfast table with a newspaper held up in front of his face, while a woman glares at the back of it, wanting to talk.

Linguistic Battle of the Sexes

How can women and men have such different impressions of communication in marriage? Why the widespread imbalance in their interests and expectations?

In the April issue of *American Psychologist*, Stanford University's Eleanor Maccoby reports the results of her own and others' research showing that children's development is most influenced by the social structure of peer interactions. Boys and girls tend to play with children of their own gender, and their sex-separate groups have different organizational structures and interactive norms.

I believe these systematic differences in childhood socialization make talk between women and men like cross-cultural communication, heir to all the attraction and pitfalls of that enticing but difficult enterprise. My research on men's and women's conversations uncovered patterns similar to those described for children's groups.

For women, as for girls, intimacy is the fabric of relationships, and talk is the thread from which it is woven. Little girls create and maintain friendships by exchanging secrets; similarly, women regard conversation as the cornerstone of friendship. So a woman expects her husband to be a new and improved version of a best friend. What is important is not the individual subjects that are discussed but the sense of closeness, of a life shared, that emerges when people tell their thoughts, feelings, and impressions.

10   Bonds between boys can be as intense as girls', but they are based less on talking, more on doing things together. Since they don't assume talk is the cement that binds a relationship, men don't know what kind of talk women want, and they don't miss it when it isn't there.

Boys' groups are larger, more inclusive, and more hierarchical, so boys must struggle to avoid the subordinate position in the group. This may play a role in women's complaints that men don't listen to them. Some men really don't like to listen, because being the listener makes them feel one-down, like a child listening to adults or an employee to a boss.

But often when women tell men, "You aren't listening," and the men protest, "I am," the men are right. The impression of not listening results from misalignments in the mechanics of conversation. The misalignment begins as soon as a man and a woman take physical positions. This became clear when I studied videotapes made by psychologist Bruce Dorval of children and adults talking to their same-sex best friends. I found that at every age, the girls and women faced each other directly, their eyes anchored on each other's faces. At every age, the boys and men sat at angles to each other and looked elsewhere in the room, periodically glancing at each other. They were obviously attuned to each other, often mirroring each other's movements. But the tendency of men to face away can give women the impression they aren't listening even when they are. A young woman in college was frustrated: Whenever she told her boyfriend she wanted to talk to him, he would lie down on the floor, close his eyes, and put his arm over his face. This signaled to her, "He's taking a nap." But he insisted he was listening extra hard. Normally, he looks around the room, so he is easily distracted. Lying down and covering his eyes helped him concentrate on what she was saying.

Analogous to the physical alignment that women and men take in conversation is their topical alignment. The girls in my study tended to talk at length about one topic, but the boys tended to jump from topic to topic. The second-grade girls exchanged stories about people they knew. The second-grade boys teased, told jokes, noticed things in the room and talked about finding games to play. The sixth-grade girls talked about problems with a mutual friend. The sixth grade boys talked about 55 different topics, none of which extended over more than a few turns.

Listening to Body Language

Switching topics is another habit that gives women the impression men aren't listening, especially if they switch to a topic about themselves. But the evidence of the 10th-grade boys in my study indicates otherwise. The 10th-grade boys sprawled across their chairs with bodies parallel and eyes straight ahead, rarely looking at each other. They looked as if they were riding in a car, staring out the windshield. But they were talking about their feelings. One boy was upset because a girl had told him he had a drinking problem, and the other was feeling alienated from all his friends.

15   Now, when a girl told a friend about a problem, the friend responded by asking probing questions and expressing agreement and understanding. But the boys dismissed each other's problems. Todd assured Richard that his drinking was "no big problem" because "sometimes you're funny when you're off your butt." And when Todd said he felt left out, Richard responded, "Why should you? You know more people than me."

Women perceive such responses as belittling and unsupportive. But the boys seemed satisfied with them. Whereas women reassure each other by implying, "You shouldn't feel bad because I've had similar experiences," men do so by implying, "You shouldn't feel bad because your problems aren't so bad."

There are even simpler reasons for women's impression that men don't listen. Linguist Lynette Hirschman found that women make more listener-noise, such as "mhm," "uhuh," and "yeah," to show "I'm with you." Men, she found, more often give silent attention. Women who expect a stream of listener noise interpret silent attention as no attention at all.

Women's conversational habits are as frustrating to men as men's are to women. Men who expect silent attention interpret a stream of listener noise as overreaction or impatience. Also, when women talk to each other in a close, comfortable setting, they often overlap, finish each other's sentences and anticipate what the other is about to say. This practice, which I call "participatory listenership," is often perceived by men as interruption, intrusion and lack of attention.

A parallel difference caused a man to complain about his wife, "She just wants to talk about her own point of view. If I show her another view, she gets mad at me." When most women talk to each other, they assume a conversationalist's job is to express agreement and support. But many men see their conversational duty as pointing out the other side of an argument. This is heard as disloyalty by women, and refusal to offer the requisite support. It is not that women don't want to see other points of view, but that they prefer them phrased as suggestions and inquiries rather than as direct challenges.

20   In his book *Fighting for Life*, Walter Ong points out that men use "agonistic" or warlike, oppositional formats to do almost anything; thus discussion becomes debate, and conversation a competitive sport. In contrast, women see conversation as a ritual means of establishing rapport.

If Jane tells a problem and June says she has a similar one, they walk away feeling closer to each other. But this attempt at establishing rapport can backfire when used with men. Men take too literally women's ritual "troubles talk," just as women mistake men's ritual challenges for real attack.

The Sounds of Silence

These differences begin to clarify why women and men have such different expectations about communication in marriage. For women, talk creates intimacy. Marriage is an orgy of closeness: you can tell your feelings and thoughts, and still be loved. Their greatest fear is being pushed away. But men live in a hierarchical world, where talk maintains independence and status. They are on guard to protect themselves from being put down and pushed around.

This explains the paradox of the talkative man who said of his silent wife, "She's the talker." In the public setting of a guest lecture, he felt challenged to show his intelligence and display his understanding of the lecture. But at home, where he has nothing to prove and no one to defend against, he is free to remain silent. For his wife, being home means she is free from the worry that something she says might offend someone, or spark disagreement, or appear to be showing off; at home she is free to talk.

The communication problems that endanger marriage can't be fixed by mechanical engineering. They require a new conceptual framework about the role of talk in human relationships. Many of the psychological explanations that have become second nature may not be helpful, because they tend to blame either women (for not being assertive enough) or men (for not being in touch with their feelings). A sociolinguistic approach by which male-female conversation is seen as cross-cultural communication allows us to understand the problem and forge solutions without blaming either party.

Once the problem is understood, improvement comes naturally, as it did to the young woman and her boyfriend who seemed to go to sleep when she wanted to talk. Previously, she had accused him of not listening, and he had refused to change his behavior, since that would be admitting fault. But then she learned about and explained to him the differences in women's and men's habitual ways of aligning themselves in conversation. The next time she told him she wanted to talk, he began, as usual, by lying down and covering his eyes. When the familiar negative reaction bubbled up, she reassured herself that he really was listening. But then he sat up and looked at her. Thrilled, she asked why. He said, "You like me to look at you when we talk, so I'll try to do it." Once he saw their differences as cross-cultural rather than right and wrong, he independently altered his behavior.

25   Women who feel abandoned and deprived when their husbands won't listen to or report daily news may be happy to discover their husbands trying to adapt once they understand the place of small talk in women's relationships. But if their husbands don't adapt, the women may still be comforted that for men, this is not a failure of intimacy. Accepting the difference, the wives may look to their friends or family for that kind of talk. And husbands who can't provide it shouldn't feel their wives have made unreasonable demands. Some couples will still decide to divorce, but at least their decisions will be based on realistic expectations.

In these times of resurgent ethnic conflicts, the world desperately needs cross-cultural understanding. Like charity, successful cross-cultural communication should begin at home.

Analyze

1. What home practice is wreaking havoc with marriage and what are the results?
2. What would DiFalco say to Tannen about conversational partner(s)?
3. What are the differences between boys' and girls' communication experiences and styles?

Explore

1. In groups made up of males and females, make a list of communication-style differences between men and women. Then, discuss why you agree or disagree with them. Have one person serve as an observer to note whether the discussion follows any of the points from the essay. Share your findings with the class.
2. In groups, create a cross-cultural communication brochure that has concrete suggestions for better communication between the sexes.
3. As a class, create a survey made up of 20 questions asking about the role of love, conversation, and sex in maintaining and terminating

relationships. The goal is to ask questions that will validate issues raised in the readings. Using the free web survey software Survey Monkey (SurveyMonkey.com), have each member of the class invite 10 people they know to participate in this anonymous survey. Set a deadline to have your participants answer. From the answers you receive, produce a PowerPoint (or other presentation form) showing the results.

Plato
Phaedrus (Selected Excerpts)

Plato was born around the year 428 BCE in Athens. Because of his family's background, he appeared destined to be in politics. However, when he began studying with Socrates, his career path changed to a focus on philosophy, and he adopted Socrates's philosophy and style and delved into their mutual interest in questions about noble character and virtue. In this excerpt, translated by Benjamin Jowett, we are shown the Socratic method of eliminating ignorance in order to arrive at truth, or in this case, what love is.

What is not love according to Plato?

Persons of the Dialogue
SOCRATES
PHAEDRUS.
Scene
Under a plane-tree, by the banks of the Ilissus.

Speech One
Phaedr. Listen. You know how matters stand with me; and how, as I conceive, this affair may be arranged for the advantage of both of us. And I maintain that I ought not to fail in my suit, because I am not your lover: for lovers repent of the kindnesses which they have shown when their passion ceases, but to the non-lovers who are free and not under any compulsion,

no time of repentance ever comes; for they confer their benefits according to the measure of their ability, in the way which is most conducive to their own interest. Then again, lovers consider how by reason of their love they have neglected their own concerns and rendered service to others: and when to these benefits conferred they add on the troubles which they have endured, they think that they have long ago made to the beloved a very ample return. But the non-lover has no such tormenting recollections; he has never neglected his affairs or quarrelled with his relations; he has no troubles to add up or excuse to invent; and being well rid of all these evils, why should he not freely do what will gratify the beloved?

If you say that the lover is more to be esteemed, because his love is thought to be greater; for he is willing to say and do what is hateful to other men, in order to please his beloved; that, if true, is only a proof that he will prefer any future love to his present, and will injure his old love at the pleasure of the new. And how, in a matter of such infinite importance, can a man be right in trusting himself to one who is afflicted with a malady which no experienced person would attempt to cure, for the patient himself admits that he is not in his right mind, and acknowledges that he is wrong in his mind, but says that he is unable to control himself? And if he came to his right mind, would he ever imagine that the desires were good which he conceived when in his wrong mind? Once more, there are many more non-lovers than lovers; and if you choose the best of the lovers, you will not have many to choose from; but if from the non-lovers, the choice will be larger, and you will be far more likely to find among them a person who is worthy of your friendship. If public opinion be your dread, and you would avoid reproach, in all probability the lover, who is always thinking that other men are as emulous of him as he is of them, will boast to some one of his successes, and make a show of them openly in the pride of his heart; he wants others to know that his labour has not been lost; but the non-lover is more his own master, and is desirous of solid good, and not of the opinion of mankind. Again, the lover may be generally noted or seen following the beloved (this is his regular occupation), and whenever they are observed to exchange two words they are supposed to meet about some affair of love either past or in contemplation; but when non-lovers meet, no one asks the reason why, because people know that talking to another is natural, whether friendship or mere pleasure be the motive.

Once more, if you fear the fickleness of friendship, consider that in any other case a quarrel might be a mutual calamity; but now, when you have given up what is most precious to you, you will be the greater loser, and therefore, you will have more reason in being afraid of the lover, for his vexations are many, and he is always fancying that everyone is leagued against him. Wherefore also he debars his beloved from society; he will not have you intimate with the wealthy, lest they should exceed him in wealth, or with men of education, lest they should be his superiors in understanding; and he is equally afraid of anybody's influence who has any other advantage over himself. If he can persuade you to break with them, you are left without friend in the world; or if, out of a regard to your own interest, you have more sense than to comply with his desire, you will have to quarrel with him. But those who are non-lovers, and whose success in love is the reward of their merit, will not be jealous of the companions of their beloved, and will rather hate those who refuse to be his associates, thinking that their favourite is slighted by the latter and benefited by the former; for more love than hatred may be expected to come to him out of his friendship with others. Many lovers too have loved the person of a youth before they knew his character or his belongings; so that when their passion has passed away, there is no knowing whether they will continue to be his friends; whereas, in the case of non-lovers who were always friends, the friendship is not lessened by the favours granted; but the recollection of these remains with them, and is an earnest of good things to come.

Further, I say that you are likely to be improved by me, whereas the lover will spoil you. For they praise your words and actions in a wrong way; partly, because they are afraid of offending you, and also, their judgment is weakened by passion. Such are the feats which love exhibits; he makes things painful to the disappointed which give no pain to others; he compels the successful lover to praise what ought not to give him pleasure, and therefore the beloved is to be pitied rather than envied. But if you listen to me, in the first place, I, in my intercourse with you, shall not merely regard present enjoyment, but also future advantage, being not mastered by love, but my own master; nor for small causes taking violent dislikes, but even when the cause is great, slowly laying up little wrath-unintentional offences I shall forgive, and intentional ones I shall try to prevent; and these are the marks of a friendship which will last.

Do you think that a lover only can be a firm friend? Reflect: if this 5 were true, we should set small value on sons, or fathers, or mothers; nor should we ever have loyal friends, for our love of them arises not from passion, but from other associations. Further, if we ought to shower favours on those who are the most eager suitors, on that principle, we ought always to do good, not to the most virtuous, but to the most needy; for they are the persons who will be most relieved, and will therefore be the most grateful; and when you make a feast you should invite not your friend, but the beggar and the empty soul; for they will love you, and attend you, and come about your doors, and will be the best pleased, and the most grateful, and will invoke many a blessing on your head. Yet surely you ought not to be granting favours to those who besiege you with prayer, but to those who are best able to reward you; nor to the lover only, but to those who are worthy of love; nor to those who will enjoy the bloom of your youth, but to those who will share their possessions with you in age; nor to those who, having succeeded, will glory in their success to others, but to those who will be modest and tell no tales; nor to those who care about you for a moment only, but to those who will continue your friends through life; nor to those who, when their passion is over, will pick a quarrel with you, but rather to those who, when the charm of youth has left you, will show their own virtue. Remember what I have said; and consider yet this further point: friends admonish the lover under the idea that his way of life is bad, but no one of his kindred ever yet censured the non-lover, or thought that he was ill-advised about his own interests.

Perhaps you will ask me whether I propose that you should indulge every non-lover. To which I reply that not even the lover would advise you to indulge all lovers, for the indiscriminate favour is less esteemed by the rational recipient, and less easily hidden by him who would escape the censure of the world. Now love ought to be for the advantage of both parties, and for the injury of neither.

I believe that I have said enough; but if there is anything more which you desire or which in your opinion needs to be supplied, ask and I will answer.

Now, Socrates, what do you think? Is not the discourse excellent, more especially in the matter of the language?

Speech Two

Soc. Come, O ye Muses, melodious, as ye are called, whether you have received this name from the character of your strains, or because the Melians are a musical race, help, O help me in the tale which my good friend here desires me to rehearse, in order that his friend whom he always deemed wise may seem to him to be wiser than ever.

Once upon a time there was a fair boy, or, more properly speaking, a youth; he was very fair and had a great many lovers; and there was one special cunning one, who had persuaded the youth that he did not love him, but he really loved him all the same; and one day when he was paying his

addresses to him, he used this very argument—that he ought to accept the
non-lover rather than the lover; his words were as follows: 10
     "All good counsel begins in the same way; a man should know what he
is advising about, or his counsel will all come to nought. But people imagine that they know about the nature of things, when they don't know
about them, and, not having come to an understanding at first because
they think that they know, they end, as might be expected, in contradict-
ing one another and themselves. Now you and I must not be guilty of this
fundamental error which we condemn in others; but as our question is
whether the lover or non-lover is to be preferred, let us first of all agree in
defining the nature and power of love, and then, keeping our eyes upon
the definition and to this appealing, let us further enquire whether love
brings advantage or disadvantage.
     Everyone sees that love is a desire, and we know also that non-lovers
desire the beautiful and good. Now in what way is the lover to be distinguished from the non-lover? Let us note that in every one of us there are
two guiding and ruling principles which lead us whither they will; one is
the natural desire of pleasure, the other is an acquired opinion which as-
pires after the best; and these two are sometimes in harmony and then
again at war, and sometimes the one, sometimes the other conquers.
When opinion by the help of reason leads us to the best, the conquering
principle is called temperance; but when desire, which is devoid of reason,
rules in us and drags us to pleasure, that power of misrule is called excess.
Now excess has many names, and many members, and many forms, and
any of these forms when very marked gives a name, neither honourable
nor creditable, to the bearer of the name. The desire of eating, for example,
which gets the better of the higher reason and the other desires, is called
gluttony, and he who is possessed by it is called a glutton—I the tyrannical
desire of drink, which inclines the possessor of the desire to drink, has a
name which is only too obvious, and there can be as little doubt by what
name any other appetite of the same family would be called; it will be
the name of that which happens to be eluminant. And now I think that
you will perceive the drift of my discourse; but as every spoken word is in
a manner plainer than the unspoken, I had better say further that the ir-
rational desire which overcomes the tendency of opinion towards right,
and is led away to the enjoyment of beauty, and especially of personal
beauty, by the desires which are her own kindred that supreme desire,
I say, which by leading conquers and by the force of passion is reinforced,
from this very force, receiving a name, is called love."
     And now, dear Phaedrus, I shall pause for an instant to ask whether
you do not think me, as I appear to myself, inspired?

Soc. The responsibility rests with you. But hear what follows, and perhaps the fit may be averted; all is in their hands above. I will go on talking to my youth. Listen:

Thus, my friend, we have declared and defined the nature of the subject. Keeping the definition in view, let us now enquire what advantage or disadvantage is likely to ensue from the lover or the non-lover to him who accepts their advances.

He who is the victim of his passions and the slave of pleasure will of course desire to make his beloved as agreeable to himself as possible. Now to him who has a mind discased anything is agreeable which is not opposed to him, but that which is equal or superior is hateful to him, and therefore the lover will not brook any superiority or equality on the part of his beloved; he is always employed in reducing him to inferiority. And the ignorant is the inferior of the wise, the coward of the brave, the slow of speech of the speaker, the dull of the clever. These, and not these only, are the mental defects of the beloved; defects which, when implanted by nature, are necessarily a delight to the lover, and when not implanted, he must contrive to implant them in him, if he would not be deprived of his fleeting joy.

15   And therefore he cannot help being jealous, and will debar his beloved from the advantages of society which would make a man of him, and especially from that society which would have given him wisdom, and thereby he cannot fail to do him great harm. That is to say, in his excessive fear lest he should come to be despised in his eyes he will be compelled to banish from him divine philosophy; and there is no greater injury which he can inflict upon him than this. He will contrive that his beloved shall be wholly ignorant, and in everything shall look to him; he is to be the delight of the lover's heart, and a curse to himself. Verily, a lover is a profitable guardian and associate for him in all that relates to his mind.

Let us next see how his master, whose law of life is pleasure and not good, will keep and train the body of his servant. Will he not choose a beloved who is delicate rather than sturdy and strong? One brought up in shady bowers and not in the bright sun, a stranger to manly exercises and the sweat of toil, accustomed only to a soft and luxurious diet, instead of the hues of health having the colours of paint and ornament, and the rest of a piece? Such a life as any one can imagine and which I need not detail at length. But I may sum up all that I have to say in a word, and pass on. Such a person in war, or in any of the great crises of life, will be the anxiety of his friends and also of his lover, and certainly not the terror of his enemies; which nobody can deny.

And now let us tell what advantage or disadvantage the beloved will receive from the guardianship and society of his lover in the matter of his property; this is the next point to be considered. The lover will be the first to see what, indeed, will be sufficiently evident to all men, that he desires above all things to deprive his beloved of his dearest and best and holiest possessions, father, mother, kindred, friends, of all whom he thinks may be hinderers or reprovers of their most sweet converse; he will even cast a jealous eye upon his gold and silver or other property, because these make him a less easy prey, and when caught less manageable; hence he is of necessity displeased at his possession of them and rejoices at their loss; and he would like him to be wifeless, childless, homeless, as well; and the longer the better, for the longer he is all this, the longer he will enjoy him.

There are some soft of animals, such as flatterers, who are dangerous and, mischievous enough, and yet nature has mingled a temporary pleasure and grace in their composition. You may say that a courtesan is hurtful, and disapprove of such creatures and their practices, and yet for the time they are very pleasant. But the lover is not only hurtful to his love; he is also an extremely disagreeable companion. The old proverb says that "birds of a feather flock together"; I suppose that equality of years inclines them to the same pleasures, and similarity begets friendship; yet you may have more than enough even of this; and verily constraint is always said to be grievous. Now the lover is not only unlike his beloved, but he forces himself upon him. For he is old and his love is young, and neither day nor night will he leave him if he can help; necessity and the sting of desire drive him on, and allure him with the pleasure which he receives from seeing, hearing, touching, perceiving him in every way. And therefore he is delighted to fasten upon him and to minister to him. But what pleasure or consolation can the beloved be receiving all this time? Must he not feel the extremity of disgust when he looks at an old shriveled face and the remainder to match, which even in a description is disagreeable, and quite detestable when he is forced into daily contact with his lover; moreover he is jealously watched and guarded against everything and everybody, and has to hear misplaced and exaggerated praises of himself, and censures equally inappropriate, which are intolerable when the man is sober, and, besides being intolerable, are published all over the world in all their indelicacy and wearisomeness when he is drunk.

And not only while his love continues is he mischievous and unpleasant, but when his love ceases he becomes a perfidious enemy of him on whom he showered his oaths and prayers and promises, and yet could hardly prevail upon him to tolerate the tedium of his company even from motives of interest. The hour of payment arrives, and now he is the servant of another master; instead of love and infatuation, wisdom and temperance are his bosom's lords; but the beloved has not discovered the change which has taken place in him, when he asks for a return and recalls to his recollection former sayings and doings; he believes himself to be speaking to the same person, and the other, not having the courage to confess the truth, and not knowing how to fulfill the oaths and promises which he made when under the dominion of folly, and having now grown wise and temperate, does not want to do as he did or to be as he was before. And so he runs away and is constrained to be a defaulter; the oyster-shell has fallen with the other side uppermost—he changes pursuit into flight, while the other is compelled to follow him with passion and imprecation not knowing that he ought never from the first to have accepted a demented lover instead of a sensible non-lover; and that in making such a choice he was giving himself up to a faithless, morose, envious, disagreeable being, hurtful to his estate, hurtful to his bodily health, and still more hurtful to the cultivation of his mind, than which there neither is nor ever will be anything more honoured in the eyes both of gods and men. Consider this, fair youth, and know that in the friendship of the lover there is no real kindness; he has an appetite and wants to feed upon you:

20   As wolves love lambs so lovers love their loves.

But I told you so, I am speaking in verse, and therefore I had better make an end; enough.

Speech Three

Soc. Know then, fair youth, that the former discourse was the word of Phaedrus, the son of Vain Man, who dwells in the city of Myrrhina (*Myrrhinusius*). And this which I am about to utter is the recantation of Stesichorus the son of Godly Man (*Euphemus*), who comes from the town of Desire (*Himera*), and is to the following effect: "I told a lie when I said" that the beloved ought to accept the non-lover when he might have the lover, because the one is sane, and the other mad. It might be so if madness were simply an evil; but there is also a madness which is a divine gift, and the source of the chiefest blessings granted to men. For prophecy is a madness, and the prophetess at Delphi and the priestesses at Dodona when out of their senses have conferred great benefits on Hellas, both in public and private life, but when in their senses few or none. And I might also tell you how the Sibyl and other inspired persons have given to many an one many an intimation of the future which has saved them from falling. But it would be tedious to speak of what everyone knows.

There will be more reason in appealing to the ancient inventors of names, who would never have connected prophecy (*mantike*) which fore-tells the future and is the noblest of arts, with madness (*manike*), or called them both by the same name, if they had deemed madness to be a disgrace or dishonour; they must have thought that there was an inspired madness which was a noble thing; for the two words, mantike and manike, are really the same, and the letter t is only a modern and tasteless insertion. And this is confirmed by the name which was given by them to the rational investigation of futurity, whether made by the help of birds or of other signs—this, for as much as it is an art which supplies from the reasoning faculty mind (*nous*) and information (*istoria*) to human thought (*oiesis*) they originally termed oionoistike, but the word has been lately altered and made sonorous by the modern introduction of the letter Omega (*oionoistike* and *oionistike*), and in proportion prophecy (*mantike*) is more perfect and august than augury, both in name and fact, in the same proportion, as the ancients testify, is madness superior to a sane mind (*sophrosune*) for the one is only of human, but the other of divine origin. Again, where plagues and mightiest woes have bred in certain families, owing to some ancient blood-guiltiness, there madness has entered with holy prayers and rites, and by inspired utterances found a way of deliverance for those who are in need; and he who has part in this gift, and is truly possessed and duly out of his mind, is by the use of purifications and mysteries made whole and except from evil, future as well as present, and has a release from the calamity which was afflicting him. The third kind is the madness of those who are possessed by the Muses; which taking hold of a delicate and virgin soul, and there inspiring frenzy, awakens lyrical and all other numbers; with these adorning the myriad actions of ancient heroes for the instruction of posterity. But he who, having no touch of the Muses' madness in his soul, comes to the door and thinks that he will get into the temple by the help of art—he, I say, and his poetry are not admitted; the sane man disappears and is nowhere when he enters into rivalry with the madman.

I might tell of many other noble deeds which have sprung from inspired madness. And therefore, let no one frighten or flutter us by saying that the temperate friend is to be chosen rather than the inspired, but let him further show that love is not sent by the gods for any good to lover or beloved; if he can do so we will allow him to carry off the palm. And we, on our part, will prove in answer to him that the madness of love is the greatest of heaven's blessings, and the proof shall be one which the wise will receive, and the witling disbelieve. But first of all, let us view the affections and actions of the soul divine and human, and try to ascertain the truth about them. The beginning of our proof is as follows:

"The soul through all her being is immortal, for that which is ever   25
in motion is immortal; but that which moves another and is moved by

another, in ceasing to move ceases also to live. Only the self-moving, never leaving self, never ceases to move, and is the fountain and beginning of motion to all that moves besides. Now, the beginning is unbegotten, for that which is begotten has a beginning; but the beginning is begotten of nothing, for if it were begotten of something, then the begotten would not come from a beginning. But if unbegotten, it must also be indestructible; for if beginning were destroyed, there could be no beginning out of anything, nor anything out of a beginning; and all things must have a beginning. And therefore the self-moving is the beginning of motion; and this can neither be destroyed nor begotten, else the whole heavens and all creation would collapse and stand still, and never again have motion or birth. But if the self-moving is proved to be immortal, he who affirms that self-motion is the very idea and essence of the soul will not be put to confusion. For the body which is moved from without is soulless; but that which is moved from within has a soul, for such is the nature of the soul. But if this be true, must not the soul be the self-moving, and therefore of necessity unbegotten and immortal? Enough of the soul's immortality.

Of the nature of the soul, though her true form be ever a theme of large and more than mortal discourse, let me speak briefly, and in a figure. And let the figure be composite—a pair of winged horses and a charioteer. Now the winged horses and the charioteers of the gods are all of them noble and of noble descent, but those of other races are mixed; the human charioteer drives his in a pair; and one of them is noble and of noble breed, and the other is ignoble and of ignoble breed; and the driving of them of necessity gives a great deal of trouble to him. I will endeavour to explain to you in what way the mortal differs from the immortal creature. The soul in her totality has the care of inanimate being everywhere, and traverses the whole heaven in divers forms appearing—when perfect and fully winged she soars upward, and orders the whole world; whereas the imperfect soul, losing her wings and drooping in her flight at last settles on the solid ground—there, finding a home, she receives an earthly frame which appears to be self-moved, but is really moved by her power; and this composition of soul and body is called a living and mortal creature. For immortal no such union can be reasonably believed to be; although fancy, not having seen nor surely known the nature of God, may imagine an immortal creature having both a body and also a soul which are united throughout all time. Let that, however, be as God wills, and be spoken of acceptably to him. And now let us ask the reason why the soul loses her wings!

The wing is the corporeal element which is most akin to the divine, and which by nature tends to soar aloft and carry that which gravitates downwards into the upper region, which is the habitation of the gods. The divine is beauty, wisdom, goodness, and the like; and by these the wing of the soul is nourished, and grows apace; but when fed upon evil and foulness and the opposite of good, wastes and falls away. Zeus, the mighty lord, holding the reins of a winged chariot, leads the way in heaven, ordering all and taking care of all; and there follows him the array of gods and demigods, marshaled in eleven bands; Hestia alone abides at home in the house of heaven; of the rest they who are reckoned among the princely twelve march in their appointed order. They see many blessed sights in the inner heaven, and there are many ways to and fro, along which the blessed gods are passing, every one doing his own work; he may follow who will and can, for jealousy has no place in the celestial choir. But when they go to banquet and festival, then they move up the steep to the top of the vault of heaven. The chariots of the gods in even poise, obeying the rein, glide rapidly; but the others labour, for the vicious steed goes heavily, weighing down the charioteer to the earth when his steed has not been thoroughly trained: and this is the hour of agony and extremest conflict for the soul. For the immortals, when they are at the end of their course, go forth and stand upon the outside of heaven, and the revolution of the spheres carries them round, and they behold the things beyond. But of the heaven which is above the heavens, what earthly poet ever did or ever will sing worthily? It is such as I will describe; for I must dare to speak the truth, when truth is my theme. There abides the very being with which true knowledge is concerned; the colourless, formless, intangible essence, visible only to mind, the pilot of the soul. The divine intelligence, being nurtured upon mind and pure knowledge, and the intelligence of every soul which is capable of receiving the food proper to it, rejoices at beholding reality, and once more gazing upon truth, is replenished and made glad, until the revolution of the worlds brings her round again to the same place. In the revolution she beholds justice, and temperance, and knowledge absolute, not in the form of generation or of relation, which men call existence, but knowledge absolute in existence absolute; and beholding the other true existences in like manner, and feasting upon them, she passes down into the interior of the heavens and returns home; and there the charioteer putting up his horses at the stall, gives them ambrosia to eat and nectar to drink.

Such is the life of the gods; but of other souls, that which follows God best and is likest to him lifts the head of the charioteer into the outer world, and is carried round in the revolution, troubled indeed by the steeds, and with difficulty beholding true being; while another only rises and falls, and sees, and again fails to see by reason of the unruliness of the steeds. The rest of the souls are also longing after the upper world and they all follow, but not being strong enough they are carried round below the surface, plunging, treading on one another, each striving to be first; and there is confusion and perspiration and the extremity of effort; and many of them are lamed or have their wings broken through the ill-driving of the charioteers; and all of them after a fruitless toil, not having attained to the mysteries of true being, go away, and feed upon opinion. The reason why the souls exhibit this exceeding eagerness to behold the plain of truth is that pasturage is found there, which is suited to the highest part of the soul; and the wing on which the soul soars is nourished with this. And there is a law of Destiny, that the soul which attains any vision of truth in company with a god is preserved from harm until the next period, and if attaining always is always unharmed. But when she is unable to follow, and fails to behold the truth, and through some ill-hap sinks beneath the double load of forgetfulness and vice, and her wings fall from her and she drops to the ground, then the law ordains that this soul shall at her first birth pass, not into any other animal, but only into man; and the soul which has seen most of truth shall come to the birth as a philosopher, or artist, or some musical and loving nature; that which has seen truth in the second degree shall be some righteous king or warrior chief; the soul which is of the third class shall be a politician, or economist, or trader; the fourth shall be lover of gymnastic toils, or a physician; the fifth shall lead the life of a prophet or hierophant; to the sixth the character of poet or some other imitative artist will be assigned; to the seventh the life of an artisan or husbandman; to the eighth that of a sophist or demagogue; to the ninth that of a tyrant—all these are states of probation, in which he who does righteously improves, and he who does unrighteously, improves, and he who does unrighteously, deteriorates his lot.

Ten thousand years must elapse before the soul of each one can return to the place from whence she came, for she cannot grow her wings in less; only the soul of a philosopher, guileless and true, or the soul of a lover, who is not devoid of philosophy, may acquire wings in the third of the recurring periods of a thousand years; he is distinguished from the ordinary good man who gains wings in three thousand years: and they who choose this life three times in succession have wings given them, and go away at the end of three thousand years. But the others receive judgment when they have completed their first life, and after the judgment they go, some of them to the houses of correction which are under the earth, and are punished; others to some place in heaven whither they are lightly borne by justice, and there they live in a manner worthy of the life which they led here when in the form of men. And at the end of the first thousand years the good souls and also the evil souls both come to draw lots and choose their second life, and they may take any which they please. The soul of a man may pass into the life of a beast, or from the beast return again into the man. But the soul which has never seen the truth will not pass into the human form. For a man must have intelligence of universals, and be able to proceed from the many particulars of sense to one conception of reason; this is the recollection of those things which our soul once saw while following God—when regardless of that which we now call being she raised her head up towards the true being. And therefore the mind of the philosopher alone has wings; and this is just, for he is always, according to the measure of his abilities, clinging in recollection to those things in which God abides, and in beholding which He is what He is. And he who employs aright these memories is ever being initiated into perfect mysteries and alone becomes truly perfect. But, as he forgets earthly interests and is rapt in the divine, the vulgar deem him mad, and rebuke him; they do not see that he is inspired.

Thus far I have been speaking of the fourth and last kind of madness, 30 which is imputed to him who, when he sees the beauty of earth, is transported with the recollection of the true beauty; he would like to fly away, but he cannot; he is like a bird fluttering and looking upward and careless of the world below; and he is therefore thought to be mad. And I have shown this of all inspirations to be the noblest and highest and the offspring of the highest to him who has or shares in it, and that he who loves the beautiful is called a lover because he partakes of it. For, as has been already said, every soul of man has in the way of nature beheld true being; this was the condition of her passing into the form of man. But all souls do not easily recall the things of the other world; they may have seen them for a short time only, or they may have been unfortunate in their earthly lot, and, having had their hearts turned to unrighteousness through some corrupting influence, they may have lost the memory of the holy things which once they saw. Few only retain an adequate remembrance of them; and they, when they behold here any image of that other world, are rapt in amazement; but they are ignorant of what this rapture means, because they do not clearly perceive. For there is no light of justice or temperance or any of the higher ideas which are precious to souls in the earthly copies of them: they are seen through a glass dimly; and there are few who, going to the images, behold in them the realities, and these only with difficulty. There was a time when with the rest of the happy band they saw beauty shining in brightness—we philosophers following in the train of Zeus, others in company with other gods; and then we beheld the beatific vision and were initiated into a mystery which may be truly called most blessed, celebrated by us in our state of innocence, before we had any experience of evils to come, when we were admitted to the sight of apparitions innocent and simple and calm and happy, which we beheld shining impure light, pure ourselves and not yet enshrined in that living tomb which we carry about, now that we are imprisoned in the body, like an oyster in his shell. Let me linger over the memory of scenes which have passed away.

But of beauty, I repeat again that we saw her there shining in company with the celestial forms; and coming to earth we find her here too, shining in clearness through the clearest aperture of sense. For sight is the most piercing of our bodily senses; though not by that is wisdom seen; her loveliness would have been transporting if there had been a visible image of her, and the other ideas, if they had visible counterparts, would be equally lovely. But this is the privilege of beauty, that being the loveliest she is also the most palpable to sight. Now he who is not newly initiated or who has become corrupted, does not easily rise out of this world to the sight of true beauty in the other; he looks only at her earthly namesake, and instead of being awed at the sight of her, he is given over to pleasure, and like a brutish beast he rushes on to enjoy and beget; he consorts with wantonness, and is not afraid or ashamed of pursuing pleasure in violation of nature. But he whose initiation is recent, and who has been the spectator of many glories in the other world, is amazed when he sees any one having a godlike face or form, which is the expression of divine beauty; and at first a shudder runs through him, and again the old awe steals over him; then looking upon the face of his beloved as of a god he reverences him, and if he were not afraid of being thought a downright madman, he would sacrifice to his beloved as to the image of a god; then while he gazes on him there is a sort of reaction, and the shudder passes into an unusual heat and perspiration; for, as he receives the effluence of beauty through the eyes, the wing moistens and he warms. And as he warms, the parts out of which the wing grew, and which had been hitherto closed and rigid, and had prevented the wing from shooting forth, are melted, and as nourishment streams upon him, the lower end of the wings begins to swell and grow from the root upwards; and the growth extends under the whole soul—for once the whole was winged.

During this process the whole soul is all in a state of ebullition and effervescence, which may be compared to the irritation and uneasiness in the gums at the time of cutting teeth, bubbles up, and has a feeling of uneasiness and tickling; but when in like manner the soul is beginning to grow wings, the beauty of the beloved meets her eye and she receives the sensible warm motion of particles which flow towards her, therefore called emotion (*imeros*), and is refreshed and warmed by them, and then she ceases from her pain with joy. But when she is parted from her beloved and her moisture fails, then the orifices of the passage out of which the wing shoots dry up and close, and intercept the germ of the wing; which, being shut up with the emotion, throbbing as with the pulsations of an artery, pricks the aperture which is nearest, until at length the entire soul is pierced and maddened and pained, and at the recollection of beauty is again delighted. And from both of them together the soul is oppressed at the strangeness of her condition, and is in a great strait and excitement, and in her madness can neither sleep by night nor abide in her place by day. And wherever she thinks that she will behold the beautiful one, thither in her desire she runs. And when she has seen him, and bathed herself in the waters of beauty, her constraint is loosened, and she is refreshed, and has no more pangs and pains; and this is the sweetest of all pleasures at the time, and is the reason why the soul of the lover will never forsake his beautiful one, whom he esteems above all; he has forgotten mother and brethren and companions, and he thinks nothing of the neglect and loss of his property; the rules and proprieties of life, on which he formerly prided himself, he now despises, and is ready to sleep like a servant, wherever he is allowed, as near as he can to his desired one, who is the object of his worship, and the physician who can alone assuage the greatness of his pain. And this state, my dear imaginary youth to whom I am talking, is by men called love, and among the gods has a name at which you, in your simplicity, may be inclined to mock; there are two lines in the apocryphal writings of Homer in which the name occurs. One of them is rather outrageous, and not altogether metrical. They are as follows:

Mortals call him fluttering love, but the immortals call him winged one, because the growing of wings is a necessity to him. You may believe this, but not unless you like. At any rate the loves of lovers and their causes are such as I have described.

Now the lover who is taken to be the attendant of Zeus is better able to bear the winged god, and can endure a heavier burden; but the attendants and companions of Ares, when under the influence of love, if they fancy that they have been at all wronged, are ready to kill and put an end to themselves and their beloved. And he who follows in the train of any other god, while he is unspoiled and the impression lasts, honours and imitates him, as far as he is able; and after the manner of his god he behaves in his intercourse with his beloved and with the rest of the world during the first period of his earthly existence. Every one chooses his love from the ranks of beauty according to his character, and this he makes his god, and fashions and adorns as a sort of image which he is to fall down and worship. The followers of Zeus desire that their beloved should have a soul like him; and therefore they seek out some one of a philosophical and imperial nature, and when they have found him and loved him, they do all they can to confirm such a nature in him, and if they have no experience of such a disposition hitherto, they learn of anyone who can teach them, and themselves follow in the same way. And they have the less difficulty in finding the nature of their own god in themselves, because they have been compelled to gaze intensely on him; their recollection clings to him, and they become possessed of him, and receive from him their character and disposition, so far as man can participate in God. The qualities of their god they attribute to the beloved, wherefore they love him all the more, and if, like the Bacchic Nymphs, they draw inspiration from Zeus, they pour out their own fountain upon him, wanting to make him as like as possible to their own god. But those who are the followers of Here seek a royal love, and when they have found him they do just the same with him; and in like manner the followers of Apollo, and of every other god walking in the ways of their god, seek a love who is to be made like him whom they serve, and when they have found him, they themselves imitate their god, and persuade their love to do the same, and educate him into the manner and nature of the god as far as they each can; for no feelings of envy or jealousy are entertained by them towards their beloved, but they do their utmost to create in him the greatest likeness of themselves and of the god whom they honour. Thus fair and blissful to the beloved is the desire of the inspired lover, and the initiation of which I speak into the mysteries of true love, if he be captured by the lover and their purpose is effected. Now the beloved is taken captive in the following manner:

35   As I said at the beginning of this tale, I divided each soul into three—two horses and a charioteer; and one of the horses was good and the other bad: the division may remain, but I have not yet explained in what the goodness or badness of either consists, and to that I will proceed. The right-hand horse is upright and cleanly made; he has a lofty neck and an aquiline nose; his colour is white, and his eyes dark; he is a lover of honour and modesty and temperance, and the follower of true glory; he needs no touch of the whip, but is guided by word and admonition only. The other is a crooked lumbering animal, put together anyhow; he has a short thick neck; he is flat-faced and of a dark colour, with grey eyes and blood-red complexion; the mate of insolence and pride, shag-eared and deaf, hardly yielding to whip and spur. Now when the charioteer beholds the vision of love, and has his whole soul warmed through sense, and is full of the prickings and ticklings of desire, the obedient steed, then as always under the government of shame, refrains from leaping on the beloved; but the other, heedless of the pricks and of the blows of the whip, plunges and

runs away, giving all manner of trouble to his companion and the charioteer, whom he forces to approach the beloved and to remember the joys
of love. They at first indignantly oppose him and will not be urged on to
do terrible and unlawful deeds; but at last, when he persists in plaguing
them, they yield and agree to do as he bids them.

And now they are at the spot and behold the flashing beauty of the
beloved; which when the charioteer sees, his memory is carried to the true
beauty, whom he beholds in company with Modesty like an image placed
upon a holy pedestal. He sees her, but he is afraid and falls backwards in
adoration, and by his fall is compelled to pull back the reins with such
violence as to bring both the steeds on their haunches, the one willing and
unresisting, the unruly one very unwilling; and when they have gone back
a little, the one is overcome with shame and wonder, and his whole soul is
bathed in perspiration; the other, when the pain is over which the bridle
and the fall had given him, having with difficulty taken breath, is full of
wrath and reproaches, which he heaps upon the charioteer and his fellow-
steed, for want of courage and manhood, declaring that they have been
false to their agreement and guilty of desertion. Again they refuse, and
again he urges them on, and will scarce yield to their prayer that he would
wait until another time. When the appointed hour comes, they make as if
they had forgotten, and he reminds them, fighting and neighing and drag-
ging them on, until at length he, on the same thoughts intent, forces them
to draw near again. And when they are near he stoops his head and puts
up his tail, and takes the bit in his teeth. and pulls shamelessly. Then the
charioteer is worse off than ever; he falls back like a racer at the barrier,
and with a still more violent wrench drags the bit out of the teeth of the
wild steed and covers his abusive tongue and jaws with blood, and forces
his legs and haunches to the ground and punishes him sorely. And when
this has happened several times and the villain has ceased from his wanton
way, he is tamed and humbled, and follows the will of the charioteer, and
when he sees the beautiful one he is ready to die of fear. And from that
time forward the soul of the lover follows the beloved in modesty and
holy fear.

And so the beloved who, like a god, has received every true and loyal
service from his lover, not in pretence but in reality, being also himself of a
nature friendly to his admirer, if in former days he has blushed to own his
passion and turned away his lover, because his youthful companions or
others slanderously told him that he would be disgraced, now as years
advance, at the appointed age and time, is led to receive him into communion. For fate which has ordained that there shall be no friendship among
the evil has also ordained that there shall ever be friendship among the

good. And the beloved when he has received him into communion and intimacy, is quite amazed at the good-will of the lover; he recognises that the inspired friend is worth all other friends or kinsmen; they have nothing of friendship in them worthy to be compared with his. And when his feeling continues and he is nearer to him and embraces him, in gymnastic exercises and at other times of meeting, then the fountain of that stream, which Zeus when he was in love with Ganymede named Desire, overflows upon the lover, and some enters into his soul, and some when he is filled flows out again; and as a breeze or an echo rebounds from the smooth rocks and returns whence it came, so does the stream of beauty, passing through the eyes which are the windows of the soul, come back to the beautiful one; there arriving and quickening the passages of the wings, watering them and inclining them to grow, and filling the soul of the beloved also with love. And thus he loves, but he knows not what; he does not understand and cannot explain his own state; he appears to have caught the infection of blindness from another; the lover is his mirror in whom he is beholding himself, but he is not aware of this. When he is with the lover, both cease from their pain, but when he is away then he longs as he is longed for, and has love's image, love for love (Anteros) lodging in his breast, which he calls and believes to be not love but friendship only, and his desire is as the desire of the other, but weaker; he wants to see him, touch him, kiss him, embrace him, and probably not long afterwards his desire is accomplished. When they meet, the wanton steed of the lover has a word to say to the charioteer; he would like to have a little pleasure in return for many pains, but the wanton steed of the beloved says not a word, for he is bursting with passion which he understands not; he throws his arms round the lover and embraces him as his dearest friend; and, when they are side by side, he is not in it state in which he can refuse the lover anything, if he ask him; although his fellow-steed and the charioteer oppose him with the arguments of shame and reason.

After this their happiness depends upon their self-control; if the better elements of the mind which lead to order and philosophy prevail, then they pass their life here in happiness and harmony-masters of themselves and orderly-enslaving the vicious and emancipating the virtuous elements of the soul; and when the end comes, they are light and winged for flight, having conquered in one of the three heavenly or truly Olympian victories; nor can human discipline or divine inspiration confer any greater blessing on man than this. If, on the other hand, they leave philosophy and lead the lower life of ambition, then probably, after wine or in some other careless hour, the two wanton animals take the two souls when off their guard and bring them together, and they accomplish that desire of their hearts which to the many is bliss; and this having once enjoyed they continue to enjoy, yet rarely because they have not the approval of the whole soul. They too are dear, but not so dear to one another as the others, either at the time of their love or afterwards. They consider that they have given and taken from each other the most sacred pledges, and they may not break them and fall into enmity. At last they pass out of the body, unwinged, but eager to soar, and thus obtain no mean reward of love and madness. For those who have once begun the heavenward pilgrimage may not go down again to darkness and the journey beneath the earth, but they live in light always; happy companions in their pilgrimage, and when the time comes at which they receive their wings they have the same plumage because of their love.

Thus great are the heavenly blessings which the friendship of a lover will confer upon you, my youth. Whereas the attachment of the non-lover, which is alloyed with a worldly prudence and has worldly and niggardly ways of doling out benefits, will breed in your soul those vulgar qualities which the populace applaud, will send you bowling round the earth during a period of nine thousand years, and leave, you a fool in the world below.

And thus, dear Eros, I have made and paid my recantation, as well and   40
as fairly as I could; more especially in the matter of the poetical figures which I was compelled to use, because Phaedrus would have them. And now forgive the past and accept the present, and be gracious and merciful to me, and do not in thine anger deprive me of sight, or take from me the art of love which thou hast given me, but grant that I may be yet more esteemed in the eyes of the fair. And if Phaedrus or I myself said anything rude in our first speeches, blame Lysias, who is the father of the brat, and let us have no more of his progeny; bid him study philosophy, like his brother Polemarchus; and then his lover Phaedrus will no longer halt between two opinions, but will dedicate himself wholly to love and to philosophical discourses.

Analyze

1. In Phaedrus's first speech (which he reads as deriving from Lysis), what are the strengths of the non-lover and the weaknesses of the lover?
2. In Speech 2 by Socrates (the speech Socrates says he can do better than Lysias's), what are the strengths of the non-lover and the weaknesses of the lover? Which speech do you think is better?
3. In Speech 3 by Socrates, what does he come to say love is? Does this coincide with what you believe and with what you have read in this chapter?

Explore

1. With a partner create a conversation between Socrates and DiFalco or between Socrates and Tannen while having lunch at a busy restaurant.
2. What are the differences and similarities between the way Socrates talks about love and the way the other writers in the chapter do?
3. What advice would Socrates give to each of the authors in this chapter about love, sex, and conversation?

Wallace Shawn
"Is Sex Interesting?"

Shawn is an American actor and playwright. In film he is best known as Wally Shawn in *My Dinner with Andre* (1981), Vizzini in *The Princess Bride* (1987), and Rex in *Toy Story*. He has written successful plays, such as *The Designated Mourner*, *Grasses of a Thousand Colors*, and *Aunt Dan and Lemon*. In this essay and in his humorous style, Shawn makes us laugh and still question why we are so uncomfortable talking and writing about sex.

Why does Shawn find sex so interesting to write about?

For whatever reason, and I don't remember how it happened, I am now what people call "sixty-four years old," and I have to admit that I started writing about sex almost as soon as I realized that it was possible to do so—say, at the age of fourteen—and I still do it, even though I was in a way the wrong age then, and in a different way I guess I'm the wrong age now. Various people who have liked me or cared about me—people who have believed in my promise as a writer—have hinted to me at different times in my life that an excessive preoccupation with the subject of sex has harmed or even ruined my writing. They've implied that it was sad, almost pitiful, that an adolescent obsession should have been allowed to marginalize what they optimistically had hoped might have been a serious body of work. Meanwhile, people I don't know very well have tended over all those decades to break into a very particular smile, one I recognize now, when they learn that I've written something that deals with sex—a winking smile that suggests a trivial, silly, but rather amusing topic has been mentioned. I suppose it goes without saying that James Joyce, D. H. Lawrence, and others were expanding the scope of literature and redrawing humanity's picture of itself when they approached this subject at the start of the twentieth century. But by the time I came along, many of my friends were embarrassed on my behalf precisely because the topic I was writing about seemed so closely associated with an earlier era.

Why is sex interesting to write about? To some, that might seem like a rather dumb question. Obviously, when someone interested in geology is alone in a room, he or she tends to think a lot about rocks. And I imagine that when many geologists were children, they put pictures having to do with rocks on their bedroom walls. And I would have to guess that geologists find it fun to sit at a desk and write about rocks. So, yes, I find it enjoyable. But apart from that, I still find myself wondering, "Why is it interesting to write about sex?"

One reason is that sex is shocking. Yes, it's still shocking, after all these years. At least, it's shocking to me. Even after all these years, most bourgeois people, including me, still walk around with an image of themselves in their heads that doesn't include—well—that. I'm vaguely aware that while going about my daily round of behavior I'm making use of various mammalian processes, such as breathing, digesting, and getting from place to place by hobbling about on those odd legs we have. But the fact is that when I form a picture of myself, I see myself doing the sorts of things that humans do and only humans do—things like hailing a taxi, going to a restaurant, voting for a candidate in an election, or placing receipts in various piles and adding them up. But if I'm unexpectedly reminded that my soul and body are capable of being swept up in an activity that pigs, flies, wolves, lions, and tigers also engage in, my normal picture of myself is violently disrupted. In other words, consciously, I'm aware that I'm a product of evolution and I'm part of nature. But my unconscious mind is still partially wandering in the early nineteenth century and doesn't know these things yet. Writing about sex is really a variant of what Wordsworth did; that is, it's a variant of writing about nature or, as we call it not, "the environment." Sex is "the environment" coming inside, coming into our homes and taking root inside our own minds. It comes out of the mud where the earliest creatures swam; it comes up and appears in our brains in the form of feelings and thoughts. It sometimes appears with such great force that it sweeps other feelings and other thoughts completely out of the way. And on a daily basis it quietly and patiently approaches the self and winds itself around it and through it until no part of the self is unconnected to it.

Sex is of course an extraordinary meeting place of reality and dream, and it's also—what is not perhaps exactly the same thing—an extraordinary meeting place of the meaningful and the meaningless. The big toe, for example, is one part of the human body, human flesh shaped and constructed in a particular way. The penis is another part of the body, located not too far away from the big toe and built out of fundamentally the same materials. The act of sex, the particular shapes of the penis and the vagina, are the way they are because natural selection has made them that way. There may be an adaptive value to each particular choice that evolution made, but from our point of view as human beings living our lives, the various details present themselves to us as arbitrary. It can only be seen as funny that men buy magazines containing pictures of breasts but not magazines with pictures of knees or forearms. It can only be seen as funny that demagogues give speeches denouncing men who insert their penises into other men's anuses—and then go home to insert their own penises into their wives' vaginas! (One might have thought it obvious that either both of these acts are completely outrageous or neither of them is.) And yet the interplay and permutations of the apparently meaningless, the desire to penetrate anus or vagina, the glimpse of the naked breast, the hope of sexual intercourse or the failure of it, lead to joy, grief, happiness, or desperation for the human creature.

5   Perhaps it is the power of sex that has taught us to love the meaningless and thereby turn it into the meaningful. Amazingly, the love of what is arbitrary (which one could alternatively describe as the love of reality) is something we human beings are capable of feeling, and perhaps even what we call the love of the beautiful is simply a particular way of exercising this remarkable ability. So it might not be absurd to say that if you love the body of another person, if you love another person, if you love a meadow, if you love a horse, if you love a painting or a piece of music or the sky at night, then the power of sex is flowing through you.

Yes, some people go through life astounded every day by the beauty of forests and animals; some are astounded more frequently by the beauty of art; and others by the beauty of other human beings. But science could one day discover that the ability to be astounded by the beauty of other human beings came first, and to me it seems implausible to imagine that these different types of astonishment or appreciation are psychologically unrelated.

Sex has always been known to be such a powerful force that fragile humanity can't help but be terribly nervous in front of it, so powerful barriers have been devised to control it—taboos of all varieties, first of all, and then all the emotions subsumed under the concepts of jealousy and possessiveness, possessiveness being a sort of anticipatory form of jealousy. (A recent survey of married people in the United States found that when asked the question "What is very important for a successful marriage?" the quality mentioned most frequently—by 93 percent—was "faithfulness," while "happy sexual relationship" came in with only 70 percent. In other words, to 23 percent of the respondents, it seemed more important that they and their partner should not have sex with others than that they themselves should enjoy sex.) Sex seems capable of creating anarchy, and those who are committed to predictability and order find themselves inevitably either standing in opposition to it or trying to pretend that it doesn't even exist.

My local newspaper, the *New York Times,* for example, does not include images of naked people. Many of its readers might enjoy it much more if it did, but those same readers still might not buy it if such images were in it, because it could no longer present the portrait of a normal, stable, adequate world—a world not ideal but still good enough—which it is the function of the *Times* to present every day. Nudity somehow implies that anything could happen, but the *Times* is committed to telling its readers that many things will *not* happen, because the world is under control, benevolent people are looking out for us, the situation is not as bad as we tend to think, and although problems do exist, they can be solved by wise rulers. The contemplation of nudity or sex could tend to bring up the alarming idea that at any moment human passions might rise up and topple the world we know.

But perhaps it would be a good thing if people saw themselves as a part of nature, connected to the environment in which they live. Sex can be a humbling, equalizing force. It's often been noted that naked people do not wear medals, and weapons are forbidden inside the pleasure garden. When the sexuality of the terrifying people we call "our leaders" is for some reason revealed, they lose some of their power—sometimes all of it—because we're reminded (and, strangely, we need reminding) that they are merely creatures like the ordinary worm or beetle that creeps along at the edge of the pond. Sex really is a nation of its own. Those whose allegiance is given to sex at a certain moment withdraw their loyalty temporarily from other powers. It's a symbol of the possibility that we might all defect for one reason or another from the obedient columns in which we march.

Analyze

1. To what other interest does Shawn compare his?
2. How does Shawn compare writing about sex to what Wordsworth wrote about?
3. If you say you love something, what does Shawn say is flowing through you?

Explore

1. Create a conversation between Shawn and Difalco, Shawn and Feldman, or Shawn and one of the other authors we have read thus far. Make sure to show where they would agree and disagree. Like Shawn's essay, you can make your writing entertaining yet at the same time informative.
2. Shawn talks about typical images he has in his mind of himself as a human being and about why places like the *New York Times* don't have pictures of people engaged in sex. Write an essay discussing why you agree or disagree with him.
3. Write an essay in the approach that Shawn uses, but ask this question as your title: Is Love Interesting?

Michelle Chen
"Farewell, June Cleaver: 'Non-Traditional Families' and Economic Opportunity"

Chen has publications in *The Nation, Newsday, Ms, Alternet, Colorlines*, and *In These Times*. She also is an editor at CultureStrike.net, and a coproducer of Asia Pacific Forum. In this essay Chen looks at current research and statistics on the possible differences of children from traditional marriages and homes compared to a single parent or alternative parent upbringing.

What do you think are similarities and differences of children, if any, from these different types of households?

As the traditional nuclear family fades into history, we've entered the era of the "non-traditional" family: single parents, pairs of moms and dads, blended families, multi-generational households, grandparent caregivers. With a growing share of babies today born outside marriage, American society seems to be finally leaving behind the *Leave It to Beaver* model.

A new study by Pew Economic Mobility Project asks how family structure—a divorced or single-parent household versus a conventional married one—affects a child's economic opportunities later in life. Society's attitude toward divorce and single parenthood has become more open over the past few generations, but has our economy?

It's easy to assume that divorce or single-parenthood would lead to some hardships, and Pew did find a link between marital status and socioeconomic advancement across generations. But the outcomes are also heavily influenced by race and class factors, which persist among poor households whether children grow up with one parent or two.

For children who start at the bottom third of the economic ladder, Pew found, "only 26 percent with divorced parents move up to the middle or top third as adults, compared to 42 percent of children born to unmarried mothers and 50 percent of children with continuously married parents."

In terms of "absolute mobility," or the potential to rise relative to their 5
parents' income level, divorce does not have a clear impact on children's mobility:

Among children who start in the bottom third, 74 percent with divorced parents exceed their parents' family income when they reach adulthood, compared to 90 percent of children with continuously married parents.

Still, the study concluded:

Perhaps surprisingly, there is no evidence that being born to an unmarried mother reduces upward absolute mobility from the bottom third of the income distribution—the rates for those children and for children with continuously married parents are statistically indistinguishable.

When you slice the data by race, a different picture emerges. Divorce appears to make a bigger difference for black children's future prospects.

Among African American children who start in the bottom third of the 10
income distribution, 87 percent with continuously married parents exceed their parents' income in adulthood, while just 53 percent of those with divorced parents do.

Among white children who start in the bottom third, about the same proportion of adult children exceed their parents' income regardless of whether their parents were continuously married (91 percent exceeding) or divorced (92 percent exceeding).

Pointing out that "family structure can explain only some of the differences in economic mobility rates between African Americans and whites," the study raises intriguing questions about how social policy interacts with parents' life choices.

The sweeping welfare reforms of the Clinton era continue to reveal the ramifications of using welfare to impose certain social norms at the expense of those who don't fit the mold. As Kate Boo explained in her trenchant 2003 *New Yorker* article "The Marriage Cure," the supposed correlation between marriage and economic well-being became perverted into the rationale that promoting marriage could reduce systemic poverty.

The "reforms" targeted urban black single mothers who were stereotyped as antithetical to the "traditional" family: degenerate, shiftless women who couldn't stop having babies. The result was a national crusade to push impoverished single mothers simultaneously into the labor market and the marriage market, for better or worse.

15   To antipoverty and racial justice activists, the pro-marriage credo has simply repackaged the old blame-the-poor canard in the rhetoric of "family values." In fact, poor single mothers have been systematically locked out of the social privileges that their middle-class married counterparts typically take for granted. Welfare rights activists since the 1960s have shown that policies intended to relieve poverty end up punishing women for not being June Cleaver.

In addition to the patriarchal conservatism inherent in pro-marriage ideology, women face practical barriers to getting hitched: Black women especially may have trouble finding long-term male partners in communities devastated by mass incarceration. Not to mention, some old-fashioned types see marriage as a matter of conjugal love rather than social engineering. Go figure.

Despite the talk of "personal responsibility" in welfare policy, the real barriers poor single mothers face are rooted in poverty itself. According to a 2002 policy paper by Stephanie Coontz and Nancy Folbre:

- Non-marriage is often a result of poverty and economic insecurity rather than the other way around.

- The quality and stability of marriages matters. Prodding couples into matrimony without helping them solve problems that make relationships precarious could leave them worse off.
- Two-parent families are not immune from the economic stresses that put children at risk. More than one third of all impoverished young children in the U.S. today live with two parents.

Pew doesn't directly critique welfare reform's legacy, but the research does point to policy changes that could help break the cycle of intergenerational poverty. The Earned Income Tax Credit, for instance, has helped lift millions of children out of poverty through targeted income supports. Paid family leave time, subsidized child care, and career training and unemployment insurance programs that recognize challenges unique to working single parents would help move non-married families toward long-awaited equity.

Regardless of what you think about the institution of marriage, there's no justification for forcing children to pay an economic penalty for their parents' decision to divorce or remain unmarried. And a parent's decision not to tie the knot shouldn't be an economic shackle on the next generation.

While our concept of the family has grown and diversified since the days   20
of Mrs. Cleaver, for households striving toward advancement, our labor market and social policy remain stuck in the past.

Analyze

1. What's a nuclear family?
2. Does family structure (divorced, single-parent household, or married) determine children's economic prospects when they are adults?
3. What are some of the suggested measures that can help lift families out of the poverty cycle?

Explore

1. This essay explores how traditional married families (a man and a woman) compare with single and alternative families on the economic impact of these families' children. Embedded in our belief that traditional married families' children will do better economically is that there is more stability. Do you think that also embedded in this view is

that traditional married families also show more love and support for their children? Write an essay defending single and alternative families' love and support for their children.

2. The article discusses the TV series *Leave It to Beaver* titled: *The nuclear option: Beaver, Wally, June, Ward Cleaver.* Create a PowerPoint of images of the families from popular TV shows generation by generation since the 1950s. How have the popular ideas of family evolved? How are the children of single and alternative families projected, well rounded, successful, or the opposite?

3. While the article explores the possible economic effect that parents in traditional married families and single and alternative families can have on their children's financial future, one idea that is not developed is that we may end up not being financially successful even though our parents (any model) loved us and were terrific role models. Write an essay arguing the latter point or argue against it.

Elizabeth Bernstein
"Sibling Rivalry Grows Up"

Early in her career Bernstein wrote for a range of newspapers and magazines, such as the *Chicago Tribune, Village Voice, Forbes, New York Magazine,* and *Publisher's Weekly.* She has been at *The Wall Street Journal* since 2010. Her writing has received numerous awards, ranging from the Education Writers Association and the New York Chapter of the Society of Professional Journalists' Deadline Club, to the American Psychoanalytic Association. In this essay Bernstein discusses the silent love-hate relationships that many siblings have and how health care professionals mostly overlook them.

Do you or someone you know have a sibling rivalry? If yes, how healthy is it?

Marianne Walsh and her sister, Megan Putman, keep track of whose kids their mother babysits more. They also compete with each other over parenting styles (Ms. Walsh is strict, Ms. Putman is laid back) and their weight.

"My kids play more instruments, so I am winning in piano," says Ms. Walsh, 38, the younger of the two by 13 months. "But she won the skinny Olympics."

Adult sibling rivalry. Experts say it remains one of the most harmful and least addressed issues in a family. We know it when we see it. Often, we deeply regret it. But we have no idea what to do about it.

Ms. Walsh and Ms. Putman have been competitive since childhood—about clothes, about boyfriends, about grades. Ms. Walsh remembers how in grammar school her sister wrote an essay about their grandfather and won a writing award. She recited it at a school assembly with her grandpa standing nearby, beaming. Ms. Walsh, seething, vowed to win the award the next year and did.

Ms. Putman married first. Ms. Walsh, single at the time, clearly recalls   5 the phone call when her sister told her she was pregnant. "I was excited because this was the first grandchild. Then I got off the phone and cried for two hours," says Ms. Walsh.

Ms. Putman, 39 and a stay-at-home-mom in Bolingbrook, Ill., remembers that she too felt jealous—of her sister's frequent travel and promotions in her marketing career. "The way my parents would go on and on about her really made me feel 'less than,'" Ms. Putman says.

Ms. Walsh eventually married, had a son and named him Jack. Seven weeks later, Ms. Putman gave birth to a son and named him Jack. The discussion? "That was always my boy name." "I never heard you say that."

Sibling rivalry is a normal aspect of childhood, experts say. Our siblings are our first rivals. They competed with us for the love and attention of the people we needed most, our parents, and it is understandable that we occasionally felt threatened. Much of what is written about sibling rivalry focuses on its effects during childhood.

But our sibling relationships are often the longest of our lives, lasting 80 years or more. Several research studies indicate that up to 45% of adults have a rivalrous or distant relationship with a sibling.

People questioned later in life often say their biggest regret is being   10 estranged from a sister or brother.

The rivalry often persists into adulthood because in many families it goes unaddressed. "Most people who have been through years of therapy have worked out a lot of guilt with their parents. But when it comes to their siblings, they can't articulate what is wrong," says Jeanne Safer, a psychologist in Manhattan and author of *Cain's Legacy: Liberating Siblings from a Lifetime of Rage, Shame, Secrecy and Regret.*

Dr. Safer believes sibling rivals speak in a kind of dialect (she calls it "sib speak"). It sounds like this: "You were always Mom's favorite." "Mom and Dad are always at your house but they never visit me." "You never call me."

"It's not the loving language that good friends have," Dr. Safer says. "It's the language of grievance collection."

It's hard to know what to say in response. "You are afraid that what you say will be catastrophic or will reveal awful truths," Dr. Safer says. "It's a lifelong walk on eggshells."

15   Sibling discord has been around since the Bible. Cain killed Abel. Leah stole Rachel's intended husband, Jacob. Joseph fought bitterly with his 10 older half brothers. Parents often have a hand in fostering it. They may choose favorites, love unevenly and compare one child with the other.

Dr. Safer draws a distinction between sibling rivalry and sibling strife. Rivalry encompasses a normal range of disagreements and competition between siblings. Sibling strife, which is less common, is rivalry gone ballistic—siblings who, because of personality clashes or hatred, can't enjoy each other's company.

Al Golden, 85, chokes up when he talks about his twin brother, Elliott, who died three years ago. The brothers shared a room growing up in Brooklyn, N.Y., graduated from the SUNY Maritime College in New York and married within a month of each other in 1947.

Yet Mr. Golden still remembers how their father often compared their grades, asking one or the other, "How come you got a B and your brother got an A?" He rarely missed a chance to point out that Elliott wasn't as good as Al in swimming.

When the boys were ready to get married, he suggested a double wedding. Mr. Golden put his foot down. "I shared every birthday and my bar mitzvah with my brother," he said. "I'll be damned if I am going to share my wedding with him."

20   Elliott Golden became a lawyer and eventually a state Supreme Court judge. Al Golden went into the mirror business, then sold life insurance. He says he always envied his brother's status and secretly took pleasure in knowing he was a better fisherman and owned a big boat. Once, Elliott asked him, "I am a lawyer. How come you make more money than me?" Mr. Golden says. "He meant: 'How come you are making more than me when you are not as successful?' But it made me feel good."

One day, Mr. Golden says, Elliott accused him of not doing enough to take care of their ailing mother. After the conversation, Mr. Golden didn't speak to his brother for more than a year. "It might have been the build-up of jealousies over the years," he says.

His brother repeatedly reached out to him, as did his nieces and nephews, but Mr. Golden ignored them.

Then one day Mr. Golden received an email from his brother telling a story about two men who had a stream dividing their properties. One man hired a carpenter to build a fence along the stream, but the carpenter built a bridge by mistake. Mr. Golden thought about the email then wrote back, "I'd like to walk over the bridge."

"I missed him," Mr. Golden says now. "I never had the chance to miss him before."

Dr. Safer says brothers' rivalries often are overt, typically focusing on things   25
like Dad's love, athletic prowess, career success, money. Women are less comfortable with competition, she says, so sister rivalries tend to be passive-aggressive and less direct. Whom did Mom love best, who is a better mother now.

Brothers often repair their rivalries with actions. When women reconcile, it's often through talking. Ms. Putman and Ms. Walsh have learned to stop arguments using a trick from childhood. When a discussion gets heated, one sister will call out "star," a code word they devised as kids to mean the conversation is over. The sister who ends it gets the last word. "You may still be mad, but you adhere to the rules of childhood," Ms. Walsh says.

For some years, the two didn't socialize much. But when Ms. Putman's husband died last fall, Ms. Walsh, now a stay-at-home-mom in Chicago, helped plan the wake and write the obituary. Arriving at her sister's house one day before the funeral, Ms. Walsh found her in bed, crying, and climbed in next to her. The sisters said, "I love you," and Ms. Putman says she realized she was going to be OK.

"Lying there, I felt that if I've got my sister, I''ve got my strength," Ms. Putman says. "She is my backbone."

Putting a Stop to Sibling Rivalry

Fix the problem by addressing it head-on, says psychologist Jeanne Safer.

- The first step is to think. Who is this person outside his or her relation-   30
ship with you? What do you like about your sibling? Remember the positive memories. Identify why you think the relationship is worth fixing—if it is.

- Take the initiative to change. It could be a gesture, like an offer to help with a sick child, a conversation or a letter. Be sincere and don't ignore the obvious. Say: "These conversations between us are painful. I would like to see if we can make our relationship better."
- Gestures count. Not everyone is comfortable talking about a strained relationship, especially men. But phone calls, invitations to spend time together, attempts to help should be seen as peace offerings.
- Consider your sibling's point of view. Try not to be defensive. What did childhood look like through his or her eyes? "You have to be willing to see an unflattering portrait of yourself," Dr. Safer says.
- Tell your sibling what you respect. "I love your sense of humor." "I admire what a good parent you are."
35 • And, finally: "It won't kill you to apologize," Dr. Safer says.

Analyze

1. What were some of the rivalries that Ms. Walsh and Ms. Putman had?
2. How do male and female sibling rivalries differ?
3. What percentage of adults has a sibling rivalry?

Explore

1. When friends part ways or couples divorce, more often than not that is the end of the relationship. What are some of the similarities and differences between friend and spousal love, and sibling love? Why is it, as Bernstein argues, that siblings can hate each other and yet tend to regret their actions and try and find a way to mend their rifts?
2. Bernstein mentions a few of the classic sibling rivalries, such as Cain and Abel, to stress that not all rivalries end well. Write an essay exploring a rivalry you are familiar with, for example, from historical, literary, film, soap opera, TV series, Facebook, etc. In the essay clearly define what their problem is/was (the source of their conflict).
3. In our essay psychologist Jeanne Safer lists six points to help heal sibling rivalry. As a follow-up to question 2, use these points to write a letter to the siblings, stating you would like to create a bridge between the two of them.

Kirun Kapur
"Anthem"

Kapur started her writing career at India's feminist magazine, *Manushi*, and since then her work has appeared in *AGNI, Poetry International, FIELD, Literary Imagination, The Christian Science Monitor, The Beloit Poetry Journal, Massachusetts Review,* and *Crab Orchard Review*. In 2012 she was awarded the Arts & Letters/Rumi Prize for Poetry. In this poem Kapur creates a metaphor of family as country.

What are some of the ways she turns family members into country traits?

> Love begins in a country
> Where oranges weep sweetness
> And men piss in the street;
>
> Your hands are forever binding
> Black strands in a plait. Your mother's
> Childhood friend has steeped
>
> Your skin in coconut oil, tucked
> Her daughter beside you—the night
> Is a womb, live with twins.
>
> Heat's body presses every body.
> Sharp chop of your uncle's cough
> Clocks the hours; your sister's washing,
>
> The rush of your thoughts. Morning
> Is nine glass bangles hoisting sacks
> Of sugar from the floor. I'm not talking
>
> About a place, but a country:
> Its laws are your mother, its walls
> Are your dreams. The flag it flies
>
> is your father, waving.

5

Analyze

1. Who are the family members that appear in the poem?
2. What are some of the images of nature in the poem?
3. What do mother and father symbolize?

Explore

1. An anthem is an uplifting song and oftentimes patriotic. What effects does this poem achieve and how does the poet's language achieve them?
2. Compare and contrast Kapur's "Anthem" with America's anthem, "The Star-Spangled Banner," or, if you are from another country, its anthem.
3. Our traditional notions of love of and for country evoke passion and battles against all odds. Kapur does away with this type of imagery and transports us into the personal yet abstract lives of family and other elements of country. Write an anthem poem to your city, region, or state with Kapur's as a model.

Forging Connections

1. Explore the relationships among love, sex, and romance that these writers have written about.
2. Argue that there is no such thing as love and we need to move on; all we have is romance, then sex, and then more of the same with other people. Come up with a new name for this concept you create.
3. Write an essay arguing that love is alive and well in the twenty-first century by using the ideas from this chapter. Also, bring in some songs, poems, or movie clips to show love in different ways.

Looking Further

1. Create a mashup of songs, poems, images, words, etc., that shows who you are in relation to the five identity themes you have explored in these five chapters.

2. If, as a couple of these essays have argued, we tend to fall in love with those in our immediate vicinity, what does this have to say with the places where we live and spend our lives, like school and work? How does the Internet change this (jump ahead to Chapter 6 to help you explore this)?

3. From the survey you conducted as a class on "20 questions asking about the role of love, conversation, and sex," use the results and essays from *Identity: A Reader for Writers* to develop an essay informing your peers about what love is or is not, how they need to think about what it is, and how to maintain (or lose) it.

6

Where Do You Draw the Line? Privacy, Socializing, & Life without Boundaries

In our final chapter we explore the new and evolving identities we create, share, and germinate with our new social technologies. With the advent of the Internet, we have opened old barriers and are in search of where our new boundaries reside. With such freedom and without rules or restrictions, we find that there are consequences that come with sharing too much about ourselves in too many open spaces. Likewise, there are consequences to the fact that many people are able to access what we share, and to the indelible nature of the information we cast into the Internet.

It is a great freedom to be able to contact friends in the time it takes to type their e-mail address, to share important moments, and to distribute our accomplishments with our friends, family, and the world. Sharing our accomplishments and special moments might seem natural, when those special moments are personal and intended for a select few. Yet sometimes they cross boundaries that we do not anticipate, and this is when we enter into gray areas whose boundaries seem nonexistent. By examining this concept from different angles, this chapter opens up several ways for us to think about and practice public sharing of ourselves, while also considering real, personal, philosophical, and legal issues about our boundary-less digital spaces.

Our first three essays offer insights into key personal freedoms that the Internet and cell phones create, as well as attempts to monitor them. In the first essay, "Don't Trip over Your Digital Footprint," Peterson and Sheninger focus on the long-term effects of young peoples' activities such as tweeting or posting on the web. Instead of talking from outside of the digital tools teens use, they monitor and are involved in what teens post and say. In this way they can intervene when necessary, as well as teach valuable lessons for young people growing up in a digital world. Turkle's "How Computers Change the Way We Think" takes the view that digital learning and experiences are creating a shallower type of learning and knowledge in which we see how things work without actually knowing how they work. This is followed by "The Way We Live Now: I Tweet, Therefore I Am," where Orenstein realizes that with her near-neurotic need to send tweets, she is constantly interpreting and performing for others, creating new identities she had never imagined she would have. The urge to be digitally connected has exploded in China with their version of Facebook, Weibo; in "East Meets Tweet," Dewoskin sheds light on the liberating role of this popular social networking site.

Our last three essays extend warnings to us about how vulnerable our privacy—our personal images and conversations—is on the Internet. Fakhoury, Opsahl, and Reitman argue the Internet needs control and limitations in "When Will Our Email Betray Us? An Email Privacy Primer in Light of the Petraeus Saga," while Fletcher sheds light into the thinking of Facebook designers and their capital-driven model (but they are our friends, right?) in "How Facebook Is Redefining Privacy." Norton's "10 Reasons Why I Avoid Social Networking Services" argues that putting all types of information about your personal and private self is a bad idea because you cannot take it back.

All of the essays in our last chapter explore digital-age notions of the images, videos, and words we share on the web, as well as the indelible consequences of our sharing.

NPR
"Don't Trip over Your Digital Footprint"

The literacy narrative for this reading comes from NPR's *Tell Me More*. In it host Michel Martin interviews Latoya Peterson, editor of the blog *Racialicious*, and Eric Sheninger, known as the New Jersey New Milford High School "Twitter Principal." When it comes to Internet use, their approach is to be immersed in the same digital cultures their students are in so they can be aware of what is taking place, teach safe Internet practices, and intervene when needed. For more on this interview in audio, text, or all three, visit National Public Radio at http://www.npr.org.

Have you ever seen or experienced online bullying?

MICHEL MARTIN, HOST:
I'm Michel Martin and this is TELL ME MORE from NPR News. Coming up, we want to take a look at this past weekend's G8 summit. We'll talk about what Europe's economic challenges could mean for the U.S. We'll have that conversation in a few minutes. But first, we want to turn our attention to social media. Facebook has been in the news, of course, because of last week's stock offering, but apart from that, Facebook has become a big part of people's everyday lives.
It boasts 900 million users. If it were a nation, it would be the third most populous in the world. And after just five years in business, Twitter has approximately 175 million users. But just because more people are using social media, it doesn't mean they understand its power. Many users are still learning the hard way how harmful it can be when millions of people can read and judge those status updates and 140 character messages.
We thought since summer is around the corner and people might be tempted to post pics of their latest beer bashes, that this might be a good time to talk about the potential pitfalls of social media. We've called Latoya Peterson. She is the editor of the blog *Racialicious*. Also with us, Eric Sheninger. He is the principal of New Milford High School in New Jersey. He's known as the Twitter principal because he is active on almost every social media network.
He also takes a hands-on approach to educating his students about the advantages and downsides of social media. He's at school, so if you hear

some school noises in the background, you'll know what that is. Welcome to you both. Thank you both so much for speaking with us.

LATOYA PETERSON: Thanks for having us.

5   **ERIC SHENINGER:** Thanks for having me.

MARTIN: Latoya, let me start with you. Twitter, of course, is a way for figures, public figures, to develop a following, but it just seems like every week we're reading about somebody stubbing his or her toe on this. I mean, of course Spike Lee had to apologize for tweeting an incorrect address for George Zimmerman, who of course is the shooter in the Trayvon Martin case.

And who could forget Anthony Weiner, a member of Congress having to resign because of a careless Twitter picture of something he should not have tweeted a picture about. So I'm just wondering what is it, do you think, about Twitter that makes people forget that the world is reading it?

> ... social media [is] blurring the boundary between ... private intimate space and public space...

PETERSON: Well, you know, my friend Dana Boyd, who is a researcher and she does a lot of work with researching teens, has a great idea on this, which is that, you know, Twitter and social media in general is kind of blurring the boundary between like this private intimate space and public space, right?

And so for most people, most people who are not in the public eye, we have this idea that we are anonymous in our daily lives. Like who really cares about your status updates except for the people who know you and people who love you? For celebrities, that becomes even more work because they know they're talking to their fans and yet they're creating this intimate space with their fans.

So you have people like Kim Kardashian tweeting, you know, what should I wear today? You know, how should I style my hair? And it becomes this very affirming relationship and at the same time it makes people feel very safe and so they start to drop their guard and say things that they really shouldn't.

10   **MARTIN:** And in a way you hear that—people say they forget that the cameras are there.

PETERSON: Exactly.

MARTIN: That kind of thing, although I don't know how you could forget that these giant microphones are in your face.

(SOUNDBITE OF LAUGHTER)

MARTIN: It's just—you know, we are on the air, folks. We are actually talking to people, millions of people. So, you know, Eric, we know that

Twitter and Facebook can actually make grown people act like teenagers, like Latoya was just saying. You actually work with teenagers as the principal at New Milford High. When did you get the idea that it was important to start incorporating social media into the educational experience?

SHENINGER: Well, I think it began with—when I sort of stuck my toe   15
into the water and quickly realized that, you know, social media could be a valuable tool for teaching and learning. You know, I was the principal that blocked, banned, prohibited, felt that social media had absolutely no place in education.

But once I began to use it and I saw the many merits associated with these forms of technology, as I became more knowledgeable and also started to hear and see all of the negative stories involving social media and— whether it be student behavior or staff behavior, I decided that, you know what, I'm in the business of education.

I need to work with my students and teach them how to be digitally responsible. I think across the country, schools, you know, fail to educate students on appropriate use of social media. Primarily they feel that, you know, it has no place in school so why bother, but you know what? It's not going away.

And what we've started to do is—I actually lead these seminars myself. We bring every single student into the auditorium. We talk about cyber-bullying. We talk about digital footprints. We talk about the negative impact that tweets or Facebook posts can eventually have in terms of getting into college or getting a job.

And we actually then share some concrete examples of situations that we've dealt with here with our students and sort of like put the students on the right path. And the end result has been a dramatic decrease in cyber-bullying. Students are actually taking down their Facebook pages. They're reporting now to us, to school officials across the district, acts of cyber bullying that they see.

And they understand that, you know what, they need to be digitally   20
responsible in this age because once it's posted out there, it doesn't go away.

MARTIN: If you're just joining us, you're listening to TELL ME MORE from NPR News. We're talking about the advantages and pitfalls of social media with Principal Eric Sheninger of New Milford High School in New Jersey. He's been called the Twitter principal because he's active on social media and also teaches about this. And also blogger Latoya Peterson. You know, we've talked a lot about the cyber-bullying with kids, but Latoya, what about the cyber-bullying among adults? I mean we've actually had experiences on this program where people—even in advance of an interview airing with someone, someone's decided that they're not going to like in advance what that person is saying and then they start attacking this person via social media.

And, you know, you say to yourself—you can't control that. I mean there's nothing you can do about that. And I'm just wondering, particularly because you have a blog that addresses sensitive issues, which race is one—are there some guidelines that you employ to help make it the kind of safe space that people would like to have so they can talk about things that are challenging? Or can you just—just have to tell people to toughen up?

PETERSON: Well, it's challenging because you don't want to tell people to toughen up because it's harassment, right? Like the same things that happen offline with slam books and gossip circles, it just migrates online and it's able to be, you know, the volume is just so much higher when it's online. Right?

25   If you make a mistake online, instead of having, like, the five people in front of you like, ooh, I hated that, now you suddenly have 500 people that might've come from Tumblr or Twitter or whatever and they're all— it feels like kind of a wave that's crashing.

But what we've tried to do to mitigate it, particularly when talking about subjects like race or gender or structural inequality at large, is really, one, to set the tone for the place and say this is what's acceptable and this is what's not. Right? So we have all these policies against personal attacks. We have policies surrounding identity. We have policies about how we talk about issues. And we tell people that do not necessarily abide by those policies to leave. Because that's a problem. Not everyone is invested in having good conversations online. Some people are invested in having these fights or stirring up this drama and they're not welcome in our space.

MARTIN: So you kick them out.

PETERSON: We do.

30   **MARTIN:** If you see these—language that you feel crosses the line, you . . .

PETERSON: Right. We don't approve the comment.

Occasionally we'll engage with things that are problematic, if we feel like, you know, so if there's like trans issues, right—they're not necessarily well-known. People might not know when they're making a mistake, and so we try to engage if that person becomes defensive or becomes aggressive.

MARTIN: And what do you say to people who feel that you're censoring them?

(SOUNDBITE OF LAUGHTER)

35   **PETERSON:** Censorship is something that's really misunderstood in our society, right? If the government was censoring you, that's one thing, but I'm on a private website and you could form your own private website

and say whatever you feel to do, but you're not going to do that on the property that I have to maintain and I have to pay for.

MARTIN: Eric, do you feel that the students are leading or following in this? For example, we've seen Twitter fights among celebrities, like, you know, Rihanna, for example.

PETERSON: Rihanna and Karrueche Tran, yeah.

MARTIN: Yes. And her ex-boyfriend and his new inamorata have gotten into some Twitter fights. Do you feel that the students look at that and think I should do that too? Or do you think—how do you think that interplay of celebrity behavior affects the student behavior?

SHENINGER: I definitely think it is playing a prominent role in students' online behavior because schools have not been proactive enough to sit their kids down and teach them about, you know, Internet etiquette, the difference between right or wrong, and the potential negative impact this could have on their lives down the road.

You know, for us what we've done is, you know, being that we're involved as 40
a school and as educators in virtually every social media space, some things have been brought to our attention. And there was one case early this year where some students started a hash tag called #NMProblems. And it was started by alumni, but some current students chimed in and they said some very derogatory remarks in regards to some present teachers.

And you know what? Immediately, when it came to our attention, we addressed it. We brought those students in, but most importantly, we brought their parents in and we let them read their public tweets before we brought the kids in. And that had such an impact on the discussions that we had with these kids because, when the parents saw, firsthand, what was being put online, they were mortified.

And, since that one point in time this year when we addressed it, we've had no other issues on Twitter throughout the entire year, because, A, the students now know, you know, that it's wrong and, B, they understand that we're out there—not policing, but making sure that they're making wise decisions in terms of the content that they are posting.

MARTIN: So good piece of advice—or why don't you leave us, Principal Sheninger, if you would, with one brief piece of advice as many students—you know, they head off into the summer and, oftentimes, they're not as closely supervised as they are during the school year. Best piece of advice for parents and for students?

SHENINGER: My piece of advice is, even though you might think it's innocent, it's not that big of a deal, that it's your private and personal information, once you put it on a social media site, it is there for anyone to, not only access, but they can then share that information, they can repurpose it, they can adapt it. Whether it's pictures, videos or your thoughts, it could lead to a potential disaster down the road where you're looking to get into that great college or looking for a job. Once it's archived, it can be accessed and, as we tell our students, that's your digital footprint. Do you want your digital footprint to be positive or negative going forward?

45 **MARTIN:** Latoya, a final word from you, 30 seconds or so. What's your final best piece of advice?

PETERSON: Definitely realize that you're always on the record and, if you're really interested in privacy and online policing, check out places like EFF, the Electronic Frontier Foundation, and they tell you kind of ways in which you can look at how people are monitoring you and how you can reduce your digital footprint.

MARTIN: Latoya Peterson is the editor of the blog *Racialicious*. She was kind enough to join us at our NPR studios in Washington, D.C. Eric Sheninger is the principal of New Milford High School in New Jersey. He was nice enough to take a short break and find some quiet corner at school to talk with us.

Thank you both so much for speaking with us.

PETERSON: Thank you, Michel.

50 **SHENINGER:** Thank you.

Analyze

1. What do the speakers mean when they say, "We have policies surrounding identity. We have policies about how we talk about issues"?

2. What are digital footprints?

3. What do the speakers say about censorship?

Explore

1. Create and describe a fictional person and profile for yourself (e.g., female, 23 years old, college student, etc.). Then, in a PowerPoint or other presentation software, create a positive and negative digital footprint. Discuss what makes them both have impact, and what the long-term effects are of the shared information.

2. In small groups, create an Internet etiquette document with either a cardboard poster or PowerPoint presentation.

3. Imagine that you have graduated and are on the job market or applying to graduate school. Your prospective employer/school asks you to write a letter describing your digital footprint. Write this letter with examples.

Sherry Turkle
"How Computers Change the Way We Think"

Sherry Turkle is the Abby Rockefeller Mauzé Professor of the Social Studies of Science and Technology at the Massachusetts Institute of Technology. Her research has focused on psychoanalysis and human–technology interaction. She has several books on the psychology of human relationships with technology, for example, *The Second Self* and *Life on the Screen*. Turkle argues that computer users need to know more about how computers operate, what is behind the GUI interfaces, and what is in the machines.

What does it mean to be a computer person?

The tools we use to think change the ways in which we think. The invention of written language brought about a radical shift in how we process, organize, store, and transmit representations of the world. Although writing remains our primary information technology, today when we think about the impact of technology on our habits of mind, we think primarily of the computer.

My first encounters with how computers change the way we think came soon after I joined the faculty at the Massachusetts Institute of Technology in the late 1970s, at the end of the era of the slide rule and the beginning of the era of the personal computer. At a lunch for new faculty members, several senior professors in engineering complained that the transition from slide rules to calculators had affected their students' ability to deal with issues of scale. When students used slide rules, they had to insert decimal points themselves. The professors insisted that that required students to maintain a mental sense of scale, whereas those who relied on calculators made frequent errors in orders of magnitude. Additionally, the students with calculators had lost their ability to do "back of the envelope" calculations, and with that, an intuitive feel for the material.

That same semester, I taught a course in the history of psychology. There, I experienced the impact of computational objects on students' ideas about their emotional lives. My class had read Freud's essay on slips of the tongue, with its famous first example: The chairman of a parliamentary session opens a meeting by declaring it closed. The students discussed how Freud interpreted such errors as revealing a person's mixed emotions. A computer-science major disagreed with Freud's approach. The mind, she argued, is a computer. And in a computational dictionary—like we have in the human mind—"closed" and "open" are designated by the same symbol, separated by a sign for opposition. "Closed" equals "minus open." To substitute "closed" for "open" does not require the notion of ambivalence or conflict.

"When the chairman made that substitution," she declared, "a bit was dropped; a minus sign was lost. There was a power surge. No problem."

The young woman turned a Freudian slip into an information-processing error. An explanation in terms of meaning had become an explanation in terms of mechanism.

5   Such encounters turned me to the study of both the instrumental and the subjective sides of the nascent computer culture. As an ethnographer and psychologist, I began to study not only what the computer was doing for us, but what it was doing to us, including how it was changing the way we see ourselves, our sense of human identity.

In the 1980s, I surveyed the psychological effects of computational objects in everyday life—largely the unintended side effects of people's tendency to project thoughts and feelings onto their machines. In the 20 years since, computational objects have become more explicitly designed to have emotional and cognitive effects. And those "effects by design" will become even stronger in the decade to come. Machines are being designed to serve explicitly as companions, pets, and tutors. And they are introduced in school settings for the youngest children.

Today, starting in elementary school, students use e-mail, word processing, computer simulations, virtual communities, and PowerPoint software. In the process, they are absorbing more than the content of what appears on their screens. They are learning new ways to think about what it means to know and understand.

What follows is a short and certainly not comprehensive list of areas where I see information technology encouraging changes in thinking. There can be no simple way of cataloging whether any particular change is good or bad. That is contested terrain. At every step we have to ask, as educators and citizens, whether current technology is leading us in directions that serve our human purposes. Such questions are not technical; they are social, moral, and political. For me, addressing that subjective side of computation is one of the more significant challenges for the next decade of information technology in higher education. Technology does not determine change, but it encourages us to take certain directions. If we make those directions clear, we can more easily exert human choice.

Thinking about privacy. Today's college students are habituated to a world of online blogging, instant messaging, and Web browsing that leaves electronic traces. Yet they have had little experience with the right to privacy. Unlike past generations of Americans, who grew up with the notion that the privacy of their mail was sacrosanct, our children are accustomed to electronic surveillance as part of their daily lives.

I have colleagues who feel that the increased incursions on privacy have   10 put the topic more in the news, and that this is a positive change. But middle-school and high-school students tend to be willing to provide personal information online with no safeguards, and college students seem uninterested in violations of privacy and in increased governmental and commercial surveillance. Professors find that students do not understand that in a democracy, privacy is a right, not merely a privilege. In 10 years, ideas about the relationship of privacy and government will require even more active pedagogy. (One might also hope that increased education about the kinds of silent surveillance that technology makes possible may inspire more active political engagement with the issue.)

Avatars or a self? Chat rooms, role-playing games, and other technological venues offer us many different contexts for presenting ourselves online. Those possibilities are particularly important for adolescents because they offer what Erik Erikson described as a moratorium, a time out or safe space for the personal experimentation that is so crucial for adolescent development. Our dangerous world—with crime, terrorism, drugs, and AIDS—offers little in the way of safe spaces. Online worlds can provide valuable spaces for identity play.

But some people who gain fluency in expressing multiple aspects of self may find it harder to develop authentic selves. Some children who write narratives for their screen avatars may grow up with too little experience of how to share their real feelings with other people. For those who are lonely yet afraid of intimacy, information technology has made it possible to have the illusion of companionship without the demands of friendship.

From powerful ideas to PowerPoint. In the 1970s and early 1980s, some educators wanted to make programming part of the regular curriculum for K-12 education. They argued that because information technology carries ideas, it might as well carry the most powerful ideas that computer science has to offer. It is ironic that in most elementary schools today, the ideas being carried by information technology are not ideas from computer science like procedural thinking, but more likely to be those embedded in productivity tools like PowerPoint presentation software.

PowerPoint does more than provide a way of transmitting content. It carries its own way of thinking, its own aesthetic—which not surprisingly shows up in the aesthetic of college freshmen. In that aesthetic, presentation becomes its own powerful idea.

15   To be sure, the software cannot be blamed for lower intellectual standards. Misuse of the former is as much a symptom as a cause of the latter. Indeed, the culture in which our children are raised is increasingly a culture of presentation, a corporate culture in which appearance is often more important than reality. In contemporary political discourse, the bar has also been lowered. Use of rhetorical devices at the expense of cogent argument regularly goes without notice. But it is precisely because standards of intellectual rigor outside the educational sphere have fallen that educators must attend to how we use, and when we introduce, software that has been designed to simplify the organization and processing of information.

In "The Cognitive Style of PowerPoint" (Graphics Press, 2003), Edward R. Tufte suggests that PowerPoint equates bulleting with clear thinking. It does not teach students to begin a discussion or construct a narrative. It encourages presentation, not conversation. Of course, in the hands of a master teacher, a PowerPoint presentation with few words and powerful images can serve as the jumping-off point for a brilliant lecture. But in the hands of elementary-school students, often introduced to PowerPoint in the third grade, and often infatuated with its swooshing sounds, animated icons, and flashing text, a slide show is more likely to close down debate than open it up.

Developed to serve the needs of the corporate boardroom, the software is designed to convey absolute authority. Teachers used to tell students that clear exposition depended on clear outlining, but presentation software has fetishized the outline at the expense of the content.

Narrative, the exposition of content, takes time. PowerPoint, like so much in the computer culture, speeds up the pace.

Word processing vs. thinking. The catalog for the Vermont Country Store advertises a manual typewriter, which the advertising copy says "moves at a pace that allows time to compose your thoughts." As many of us know, it is possible to manipulate text on a computer screen and see how it looks faster than we can think about what the words mean.

Word processing has its own complex psychology. From a pedagogical   20 point of view, it can make dedicated students into better writers because it allows them to revise text, rearrange paragraphs, and experiment with the tone and shape of an essay. Few professional writers would part with their computers; some claim that they simply cannot think without their hands on the keyboard. Yet the ability to quickly fill the page, to see it before you can think it, can make bad writers even worse.

A seventh grader once told me that the typewriter she found in her mother's attic is "cool because you have to type each letter by itself. You have to know what you are doing in advance or it comes out a mess." The idea of thinking ahead has become exotic.

Taking things at interface value. We expect software to be easy to use, and we assume that we don't have to know how a computer works. In the early 1980s, most computer users who spoke of transparency meant that, as with any other machine, you could "open the hood" and poke around. But only a few years later, Macintosh users began to use the term when they talked about seeing their documents and programs represented by attractive and easy-to-interpret icons. They were referring to an ability to make things work without needing to go below the screen surface. Paradoxically, it was the screen's opacity that permitted that kind of transparency. Today, when people say that something is transparent, they mean that they can see how to make it work, not that they know how it works. In other words, transparency means epistemic opacity.

The people who built or bought the first generation of personal computers understood them down to the bits and bytes. The next generation of operating systems were more complex, but they still invited that old-time reductive understanding. Contemporary information technology encourages different habits of mind. Today's college students are already used to taking things at (inter) face value; their successors in 2014 will be even less accustomed to probing below the surface.

Simulation and its discontents. Some thinkers argue that the new opacity is empowering, enabling anyone to use the most sophisticated technological tools and to experiment with simulation in complex and creative ways. But it is also true that our tools carry the message that they are beyond our understanding. It is possible that in daily life, epistemic opacity can lead to passivity.

25   I first became aware of that possibility in the early 1990s, when the first generation of complex simulation games was introduced and immediately became popular for home as well as school use. SimLife teaches the principles of evolution by getting children involved in the development of complex ecosystems; in that sense it is an extraordinary learning tool. During one session in which I played SimLife with Tim, a 13-year-old, the screen before us flashed a message: "Your orgot is being eaten up." "What's an orgot?" I asked. Tim didn't know. "I just ignore that," he said confidently. "You don't need to know that kind of stuff to play."

For me, that story serves as a cautionary tale. Computer simulations enable their users to think about complex phenomena as dynamic, evolving systems. But they also accustom us to manipulating systems whose core assumptions we may not understand and that may not be true.

We live in a culture of simulation. Our games, our economic and political systems, and the ways architects design buildings, chemists envisage molecules, and surgeons perform operations all use simulation technology. In 10 years the degree to which simulations are embedded in every area of life will have increased exponentially. We need to develop a new form of media literacy: readership skills for the culture of simulation.

We come to written text with habits of readership based on centuries of civilization. At the very least, we have learned to begin with the journalist's traditional questions: who, what, when, where, why, and how. Who wrote these words, what is their message, why were they written, and how are they situated in time and place, politically and socially? A central project for higher education during the next 10 years should be creating programs in information-technology literacy, with the goal of teaching students to interrogate simulations in much the same spirit, challenging their built-in assumptions.

Despite the ever-increasing complexity of software, most computer environments put users in worlds based on constrained choices. In other words, immersion in programmed worlds puts us in reassuring environments where the rules are clear. For example, when you play a video game, you often go through a series of frightening situations that you escape by mastering the rules—you experience life as a reassuring dichotomy of scary and safe. Children grow up in a culture of video games, action films, fantasy epics, and computer programs that all rely on that familiar scenario of almost losing but then regaining total mastery: There is danger. It is mastered. A still-more-powerful monster appears. It is subdued. Scary. Safe.

Yet in the real world, we have never had a greater need to work our way   30 out of binary assumptions. In the decade ahead, we need to rebuild the culture around information technology. In that new sociotechnical culture, assumptions about the nature of mastery would be less absolute. The new culture would make it easier, not more difficult, to consider life in shades of gray, to see moral dilemmas in terms other than a battle between Good and Evil. For never has our world been more complex, hybridized, and global. Never have we so needed to have many contradictory thoughts and feelings at the same time. Our tools must help us accomplish that, not fight against us.

Information technology is identity technology. Embedding it in a culture that supports democracy, freedom of expression, tolerance, diversity, and complexity of opinion is one of the next decade's greatest challenges. We cannot afford to fail.

When I first began studying the computer culture, a small breed of highly trained technologists thought of themselves as "computer people." That is no longer the case. If we take the computer as a carrier of a way of knowing, a way of seeing the world and our place in it, we are all computer people now.

Analyze

1. What does Turkle describe as happening at a lunch with engineers?
2. Why does Turkle say that she started to study our use of computers?
3. How are computers being designed and with what types of roles?

Explore

1. Turkle states, "I have colleagues who feel that the increased incursions on privacy have put the topic more in the news, and that this is a positive change. But middle-school and high-school students tend to be willing to provide personal information online with no safeguards,

and college students seem uninterested in violations of privacy and in increased governmental and commercial surveillance." Drawing from the essays from this chapter, write a letter to Turkle telling her that we are way beyond incursions, and some news stories about privacy issues.

2. At one point Turkle says, "Online worlds can provide valuable spaces for identity play." Using this quote, create a comic showing either the positive side, which she alludes to, or the negative side, which is not a matter of play, but a serious business with traumatic consequences.

3. Explore what this quote means for you in terms of your identity and reputation: "When I first began studying the computer culture, a small breed of highly trained technologists thought of themselves as 'computer people.' That is no longer the case. If we take the computer as a carrier of a way of knowing, a way of seeing the world and our place in it, we are all computer people now."

Peggy Orenstein
"The Way We Live Now: I Tweet, Therefore I Am"

Peggy Orenstein is the author of several books, including the best-selling *School Girls: Young Women, Self-Esteem and the Confidence Gap*, and her recent best-seller, *Cinderella Ate My Daughter: Dispatches from the Front Lines of the New Girlie-Girl Culture*. She also is a writer for *The New York Times Magazine* and has written for such publications as *The Los Angeles Times, Mother Jones, Discover, USA Today*, and *Vogue*. She has appeared on talk shows such as NPR's *Fresh Air* and *Morning Edition, Nightline, Good Morning America*, and *The Today Show*. In Orenstein's essay she shares how tweeting has become a "normal" part of her life; she describes this as if it were a normal appendage of her body and psyche responding to life.

If you have a Twitter account, how close do your tweets reflect your life at the moment?

On a recent lazy Saturday morning, my daughter and I lolled on a blanket in our front yard, snacking on apricots, listening to a download of E. B. White reading "The Trumpet of the Swan." Her legs sprawled across mine; the grass tickled our ankles. It was the quintessential summer moment, and a year ago, I would have been fully present for it. But instead, a part of my consciousness had split off and was observing the scene from the outside: this was, I realized excitedly, the perfect opportunity for a tweet.

I came late to Twitter. I might have skipped the phenomenon altogether, but I have a book coming out this winter, and publishers, scrambling to promote 360,000-character tomes in a 140-character world, push authors to rally their "tweeps" to the cause. Leaving aside the question of whether that actually boosts sales, I felt pressure to produce. I quickly mastered the Twitterati's unnatural self-consciousness: processing my experience instantaneously, packaging life as I lived it. I learned to be "on" all the time, whether standing behind that woman at the supermarket who sneaked three extra items into the express check-out lane (you know who you are) or despairing over human rights abuses against women in Guatemala.

Each Twitter post seemed a tacit referendum on who I am, or at least who I believe myself to be. The grocery-store episode telegraphed that I was tuned in to the Seinfeldian absurdities of life; my concern about women's victimization, however sincere, signaled that I also have a soul. Together they suggest someone who is at once cynical and compassionate, petty yet deep. Which, in the end, I'd say, is pretty accurate.

Distilling my personality provided surprising focus, making me feel stripped to my essence. It forced me, for instance, to pinpoint the dominant feeling as I sat outside with my daughter listening to E.B. White. Was it my joy at being a mother? Nostalgia for my own childhood summers? The pleasures of listening to the author's quirky, underinflected voice? Each put a different spin on the occasion, of who I was within it. Yet the final decision ("Listening to E.B. White's 'Trumpet of the Swan' with Daisy. Slow and sweet.") was not really about my own impressions: it was about how I imagined—and wanted—others to react to them. That gave me pause. How much, I began to wonder, was I shaping my Twitter feed, and how much was Twitter shaping me?

Back in the 1950s, the sociologist Erving Goffman famously argued that   5 all of life is performance: we act out a role in every interaction, adapting it based on the nature of the relationship or context at hand. Twitter has extended that metaphor to include aspects of our experience that used to be considered off-set: eating pizza in bed, reading a book in the tub, thinking a thought anywhere, flossing. Effectively, it makes the greasepaint permanent, blurring the lines not only between public and private but also between the authentic and contrived self. If all the world was once a stage, it has now become a reality TV show: we mere players are not just aware of the camera; we mug for it.

The expansion of our digital universe—Second Life, Facebook, MySpace, Twitter—has shifted not only how we spend our time but also how we construct identity. For her coming book, *Alone Together*, Sherry Turkle, a professor at M.I.T., interviewed more than 400 children and parents about their use of social media and cellphones. Among young people especially she found that the self was increasingly becoming externally manufactured rather than internally developed: a series of profiles to be sculptured and refined in response to public opinion. "On Twitter or Facebook you're trying to express something real about who you are," she explained. "But because you're also creating something for others' consumption, you find yourself imagining and playing to your audience more and more. So those moments in which you're supposed to be showing your true self become a performance. Your *psychology* becomes a performance." Referring to "The Lonely Crowd," the landmark description of the transformation of the American character from inner- to outer-directed, Turkle added, "Twitter is outer-directedness cubed."

The fun of Twitter and, I suspect, its draw for millions of people, is its infinite potential for connection, as well as its opportunity for self-expression. I enjoy those things myself. But when every thought is externalized, what becomes of insight? When we reflexively post each feeling, what becomes of reflection? When friends become fans, what happens to intimacy? The risk of the performance culture, of the packaged self, is that it erodes the very relationships it purports to create, and alienates us from our own humanity. Consider the fate of empathy: in an analysis of 72 studies performed on nearly 14,000 college students between 1979 and 2009, researchers at the Institute for Social Research at the University of Michigan found a drop in that trait, with the sharpest decline occurring since 2000. Social media may not have instigated that trend, but by encouraging self-promotion over self-awareness, they may well be accelerating it.

None of this makes me want to cancel my Twitter account. It's too late for that anyway: I'm already hooked. Besides, I appreciate good writing whatever the form: some "tweeple" are as deft as haiku masters at their craft. I am experimenting with the art of the well-placed "hashtag" myself (the symbol that adds your post on a particular topic, like #ShirleySherrod, to a stream. You can also use them whimsically, as in, "I am pretending not to be afraid of the humongous spider on the bed. #lieswetellourchildren").

At the same time, I am trying to gain some perspective on the perpetual performer's self-consciousness. That involves trying to sort out the line between person and persona, the public and private self. It also means that the next time I find myself lying on the grass, stringing daisy chains and listening to E. B. White, I will resist the urge to trumpet about the swan.

Analyze

1. How did Orenstein become an active tweeter?
2. Do you agree with Orenstein's observation about people who tweet, that they're "at once cynical and compassionate, petty yet deep"?
3. What does Orenstein mean when she asks, "How much, I began to wonder, was I shaping my Twitter feed, and how much was Twitter shaping me?" Do you think that her concern is the same as people who videotape everything happening around them, even if others are being hurt in the process?

Explore

1. Orenstein states that "all of life is performance: we act out a role in every interaction, adapting it based on the nature of the relationship or context at hand. Twitter has extended that metaphor to include aspects of our experience that used to be considered off-set: eating pizza in bed, reading a book in the tub, thinking a thought anywhere, flossing." Whether you use Twitter, Facebook, Tumblr, or some other social media, write an essay or a comic book depicting the life the author projects from either a positive, negative, or "just the way it is" viewpoint.
2. Conduct an informal interview, like the one Orenstein says Sherry Turkle conducted, in class on the class's use of social media and cellphones. State your findings and how they conform with, dispute, or go beyond what Turkle found, for example, "Among young people especially she found that the self was increasingly becoming externally manufactured rather than internally developed: a series of profiles to be sculptured and refined in response to public opinion."

3. Write an argument either in agreement or disagreement with this claim from the essay: "performance culture, of the packaged self, is that it erodes the very relationships it purports to create, and alienates us from our own humanity. Consider the fate of empathy: in an analysis of 72 studies performed on nearly 14,000 college students between 1979 and 2009, researchers at the Institute for Social Research at the University of Michigan found a drop in that trait, with the sharpest decline occurring since 2000. Social media may not have instigated that trend, but by encouraging self-promotion over self-awareness, they may well be accelerating it."

Rachel Dewoskin
"East Meets Tweet"

Dewoskin has published two novels, *Repeat after Me*, and *Big Girl Small*, which won the 2012 American Library Association's Alex Award. Her memoir, *Foreign Babes in Beijing*, tells the story of her accidental notoriety from her starring role in a Chinese soap opera. She has published on an array of topics in many magazines, including the *Boston Globe, Boston Magazine, Seneca Review, Ann Arbor Observer, New Delta Review*, and *Teachers & Writers Magazine*. She is the recipient of an American Academy of Poets Award and a Grolier Poetry Prize. In "East Meets Tweet" she explores the influential Chinese version of Twitter, called Weibo, and the role it plays in opening up a normally closed society.

How is Weibo transforming and informing the entire country of China?

In February 2011, Tom Cruise tweeted to his followers on Twitter: "We're having fun talking to you & our new friends at http://t.sina.com.cn/. It's the Chinese Twitter, but with a lot more functionality." The fun he was having with his new, superior Twitter delighted China, since it was evidence that Weibo (which translates from Chinese literally as "microblog") is the belle of the global microblogging ball. Cruise wrote in his giddy inaugural "weibos": "It's exciting to be here with you. We look forward to learning more about Weibo" and "Hello! We have some questions about adding a background and posting etiquette. Is this where we should ask? Thank you!" Thousands of eager fans offered instant advice, including: "I can teach you Chinese if you come to Shanghai," and "Dear Mr. Cruise, As for posting etiquette, I don't think you should have to worry about that. As long as you don't post anything offensive religiously, politically, culturally): Welcome to Weibo."

To his now 3.2 million Weibo followers, Cruise is known as "Tom Brother." And Tom Brother is not the only Western star with love to show the East; British actress Emma Watson wrote her first Weibo post on July 8, 2011: "Hi everyone, this is the Real Me (@ EmWatson)! Very excited about my new Weibo page"; N.B.A. star Kevin Durant "weiboed": "I love China, cannot wait to go there again"; President Bush's brother Neil joined in with: "In the past 35 years, I have been to China 80 times and am in awe of China's development." And Radiohead, in spite of the band's history of criticizing the Chinese government, arrived with a shy first post: "testing the weibo . . ."

"It's like ET," says Cai Jinqing, a Beijinger with more than 120,000 followers. She imitates a foreigner arriving on Weibo by putting her hands in the air and then landing them in front of her in a gesture of fresh arrival and tremendous confusion. "I'm going to touch down into this world and see what it's like!" Because the Chinese find Western curiosity and friendliness endearing, they celebrate posts like Cruise's early ones for what Cai calls "willingness to show vulnerability" or "authenticity." "Especially if you're famous," Cai says, "you have to loosen up your language. You have to show China your real self."

The Chinese social-networking scene is crowded with microblogging sites for China's 500 million Internet users. Sina Weibo, launched in August 2009 as an accessory to Sina, one of China's most established portals, is the fastest growing and most talked about, home to more than 250 million users and growing at a rate of about 10 million a month.

Sina is listed on NASDAQ. But since the Chinese government restricts foreign direct investment in certain sectors, Sina uses a variable interest entity (V.I.E.) to filter capital through a Cayman Islands bridge company and a chain of intermediaries. The founders in China sort of own it; the investors in New York sort of own it. Sina is run by Charles Chao, a

Chinese-born, American-educated journalist and accountant who joined Sina in 1999 as a V.P. of finance and rose through the ranks to become C.E.O. in 2006. In other words, Sina is a perfect example of 21st-century global capitalism; it's both public and private, local and international, American and Chinese. The site's dominance owes a great deal to its courtship of celebrity users; Sina focused on gathering and "verifying" stars, and fans flocked to the site. (It's a strategy that Western newcomers to the microblogging/social-networking business, like Google+, have attempted in various ways, and with varying degrees of success). Sina Weibo verifies the authenticity of celebrities' identities by putting a gilded V next to the profiles of public people who meet the requirements for verification—that is, who can prove they're who they say they are. The rest of us end up relegated to slightly inferior status, with commoner accounts. This two-tier system of verification may seem ironic in a society (and on a microblog platform) that purports to promote social equality, but it both reflects and begets a powerful desire for "authenticity" on the site and in Chinese culture generally. Verification suggests the possibility of distinguishing - on Weibo and beyond - between true and false, original and mimicked, real and fake.

Sylvia Wang, a 25-year-old former project executive for Hachette Advertising,showed me the Weibo page of a beauty with a yearning look, named "Jessie-whowants-to-be-a-flight-attendant." Jessie blogs about fashion and her life and has more than 42,000 fans. But it turns out she's not real. "I made her up," Wang said, "For advertising. You can make up followers, too; they're called zombie fans." The Chinese government announced recently that real-name registration will be required from all Weibo users by March 16, 2012. (Unregistered users may read but won't be allowed to post or forward tweets. Names will ostensibly be kept confidential by Sina and other Weibo hosts, but there is speculation that having to register may scare off not only zombies but also real Weibo users.)

Wang recently weiboed: "Not everyone has the ability to distinguish between true and false, but everyone has freedom of speech." It could be the slogan of Weibo, or of China's youth. Because most Chinese are mistrustful of officialdom and mainstream media, the desire for access to "real" information is particularly acute. And Weibo has provided a taste of that access. In modern China, and especially on Weibo, ordinary people can have a voice, but the Weibo verification team and government officials retain the power to determine what is widely read, what is deemed "true,"and what gets rooted out.

Sina Weibo looks and behaves like a Chinese love child of Facebook and Twitter (both blocked by the government in an effort to control political content and protect Chinese brands). Made mostly of Chinese characters, the site can be navigated via a combination of Chinese and English, with the help of translation services including Google's. Weibo posts are 140-character, blog-like comments, packed with the power of the Chinese language to include multiple meanings in single syllables. Weibo also supports embedded videos, photos, voicemail tweets, and a comprehensive, colorful portal page streaming with hot topics, scandals, photos of "interesting people," polls, and an endless supply of gossip. On any given day the home page might be bubbling over with everything from analysis of basketball star Jeremy Lin's breakout season to celebrations of China's mid-autumn festival, to vigorous arguments about government corruption. Weibo is often described by Westerners as "Twitter with Chinese characteristics." Those characteristics include breakneck growth, a delicate balance between government interference and free speech, and a sometimes frenetic search for identity and individuality. In fact, Weibo is "Twitter with Chinese characteristics" in the same way that China is a free market with Chinese characteristics, or the Chinese reality-TV show *Mongolian Cow Sour Yogurt Super Girl Contest was American Idol* with Chinese characteristics—that is, adapted from the outside but utterly Chinese.

The sheer force of its numbers is arguably Weibo's most distinguishing and tempting characteristic. Twitter's 2006 launch gave it a three-year head start, and yet, only two Twitter stars (Lady Gaga and Justin Bieber) can top Weibo's No. 1 blogger, Chinese actress Yao Chen, who has more than 17 million followers, putting her ahead of the Twitter totals for President Obama, Britney Spears, and Kim Kardashian. "The scale on Weibo is beyond anything I've ever seen," says Kai Lukoff, editor in chief at iChinaStock, an English-language site that covers Chinese stocks listed in the U.S. "On Twitter something might get retweeted 50 times. On Weibo it's 1,000 times."

Weibo can be used for frivolous socializing and celebrity watching, but what has caught the world's attention is the site's powerful twin forces of subversion and surveillance. "Weibo is a magnifying glass for China's social issues," says Bill Bishop, a Beijing-based independent analyst who follows

China's Internet market. "It's raising the pressure, adding some catalyst into an incredibly volatile mix."

Hung Huang, an outspoken writer and publisher with 3.9 million followers and the nickname "China's Oprah," puts it simply: "Freedom of speech was repressed for so long, Weibo is an outburst. People want to express themselves and before social media, they had no way to do it."

"I'm in denial that I'm in a totalitarian society," Huang told me over lunch in Beijing. "I'll pretend I can function how I want to function and see how far I can get. I get messages from my followers whenever I state the obvious, saying, 'Huang, be careful! We want you around!'"

Huang once posted the entire text (in 140-character excerpts) of a letter by controversial artist Ai Weiwei, who was detained by police last year and was allegedly tortured and intimidated before being released. As Huang weiboed, she and her millions of fans watched the posts go up and then, within seconds, come down. "It was fun," she said. "It gave me adrenaline. In China you can be naughty and Big Brother still cares. In most countries, no one cares what you say."

Because authorities do care in China, Weibo has given birth to a new and rapidly evolving language, of abbreviations, neologisms, and substitute words. As Huang's Ai Weiwei weibos vanished along with any others containing his name, savvy Weibo'ers were evading censors by bending the language, transforming "Ai Weiwei" into the cheerful slogan "Ai Wei Lai," or "Love the future." A close enough homonym that users knew what they meant, the characters were still safe enough to be weiboed and re-weiboed thousands of times: "I love the future," "To love the future is to love yourself," "I really don't dare believe that in this society, even love for the future can disappear." Filmmaker Alex Jia, who formerly taught Chinese language at Harvard, calls the language on Weibo "a kind of revolution. People can invent words and use them in front of an audience. That's unprecedented."

"Until I signed on to Weibo, I never saw the real China," says Cai Jinqing. "Now I can follow what's happening with a village head in Jiangsu province. Grassroots incidents are gaining momentum, becoming the talk of the day. People can speak for themselves, and be heard." A student leader at Beijing University during the Tiananmen Square uprising in 1989, Cai left China that summer, studied at Wellesley, and completed a master's degree at Princeton before returning to China. "Weibo is a genie in a bottle," she says. "The power is huge, but if it becomes too powerful, the government will shut it down. The government also has to be careful; if they shut

Weibo down it will cause a riot. It's an unspoken, collective agreement that everyone has to behave."

Part of that quiet pact is that no one touches the "3Ts and 1F": Tiananmen, Taiwan, Tibet, and Falun Gong; those terms are scrubbed from the Internet in China. And yet information is making it through, and users exert real measures of control over the site. When Fang Binxing, widely considered to be the father of China's Great Firewall (GFW), the technology that blocks users from accessing sensitive sites, opened a Weibo account, furious Weibo'ers nicknamed him "Eunuch Fang" and within 30 seconds posted hundreds of messages including: "Before, the GFW deprived people's right to freely access the Internet, now people will deprive your right to use microblog," and "f–k you 404 times"—a barbed reference to "404 error" messages, which appear when you search the Chinese Internet for blocked terms. Censors couldn't keep up, and Fang's account was shut down in less than an hour.

Not all officials get shouted off the site; more than 20,000 government departments and officials have Weibo accounts, the most active of which are police. This is the great surprise of Weibo, says Dylan Myers, former project manager at Google China. "Government officials are being encouraged to get on. It's a gigantic threat to the propaganda department. Weibo is a great communication tool, a symbol that you're closer to the people. It's grassroots. But it's stripped the party of the ability to control communication. And that's revolutionary." Yet it may also be the best service ever provided to the Chinese government. Want to know what your citizens are saying, doing, thinking? Check their weibo's.

The site was instrumental in channeling both information and rage over news of the scandal-plagued Chinese bullet train in July—beset first by power outages and delays and then by a fatal accident in Zhejiang province. When a signaling failure led to a head-on collision, throwing cars off a bridge, 40 people were killed and close to 200 injured. SOS messages from inside the trains poured into Weibo, and were forwarded hundreds of thousands of times. Within minutes, Weibo became the channel of choice for survivors and witnesses to report the crash and rescue effort; for hospitals to make requests for blood donations; and for users to create and update lists of the injured and dead. But posts turned quickly into furious demands that the railway ministry take responsibility, that the government answer questions, and that someone be held accountable for both the accident and what, after being followed with rapt attention by millions on Weibo, was widely considered to be an inadequate rescue response. Tens of thousands of posts went up in the days following the crash, so many that the Department of Propaganda issued an edict that official media stop covering the accident. But long after the media stopped covering the crash, the conversation on Weibo raged on.

At the Sina offices in Beijing, housed in two giant skyscrapers in Zhongguancun, a sprawling neighborhood of corporate headquarters, visitors are greeted with a poem entitled YOU ARE THE ONE. Painted in rainbow colors, in Chinese and English, right across from reception, it begins: "Here is the impactful galaxy, growing in the center of the Chinese cyber world. Each of us is a star shines in the sky of Sina." It celebrates "an admirable, super big family that influences China impressively," and ends: "Here, we are all rising, shining stars, we keep trying to become a better us. YOU ARE THE ONE!"

Selves used to be suppressed in China, morphed into larger units (family units, work units) that operated in service to the state; these days, thanks in large part to Weibo, selves are being carved out, branded, made, re-made, and celebrated. This leads to both exhilarating freedom and tremendous anxiety about what it means to be an individual in modern China.

An aspiring actress named Guo Meimei found herself at the center of one of the biggest Weibo scandals of 2011 after she posted pictures of her palatial villa, luxury cars, and designer handbags. Flaunting wealth on Weibo would have been nothing special, except that Guo Meimei had a verified account, which announced that she worked for China's Red Cross. (The Red Cross Society of China denied she was an employee.) Weibo'ers posted more than 640,000 furious messages, many demanding audits and vowing never to give to charity again. Much of the torrent came close to being direct criticism of the government, since China's Red Cross is state run. In August, when someone posted comments accusing the Red Cross of selling blood for profit, Weibo sent a notice to every one of its then 200 million users, informing them that the rumor was false and that the user's account had been suspended for a month. A party secretary paid a visit to Sina, bearing warnings about the need to be active and resolute in blocking the spread of "false and harmful information." And Xinhua, China's official news agency, has called for a crackdown on "toxic rumors."

In America, losing one's Twitter account would be insulting and might, for the most addicted, even cause a moment of painful withdrawal. But there are plenty of other social-networking and publishing possibilities, not to mention news sources. In China, where Weibo has become one of the only venues of relatively free speech, and the channel for real information, banishment from the site carries the acute sting of being forcibly cut off and silenced.

At the end of our lunch together, Huang—"China's Oprah"—was trying to start following the Weibo for Sora Aoi, a Japanese porn star with close to 10 million followers. (I had just shown Huang an irresistible picture of Aoi's lunch, a bright green, tumescent pickle rising from two tomatoes.) But Huang kept getting an error message. Half joking, but with a hint of genuine anxiety, she asked, "Have I done something wrong? Am I kicked off? I'm getting a bad connection message. Maybe they're making sure I don't get porn, taking care of me." She feverishly tried to get on until she realized that she hadn't signed the restaurant's wi-fi user agreement. As she connected successfully, she smiled and clutched her iPhone so she could watch her Weibo page as she said, "It was just a connection error. I'm still alive."

Analyze

1. What does Weibo mean?
2. Who are some celebrities "Weiboing"?
3. What is the big deal about authenticity and how does Weibo achieve this?

Explore

1. Weibo encourages zombie fans, like the one advertiser Sylvia Wang created of an alluring young woman with the name, "Jessie-who-wants-to-be-a-flight-attendant." Her zombie has more than 42,000 fans! Users create zombies as a way to create the illusion of their popularity. Write an essay arguing either that this practice is an acceptable deception to create a stronger, more popular identity, or that it is an unacceptable deception encouraging the creation of fictitious accomplishments.
2. Sign up for a Weibo account and report on what makes it similar and different from mainstream social media sites in the United States. Are the protections and monitoring by the Chinese government something the United States should consider?
3. Dewoskin makes the point that "The Selves used to be suppressed in China, morphed into larger units (family units, work units) that operated in service to the state; these days, thanks in large part to Weibo, selves are being carved out, branded, made, re-made, and celebrated. This leads to both exhilarating freedom and tremendous anxiety about what it means to be an individual in modern China." We have been reading in this chapter about the ways that the "individuals" we create on SNSs can have a variety of effects and consequences. Write a persuasive Weibo (or Tweet) advocating more or less control over what Weibo users can post.

Hanni Fakhoury, Kurt Opsahl, and Rainey Reitman
"When Will Our Email Betray Us? An Email Privacy Primer in Light of the Petraeus Saga"

Hanni Fakhoury writes and speaks on subjects involving technology, criminal law, privacy, and free speech. He is a staff attorney with the Electronic Frontier Foundation and in this role has argued before the Fifth Circuit Court of Appeals on warrantless cell tracking. Kurt Opsahl focuses on civil liberties, free speech, and privacy law as senior staff attorney with the Electronic Frontier Foundation. He is the coauthor of the *Electronic Media and Privacy Law Handbook*. Rainey Reitman studies the effects of technology on personal privacy, especially with social networking. At Electronic Frontier Foundation, she heads the activism team. She is a steering committee member for the Internet Defense League and on the board of directors for the Bill of Rights Defense Committee. While e-mail almost seems like an antique communication technology, it can, as scandals still regularly unfold, create powerful digital footprints, as the growing number of scandals make us aware.

Should law enforcement be allowed to trace all electronic information we share and post, such as e-mail and pictures?

The unfolding scandal that led to the resignation of Gen. David Petraeus, the Director of the Central Intelligence Agency, started with some purportedly harassing emails sent from pseudonymous email accounts to Jill Kelley. After the FBI kicked its investigation into high gear, it identified the sender as Paula Broadwell and, ultimately, read massive amounts of private email messages that uncovered an affair between Broadwell and Petraeus (and now, the investigation has expanded to include Gen. John Allen's emails with Kelley). We've received a lot of questions about how this works—what legal process the FBI needs to conduct its email investigation. The short answer? It's complicated.

The Electronic Communications Privacy Act (ECPA) is a 1986 law that Congress enacted to protect your privacy in electronic communications, like email and instant messages. ECPA provides scant protection for your identifying information, such as the IP address used to access an account. While Paula Broadwell reportedly created a new, pseudonymous account for the allegedly harassing emails to Jill Kelley, she apparently did not take steps to disguise the IP number her messages were coming from. The FBI could have obtained this information with just a subpoena to the service provider. But obtaining the account's IP address alone does not establish the identity of the emails' sender.

Broadwell apparently accessed the emails from hotels and other locations, not her home. So the FBI cross-referenced the IP addresses of these Wi-Fi hotspots "against guest lists from other cities and hotels, looking for common names." If Broadwell wanted to stay anonymous, a new email account combined with open Wi-Fi was not enough. The ACLU has an in-depth write-up of the surveillance and security lessons to be learned from this.

After the FBI identified Broadwell, they searched her email. According to news reports, the affair between Petraeus and Broadwell lasted from November 2011 to July 2012. The harassing emails sent by Broadwell to Jill Kelley started in May 2012, and Kelley notified the FBI shortly thereafter. Thus, in the summer of 2012, when the FBI was investigating, the bulk of the emails would be less than 180 days old. This 180 day old dividing line is important for determining how ECPA applies to email.

Compared to identifying information, ECPA provides more legal 5 protection for the contents of your email, but with gaping exceptions. While a small but increasing number of federal courts have found that the Fourth Amendment requires a warrant for all email, the government claims ECPA only requires a warrant for email that is stored for 180 days or less.

But as the Department of Justice Manual for searching and seizing email makes clear, the government believes this only applies to unopened email. Other email is fair game with only a subpoena, even if the messages are less than 180 days old. According to reports, Patraeus and Broadwell adopted a technique of drafting emails, and reading them in the draft folder rather than sending them. The DOJ would likely consider draft messages as "opened" email, and therefore not entitled to the protection of a search warrant.

In a nutshell, although ECPA requires a warrant for the government to obtain the contents of an email stored online for less than 180 days, the government believes the warrant requirement doesn't apply for email that was opened and left on the server—the typical scenario for webmail systems like Gmail—even if the messages are less than 180 days old. So, under the government's view, so long as the emails had been opened or were saved in the "drafts" folder, only a subpoena was required to look at contents of Broadwell's email account.

Confused? Well, here's where things get really complicated. The government's view of the law was rejected by the Ninth Circuit Court of Appeals, the federal appellate court that covers the western United States, including California, and the home to many online email companies and the servers that host their messages. As a result, the DOJ Manual notes that "Agents outside of the Ninth Circuit can therefore obtain such email (and other stored electronic or wire communications in "electronic storage" more than 180 days) using a subpoena . . ." but reminds agents in the Ninth Circuit to get a warrant.

News reports show that the FBI agents involved in the Petraeus scandal were in Tampa, Florida. Thus, according to the DOJ Manual, they did not need to get a warrant even if the email provider was in California (like, for example, Gmail): "law enforcement elsewhere may continue to apply the traditional narrow interpretation of 'electronic storage,' even when the data sought is within the Ninth Circuit."

A subpoena for email content would generally require notice to the subscriber, though another section of ECPA allows for delayed notice, for up to 90 days. The FBI interviewed Broadwell for the first time in September, about 90 days after the investigation began in June.

However, many providers nevertheless protect their users by following the Ninth Circuit rule, and insist upon a warrant for the contents of all email. In EFF's experience, the government will seek a warrant rather than litigate the issue. Thus, assuming the service provider stepped up, it is likely that the government used a warrant to obtain access to the emails at issue.

10   If a warrant was used, note that a warrant is often quite broad, and the government may well have obtained emails from other accounts under the same warrant. And as result, there's no telling how much email the FBI actually read.

The government is required to "minimize" its collection of some electronic information. For example, under the Wiretap Act, the government is supposed to conduct its wiretapping in a way that "minimize[s] the interception of communications not otherwise subject to interception." This ensures the government isn't listening to conversations unrelated to their criminal investigation.

But when it comes to email, such minimization requirements aren't as strong. The DOJ Manual suggests that agents "exercise great caution" and "avoid unwarranted intrusions into private areas," when searching email on ISPs but is short on specifics. *The New York Times* reported that FBI agents obtained access to Broadwell's "regular e-mail account." They could have read every e-mail that came through as they investigated the affair. Possibly, the FBI could have read an enormous amount of email from innocent individuals not suspected of any wrongdoing.

And while the Fourth Amendment requires search warrants to be specific and particular, as noted earlier, it's not entirely clear whether the FBI got a search warrant to search Broadwell's email. Even if it did get a warrant, the government has argued that broad warrants are needed in electronic searches because evidence could be stored anywhere. While some courts have pushed back on this broad search authority when it comes to email, many courts still give the government wide access to email and other forms of electronic content.

Sound confusing? It is. ECPA is hopelessly out of date, and fails to provide the protections we need in a modern era. Your email privacy should be simple: it should receive the same protection the Fourth Amendment provides for your home.

So why hasn't Congress done anything to update the law? They've tried a few times but the bills haven't gone anywhere. That's why EFF members across the country are joining with other advocacy groups in calling for reform. This week, we're proud to launch a new campaign page to advocate for ECPA reform. And we're asking individuals to sign EFF's petition calling on Congress to update ECPA for the digital era so that there can be no question that the government is required to go to a judge and get a warrant before it can rummage through our email, online documents, and phone location histories.

We know that major privacy scandals can prompt Congress to get serious 15 about updating privacy law. The Video Privacy Protection Act was inspired by the ill-fated Supreme Court nomination of Judge Robert Bork, after a local Washington reporter obtained Bork's video rental records. And the Foreign Intelligence Surveillance Act was inspired by the findings of the Church Committee, which showed that the FBI had warrantlessly surveilled Dr. Martin Luther King, Jr. and many other activists. If we learn nothing else from the Petraeus scandal, it should be that our private digital lives can become all too public when over-eager federal agents aren't held to rigorous legal standards.

Congress has dragged its feet on updating ECPA for too long, resulting in the confusing, abuse-prone legal mess we're in today. Join EFF in calling on Congress to fix the law.

Analyze

1. What is the 1986 Electronic Communications Privacy Act (ECPA)?
2. What led the FBI to Broadwell and how did they track her?
3. What is the 180-day guideline the ECPA applies to e-mail?

Explore

1. Petraeus and Broadwell would write e-mails to each other but not send them. They would post them to the draft folder of a shared e-mail account. The Department of Justice, according to this essay, would likely consider draft messages as "opened" e-mail and would therefore not consider them to be entitled to the protection of a search warrant. In groups, research and discuss this rule and take a stand on whether you agree with it or not.
2. Explore what the Fourth Amendment is and write an essay explaining why e-mail privacy should fall under the same protections that the Fourth Amendment protects.
3. A few of the essays in this chapter have argued that we need to be careful with what we put up and send out in our digital worlds. Create a visual or video that educates people to the personal, social, professional, and legal dangers of putting too much information out there.

Dan Fletcher
"How Facebook Is Redefining Privacy"

In 2010 at 22 years old, Fletcher was the youngest person to write a *Time* cover story, where he also created Time.com's News Feed and *Time's* social media feeds. At Bloomberg a few years later he created and staffed the editorial social media teams for Bloomberg News and Bloomberg Businessweek. He recently left Facebook as its managing editor. In this essay Fletcher shares insights with us into how Facebook has made getting and sharing our private information into a scientific process that makes a lot of money.

Because Facebook is free, do you think the company should have the rights to our information and the ability to share it?

S ometime in the next few weeks, Facebook will officially log its 500 million active citizen. If the website were granted terra firma, it would be the world's third largest country by population, two-thirds bigger than the U.S. More than 1 in 4 people who browse the Internet not only have a Facebook account but have returned to the site within the past 30 days.

Just six years after Harvard undergraduate Mark Zuckerberg helped found Facebook in his dorm room as a way for Ivy League students to keep tabs on one another, the company has joined the ranks of the Web's great superpowers. Microsoft made computers easy for everyone to use. Google helps us search out data. YouTube keeps us entertained. But Facebook has a huge advantage over those other sites: the emotional investment of its users. Facebook makes us smile, shudder, squeeze into photographs so we can see ourselves online later, fret when no one responds to our witty remarks, snicker over who got fat after high school, pause during weddings to update our relationship status to Married or codify a breakup by setting our status back to Single. (I'm glad we can still be friends, Elise.)

Getting to the point where so many of us are comfortable living so much of our life on Facebook represents a tremendous cultural shift, particularly since 28% of the site's users are older than 34, Facebook's fastest-growing demographic. Facebook has changed our social DNA, making us more accustomed to openness. But the site is premised on a contradiction: Facebook is rich in intimate opportunities—you can celebrate your niece's first steps there and mourn the death of a close friend—but the company is making money because you are, on some level, broadcasting those moments online. The feelings you experience on Facebook are heartfelt; the data you're providing feeds a bottom line.

The willingness of Facebook's users to share and overshare—from descriptions of our bouts of food poisoning (gross) to our uncensored feelings about our bosses (not advisable)—is critical to its success. Thus far, the company's m.o. has been to press users to share more, then let up if too many of them complain. Because of this, Facebook keeps finding itself in the crosshairs of intense debates about privacy. It happened in 2007, when the default settings in an initiative called Facebook Beacon sent all your Facebook friends updates about purchases you made on certain third-party sites. Beacon caused an uproar among users—who were automatically enrolled—and occasioned a public apology from Zuckerberg.

And it is happening again. To quell the latest concerns of users—and of   5 elected officials in the U.S. and abroad—Facebook is getting ready to unveil enhanced privacy controls. The changes are coming on the heels of a complaint filed with the Federal Trade Commission (FTC) on May 5 by the Electronic Privacy Information Center, which takes issue with Facebook's frequent policy changes and tendency to design privacy controls that are, if not deceptive, less than intuitive. (Even a company spokesman got tripped up trying to explain to me why my co-worker has a shorter privacy-controls menu than I do.) The 38-page complaint asks the FTC to compel Facebook to clarify the privacy settings attached to each piece of information we post as well as what happens to that data after we share it.

Facebook is readjusting its privacy policy at a time when its stake in mining our personal preferences has never been greater. In April, it launched a major initiative called Open Graph, which lets Facebook users weigh in on what they like on the Web, from a story on TIME.com to a pair of jeans from Levi's. The logic is that if my friends recommend something, I'll be more inclined to like it too. And because Facebook has so many users—and because so many companies want to attract those users' eyeballs—Facebook is well positioned to display its members' preferences on any website, anywhere. Less than a month after Open Graph's rollout, more than 100,000 sites had integrated the technology.

"The mission of the company is to make the world more open and connected," Zuckerberg told me in early May. To him, expanding Facebook's function from enabling us to interact with people we like on the site to interacting with stuff our friends like on other sites is "a natural extension" of what the company has been doing.

In his keynote announcing Open Graph, Zuckerberg said, "We're building a Web where the default is social." But default settings are part of the reason Facebook is in the hot seat now. In the past, when Facebook changed its privacy controls, it tended to automatically set users' preferences to maximum exposure and then put the onus on us to go in and dial them back. In December, the company set the defaults for a lot of user information so that everyone—even non-Facebook members—could see such details as status updates and lists of friends and interests. Many of us scrambled for cover, restricting who gets to see what on our profile pages. But it's still nearly impossible to tease out how our data might be used in other places, such as Facebook applications or elsewhere on the Web.

There's something unsettling about granting the world a front-row seat to all of our interests. But Zuckerberg is betting that it's not unsettling enough to enough people that we'll stop sharing all the big and small moments of our lives with the site. On the contrary, he's betting that there's almost no limit to what people will share and to how his company can benefit from it.

Since the site expanded membership to high schoolers in 2005 and to   10
anyone over the age of 13 in 2006, Facebook has become a kind of virtual pacemaker, setting the rhythms of our online lives, letting us ramp up both the silly socializing and the serious career networking. Zuckerberg's next goal is even more ambitious: to make Facebook a kind of second nervous system that's rapid-firing more of our thoughts and feelings over the Web. Or, to change the metaphor, Facebook wants to be not just a destination but the vehicle too.

"I'm CEO . . . Bitch"

Facebook's world headquarters in Palo Alto, Calif., looks like an afterthought, a drab office building at the end of a sleepy stretch of California Avenue. Lacking the scale of Microsoft's sprawling campus or the gleaming grandeur of Google HQ, Facebook's home base is unpretentious and underwhelming. The sign in front (colored red, not the company's trademark cobalt blue) features a large, boldface address with a tiny Facebook logo nestled above.

Inside the building, Facebook crams in hundreds of employees, who work in big, open-air bullpens. Without cubicles or walls, there isn't much privacy, so each desk seems like, well, a Facebook profile—small, visible-to-all spaces decorated with photos and personal sundries. Zuckerberg spent the past year in a dimly lit bullpen on the ground floor. But perhaps in a concession to the fact that the CEO needs some privacy, the 26-year-old billionaire recently moved upstairs to a small office, albeit one with a glass wall so everyone can see what he's doing in there.

Steve Jobs has his signature black turtlenecks; Zuckerberg usually sports a hoodie. In Facebook's early years, he was the cocky coder kid with business cards that read, "I'm CEO . . . Bitch." (Zuckerberg has said publicly they were a joke from a friend.) And elements of the Palo Alto headquarters—snack tables, Ping-Pong—still impart some semblance of that hacker-in-a-dorm-room feel.

The office's design reflects Facebook's business model too. Openness is fundamental to everything the company does, from generating revenue to its latest plans to weave itself into the fabric of the Web. "Our core belief is that one of the most transformational things in this generation is that there will be more information available," Zuckerberg says. That idea has always been key to Facebook's growth. The company wants to expand the range of information you're sharing and get you to share a lot more of it.

15   For this to happen, the 1,400 Facebook employees in Palo Alto and around the world (Dublin, Sydney, Tokyo, etc.) work toward two goals. The first is expansion, something the company has gotten prodigiously good at. The site had 117 million unique visitors in the U.S. in March, and the company says some 70% of its users are in other countries. In cellular-connected Japan, the company is focusing on the mobile app. In cricket-crazed India, Facebook snared fans by helping the Indian Premier League build a fan page on Facebook's site.

There's a technical aspect too. The slightest fraction of a second in how long it takes to load a Facebook page can make the difference between someone's logging in again or not, so the company keeps shaving down milliseconds to make sure you stay. It also mobilized Facebook users to volunteer to help translate the site into 70 languages, from Afrikaans to Zulu, to make each moment on Facebook feel local.

The Aha! Moment

Facebook did not invent social networking, but the company has fine-tuned it into a science. When a newcomer logs in, the experience is designed to generate something Facebook calls the aha! moment. This is an observable emotional connection, gleaned by videotaping the expressions of test users navigating the site for the first time. My mom, a Facebook holdout whose friends finally persuaded her to join last summer, probably had her aha! moment within a few minutes of signing up. Facebook sprang into action. First it asked to look through her e-mail address book to quickly find fellow Facebook users she knew. Then it let her choose which of these people she wanted to start getting short status updates from: Details about what a long-lost friend from high school just cooked for dinner. Photos of a co-worker's new baby. Or of me carousing on a Friday night. (No need to lecture, Mom.)

Facebook has developed a formula for the precise number of aha! moments a user must have before he or she is hooked. Company officials won't say exactly what that magic number is, but everything about the site is geared to reach it as quickly as possible. And if you ever try to leave Facebook, you get what I like to call the aha! moment's nasty sibling, the oh-no! moment, when Facebook tries to guilt-trip you with pictures of your friends who, the site warns, will "miss you" if you deactivate your account.

So far, at least, the site has avoided the digital exoduses that beset its predecessors, MySpace and Friendster. This is partly because Facebook is so good at making itself indispensable. Losing Facebook hurts. In 2008 my original Facebook account was shut down because I had created multiple Dan Fletchers using variants of the same e-mail address, a Facebook no-no but an ingenious way to expand my power in the Mob Wars game on Facebook's site. When Facebook cracked down and gave me and my fictional mafia the kiss of death, I lost all my photos, all my messages and all my status updates from my senior year of high school through the first two years of college. I still miss those digital mementos, and it's both comforting and maddening to know they likely still exist somewhere, sealed off in Facebook's archives.

Being excommunicated from Facebook today would be even more painful.   20
For many people, it's a second home. Users share more than 25 billion pieces of information with Facebook each month. They're adding photos—perhaps the most intimate information Facebook collects—at a rate of nearly 1 billion unique images a week. These pics range from cherished Christmas mornings to nights of partying we, uh, struggle to remember. And we're posting pictures not just of ourselves but also of our friends, and naming, or tagging, them in captions embedded in the images. Not happy someone posted an unflattering shot of you from junior high? Unless the photo is obscene or otherwise violates the site's terms of use, the most you can do is untag your name so people will have a harder time finding the picture (and making fun of you).

With 48 billion unique images, Facebook houses the world's largest photo collection. All that sharing happens on the site. But in two giant leaps, the company has made it so that users can register their opinions on other sites too. That first happened in 2008, when the company released a platform called Facebook Connect. This allows your profile to follow you around the Internet from site to site, acting as a kind of passport for the Web. Want to post a comment about this article on TIME.com? Instead of having to register specifically with that site, Facebook users just have to click one button. This idea of a single sign-on—a profile that obviates the need for multiple user names and passwords—is something a lot of other companies have attempted. But Facebook had the critical mass to make it work.

Targeting Your Likes

Zuckerberg unveiled the second big initiative, Open Graph, this spring. It's a nerdy name for something that's surprisingly simple: letting other websites place a Facebook Like button next to pieces of content. The idea is to let Facebook users flag the content from as many Web pages as possible. For example, if I'm psyched about *Iron Man 2*, I can click the Like button for that movie on IMDB, and the film will automatically be filed under Movies on my Facebook profile. I can set my privacy controls so that my friends can find out in one of three ways that this is a movie I like. They can go to IMDB, where my charming profile picture will display on the page. They can get a status update about my liking this movie. Or they can see it on my Facebook profile.

Facebook wants you to get into the habit of clicking the Like button anytime you see it next to a piece of content you enjoy. Less than a month after launching Open Graph—which made its debut with some 30 content partners, including TIME.com—Facebook is quickly approaching the point where it will process 100 million unique clicks of a Like button each day.

The company's goal with Open Graph is to give you ways to discover both new content and more common ground with the people you're friends with. That's the social benefit Zuckerberg sees, and it's shared by those in his employ. Sheryl Sandberg, Facebook's chief operating officer, is at her most enthusiastic when she's describing Peace.Facebook.com, part of the website that tracks the number of friendships made each day between members of groups that have historically disagreed, such as Israelis and Palestinians and Sunnis and Shi'ites. "We don't pretend Facebook's this profound all the time," Sandberg says. "But is it harder to shoot at someone who you've connected to personally? Yeah. Is it harder to hate when you've seen pictures of that person's kids? We think the answer is yes."

25   Helping bring about world peace would be nice, but Facebook is not a philanthropic organization. It's a business, and there's a tremendous business opportunity around Facebook's member data. And Sandberg knows it. She joined the company in 2008 after helping Google build its ad platform into a multibillion-dollar business. Much like Google, Facebook is free to users but makes a lot of money (some analysts estimate the privately held company will generate $1 billion in revenues in 2010) from its robust ad system. According to the Web-research firm comScore, Facebook flashed more than 176 billion banner ads at users in the first three months of this year—more than any other site.

The more updates Facebook gets you to share and the more preferences it entreats you to make public, the more data it's able to pool for advertisers. Google spearheaded targeted advertisements, but it knows what you're interested in only on the basis of what you query in its search engine and, if you have a Gmail account, what topics you're e-mailing about. Facebook is amassing a much more well-rounded picture. And having those Like buttons clicked 100 million times a day gives the company 100 million more data points to package and sell.

The result is that advertisers are able to target you on an even more granular level. For example, right now the ads popping up on my Facebook page are for *Iron Man 2* games and no-fee apartments in New York City (I'm in a demographic that moves frequently); my mom is getting ads for in-store furniture sales (she's in a demographic that buys sofas).

This advertising platform is even more powerful now that the site can factor in your friends' preferences. If three of your friends click a Like button for, say, Domino's Pizza, you might soon find an ad on your Facebook page that has their names and a suggestion that maybe you should try Domino's too. Peer-pressure advertising! Sandberg and other Facebook execs understand the value of context in selling a product, and few contexts are more powerful than friendship. "Marketers have known this for a really long time. I'm much more likely to do something that's recommended by a friend," Sandberg says.

As powerful as each piece of Facebook's strategy is, the company isn't forcing its users to drink the Kool-Aid. It's just serving up nice cold glasses, and we're gulping it down. The friends, the connections, the likes—those are all produced by us. Facebook is the ultimate enabler. It's enabling us to give it a cornucopia of information about ourselves. It's a brilliant model, and Facebook, through its skill at weaving the site into the fabric of modern life, has made it work better than anyone else.

What Voldemort Is to Harry Potter

Zuckerberg believes that most people want to share more about themselves online. He's almost paternalistic in describing the trend. "The way that people think about privacy is changing a bit," he says. "What people want isn't complete privacy. It isn't that they want secrecy. It's that they want control over what they share and what they don't."   30

Unfortunately, Facebook has a shaky history of granting people that control. In November 2007, when the company tried to make its first foray into the broader Web, it rolled out Facebook Beacon, in which users were automatically signed up for a program that sent a notice to all their friends on Facebook if, say, they made a purchase on a third-party site, like movie tickets on Fandango. Initially, users couldn't opt out of the service altogether—they had to click No Thanks with each individual purchase. And, worse, investigations by security analysts found that even after users hit No Thanks, websites sent purchase details back to Facebook, which the company then deleted. Amid a torrent of complaints, Facebook quickly changed Beacon to be an opt-in system, and by December 2007, the company gave users the option of turning off Beacon completely. Ask Zuckerberg and other executives about the program now, and you'll notice that Beacon has become to Facebook what Voldemort is to Harry Potter's world—the thing that shall not be named.

Facebook isn't the only company to have made a serious social-networking infraction. In February, Google apologized after the rollout of its Twitter-esque Buzz application briefly revealed whom its users e-mailed and chatted with most, a move that alarmed, among others, political dissidents and cheating spouses. But at Facebook, the Beacon debacle didn't stop the company from pushing to make more information public. This winter, the company changed its privacy controls and made certain profile details public, including a user's name, profile photo, status updates and any college or professional networks. During the transition, Zuckerberg's private photos were briefly visible to all, including several pictures in which he looks, shall we say, overserved. He quickly altered his settings.

In April, the site started giving third-party applications more access to user data. Apps like my beloved Mob Wars used to be allowed to keep your data for only 24 hours; now they can store your info indefinitely—unless you uninstall them. This spring, Facebook also launched something called Instant Personalization, which lets a few sites piggyback onto Facebook user data to create recommendation engines. Once again, as with Beacon, users were automatically enrolled.

With each set of changes to Facebook's evolving privacy policy, protest groups form and users spread warnings via status messages. In some cases, these outcries have been quite sizable. Zuckerberg points to 2006, when users protested the launch of Facebook's News Feed, a streaming compilation of your friends' status updates. Without much warning, tidbits that you used to have to seek out by going to an individual's profile page were suddenly being broadcast to everyone on that person's list of friends. "We only had 10 million users at the time, and 1 million were complaining," Zuckerberg says. "Now, to think that there wouldn't be a news feed is insane." He's right—protesting the existence of a news feed seems silly in hindsight; Twitter built its entire site around the news-feed concept. So give Zuckerberg some credit for prescience—and perseverance. "That's a big part of what we do, figuring out what the next things are that everyone wants to do and then bringing them along to get them there," he says.

But corralling 500 million people is a lot harder than corralling 10 million. And some users are ready to pull the plug entirely. Searches for "how to delete Facebook" on Google have nearly doubled in volume since the start of this year.

The Web's Sketchy Big Brother

f Facebook wants to keep up the information revolution, then Zuckerberg   35
needs to start talking more and make his case for an era of openness more transparently. Otherwise, Facebook will continue to be cast in the role of the Web's sketchy Big Brother, sucking up our identities into a massive Borg brain to slice, dice and categorize for advertisers.

But amid all the angst, don't forget that we actually like to share. Yes, Facebook is a moneymaking venture. But after you talk to the company's key people, it's tough to doubt that they truly believe that sharing information is better than keeping secrets, that the world will be a better place if you persuade (or perhaps push) people to be more open. "Even with all the progress that we've made, I think we're much closer to the beginning than the end of the trend," Zuckerberg says.

Want to stop that trend? The onus, as always, is on you to pull your information. Starve the beast dead. None of Facebook's vision, be it for fostering peace and harmony or for generating ad revenue, is possible without our feeding in our thoughts and preferences. "The way that people decide whether they want to use something or not is whether they like the product or not," Zuckerberg says. Facebook is hoping that we're hooked. As for me? Time to see if the ex-girlfriend has added new photos.

Analyze

1. Fletcher tells us, "Google helps us search out data. YouTube keeps us entertained. But Facebook has a huge advantage over those other sites . . ." What is the advantage he says?
2. What is Facebook's fastest-growing demographic?
3. How many pieces of information do Facebook users share each month?

Explore

1. Create categories and then categorize the types of updates people in your social network make during a week. Put your findings in a Power-Point and share them with your class.

2. In our reading by Dewoskin, "East Meets Tweet," she brings up the concerns the Chinese have about its government controlling what people can post to Weibo, and removing posts. How does this compare with the ongoing struggles Facebook users have with Facebook taking and sharing information without our permission? Do you agree with the Federal Trade Commission stepping in to control Facebook a little?

3. At one point Fletcher argues, "If Facebook wants to keep up the information revolution, then Zuckerberg needs to start talking more and make his case for an era of openness and more transparently. Otherwise, Facebook will continue to be cast in the role of the Web's sketchy Big Brother, sucking up our identities into a massive Borg brain to slice, dice and categorize for advertisers." Write a researched argument for or against allowing sites like Facebook access to our personal lives, which they let us post for free, as long as they can use and share our personal information. Are we becoming, as Fletcher implies, part of the collective hive?

Alan Norton
"10 Reasons Why I Avoid Social Networking Services"

Norton writes for *TechRepublic* primarily creating practical "10 Reasons" columns of advice on how to survive and succeed in the business world. In this essay he lists ten reasons why we should avoid online social networking.

Of the ten reasons Norton lists, which ones do you dis/agree with and why?

I have a confession to make. I don't do social networking. That's not *that* unusual for someone my age. Just 8% of all Facebook users fall into my age group. Nonetheless, according to the Pew Internet & American Life

Project, social networking is popular and still growing. While only 8% of adult Internet users used social networking sites in 2005, that number had grown to 65% by 2011. Why then do some people in general and older Internet users in particular avoid social networking services? I can give you 10 reasons why this experienced ancient one doesn't use them.

1. I have privacy concerns

   The recent IPO of Facebook wasn't as successful as its backers wanted. But it was successful bringing to the public's attention Facebook's privacy concerns. I, like many others, don't fully understand how serious those concerns are. It does make for a great excuse though to avoid Facebook altogether. Putting your personal information in the care of others, no matter how diligent their stewardship, increases your risk of that information getting into the hands of third parties.

   Our image is, in part, defined by our words. Each of us should ask how much of ourselves we want to give to people we don't even know. Once gone, that private piece of our lives can never be retrieved.

2. Ownership of content is unclear

   Who actually owns and who controls "your" intellectual content that you post is not as clear as you might think. Terms vary by social networking service, but typically you give up control of how your content may be used. Which raises the question: If you don't control it, do you really own it? It *isn't* clear who legally owns your content. The Twitter Terms of Service as of July 4, 2012, clearly states that you own the content you post:

   "You retain your rights to any Content you submit, post or display   5
   on or through the Services.... But what's yours is yours—you own your Content (and your photos are part of that Content)."

   According to a New York judge, however, Twitter owns your Tweets. That should at least cause you to pause before posting *anything* at any site other than your own. I am not a lawyer, but it appears that the legal ownership of your Tweets and other posted content may not be fully determined for years.

3. It's too impersonal

   Social networking offers an easy way to meet people—perhaps too easy. No commitment is required, and you can invest as much or as little of your time as you wish. Social networking services can be a great way to keep people at a distance: Interact only when and where you want with whom you want. That may be great for some people. I prefer more meaningful ways to interact, like face-to-face and over the phone.

People value your full attention and time. Social interaction is only as rewarding as you are willing to make it, whether in person or online.

4. I want to minimize online gaffes

There is that risqué limerick you shared while in high school or those embarrassing statements you made about a former employer that can be found with a simple Web search. Pity the poor job interviewee grilled by an interviewer who did his homework and found your ignorance, or worse, the bad information you posted about a topic for which you are supposed to be an expert. If you must post, practice safe posting. Of course, abstinence means never having to say you're sorry.

5. I want to minimize data points for possible data mining

Make a spelling mistake or grammatical error and you can be dinged for it forever. For me, it would be embarrassing as a writer and a blow to my ego but not a great loss. To a younger person interviewing for a job, consider what this report would do for a first impression:

10   It's not likely that you will run across this level of detail at your next job interview. But it isn't that difficult to collect such data—and you can bet that if it can be done, it will be done. Never mind the fact that such data is fraught with problems.

6. I don't subscribe to social fads

Call me a rebel, please. I don't like following the sheep to gain their acceptance. Clothing from Sears has always been my fashion statement, though the local thrift store has of late been getting my business. Twitter and Facebook may just be another fad that comes and goes, like AIM and MySpace.

7. I don't like being pressured to join

The sinister way that social networking services sneak into even the most ardent holdout's daily life is through invitations from friends and family members. Yes, I am now a lousy brother in law because I ignored an invitation from my brother's wife to join her inside circle at Facebook. I became a rotten friend when I politely turned down a request to be in a friend's LinkedIn professional network. Thank goodness my nephews and nieces have yet to ask me to "join up." I would hate to be a terrible uncle too.

8. I don't need the abuse

I used to think that posting at services like Usenet was something akin to self flagellation. Why would I risk being verbally flogged for posting what others might perceive as flame bait? I still don't need the abuse but, thankfully, I no longer take name calling like "idiot" or

User Name - Alan Norton For the period Jul-01-11 to Jun-30-12	Average # of posts per month	Average # of words per month	Avg #/% of misspellings per month	Avg #/% of grammatical errors per month
Facebook	0	0	0/0%	0/0%
Twitter	52	520	18/3.5%	4/0.8%
Google+	0	0	0/0%	0/0%
Usenet - alt.comp.hardware	11	506	22/4.3%	12/2.4%
Usenet - alt.support.depression	28	980	59/6.0%	33/3.4%
Other	76	2204	76/3.4%	62/2.8%
Totals	167	4210	175/4.2%	111/2.6%

"nimrod" as personally as I once did. Being flamed has instead become part of the profession "writer" and a badge of honor. Those who post on TechRepublic are a class act by comparison—people who disagree with me here call me "Mr. Norton."

9. It's more work

If your work is anything like my experiences in the cubicle, you already spend enough time typing when you answer emails, update status reports, and write code. It's just no fun coming home to more of the same.

This may not apply to you, but when you write for a living, it's not a   15
lot of fun interacting socially with the written word. After calculating the amount of wisdom I spew forth per dollar received, I have to tell you, I am working cheap (1:51—2:23). I just can't afford to give away my wisdom for free.

The Bottom Line . . .

Is that it's just not me (**#10**). Some of us prefer to keep ourselves to our self. I have heard about certain sites that cater to the courtship rituals of modern *Homo sapiens,* but every day that goes by I become less modern than the day before. Neither do I need to network for a job, though I *used* to believe that getting published was far better than social networking when it came to that big job interview. My notoriety, or lack thereof, has me now questioning the accuracy of that belief. Then there's the fact that I have yet to find a reason why I should tell countless others how totally devoid of meaning my life really is.

According to an analysis of tweets by Pear Analytics, 40% of all tweets are pointless babble. I have better ways to atrophy my brain, better ways to slowly turn my gray matter into mush. Is it possible that we will prefer communicating via machine rather than one on one? Personal social interaction could become a lost art. And it would be a shame for humanity to become so impersonal.

I can guess that some of you more analytical thinkers are saying, "Hold on there just a minute, Alan. You participate in the forums at TechRepublic. Doesn't that make you a hypocrite?" I believe that every writer should be available to answer any questions that you, the patient reader, might have. What you may perceive as hypocrisy is merely *relativistic disingenuous behavioral prioritization*. I would be hypocritical if I didn't participate. Besides, sometimes you've just gotta throw 10 silly reasons to the wind and risk acting the goat so you can help someone.

Analyze

1. What percent of Tweets are pointless babble?
2. What is "relativistic disingenuous behavioral prioritization"?
3. The author shares with us a statistic about his age: "Just 8% of all Facebook users fall into my age group." How old does that make him?

Explore

1. Norton argues that "Our image is, in part, defined by our words. Each of us should ask how much of ourselves we want to give to people we don't even know. Once gone, that private piece of our lives can never be retrieved." Drawing from the essays in this chapter and from your own experience on social networking sites, write an essay agreeing or disagreeing with this view.
2. In the following quote from the essay, does Norton contradict himself? "Social networking services can be a great way to keep people at a distance: Interact only when and where you want with whom you want. That may be great for some people. I prefer more meaningful ways to interact, like face-to-face and over the phone. People value your full attention and time. Social interaction is only as rewarding as you are willing to make it, whether in person or online." Think about what makes face-to-face interaction rewarding, and what makes social network interactions rewarding.

3. At the end of the essay Norton invites us to dialogue with him: "Do you share some of these objections and concerns? Or have you come to rely on social networking as a means of enriching your life and advancing your career?" To do so we can sign up with *TechRepublic's* 10 Things Newsletter. Create your own List of 10 Reasons Why I Love or Hate Social Networking (or a combination of the two, Why I Have a Love-Hate Relationship with Social Networking).

Forging Connections

1. How has the Internet changed the way we find out more about ourselves through our names (e.g., ancestry.com), about how important places are in relation to our notions of ourselves, about the schooling we receive and what we learn, how we become our jobs (I am a teacher, accountant, etc.), the investments we place in our relationships in defining our happiness or sadness or stability, and how we share all this indelible information, unfiltered, to the Internet with everyone?

2. Using essays from this chapter, prepare a letter to Latoya Peterson and Eric Sheninger ("Don't Trip over Your Digital Footprint") easing their worries about safety and privacy on the Internet.

3. Pick a recent situation from the news where someone's Internet identity became public and this resulted in arrest, exposure, criminal prosecution, or jail time. Gather as much information as you can about the story you select. Write an essay describing why, based on your focus, the "open" Internet where all information is available is working the way it should, or use the case as an example of why it needs to be protected more.

Looking Further

1. In the last chapter, Orenstein stated, "When friends become fans, what happens to intimacy? The risk of the performance culture, of the packaged self, is that it erodes the very relationships it purports to create, and alienates us from our own humanity." She is arguing that our personality and our way of behaving change us. Create a comic that shows the evolution or metamorphosis that you perceive humans undergoing as a result of sharing everything about themselves on social networking and cell phones.

2. Write a letter, a tweet, a text, and a six-word description to someone telling them about the various identities you have, how they evolve, and how they simply change based on where you are. Draw from the understandings of identity that you learned throughout the chapters. Do you see a different identity emerge based on the form you put your message in?

3. Going back to Chapter 1 with a focus on our names, Chapter 2 with a focus on where we are from, Chapter 3 with a focus on where we went to school, Chapter 4 with a focus on where we work, Chapter 5 with a focus on whom we love, and Chapter 6 with a focus on our Internet identities, we have explored many ways to think about how we think of ourselves and how others think of us, in good and bad ways. Write an essay that uses ideas from all of the chapters in which you reflect on the many nuanced ways that your identity is important to you on personal and social levels.

Researching and Writing About Identity

Research-based writing is important to understand and practice if we wish to be successful in our classes. Because we will be practicing research-based projects throughout our educational and professional lives, it is important that we enjoy the discovery process and recognize the ways we grow and learn in our thinking. As college students, it is through writing and research that we become active participants in intellectual communities. Doing research in college involves engaging with ideas in a variety of ways.

Because feeling nervous about all the ideas we read, talk, write, and share with others is normal, we offer strategies that demystify and make clear effective writing and research processes, breaking down some of the steps scholars take when they undertake research projects and write about them. We will see that writing a researched essay is a form of scholarship. To get started, we share effective strategies about writing and researching that can be learned and practiced.

Throughout this Appendix we imagine writing and doing research as engaging in a scholarly process and conversation. When we read academic writing, we see that scholars refer to studies that came before their own by alluding to them in the form of quotations, paraphrases, and summaries. When we think of research as engaging in a conversation, we quickly realize that scholarship has a social connection. Even if we like to search for books in the remotest corner of the library, and draft our essays hidden alone in a special place, we are always conversing with the ideas we read from others and, as we write, asking, How will so and so respond to this, or

Does that sound right? In other words, we ask questions to ourselves about readers who might not be present; this is a process experienced writers practice and so can we.

What does it mean to have an open mind when we're doing research? After all, shouldn't we find evidence that supports our thesis? We'll return to this question soon, but the quick answer is we need to have an open mind while we start doing research because we will not have a focused claim at this point. We realize this may be a big change from the way you think about research. The fact is, though, scholars often do research before they know any of the arguments they will be making in their papers. Oftentimes, scholars begin research even though they only have a general focus on what they will write about.

When scholars do research, they are already exploring their topic through writing in various ways. When they are hunting for useful scholarship, they may not know exactly what they are hunting for, but they have techniques that help them define projects, think about their readers, and ask questions throughout their research. Our Appendix focuses on two key strategies to help you produce researched essays. First, we will help you understand several strategies and ways to practice writing, and, second, how to move through the various kinds of research that you will need at the different stages of your project.

Writing as Art and Technique

Just as we have skills and abilities that become more advanced with practice, training, and teaching, the same holds true with our reading and writing skills. With anything we want to improve upon, we need to have a strategy, and we need to practice. Think about any activity or hobby you have ever become involved in and improved at. You had a routine, a process, or a method to get better.

When we ask ourselves who is writing about a topic in a particular publication, we are the audience, and they are directing their content to us. The writers, producers, speakers, and news anchors are all the authors, and we should study the way they project themselves because such understanding is a big leap in knowing the positions of the authors we read and listen to.

The scenario of writers, audience, and subject is what makes up part of the *Rhetorical Situation*. To begin, then, we need to delve into what a rhetorical situation is, what the *Rhetorical Modes* are, and what a *Composing*

Process entails. With an understanding of these topics, we will begin to appreciate the diversity of experiences and views throughout our literacy encounters.

The Rhetorical Situation

We are never just a reader, writer, or researcher. We are typically all of these. We read things on Facebook, Tumblr, e-magazines, e-books, e-journals, e-texts, and we watch shows on TV and the web. When we engage in these activities, most of us have an urge to respond, whether it is with a text to friends, an essay, an Op Ed, a book, a tweet, or a shout, "OMG!"

We are always interacting and shifting roles from writers of tweets, to readers of them, and on and on. Take a moment to think about how you read and write in the following situations:

1. Describe a Twitter event that you recently followed. What was the subject about? Did you read as well as write about it? Describe what you read and what you wrote. What about the subject made you get into the tweet thread? Why do you think others responded to the tweet?
2. What was the last school essay you wrote? Describe how you went about learning about the subject. Before you read anything, how did you feel about writing your essay? How about after? What did reading about the subject do to help you write about the subject?

In the scenarios above, one way to think about our entrance into a subject is based on the rhetorical situation. In the two instances we went from general knowledge of our subject to a level of competence or understanding that allowed us to enter into the conversation and write about the subject.

These two scenarios are rhetorical situations. Understanding that rhetorical situations exist in any communication act is important to becoming a knowledgeable and listened-to writer. In other words, we decided on a topic that interested us, or maybe even one that we have heard others talking about, and felt we needed to get up to speed in order to get into the conversation. When we begin thinking and reading about a subject, this is the first step in understanding and defining our rhetorical situation.

As we go about finding readings on subjects we want to learn about, we should have an idea of what our *audience* and *purpose* will be when we decide to write and become part of the conversation on a chosen subject.

For *audience,* we need to ask, Who am I writing to or for, and why? Often times, we correctly think of audience with the people who watch a theatrical play or watch a TV program, but as readers and writers we also consider those who read what we write as our audience (or conversely, we are the audience when we read others' writing). We need to consider our audience, those we want to influence with our writing, because when we do this it helps us to realize what types of information we need to include, how much background explanation, and even the type of language and words we select. We should be able to answer questions such as: Who am I writing this essay, tweet, text, love letter to? What do readers already know about the subject? What is the typical length of a similar type essay? Once we answer questions like these we have begun honing in on our subject and audience and it is time to then ask ourselves why we are writing this.

Our "why" question is our *purpose.* We need to ask, What do I wish to achieve with my writing? Several responses come to mind. **Persuade**: This is the most common purpose any writer undertakes. The goal is to convince readers to see or believe something other than what they believed before reading our essay; **Reflect**: With the entire essay or parts of it, by bringing in anecdotal or historical information and reflections, our purpose is to have readers identify with our examples. When readers identify with our examples, they feel connected to us and are more likely to agree with our ideas; **Understand**: We want readers to read our essay and feel they now realize the full scope of a particular issue, or how to construct something as in a set of instructions. If they feel what we write helps them understand a subject, we will be seen as smart and believable writers; **Consent**: This is part of persuasion in that we want readers, who, up until reading our essay, were not open to a certain idea or ways of doing something. Once they read our essay, they will approve or agree with what we propose; **Inform**: Readers often look to better understand something, like the changing role of social networking in their life, or the positions of political candidates; **Commit**: This is part of persuasion as well, but our purpose is not only to convince or change readers' beliefs but also we want them to "sign on the line" to help a cause or vote a particular way, for example; **Change Attitude**: Readers' stances on a particular issue or way of supporting a subject are part of persuasion. In this case, readers can have an exaggerated vision about a subject, like a school's sport team being the best, to having a strong view about not having a view on something. From a persuasive stance, this is one of the most difficult to attempt to alter because having a position with attitude is an emotional one; **Change Behavior**: This ranges from, for example, stopping a bad behavior, such as smoking, to starting a healthy one, like exercise. This also falls into the category of persuasion; **Entertain**: We want our readers to feel we know our subject well and can joke about it in a way that is not insulting or derogatory.

Knowing our purpose, then, when writing an essay asks us to think about our readers, so that we can then figure out what we would like them to walk away with from our thoughts on the subject. In all of the instances above, the two most common purposes are to persuade and inform. We are constantly attempting to convince people to see things our way, in a new way, or to do something in a different (safer, faster) way, or how to do it, and so forth.

The Rhetorical Modes

Rhetorical modes are more tools at our disposal. Video gamers, for example, as they become more experienced want more tools to unlock special powers or benefits, like achieving more health, or entering unknown realms, etc. As readers and writers, we will want more tools as well to allow us to critically understand what we read (unlock) and to effectively write our views.

These rhetorical techniques are effective in helping us and others see or experience an idea the way we want them to. Subtly, we get readers to see and focus on what we want them to. These are the most common rhetorical modes: **Argument**: When reading or writing an argument, generally both sides of an issue are presented fairly and in balanced fashion. As writers, then, we lead readers to a conclusion based on the information we present. As writers, nevertheless, the key is to at least make our argument appear balanced; **Cause-Effect** (also called Cause-Result): Cause and effect can be as brief as a sentence, or as long as an essay. When this mode is used, it explains to readers why something happened, for example, "excessive gasses like CO_2 (cause) are speeding up global warming (effect)." When we write a cause-effect essay, typically we first develop the cause we wish to explain to readers with facts, statistics, and quotes from experts, and so forth, and then finalize with the effects. When we use cause and effect as a technique, we are telling readers that there is no random or coincidental reason why something happened; **Classification/Division**: This mode asks that we group all similar ideas, elements, people, and things into their respective category of classification, or conversely that we divide all ideas into similar divisions; **Comparison/Contrast**: When we compare things—peoples, places, and things—we are pointing out how they are similar. For example, we might watch two TV shows that are both sit-coms, both in New York, and both with dysfunctional friendships. Contrast points out the differences between things; in reference to the sit-coms, the friendships might be all women in one, working class in another, and white collar in yet another; **Description**: In description we help readers see how a person, a setting, or an object is unique and we communicate this so the reader can visualize what we describe; **Definition**: In writing we often define an issue that is the focus of our research subject. Dictionaries can be useful in helping us fully understand a word, but oftentimes a concept or issue we study might be better defined through the current scholarship; **Narration**: An essay using this mode works chronologically, which means it can start at the beginning or the end of an event, a happening, an observation, or an experience. The narration of the event, happening, observation, or experience can be personal, as in "I felt the following things when I started college . . ." or neutral and more technical as in a lab report or newspaper account, "The mold spores under the microscope began dormant, but quickly initiated . . ."; **Process**: The standard process essay is a set of instructions because they explain how to do something from start to finish. The sciences typically use process for lab reports to explain how or why something happened.

Claim/Thesis/Main Point

The three titles we use here are essentially the same thing: Claim/Thesis/Main Point. We will use claim to mean all three of these. As writers, we need to be aware that we have a purpose in all communications with others and our claims allow us to state clearly and concisely what our purpose is. Sometimes it is difficult to know if we have written an effective claim, but one simple question can help us, "Can a reasonable person disagree with my claim?" If the answer is no, then we likely have written an observation rather than an argument. For instance, the statement, "There are six official languages of the UN" is not a thesis, since this is a fact. A reasonable person cannot disagree with this fact, so it is not an argument. The statement, "Arabic became an official language of the UN for economic reasons" is a thesis, since it is a debatable point. A reasonable person might disagree (by arguing, for instance, that "Arabic became an official language of the UN for political reasons"). We should regularly return to our claim while writing. Not only will we be able to make sure that our writing remains on a clear path, but we will also be able to keep refining our claim so that it becomes clearer and more precise.

The Composing Process

This is, perhaps, the easiest notion to grasp but the most difficult to practice. Good writing, like any activity we want to become polished at, takes practice, dedication, and time. Like any activity, we have to constantly make how we write fresh and interesting.

Writers prefer to have time to craft their documents. Research in the field of Rhetoric and Composition has taught us much about what is commonly called "the writing process." While we may have encountered other terms to express the stages strong writers go through, we use the following seven terms to capture traditional and new ways to see ourselves as practicing writers.

1. Recognition

When we write on a variety of topics, we usually begin at differing knowledge levels about them, so as soon as we are assigned a topic or are thinking of one, we should access our knowledge about the subject. Two common recognition points most writers find themselves in are these:

1. Maria has been researching and writing on a subject for three years. Her background knowledge level is deep. Because of this, she can begin with clear notions of some of the points she wants to make and she has scholarly sources on hand.
2. The recent mixed messages over global warming have Betty confused. She knows she is not well versed on this subject. While she is for protecting the planet and has heard that some scientists and specialists both agree and disagree with this, she has mostly heard from politicians. She doesn't know what to say or argue. "All I could say is, let's be careful, while someone else, who may believe one way or another, could easily persuade me to what is not true." This is exactly what happens with many current issues. In this case, before she can jump into the conversation and make a convincing argument, she would need to read up on what global warming is, how it is defined, and what are opposing

views. Then, after she has read and understood the issues and arguments from both sides, she could argue her view on global warming.

In these examples, the writers start at different places for each topic. With the readings in *Identity: A Reader for Writers,* we might find ourselves at different knowledge levels for each subject area as well. Reading more and educating ourselves on a subject will allow us to better educate others to what we have found and believe is the correct way to view our subject. When others try to disagree, we will know where they are coming from. We can show other counter points to the ones they bring up. In the two cases above, the first writer was already knowledgeable on the subject and was ready to begin writing, and the second knew she had a goal to learn more about the subject and then begin writing about it.

When we work to discover and understand a subject from as many angles as we can and as best we can, this is called *invention,* or, in more common language, "background research." Once we complete this background reading, we then are ready to begin exploring what we want to say. Remember, we start subjects at different knowledge and understanding levels.

An effective strategy to use while reading is to take notes about what we are learning and thinking about. By engaging with a text, we are, in a way, getting into a conversation with the author about what we are reading. One effective technique to engage with what we read combines the visual with writing: *Skriting.*

2. Skriting Log

Skriting is a combination of sketching and writing. The textual and visual transformation looks like this:

$$\text{Sketching Writing} =$$
$$\text{"Sk" } \cancel{\text{"riting"}} \text{ (etching W)}$$
$$\textit{Skriting}\text{———}$$

Have you ever seen artists sketch images of an idea? It's fast, has pauses, is sloppy, and is far from perfect! At the early stage of thinking and reading about a subject or topic there is no commitment. From sketches, artists begin to discover what and how they want to communicate in an eventual painting, without actually doing a whole painting. Skriting works the same way, but it is for writers. The key idea behind skriting is that we are using words, arrows, images (ones we sketch or download, or take ourselves) to begin writing about our subject and making multimodal connections.

When we begin writing, this is often called prewriting and drafting. For writers, these early moments are time for skriting about our thoughts on the subject. We sketch our ideas in words, we use arrows to bring similar ideas together, we sketch rough images, we paste and scan images we have collected from the computer, and we mix our words and images. We cross out and recreate thoughts and connections as we go along. Through all these actions, we are connecting our ideas as they come to us.

For example, student Elsa Martin uses her smart phone to keep her skrite log (see Insert B).

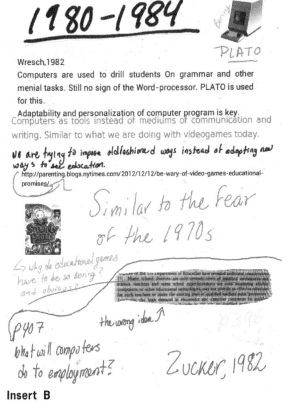

Insert B

Notice how she interacts with the text in a variety of ways. Does she know where she is going with her insertions and comments? No, and this is okay. By doing this she is reading closer, remembering more, and creating a roadmap of interconnecting ideas and questions. Others have made skrite logs with Word or Acrobat Pro by using images, arrows, and hyperlinks to connect ideas among the things they read and viewed. Some did the same but without using digital technology by working with low-tech scrapping materials.

There is no one way to skrite, and the example in Insert B shows one way to create a Skrite Log. Skriting can be done on a napkin (have you ever drawn a picture on a napkin and written something on it?), on cardboard, on paper. At this stage, how we do skriting and say it is our private language. We are getting our ideas down while trying to make sense of all we have read. A Skriting Log is a powerful technique to expanding our understanding and connection to the ideas with which we come into contact.

3. Writing

We cull the threads, chunks of sentences, and images from our readings, and begin writing now with a focus. We start writing our first draft, sometimes called prewriting. Since we always start someplace when we write an essay, it is normal that we start with a draft of our introduction. It is important that we do not feel tied to our drafted introduction. Instead we need to see the introduction as a work in progress, one that will evolve as we write and revise our essay. Peter Elbow tells us that "Writing is a way to end up thinking something you couldn't have started out thinking" (16) and we need to see our introductions, like our essays, as what we evolve them to be in relation to the content of our essays.

We have all had the opportunity to read introductions that pull us into the subject matter, making us want to read more, while also creating a sense of known anticipation. That is, with good writing we begin to anticipate what the author's next ideas will be. For readers this makes the reading easy and makes us feel smart as well (like really good readers). Good writers spend a lot of time and many drafts making their writing easy for us to flow into.

The number of drafts we can write depends on how much time we have and how well we are able to express our thoughts. Typically, good writers will go through 3–5 drafts before arriving at a close-to-finished essay. If this sounds time-consuming, it *is*—and it is *not*. It is, if we try and do all our writing in one shot. If we write our drafts in stages and create a reasonable time frame, we will see that our writing is manageable. If we have time to let the essay sit for a few hours, a few days, or even months, when we revisit our writing after a break, we usually see sentences and ideas we do not like or places where the essay needs to be developed or clarified.

4. Peer Feedback (In Classrooms This Is Often Called Peer Review)

Getting feedback on a draft of our developing essay is common among writers because we can become blindly in love with our ideas and words, overlooking places where readers might be confused or need more information. When we receive feedback from others, we call this peer feedback, whether it is by fellow classmates, teachers, friends, tutors in our writing center, or by professionals. *All good writers seek feedback.* The feedback we receive allows us to see what we have done from a reader's perspective and allows us to move forward with revision.

Revising is an important step in writing for any level and ability of writer. This stage in our writing is important because we have worked to produce the first complete statement of our ideas and now have them tested. Be aware that peer reviewers might give us a lot of feedback, and we should not take this poorly or feel offended. We need to look at what the comments are and think of how we can use them to make our essay better. In your class, your teacher will most likely give everyone a set of questions to ask about the essays they will read and evaluate. These questions are called a rubric. Let's take a look at a sample rubric (Insert C).

So our peer reviewer reads our essay and has responded that the essay at certain sections is confusing because of something we said, that she did not understand what we meant in another two to three parts, and loved another section. At the end, she says she was unclear about the direction. Let's not panic! This happens to writers all the time. We need to look at such comments as helpful, so what do we do? A. Get mad. B. Get even. C. Think she is dense. D. Read her comments again and look at our essay with her points in mind. Of course, A, B, and C might be what initially come to mind, but remember anyone who reads our work and makes suggestions is doing us a favor. So instead we read her comments and look again at our essay. At this point, we are transitioning to being a critical reader by reading our own essay as if we were reading someone else's.

Sample Workshop Rubric

Writer's Name:

Evaluator's Name:

Read the writer's essay from start to finish. Do not make any comments yet. Get a feel for the essay as a whole and then answer the following questions.

1. In three minutes write or type everything and anything in response to the essay, answering, What did the writer's ideas cause you to think as soon as you finished reading it?

2. What are three good points or things the writer does?

3. What is the writer's main idea or point? What is he/she trying to make you feel or believe?

4. What rhetorical modes does the writer employ in the writing? Are they effective?

5. What are three points or things the writer needs to work on between now and the next draft?

6. If the essay were graded today, what grade would you give it and why?

Insert C

5. Rewriting and Revising

As soon as we return to look at the suggestions our peer reviewer (or tutor, teacher, or friend) has made, we have started rewriting and revising. As we begin this important task, we can ask ourselves questions like this that put us in dialogue: How can I say this, or develop that, or add/take away from my present draft, so that if she reads my essay again, her concerns will not be there? As we work with the suggested revisions on our essay, we should also ask ourselves, How can I address each of the concerns? Now we begin writing down how we will address concerns so that we can refer to them as we set about revising the essay. We can use the list of concerns when we actually are revising the essay.

An important strategy during revision is to break down the process into stages. We look at our list of changes and then set concrete time frames to accomplish them. For example, to address a criticism like "introduction is unclear as to how it relates to the actual essay." This suggestion is telling us that the introduction needs to be substantially, if not completely, rewritten, so we set aside forty-five minutes to an hour to work just on this. The suggestion does not mean the subject needs to change. We need to make sure we read the whole essay over so we understand the suggested revisions, seeing how the actual essay and the introduction do not work well together. For each of the other revisions, we break the tasks down so they are manageable, and so that we can do them at different times that fit into our demanding schedules.

Once we are in the heat of rewriting our essay, we will most likely have additional things we would like to add and take away. This is normal and even good.

6. Editing

Once we feel we are done with our essay, it is time to edit as closely as possible. When we were revising the essay, the odds are we were editing as well, but we were mainly focused on the development and expression of our ideas. The editing stage is when we are looking for misspellings, sentence mistakes, and making active sentences. If you have access to someone who can look over your paper (e.g., your writing center or a friend who writes well), this is a good time to do so.

7. Turning It In (Sometimes Called Publishing)

Once again, when we write we are putting our ideas out there, and we will see how others, various audiences, respond to our ideas. This is an exciting and scary time. In school it usually means a grade. If it is a submission for possible publication, it could be a time of acceptance or rejection. *Turning It In* is a normal part of the writing process. We need to view it as such and, once submitted, forget about it and focus on other tasks. When we receive our essay back, a good practice is to examine the types of comments we have received. If we are allowed to revise, this is a good moment to use our teachers' comments to guide us.

Stepping Into the Conversation to Generate Ideas

When we want to find the answer to something that we need to learn about, many of us do not start with our library or its research tools. The first places we go to are Google, Wikipedia, or social media sites such as Facebook and Twitter. These sites are acceptable places to start because they can orient us, that is, we need a place to stand, to look around at the panorama of ideas, before we can begin to understand our subject. Think of this step as listening to a conversation at a social event; once we get the feel and flow of our subject, then we can begin to talk. In the case of our researched essay, to take another step we need to find resources that will inform us on what has been said on our subject.

To begin our process with a focus on identity and social media, let's launch Google. We use Google because we know it is a familiar search interface and that our search will produce many results. These results may not be completely relevant to your topic, but Google helps us in our discovery. For example, our student essay, written by Monica Calderas, focused on "Chapter 6: Where Do You Draw the Line? Privacy, Socializing, and Life without Boundaries." The title of her essay is "Identity and Social Media." A Google search on identity and social media produced 264,000 hits!

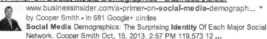

Identity and social media

Web   Images   Maps   Shopping   More ▾   Search tools

About 221,000,000 results (0.23 seconds)

Social Media Spheres: The Dual **Identity** Conundrum
socialmediatoday.com/.../social-media-spheres-dual-identity-conundrum ▾
6 days ago - Finding the point of optimal convergence for the three overlapping spheres of **social media** engagement is tricky. Employees of companies will ...

A Primer On **Social Media** Demographics - Business Insider
www.businessinsider.com/a-primer-on-social-media-demograph... ▾
by Cooper Smith - in 681 Google+ circles
Social Media Demographics: The Surprising **Identity** Of Each Major Social Network. Cooper Smith Oct. 15, 2013, 2:57 PM 119,573 12 ...

Performing and undoing identity online: Social networking, identity ...
con.sagepub.com/content/18/2/177.abstract ▾
by R Cover - 2012 - Cited by 4 - Related articles
Abstract. This article aims to expand the critical frameworks by which online **social networking** can be contextualised and understood within the broader cultural ...

Insert D

This Google search will produce articles from diverse sources—magazines, academic articles, government sites, and corporate reports among them. We use these results to begin honing in on our topic. A quick look through these results yields some focused topics such as how identity and social media lead to a new era of identity, and the effects of identity theft. Take the time to read through some of these pieces to gather a panoramic look at how people think about this subject.

Wikipedia

A Wikipedia search on identity and social media will lead us to articles that address both concepts. The great thing about Wikipedia is that it is an easy way to gain access to a wealth of information about thousands of topics. However, it is crucial to realize that Wikipedia itself is not an authoritative source in a scholarly context. Even though we may see Wikipedia cited in mainstream newspapers and popular magazines, as academic researchers we should not consider Wikipedia a reliable source or cite it in our research. Wikipedia itself says that "Wikipedia is not considered a credible source . . . This is especially true considering that anyone can edit the information given at any time." For research papers in college, however, Wikipedia is a valuable source to broadly understand a subject, and then find additional information about our topic through its references to scholarly articles. Wikipedia and Google are useful, then, for getting oriented about the panorama of thought on a subject.

Search results

For search options, see Help:Searching.

| identity and social media | × | Search |

Content pagesMultimediaHelp and Project pagesEverythingAdvanced

Results 1–20 of 9,137 for **identity and social media**

The page "Identity and social media" does not exist. You can ask for it to be created, but consider checking the search results below to see whether the topic is already covered.
For search help, please visit Help:Searching.

Social media
Social media refers to the means of interactions among people in which they create, ... **Identity**:
The **identity** block represents the extent to ...
59 KB (8,683 words) - 15:58, 16 October 2013

Public relations (redirect from **Media** training)
bookmarking, new **media** relations, blogging and **social media** marketing . ... of destroying the target's reputation and/or corporate **identity** . ...
19 KB (2,597 words) - 18:02, 16 October 2013

Social networking service (redirect from **Social** networking **media**)
A **social** networking service is a platform to build **social** network s or **social** ... major uses for businesses and **social media**: to create brand ...
98 KB (14,353 words) - 16:01, 14 October 2013

Arab Spring (section **Social media** and the Arab Spring)
well as the effective use of **social media** to organize, communicate, ... protests and fighting under Berber **identity** banners, some Berbers in ...
194 KB (23,325 words) - 18:40, 15 October 2013

Insert E

Using Social Media

Social media such as Facebook and Twitter can also be useful when we are starting out. The key is to use them in ways we may have never thought. Most of us use Facebook or Twitter accounts to keep in touch with friends, family, and colleagues, but both Facebook and Twitter have powerful search functions that can lead us to resources.

After logging in to Facebook, use the "Search for people, places, and things" bar at the top of the page to begin. When we type search terms into this bar, Facebook will first search our own social network. To extend beyond this network, try adding the word "research" after your search terms. For instance, a search on Facebook for "identity and social media research" will lead us to a Facebook page similar to a Google search results page. Two interesting leads surfaced for us, one titled "2012 Identity Fraud Industry Report: Social Media and Mobile Forming the New Fraud Frontier," and another "The Networked Academic: Social Media and your Research Identity." The posts on this page link to current news stories, links to research centers, and topics of interest in the field of identity and social media research. These search results are a way to see, read, and become part of the conversation about our budding research topic.

Many of us use or are familiar with Twitter, so we understand it as an information network where users can post short messages (or "tweets"). While many of us use Twitter simply to update our friends ("Eating a terrific pizza" or "Running in the hot sun and baking!"), more and more people and organizations use Twitter to comment on noteworthy events or link to interesting articles.

We can use Twitter early in our search because it aggregates links to sites, people in a field of research, and useful sources. Communities, sometimes even scholarly communities, form around topics on Twitter. Have you ever formed a community? User groups post together by using hashtags—words or phrases that follow the "#" sign. Users can respond to other users by using the @ sign followed by a user's twitter name. When searching for specific individuals or organizations on Twitter, we search using their handle (such as @USNewsEducation, or @whitehouse). We retrieve tweets that were created either by the person or organization, or tweets that mention the person or organization. When searching for a topic to find discussions, we search using the hashtag symbol, #. For instance, a search on #identity will take you to tweets and threaded discussions on the topic of identity. (A useful reference article to also help you locate information is *10 Twitter Handles to Help With Your Scholarship Search* (usnews.com).

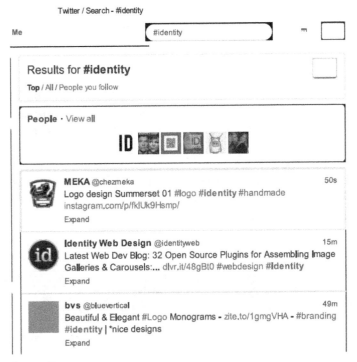

Insert F

There are two ways to search Twitter. You can use the search book in the upper right-hand corner and enter either a @ or # search as described above. Once you retrieve results, you can search again by clicking on any of the words that are hyperlinked within your results such as #antiidentity.

If you consider a hashtag (the # sign) as an entry point into a community, you will begin to discover a conversation around topics. For instance, a search on Twitter for #identity leads you to Elite Lifestyle Design (@Lukehavard), a community that explores identity and growth for professionals, "coaching for elite professionals and public figures." News agencies such as Reuters are also active in Twitter, so an article from a Reuter's publication will be retrieved in a search. Twitter, like Wikipedia and Google, is a starting point to help us get a sense of the spectrum of topics early on.

Create a Concept Map

Once we have settled on a topic that interests us, the next step is to generate search terms, or keywords, for effective searching. Keywords are the crucial terms or phrases that locate the content of any given source and are the building blocks of our search for information. We have already seen a few basic keywords such as "identity" and "social media." A concept map can help us generate more keywords and, in many cases, narrow our topic to make it more manageable.

A concept map is a way to visualize the relationship between concepts or ideas. We can create a concept map on paper, or there are free programs online that can help us do this. The concept map here was created using the app SimpleMind. First, we begin with a term like identity. We put that term in the first box and then think of synonyms or related words to describe identity such as "ethos," "identity formation," "character," "identity destruction," "multiple identities," "persona," and "personality." This brainstorming process will help us develop keywords for searching.

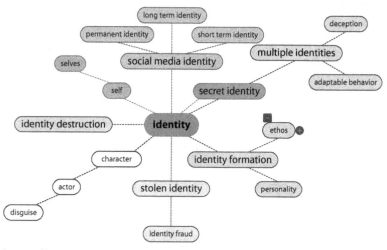

Insert H

After some practice, we discover that some phrases make for excellent keywords. The best keywords are precise enough to narrow our topic so that all of our results are relevant but are not so specific that we might miss helpful results. Concept maps created using apps such as SimpleMind allow us to use templates, embed hyperlinks, and attach notes, among other useful functions.

Keyword Search

Keyword searches are most effective at the beginning stages of our research. They generally produce the most number of results and can help us determine how much has been written on our topic. We want to use keyword searches to help us achieve a manageable number of results. What is manageable? This is a key question when beginning our research. Our keyword search in Google on identity and social media produced over 264 million results. The same search in JSTOR.org, which many university libraries have access to, produces over 97,187 results. These are not manageable results sets. Let us see how we can narrow our search.

Keyword searches, in library resources or even on Google, are most effective if we employ a few search strategies that focus our results.

1. Use AND when combining multiple keywords. We have used this search construction previously:

Identity AND Social Media

The AND ensures that all our results will contain both the term "identity" and "social media." Many search engines and databases will assume an AND search, meaning if we type

Identity Social Media

the search will automatically look for both terms. However, in some cases the AND will not be assumed and "identity social media" will be treated as a phrase. This means that "identity" will have to be next to the word "social media" to return results. Worse yet, sometimes the search automatically assumes an OR. That would mean that all our results would come back with either "identity" OR "social media." This will produce a large and mostly irrelevant set of results. Therefore, we use AND whenever we want two or more words to appear in a result.

2. Using OR can be very effective when we want to use several terms to describe a concept such as:

Identity or Social Media or Internet

The following search casts a broader net because results will come back with "identity" and either "social media" or "Internet." Our search with

identity OR social media **OR Internet** found 1,013,296 sources when we leave all sources open. When we select articles and books, we hit 664,472 (see insert below).

Insert I

Not all of these words will appear in each record. Note also that the parentheses set off the OR search indicating that "identity" must appear in each record and then either "social media" or "Internet" needs to appear.

3. We use quotation marks when looking for a phrase. For instance, if we are looking for information on identity and formation in Internet settings, we can ensure that the search results will include all of these concepts and increase the relevance by using the following search construction:

Identity AND formation AND "Internet settings"

This phrasing will return results that contain both the word "identity" and the phrase "Internet settings."

4. We use NOT to exclude terms that will make our search less relevant. We may find that a term keeps appearing in our search that is not useful. Try this:

Identity NOT literacy

If we are interested in the psychological side of this debate, getting a lot of results that discuss the politics of literacy may be distracting. By excluding the keyword "literacy," we will retrieve far fewer sources, and hopefully more relevant results.

Researchable Question

In a college research paper, it is important that we make an argument. This means that we have to go beyond writing a report that lists or catalogues the information, we find, or showing a series of findings to show our teacher that we have investigated our topic. In college, readers are interested in data or information, but they will want to know what we make of this data and why they should care.

In order to satisfy the requirements of a college paper, we need to distinguish between a topic and a research question. We will likely begin with a topic, but it is only when we move from a topic to a question that our research will begin to feel motivated and purposeful. A topic refers only to the general subject area that we will be investigating. A researchable question, on the other hand, points toward a specific problem in the subject area that we are attempting to answer by making a claim about the evidence we examine.

"Identity and Internet" is a topic, but not a researchable question. It is important that we ask, "What aspect of the topic is most interesting to us?" It is even more important to ask, "What aspect of the topic is most important that we illuminate for our audience?" Ideally, our skriting log and early use of Google, Wikipedia, or Twitter will yield questions about identity and Internet that we will want to investigate.

A strong researchable question will not lead to an easy answer, but rather will lead us into a scholarly search and conversation in which there are many competing claims. For instance, the question, "What is the percent of college students who use the Internet?" is not a strong research question, because there is only one correct answer and thus there is no scholarly debate surrounding the topic. It is an interesting question (the answer is 72%), but it will not lead us into a scholarly conversation.

When we are interested in finding a scholarly debate, we use the words "why" and "how" rather than "what." Instead of leading to a definitive answer, the words "why" and "how" will often lead to complex, nuanced answers for which we will need to intertwine evidence in order to be convincing. "How does the Internet affect identity?" is a question that has a number of complex and competing answers that might draw from a number of different disciplines (psychology, rhetoric, communications, political science, and history, among others).

Once we have come up with an interesting researchable question, our first task as researchers is to figure out how scholars are discussing our question. At the beginning stages of a research project we do not need to articulate an argument, and then find sources to confirm it. Instead, experienced researchers and writers know that they cannot possibly come up with a strong central argument until they have done sufficient research. So instead of looking for sources that confirm a preliminary claim we might want to make, we look to enter into the scholarly conversation on our subject. If our question is so broad that there are thousands of books and articles participating in the scholarly conversation, it is a good idea for us to focus our question so that we are asking something more specific. On the other hand, if we are asking a research question that is so obscure that we cannot find a corresponding scholarly conversation, we will want to broaden the scope of our project by asking a slightly less specific question.

Campus Libraries

College libraries are typically much larger than any library we have used and have more tangible resources like books and journals, and digital sources like eBooks, and streaming video. The most important thing to know before and during the research process is that there are people—librarians—to help us. While most libraries now have an e-mail or chat service set up so we can ask questions without even setting foot in a library, help can also come in the form of scheduled consultations. No question is too basic or too specific. Librarians' jobs are to help us find answers to all our questions. Among the many questions fielded by reference librarians, the following three are most often asked.

1. How do I find a book relevant to my topic?

The answer to this question will vary from library to library, but the thing to remember is that finding a book can be either a physical or virtual process. Libraries have books on shelves in many locations, and the complexity of how those shelves are organized and accessed depends on factors of size, number of libraries on campus, and the system of organization. However, we initially locate books by using our library's online catalog and noting the call number.

Libraries are also increasingly likely to offer electronic books or ebooks. These books are also discoverable in our library's online catalog, but in this case we see a link to ebook versions. While we will not find an ebook in every search, when we do we can immediately access it, and the content is searchable, making our job of finding relevant material easier. If we find one solid book on our topic, a great strategy is to use it as a jumping-off point for finding more books or articles on that topic. Book authors compile all the sources they used in bibliographies either at the end of each chapter or the end of the book. These sources can be a tremendous asset to our research because they are focused on our subject.

Another efficient way to find more sources once we have identified a particularly authoritative and credible book is to go back to the book's listing in our library's online catalog. Once we find the book, if we look carefully at the record for links to subjects and click on a subject link, we can find other items in the library on the same subject. For instance, a search on "Identity and Internet" will lead us to items with subjects such as "Protecting your Internet identity," "Identity and privacy in the Internet age," and "Cybertypes."

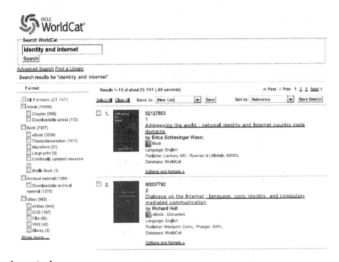

Insert J

2. What sources can I use as evidence in my paper?

There are many types of resources out there to help us as we orchestrate a scholarly search and select sources to support our argument. Books, which we discussed earlier, are great sources if we can find them on our topic, but often our research question will be something that is either too new or too specific for a book to cover. Books are very good for historical questions and overviews of large topics, but for current topics, we will want to explore articles from magazines, journals, and newspapers.

Magazines or periodicals (we will hear these terms interchangeably) are published on a weekly or monthly schedule and contain articles of popular interest. These sources can cover broad topics like the news in magazines such as *Newsweek, Time,* and *U.S. News and World Report,* or they can be more focused for particular groups like photographers (e.g., *Creative Photography*). Though articles in magazines or periodicals are by professional writers, who may or may not be experts on the subject, they typically are not considered scholarly and generally do not have bibliographies, endnotes, or footnotes. This does not mean they are not good sources for our research. In fact, there may be good reasons to use a magazine article to help support our argument. Magazines capture the point of view of a particular group on a subject, like how people feel about the Internet and privacy. Additionally, magazines can also highlight aspects of a topic at a particular point in time. Comparing a *Newsweek* article from 1990 on views on the Internet to an article on the same topic in 2013 allows us to draw conclusions about the changing relationship between perceptions of Internet privacy over that 20-year period.

Journals are intended for a scholarly audience of researchers, specialists, or students of a particular field. Journals such as *College Composition and Communication, Computers and Writing,* or *American Indian Quarterly* are examples of scholarly journals focused on a particular field or research topic. You may hear the term "peer-reviewed" or "referred" in reference to scholarly journals. This means that the articles contained in a journal have been reviewed or vetted by a group of scholars in the same field before the article is published in the journal. By citing scholarly articles we bolster our argument and enter into the scholarly conversation.

Newspaper articles are generally published daily. There is a broad range of content in newspapers ranging from articles written by staff reporters; editorials written by scholars, experts, and general readers; to reviews and commentary written by experts. Newspapers are published more frequently and locally than magazines or journals, making them excellent sources for recent topics and events as well as those with regional significance.

Newspaper articles can provide us with a point of view from a particular part of the country or world (How do Americans feel about identity zombies in the social media site Wiebo vs. the Chinese?).

A good argument uses evidence from a variety of sources to fill out our argument, and our instructors will usually provide us with guidelines about the number and types of sources we need.

3. Where should we look for articles on our topic?

The best way to locate journal, magazine, or newspaper articles is to use a database. A database is an online resource that organizes research material of a particular type or content area. For example, *PsycINFO* is a psychology database where we would look for journal articles (as well as other kinds of sources) in the discipline of psychology. Our library licenses or subscribes to databases so we can locate scholarly sources. Finding the right database for our topic will depend upon what is available at our college or university. Many libraries will provide subject or research guides (often available on the library website) that can help us determine what database would be best for our topic.

Our library's website will have a way to search databases in a section on databases where we should see a search box. For instance, if we type "identity" in a database search box, we may find that our library licenses a database called *MLA International Bibliography* (Modern Language Association). A search for "history" in the database search box may yield *American History and Life* or *Historical Abstracts*. In most instances, our best bet is to ask a librarian which database or databases are most relevant to our research.When we use the databases that our library provides for us, we will know that we are starting to sufficiently narrow or broaden our topic when we begin to retrieve thirty to fifty sources during a search. Databases help us determine when we have begun to ask a manageable question. When we whittle down to thirty to fifty sources in our result list, this is a good time to begin to look through these results to see what aspects of our topic are being written about.

Using Evidence

The quality of evidence and our use of it is important to persuading readers to believe our arguments. If we look at any scholarly book or article, we will see that evidence can be used in a number of different ways. Evidence can be used to provide readers with crucial background information, to inform readers what scholars have commonly thought about a topic, propose a theory that we use as a lens, or set forth a methodology that we would like to use. And finally, evidence can be used to back up the claim that we will be making in our paper.

Other Forms of Evidence

We have talked about finding evidence in books, magazines, journals, and newspapers. Here are a few other kinds of evidence we may want to use.

Interviews

Interviews can be a powerful form of evidence, especially if the person we interview is an expert in the field we are investigating. Most scholars are deeply interested in spreading knowledge, so we should feel comfortable asking them for their ideas. We need to remember to be as courteous as possible when we are planning to interview someone. This means sending a polite e-mail that fully introduces our project and us before we begin asking questions. It is a good idea to write down a number of questions before the interview. Make sure not just to get facts (which we can likely get somewhere else). E-mail interviews may be convenient, but an in-person interview is best, since this allows the interviewee and us to engage in a conversation that may take surprising and helpful turns. In several of the activities throughout *Identity: A Reader for Writers* we have even asked you to interview classmates so you have quick and easy access.

If we do conduct an in-person interview, we need to act professionally by arriving on time, dressing respectfully, and showing sincere interest and gratitude. If you have access to a recorder, bring it to record the interview. Many reporters still use pens and a pad, since these feel unobtrusive and are portable. We should write down the interviewee's name, the date, and the location of the interview, and have our list of questions ready. At the same time we should not be afraid to veer from our questions. If we want to record the interview, we need to make sure to ask permission. It is always nice to send a brief thank-you note or e-mail after the interview, which allows us to ask any brief follow-up questions.

Images and Multimedia

Because we live in a visual age, we tend to take images and multimedia for granted. We see them in magazines, on TV, and on the Internet. We don't often think about them as critically as we think about words on a page. Yet a critical look at an image or video can uncover helpful evidence for a claim. For example, if we are writing about the impact of identity theft or cyber bullying, we could introduce an image such as the one below.

Insert K

This is an image of a young man in anguish while looking at his Facebook site. Many readers can identify with him and make the connection to Facebook. The image enables us to discuss how visual elements (body posture, anguish, intense stare at the computer screen, etc.) can be read like a language—a language that is easily understandable. Images and multimedia can add depth and variety to our argument and they are generally easy to find on the Internet. Using the same keywords we used to find books and articles, for images we can use Google Image search or flickr.com, and for audio and video there are several search engines available such as Vimeo (vimeo.com), Blinkx (blinkx.com), and the BBC, Reuters, and the Associated Press, among others, have search engines for audio and video. Like articles and books, we need to document the images and multimedia we use. If we want to present our research outside of a classroom project (for example, publish it on a blog or share it at a community event), ask a research librarian for guidance on avoiding any potential copyright violations.

Evaluating Sources

A common problem in research is not a lack of sources, but an overload of information. How do we know what is good information? Librarians and teachers can help. Evaluating online sources is more challenging than traditional sources because it is harder to make distinctions between good and bad online information than with print sources. It is easy to tell that *Newsweek* magazine is not as scholarly as an academic journal, but online everything may look the same. There are markers of credibility and authoritativeness when it comes to online information. Here are a few tips here, but whenever we are uncertain about the reliability of a source we should ask our librarians or teachers.

1. **Domain**—The "domain" of a site is the last part of its URL. The domain indicates the type of website. Noting the web address can tell you a lot. An ".edu" site indicates that an educational organization created that content. This is no guarantee that the information is accurate, but it does suggest less bias than a ".com" site, which is commercial in nature with a motive to sell us something.
2. **Date**—Most websites include a date somewhere on the page. This date may indicate a copyright date, the date something was posted, or the date the site was last updated. These dates tell us when the content on the site was last changed or reviewed. Older sites might be outdated or contain information that is no longer relevant.
3. **Author or editor**—Does the online content indicate an author or editor? Like print materials, authority comes from the creator or the content. It is now easier than ever to investigate an author's credentials with a Google search. If an author is affiliated with an educational institution, we should try visiting the institution's website for more information.

Managing Sources

Once we have found sources, we need to think about where we are going to keep track of them and prepare the bibliography that will accompany our paper. Managing sources is called "bibliographic citation management," and we sometimes see references to bibliographic citation management at libraries' websites. Managing citations from the start of our research will make our life much easier during the research process and especially the night before the paper is due while we are compiling our bibliography.

When we manage our sources, we are putting them in the correct citation format as we use them. This process avoids backtracking—trying to rediscover the source—and incorrect format.

EndNote and RefWorks

Chances are our college library provides software, such as *EndNote* or *RefWorks*, to help us manage citations. These are two commercially available citation management software packages. *EndNote* or *RefWorks* enables us to organize our sources into personal libraries. These libraries help us manage our sources and create bibliographies. Both *EndNote* and *RefWorks* also enable us to insert endnotes and footnotes directly into a Microsoft Word document.

Zotero

If our library does not provide *EndNote* or *RefWorks,* a freely available software called *Zotero* (Zotero.org) will help us manage our sources. *Zotero* helps us collect, organize, cite, and share our sources and it lives right in our web browser where we do our research. As we search *Google,* the library catalog, or library database, *Zotero* enables us to add a book, article, or website to our personal library with one click. As we add items to our library, *Zotero* collects the information we need for our bibliography and any full-text content. This means that the content of journal articles and e-books will be available to us right from our *Zotero* library.

Taking Notes It is crucial that we take good, careful notes while we are doing our research. Not only is this necessary to avoid plagiarism, careful note taking can help us think through our project while we are doing research.

While many researchers used to take notes on index cards, most now use computers. An effective strategy we can use is to open a new document for each source we are considering using. The first step in taking notes is to make sure that we gather all the information we might need in our bibliography or works cited. If we are taking notes from a book, for instance, we will need the author, the title, the place of publication, the press, and the year. We should make sure to check the style guide assigned by our instructor to make sure we are gathering all the necessary information.

After we have recorded the bibliographic information, we should add one or two keywords that can help us sort this source. Next, we should write a one- or two-sentence summary of the source. When we write down a quote, we need to remember to be careful that we are capturing it exactly as it is written—and that we enclose it in quotation marks; if possible, we can use copy and paste to ensure accuracy. We should not use abbreviations or change the punctuation. We need to remember, too, to write down the exact page numbers from the source we are quoting. Being careful with small details at the beginning of our project can save us a lot of time and frustration in the long run. Once we learn an effective and efficient strategy, it gets easier the more we do it.

Integrating Our Research

Using evidence is a way of gaining authority. Even though we may not have known much about our topic before we started researching, the way we use evidence in our paper will allow us to establish a voice that is authoritative and trustworthy. We have three basic choices to decide how best we would like to present information from our sources: summarize, paraphrase, and quote.

Summary We should summarize a source when the source provides helpful background information for our research. Summaries can be helpful if we need to chart the scholarly conversations of our subject. Summaries must be accurate and honest to the scholar's ideas so that we remain unbiased and ethical in our own work.

Let's say we come across the following quote that we would like to summarize from *The Language Wars: A History of Proper English*, by Henry Hitchings:

> No language has spread as widely as English, and it continues to spread. Internationally the desire to learn it is insatiable. In the twenty-first century the world is becoming more urban and more middle class, and the adoption of English is a symptom of this, for increasingly English serves as the lingua franca of business and popular culture. It is dominant or at least very prominent in other areas such as shipping, diplomacy, computing, medicine and education. (300)

Professor of Anthropology David Harvey explains that . . .
In a recent book by Harvey, he contends . . .

Each of these examples introduces the quote in such a way that readers are likely to recognize it as an authoritative source.

2. The next step is to **Cite** the quote (C). Here is where we indicate the origin of the quotation so that our readers can easily look up the original source. Citing is a two-step process that varies slightly depending on the citation style that we are using. Here is an example using MLA style. The first step involves indicating the author and page number in the body of our essay. The following is an example of a parenthetical citation which gives the author and page number after the quote and before the period that ends the sentence:

> One expert on the relationship between economics and politics claims that neoliberal thinking has "long dominated the US stance towards the rest of the world" (Harvey 7).

Note that if it is already clear to readers which author we are quoting, we need only to give the page number:

> In *A Brief History of Neoliberalism,* David Harvey contends that neoliberal thinking has "long dominated the US stance towards the rest of the world" (7).

The second step of citing the quote is providing proper information in the works cited or bibliography of our paper. This list should include the complete bibliographical information of all the sources we have cited.

3. Finally, the most crucial part of integrating a quote is **Explaining (E)** it. The E in ICE is often overlooked, but a strong explanation is the most important step in involving our ideas in the scholarly conversation. Here is where we explain how we interpret the source, and how it pertains to our own project. For example:

> David Harvey writes, "The assumption that individual freedoms are guaranteed by freedom of the market and of trade is a cardinal

feature of neoliberal thinking, and it has long dominated the US stance towards the rest of the world" (7). As Harvey explains, neoliberalism suggests that free markets do not limit personal freedom but actually lead to free individuals.

Or:

David Harvey writes, "The assumption that individual freedoms are guaranteed by freedom of the market and of trade is a cardinal feature of neoliberal thinking, and it has long dominated the US stance towards the rest of the world" (7). For Harvey, before we understand the role of the United States in global politics, we must first understand the philosophy that binds personal freedom with market freedom.

A good practice is to avoid ending a paragraph with a quote because we end up leaving it to speak for itself and it will seem disjointed from our idea. In the above examples, notice that the first explanation suggests that the writer quoting Harvey is centrally concerned with neoliberal philosophy, while the second explanation suggests that the writer is centrally concerned with United States politics. The explanation, in other words, is the crucial link between our source and the main idea of our paper.

Avoiding Plagiarism

Scholarly conversations are what drive knowledge in the world. Scholars using each other's ideas in open, honest ways form the bedrock of our intellectual communities and ensure that our contributions to the world of thought are important. It is crucial that all writers do their part in maintaining the integrity and trustworthiness of scholarly conversations. It is crucial that we never claim someone else's ideas as our own, and that we always are extra-careful to give the proper credit to someone else's thoughts. This is responsible scholarship.

The best way to avoid plagiarism is to plan ahead and keep careful notes as you read your sources. Remember the advice (above) on *Zotero* and taking notes: find the way that works best for keeping track of what ideas are our own and what ideas come directly from the sources we are reading. Most acts of plagiarism are accidental. It is easy when we are drafting a paper to lose track of where a quote or idea came from; plan ahead and this won't happen. Here are a few tips for making sure that confusion doesn't happen.

1. Know what needs to be cited. We do not need to cite what is considered common knowledge such as facts (the day Lincoln was born), concepts (the earth orbits the sun), or events (the day Martin Luther King was shot). We do need to cite the ideas and words of others from the sources we are using in our essay.
2. Be conservative. If we are not sure if we should cite something, we should ask our instructor, a librarian, or cite it. It is better to cite something we do not have to than not cite something we should.
3. As direct quotations from our sources need to be cited, so, too, do our paraphrases of others' ideas.
4. Finally, extensive citation not only helps us avoid plagiarism, but it also boosts our credibility and enables our readers to trace our scholarship.

Citation Styles

It is crucial that we adhere to the standards of a single citation style when we write our essay. The most common styles are Modern Language Association (MLA, generally used in the humanities), American Psychological Association (APA, generally used in the social sciences), and Chicago Manual of Style (Chicago). When unsure which style we should use, we must ask our instructor. Each style has its own guidelines regarding the format of the essay. There are a number of useful free online guidebooks that will help us with documentation rules we need to know in order to follow the standards for various citation styles. Here are a few online resources:

- Purdue Online Writing Lab: owl.english.purdue.edu/
- Internet Public Library: ipl.org/div/farq/netciteFARQ.html
- Modern Language Association (for MLA style): mla.org/style
- American Psychological Association (for APA style): apastyle.org/
- The Chicago Manual of Style Online: chicagomanualofstyle.org/ tools_citationguide.html

Sample Student Research Paper

Monica J. Calderas
April 2013
Chapter 6

Identity and Social Media

Technology advances every day, changing the way we communicate and the way we live. The Internet has taken over most of the electronic products we use in our daily lives, such as computers, cellphones, and tablets. Most people cannot be a day without them. The Internet has changed the way we send and receive information; the way we communicate with our friends, family, and others. Not so long ago, however, people would communicate privately with friends and family through cell phone, text message, or email.

Now with social media there seems to be no limit, as the whole world can know what we are doing anytime and anywhere. Facebook and Twitter have taken over and their users vary from children to adults. These new social networks help people create "new and evolving identities" to portray to the whole world. However, this creates a potential problem because "there are consequences that come with sharing too much about ourselves in too many open spaces" (Scenters-Zapico). The reason for this is that everyone can have access to everything we post. For example, in face-to-face interactions the Internet is not only used for good, as in socialization, but also for bad, as in cyber-bullying and stalking. The type of problems people find themselves in depends on the way social networks are used. Being aware of the short-term and long-term dangers they face on the Internet, and knowing how to set boundaries for the way they portray themselves to the world, are simple to preach yet difficult to practice.

Social Media Changing People

Social media is the new way people communicate with others, from next door to another country, and they share lots of details about their personal lives. For this reason social media such as Twitter and "Facebook [have] become a big part of people's everyday lives. . . . But just because more people are using social media, it does not mean they understand its power," as Martin says in *Don't Trip Over Your Digital Footprint.* In these two social media, Facebook and Twitter, users create a profile and they can be whoever they want, *follow* or *friend* who they want, and in the process create unique identities.

Identities are created with posts, images, and tweets. Someone may be walking on the beach looking at the sunset and suddenly decide that this is "the perfect opportunity for a tweet" as Peggy Orenstein tells us. What we may not realize is how our likes, tweets, posts, and images do not basically shape our Facebook or Twitter accounts but, reciprocally, "how much [is] Twitter shaping me" because the "expansion of our digital universe . . . has shifted not only how we spend our time but also how we construct identity" (Orenstein). This is because with social media more people can spend more time on their preferred media—on their cell phone, tablet, laptop, desktop computer, and even television.

Because of quick and easy access, it is likely for people to post and update their status on Facebook or Twitter regularly, constructing a profile and personality that depicts who they are . . . or who they pretend to be. I call these users *pretenders* because as they write a post they are also "creating something for others' consumption . . . So those moments in which you're supposed to be showing your true self becomes a performance" (Turkle). These posts not only affect people's personality but also their privacy.

Privacy and social media

Privacy is one thing we have lost with social media. On Tweeter and Facebook people's identity is based on posts or tweets, images and likes, just as "the web creates personalities for us based on everything we click, view, visit, and purchase on the web" (Koppell). People mainly use such sites "to share important moments, and to distribute our accomplishments," which are intended mainly for "friends [and] family" but oftentimes people forget the other person they are sharing their posts with may be "the World" (Scenters-Zapico). People somehow tend to forget this because "Twitter and social media in general is . . . blurring the boundary between . . . this private intimate space and public space"; therefore they share everything they think is friends and family likable, not knowing they are sharing it with the whole world. Posts can later have a negative impact "in terms of getting into college or getting a job," as Sheninger, principal of New Milford High School, says in *Don't Trip Over Your Digital Footprint*. Posts have affected even people in Congress such as Anthony Weiner, a member of Congress who had to resign "because of a careless Twitter picture of something he should not have tweeted a picture about" (Martin).

Our posts are being seen not only by our Facebook friends and family, but also by the employees working at these social media companies. Popkin explains in *Privacy is Dead on Facebook: Get Over It* that an anonymous Facebook employee said that whatever people post on Facebook is "forever on a Facebook database" and "just a search query" is needed to access such information. Therefore, even though we may set our pictures and profiles to private mode, they are not really private to all people, revealing our privacy and exposing who we really are or appear to be can be a problem, but it also makes us vulnerable to cyber bullying.

Another way of bullying: cyber bullying

Bullying has become a big issue for schools, especially for middle and high schools. Now with social media, cyber-bullying is another way to bully. The problem is that "schools have not been proactive enough to sit their kids down and teach them about . . . Internet etiquette," as Principal Sheninger says. Schools have usually "blocked, banned, [or] prohibited . . . social media" since principals feel it has "no place in education" (Sheninger). Students want to be on those sites (and will be), and the right thing to do is to incorporate "social media into the educational experience" (Martin). Schools need to "talk about cyber-bullying . . . about digital footprints . . . the negative impact that tweets or Facebook posts can eventually have in terms of getting into college or getting a job." This way, Sheninger adds, students will think twice before posting something on Facebook or on Twitter because "once it's posted out there, it doesn't go away." An added benefit to learning about the destructive effects of cyber bullying is that students who become aware of the problem will start reporting cyber-bullying to faculty in school and "understand that . . . they need to be digitally responsible in this age" (Sheninger).

Sadly, not only kids use the Internet for cyber-bullying; adults do too. Adults are involved in "these fights or stirring up this drama" that may start in "gossip circles [and] it just migrates online" (Peterson). The problem is that children may learn from watching their parents' online behavior. Still, parents are not the only ones that may affect their children's behavior. Celebrities have even "more work because they know they're talking to their fans and yet they're creating this intimate space with their fans," and sometimes "they forget that the cameras are there," and their fans are watching. For example, Rihanna and her former boyfriend "and his new inamorata have gotten into some Twitter fights" and "that interplay of celebrity behavior affects the student behavior" (Peterson). This is due to the fact that some students may look up to them, and want to be like them, but in the end it all comes down to the education they have had about correct Internet and social media use.

Conclusion

With advances in technology our communication has changed and so have the identities we create for ourselves. Social media is essential in our lives in the 21st Century, and it is being used for good and bad. With social media we are able to share everything and anything with the world, from who we are and what we do, to how we create unique identities that may be different from real life. An important and overlooked concern is that people are taking little interest in the effects that may come in the near future. Online notions of privacy may ultimately be public, and this will likely have long-term effects on younger generations. Making social media users aware of the consequences of what seem like innocent posts will save them a lifetime of scarlet letters.

credits

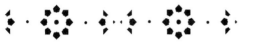

index